Sisters in Arms

During the Second World War some 600,000 women were absorbed into the Women's Auxiliary Air Force, the Auxiliary Territorial Service, and the Women's Royal Naval Service. These women performed important military functions for the armed forces, both at home and overseas, and the jobs they undertook ranged from cooking, typing and telephony to stripping down torpedoes, overhauling aircraft engines and operating the fire control instruments in anti-aircraft gun batteries. In this wide-ranging study, which draws on a multitude of sources and combines organisational history with the personal experiences of servicewomen, Jeremy Crang traces the wartime history of the WAAF, ATS and WRNS and the integration of women into the British armed forces. Servicewomen came to play such an integral wartime role that the military authorities established permanent regular post-war women's services and, in so doing, opened up a military career for women for the first time.

Jeremy A. Crang is Professor of Modern British History at the University of Edinburgh. He is the author of *The British Army and the People's War, 1939–1945* (2000) and co-editor (with Paul Addison) of *The Burning Blue: a New History of the Battle of Britain* (2000); *Firestorm: the Bombing of Dresden, 1945* (2006); *Listening to Britain: Home Intelligence Reports on Britain's Finest Hour, May to September 1940* (2010); and *The Spirit of the Blitz: Home Intelligence and British Morale, September 1940–June 1941* (2020). He is also co-editor (with Edward Spiers and Matthew Strickland) of *A Military History of Scotland* (2012).

T0384602

Studies in the Social and Cultural History of Modern Warfare

General Editor

Robert Gerwarth, *University College Dublin*

Jay Winter, *Yale University*

Advisory Editors

Heather Jones, *University College London*

Rana Mitter, *University of Oxford*

Michelle Moyd, *Indiana University Bloomington*

Martin Thomas, *University of Exeter*

In recent years the field of modern history has been enriched by the exploration of two parallel histories. These are the social and cultural history of armed conflict, and the impact of military events on social and cultural history.

Studies in the Social and Cultural History of Modern Warfare presents the fruits of this growing area of research, reflecting both the colonization of military history by cultural historians and the reciprocal interest of military historians in social and cultural history, to the benefit of both. The series offers the latest scholarship in European and non-European events from the 1850s to the present day.

A full list of titles in the series can be found at:

www.cambridge.org/modernwarfare

Sisters in Arms

Women in the British Armed Forces during the Second World War

Jeremy A. Crang
University of Edinburgh

CAMBRIDGE
UNIVERSITY PRESS

CAMBRIDGE
UNIVERSITY PRESS

Shaftesbury Road, Cambridge CB2 8EA, United Kingdom

One Liberty Plaza, 20th Floor, New York, NY 10006, USA

477 Williamstown Road, Port Melbourne, VIC 3207, Australia

314–321, 3rd Floor, Plot 3, Splendor Forum, Jasola District Centre, New Delhi – 110025, India

103 Penang Road, #05–06/07, Visioncrest Commercial, Singapore 238467

Cambridge University Press is part of Cambridge University Press & Assessment, a department of the University of Cambridge.

We share the University's mission to contribute to society through the pursuit of education, learning and research at the highest international levels of excellence.

www.cambridge.org
Information on this title: www.cambridge.org/9781107601116

DOI: 10.1017/9781139004190

First published 2020
First paperback edition 2023

A catalogue record for this publication is available from the British Library

Library of Congress Cataloging-in-Publication data
NAMES: Crang, Jeremy A., author.
TITLE: Sisters in arms : women in the British Armed Forces during the Second World War / Jeremy A. Crang, University of Edinburgh.
OTHER TITLES: Women in the British Armed forces during the Second World War
DESCRIPTION: Cambridge ; New York : Cambridge University Press, 2020. | Series: Schw studies in the social and cultural history of modern warfare | Includes bibliographical references and index.
IDENTIFIERS: LCCN 2020014751 (print) | LCCN 2020014752 (ebook) | ISBN 9781107013476 (hardback) | ISBN 9781139004190 (ebook)
SUBJECTS: LCSH: World War, 1939–1945 – Women – Great Britain. | World War, 1939–1945 – Participation, Female. | Great Britain. Auxiliary Territorial Service – History. | Great Britain. Women's Auxiliary Air Force – History. | Great Britain. Royal Navy. Women's Royal Naval Service (1939–1993) – History. | Great Britain – Armed Forces – History. | National service – Great Britain – History – 20th century.
CLASSIFICATION: LCC D810.W7 C73 2020 (print) | LCC D810.W7 (ebook) | DDC 940.54/1241082–dc23
LC record available at https://lccn.loc.gov/2020014751
LC ebook record available at https://lccn.loc.gov/2020014752

ISBN   978-1-107-01347-6   Hardback
ISBN   978-1-107-60111-6   Paperback

For Fiona and Emily
and
in loving memory of my mother,
Elizabeth

CONTENTS

List of Figures   *page* viii
Acknowledgements   xi

Prologue   1

1   Revival   7

2   Organisation and Recruitment   25

3   Training and Selection   43

4   Work   60

5   Status and Discipline   93

6   Necessities of Life   112

7   Medical Matters   124

8   Off Duty   141

9   Overseas Service   174

10 Demobilisation and the Creation of the Permanent
    Women's Services   201

    Conclusion   235

    Notes   248
    Appendix   310
    Bibliography   313
    Index   332

FIGURES

P.1   Section Officer Daphne Pearson with her George Cross
       after her investiture by King George VI at
       Buckingham Palace, 1941   *page* 2
P.2   Princess Elizabeth undertaking ATS training in
       vehicle maintenance, 1945   4
P.3   Dame Laura Knight's portrait of Daphne Pearson, 1940   6
1.1   The Marchioness of Londonderry in the uniform of the
       Women's Legion, 1918   9
1.2   Dame Helen Gywnne-Vaughan, Director of the ATS
       1939–41, inspects members of her force   18
1.3   Jane Trefusis Forbes, Director of the WAAF 1939–43   21
1.4   Vera Laughton Mathews, Director of the WRNS
       1939–46   23
2.1   ATS recruitment office, 1941   28
2.2   'Free a Man for the Fleet': WRNS recruiting poster   29
2.3   Jean Knox, Director of the ATS 1941–3   33
2.4   Violet Markham, 1938, who chaired the committee
       of inquiry into amenities and welfare conditions in
       the women's services   41
3.1   WAAF recruits being issued with service shoes, 1941   45
3.2   Waafs on parade at a RAF Fighter Command station,
       1940   48
3.3   Wrens learning morse code at HMS *Mercury*, the Royal
       Navy's signal training establishment, 1943   50

3.4   The Duchess of Kent, Commandant of the WRNS,
       inspects WRNS officer cadets at the Royal Naval
       College, Greenwich, London, 1941   53
4.1   WAAF flight mechanics and armourers service a RAF
       Hawker Hurricane, 1943   62
4.2   Wrens move a torpedo in readiness for loading onto
       a submarine, 1943   63
4.3   Waafs learning how to handle a barrage balloon   64
4.4   WAAF plotters at work in the Operations Room at the
       headquarters of the RAF's No. 11 Group, 1942   65
4.5   An ATS cook stirs a cauldron of stew at an army
       cookhouse, 1942   66
4.6   An ATS teleprinter operator at a London HQ, 1942   67
4.7   ATS personnel serving at a 3.7-inch anti-aircraft gun
       site, Wormwood Scrubs, London, 1941   72
4.8   Winston Churchill; his daughter, ATS officer Mary
       Churchill; and General Sir Frederick Pile,
       Commander-in-Chief of Anti-Aircraft Command,
       watch a demonstration of measures used to combat
       flying bombs over the south of England, 1944   75
4.9   Leslie Whateley, Director of the ATS 1943–6   77
4.10   ATS officer Mary Thomson (then Mary Dixon), c.
       1945, who served as a staff officer in Anti-Aircraft
       Command. She ended the war with the rank of Controller
       (Colonel), later becoming Deputy Director, ATS, Middle
       East Land Forces   81
4.11   Bomber Command aircrew being interviewed by a
       WAAF intelligence officer at RAF Lakenheath, after
       returning from a mine-laying operation on the enemy
       coastline   85
4.12   Lady Mary Welsh, Director of the WAAF 1943–6   92
5.1   An ATS military policewoman on patrol, 1943   101
5.2   WAAF police take part in a demonstration court martial
       at the RAF police school   104
6.1   ATS recruits at a hutted camp, 1941   116
6.2   Mealtime in a WRNS mess   119
6.3   Wrens receiving their pay, 1942   122
7.1   Members of the ATS have their feet examined by a
       nurse, 1941   130

8.1   Waafs watch their colleagues competing at a RAF sports
        meeting, 1941   144
8.2   Members of the ATS apply make-up, 1941   149
8.3   Staff Sergeant-Major Twist of the ATS embraces her
        husband, Lance Bombardier Twist, 1941   164
9.1   WRNS officers in Alexandria, Egypt, 1942   176
9.2   West Indian ATS recruits in the UK, 1943   181
9.3   Waafs and airmen dancing at the Lady Rosalinde
        Tedder Club in Cairo, Egypt, 1944–5   192
9.4   Admiral Sir James Somerville, the Commander-in-Chief
        of the Eastern Fleet, inspects Wrens serving in Colombo,
        Ceylon, 1944   197
9.5   ATS telephonists, Minden, Germany, 1945   199
9.6   Waafs survey the damaged Hall of Mosaics in the Reich
        Chancellery after the fall of Berlin   200
10.1   Wrens being taught 'mothercraft' by the Mothercraft
        Training Society   205
10.2   A mother welcomes home her daughter, demobbed
        from the WAAF, 1945   211
10.3   WRNS officers' mess dress designed by Victor Stiebel,
        1951   233
C.1   WRNS officer Audrey Roche (then Audrey Coningham)
        who saved the life of Leading Seaman Leslie Crossman in
        1942   246

ACKNOWLEDGEMENTS

I have accumulated many debts during the writing of this book. I am grateful to the School of History, Classics and Archaeology at the University of Edinburgh for providing such a congenial academic home; to the Arts and Humanities Research Council for awarding me a period of sabbatical leave to undertake research; and to Churchill College, Cambridge and Pembroke College, Oxford, for electing me to visiting fellowships.

I am also indebted to the staffs of the National Archives, the Imperial War Museum, the Churchill Archives Centre, the Liddell Hart Centre for Military Archives, the London School of Economics Women's Library, the Mass Observation Archive, the National Army Museum, the National Maritime Museum, the National Museum of the Royal Navy, the RAF Museum, the Wellcome Library, the National Library of Scotland and Edinburgh University Library, for their unfailing courtesy and helpfulness. In particular, warm thanks are due to Peter Elliot, Victoria Ingles, Alastair Massie, Simon Offord, Allen Packwood, Sarah Paterson, Harry Raffal, Andrew Riley, Jessica Scantlebury, Natasha Swainston, Lucia Wallbank and Stephen Walton, for their archival assistance. Material from the Mass Observation Archive is reproduced with permission of Curtis Brown Group Ltd, London, on behalf of the Trustees of the Mass Observation Archive. The author has made every effort to contact relevant copyright holders but apologises to any he has failed to trace.

I owe a further debt of gratitude to colleagues, friends, family and others who provided information, advice and support: Rosy

Addison, Martin Alexander, Rosalie Alexander, Robert Anderson, Ewen Cameron, Martin Chick, Joan Cole, Terry Cole, Christopher Crang, the late Colin Crang, Elizabeth Crang, Jacqueline Crang, John Culling, Margaret Culling, Roger Davidson, Gayle Davis, Tom Devine, Harry Dickinson, Frances Dow, Owen Dudley Edwards, Alastair Duthie, Amy Forrest, Trevor Griffiths, Alvin Jackson, Louise Jackson, Joan Kemp, Lisa Kendall, the late Peter Larcombe, Paul MacKenzie, Catherine Martin, Bob McKean, the late Jim McMillan, Dorothy Miell, Stana Nenadic, Paul Norris, Douglas Rodgers, Lindy Rodgers, Sabine Rolle, Gary Sheffield, Kathleen Sherit, Andrew Skinner, Gabriella Skinner, Sarah Skinner, Toby Skinner, Edward Spiers, David Stafford, Jill Stephenson, Matthew Strickland, Pat Thane, Pam Webster, Naomi Walker, Allan Williams and Vicky Watters. I am especially grateful to Wendy Ugolini and Richard Thomson who read the manuscript and provided many helpful comments (and to the anonymous CUP referees who did likewise). All errors of fact and interpretation are of course my own.

I must pay special tribute to the late Mary Thomson, who as a former senior officer in the ATS encouraged me to pursue this project and was in many ways the inspiration behind it; to the late Paul Addison, my incomparable colleague at Edinburgh, for many stimulating insights on the topic and his wonderful comradeship and wise counsel over many years; and to Michael Watson, my publisher at Cambridge University Press, for his invaluable guidance and infinite patience. Grateful thanks also go to Emma Sullivan and Amanda Speake for their meticulous copy-editing and indexing, and to Emily Sharp, Ruth Boyes, Ian McIver, Stanly Emelson and Akash Datchinamurthy, for seeing the book through the press with such skill and conviviality.

My greatest debts are to my late in-laws, Allan and Isabel Douglas, who were a constant source of encouragement during the writing of this volume; to my mother, Elizabeth, who very sadly passed away just before the book was finished, but whose support was fundamental to its completion in so many different and unspoken ways; and, above all, to my wife, Fiona, and our daughter, Emily, for their unstinting love and forbearance.

JAC
Edinburgh and Dundee

PROLOGUE

*When you see a girl in khaki or air-force blue with a bit of ribbon on
her tunic – remember she didn't get it for knitting more socks than
anyone else in Ipswich.*[1]

At 1.00 am on 31 May 1940 twenty-nine-year-old Corporal Daphne
Pearson, a medical orderly in the Women's Auxiliary Air Force and
former manager of the Ditton Court farm shop near Maidstone in Kent,
was asleep in her bunk in the women's quarters at RAF Detling.
Suddenly she was woken by the noise of an Avro Anson – of Coastal
Command's 500 Squadron – returning from operations. Although she
was accustomed to the drone of these aircraft, the tone of the engines
indicated that something was wrong. Instinctively, Pearson pulled
a jersey and pair of trousers over her pyjamas and, clad in tin hat and
wellington boots, rushed outside in time to see the stricken Anson crash-
land in flames in an adjacent field. Ignoring calls for her to keep away,
she scrambled through a ditch of nettles towards the red glow of the
crash site. On arriving at the scene, two of the injured aircrew had
managed to extract themselves from the aircraft, but the pilot, Pilot
Officer David Bond, was more seriously hurt. Although the Anson was
ablaze, and there were fuel and bombs on board ready to detonate,
Pearson courageously stood on the burning wreckage, roused the
stunned pilot and assisted in getting him clear. When Bond had been
moved some thirty yards away from the aircraft, a 120 lb bomb went off
and Pearson threw herself on top of the pilot in order to protect him
from the splinters and debris of the explosion. The blast was so strong

that others arriving to assist were said to have been blown over like tents in a gale force wind. After helping Bond onto a stretcher, and despite the risk of further detonations, Pearson returned to the Anson to search for the missing wireless operator, but found him dead. She then helped to remove fragments of metal from the injured airmen in a makeshift operating theatre at the base before they were transferred elsewhere. Having snatched a few hours sleep, she calmly reported back to the sick bay at 8.00 am to resume her normal duties. In recognition of her role in helping to save Bond's life that night, Pearson was awarded the Empire Gallantry Medal. The following year she was presented with the George Cross, which had superseded the EGM. She was the first woman to receive the GC: the nation's highest civilian award for gallantry and equal in status to the Victoria Cross.[2] 'The bravery of Corporal Joan Daphne Pearson', wrote one wartime commentator, ' ... has become a matter of national pride.'[3]

During the Second World War approximately 600,000 women were absorbed into three British women's auxiliary services: the

Figure P.1 Section Officer Daphne Pearson with her George Cross after her investiture by King George VI at Buckingham Palace, 1941 (PNA/Hulton Archive via Getty Images)

Women's Auxiliary Air Force (WAAF), the Auxiliary Territorial Service (ATS) and the Women's Royal Naval Service (WRNS). At their peak strengths, the WAAF numbered 182,000, the ATS 213,000 and the WRNS 74,000 (see Table 1 in appendix).[4] Women from all parts of the United Kingdom, and beyond, served in these forces. In the ATS, for example, of the approximately 208,000 auxiliaries embodied at the end of 1943, 162,900 had been born in England, 25,700 in Scotland, 7,300 in Wales, 1,900 in Northern Ireland, 3,000 in Eire and 3,500 in India, the Dominions or the British colonies. An additional 1,300 personnel were of British nationality born outside the British empire and a further 2,200 were of foreign nationality (chiefly German, Polish, Austrian, Czech and Russian).[5] These servicewomen were generally young in age. Of the 445,200 female personnel across the three women's services in the summer of 1943, over half were aged twenty-two or under. A quarter were twenty or under.[6]

The WAAF, ATS and WRNS performed a variety of military functions in support of the RAF, army and Royal Navy, both at home and overseas, and in many cases women served alongside men. The jobs they undertook ranged from cooking, typing and telephony, to stripping down torpedoes, overhauling aircraft engines and operating the fire control instruments in anti-aircraft gun batteries. Some 1,500 women died during their war service.[7] Churchill himself contributed a daughter to each of these forces – Sarah to the WAAF, Mary to the ATS and Diana to the WRNS[8] – but perhaps the most notable recruit was the King's elder daughter: eighteen-year-old Princess Elizabeth. She joined the ATS in early 1945 as No. 230873 Second Subaltern Windsor and was trained as a driver, and in vehicle maintenance, at No. 1 Mechanical Transport Training Centre in Camberley. Although the heir to the throne could never be just 'one of the girls', and returned to Windsor each night to sleep, she reminisced that it was the first time in her life that she had been able to measure herself against her contemporaries in any collective activity.[9] The ATS provided a contingent for the guard of honour at her wedding in Westminster Abbey in 1947.[10]

This book is intended as a contribution to the historiography of the wartime British armed forces. Military historians have, perhaps understandably, concentrated their attention on the male services.[11] The aim here is to investigate their female counterparts. A number of valuable historical studies have been published of these forces during the war, but they have tended to focus on individual services,[12] or on

Figure P.2 Princess Elizabeth undertaking ATS training in vehicle maintenance, 1945 (Bettmann via Getty Images)

particular servicewomen, such as the much-publicised ATS 'gunners' (of whom Mary Churchill was one) who helped to engage German aircraft and flying bombs over Britain.[13] This volume deals with all three services and investigates a range of aspects of service experience, in the hope of broadening our understanding of these wartime auxiliary institutions and the integration of women into the British armed forces. Drawing on a variety of sources, it begins with a discussion of the re-establishment of the three women's services shortly before the outbreak of hostilities. It then moves onto an examination of the wartime history of these forces. This is explored in a series of thematic chapters covering various features of service life during the conflict. It ends with the creation of the permanent regular post-war women's services which, for the first time, offered a career for women with their 'parent' armed forces.

At the end of the war, Flight Officer Daphne Pearson (as she then was after receiving a commission in 1940) was demobilised from the WAAF. After a period as an assistant governor at H. M. Prison, Aylesbury, she joined the staff of the Herbarium at the Royal Botanic

Gardens, Kew, and established her own plant nursery and shop in the village. In the late 1950s Pearson, who was not in the best of health, moved to Australia. There she worked as a horticulturist for the Department of Civil Aviation and helped create international-standard gardens around the new Tullamarine (Melbourne) airport. She, however, returned to Britain regularly for reunions of the Victoria Cross and George Cross Association and in 1995, during a visit to take part in the commemorative events to mark the fiftieth anniversary of victory in Europe, enjoyed an emotional meeting with the family of Pilot Officer Bond. After the conflict, Bond had founded what would become the world's largest civilian helicopter group with its headquarters in Aberdeen. Although he had died in 1977 without having had the opportunity of seeing Pearson again, his sons, who had seen pictures of her in the press being presented to the Queen Mother along with the story of her award, wished to thank her in person for her part in saving their father in 1940. They therefore arranged to fly the eighty-three-year-old wartime heroine up to Scotland for a special celebratory lunch at the Raemoir House Hotel in Banchory.[14] 'We owe a great debt to Daphne', they later wrote ' – our very existence'.[15] For her, it was an equally memorable occasion: 'I just wanted to cry when they got in touch with me. I have found a whole new family.'[16]

In 2000 Daphne Pearson passed away. Her GC is now among the collections of the Imperial War Museum, as is Dame Laura Knight's evocative wartime portrait of her. This picture was painted for the Ministry of Information's War Artists' advisory committee during the height of the Battle of Britain in late August and early September 1940.[17] During the sitting, Pearson, who was 'full of conflictions' because she was absent from her RAF station while the battle was raging, stayed at the British Camp Hotel at Wynd's Point near Malvern and it seems likely that the picture was painted in the nearby garden of Sir Barry Jackson, a close friend of Knight and her husband. A sun-burned Pearson reported in a letter to her mother that Knight had initially depicted her holding a rifle which, in tandem with the tin helmet perched on the back of Pearson's head like a woman's bonnet, would make 'a good line'. Pearson was much in favour of this combative portrayal: 'If Germans kill women and children deliberately in their homes and in the streets, machine-gunning – then the women must be prepared to kill to protect their children'. But such an image was controversial since airwomen were not permitted to carry arms and she admitted that 'the Air Min. will be furious'.[18] In the end, a respirator was inserted in place of the rifle. 'The irony of the gun was over-ruled by using a gas mask', recalled Pearson, '[but] in truth no way would one open up a gas mask in such an artistic manner.'[19] The replacement of a rifle with a respirator – the apparatus of life over that of death – tells us something about the gender tensions surrounding the service of women with the British armed forces during the war and the challenges they faced in entering the male military bastion.

Figure P.3 Dame Laura Knight's portrait of Daphne Pearson, 1940 (© Imperial War Museum)

1 REVIVAL

The First World War and Its Immediate Aftermath

During the First World War, various independent women's organisations assisted the armed forces. These included such bodies as the First Aid Nursing Yeomanry (FANY), which ran an ambulance service, and the Women's Legion, which deployed cookery and motor transport sections. Faced, however, with a manpower crisis as a result of the casualties on the western front, the military authorities were forced to establish their own official uniformed women's auxiliary services with the aim of combing out non-combatant servicemen who were fit for frontline service. The Women's Army Auxiliary Corps (WAAC) was established in March 1917, the Women's Royal Naval Service (WRNS) in November 1917 and the Women's Royal Air Force (WRAF) in April 1918 – the latter being created on the same day as the RAF. The members of these women's services retained their civilian status and performed mainly 'feminine' roles, such as domestic, clerical and telephonist work, in support of their male 'parent' forces. Some 95,000 women served in these organisations at home and overseas.[1]

In the immediate aftermath of the war there was some discussion in military circles over whether the women's services should be retained as part of the permanent strength of the armed forces. But against a backdrop of contracting defence spending, as well as an antifeminist reaction in some quarters towards women in uniform which associated them with 'unnatural' masculine traits, this was not considered a priority by the male service establishment. The WRNS, the WRAF and the WAAC (which had been renamed Queen Mary's Army Auxiliary Corps) were thus disbanded during the period 1919–21.² The creation of a women's reserve organisation might have been a cheaper and less contentious alternative. In 1920 a War Office committee under Major-General Basil Burnett-Hitchcock put forward proposals for the establishment of a 'Queen's Reserve' of women which would be affiliated to the Territorial Army and would act as the cadre for an expanded women's service in time of war. The Army Council concluded, however, that such a body was 'not desirable at the present time' and let the matter drop.³ Although the FANY (which increasingly became a general transport unit rather than a purely ambulance corps) and the Women's Legion (whose motor transport section remained active) continued to offer a quasi-military role for a few middle- and upper-class enthusiasts in the post-war years – both bodies turning out to support the army during the general strike of 1926 – no official women's service existed.⁴ Women were once more excluded from the servicemen's sphere.

The (New) Women's Legion and the Emergency Service

The first tentative steps that would eventually lead to a revival of the women's auxiliary services were taken in the early 1930s. The initiative came from the Marchioness of Londonderry, the renowned political and society hostess, who had founded the Women's Legion in 1915 and continued to preside over it after the war. Londonderry was anxious about growing tensions in Europe and the need for women to prepare for a role in national defence in a future conflict. She was also agitated by the formation of a new rival paramilitary women's organisation: the Women's Reserve. The brainchild of 'Commandant' Mary Allen, a former wartime policewoman and jackbooted fascist sympathiser, this shadowy enterprise was intended to combat left-wing subversion and threatened to undermine the Marchioness's own organisation, the Women's Legion, as well as the FANY. As a result of these concerns, Londonderry, whose Unionist husband was serving in Ramsay MacDonald's cabinet as Secretary of State for Air, sought the approval of the military authorities in late 1933 for a new and expanded Women's Legion under her presidency. This would act as an umbrella organisation for the established independent women's bodies and

Figure 1.1 The Marchioness of Londonderry in the uniform of the
Women's Legion, 1918 (© National Portrait Gallery, London)

provide a national pool of trained women who could be mobilised to
perform ancillary tasks for the armed forces in an emergency.[5]

The service ministries could see the advantages of dealing with
one representative organisation and gave a guarded welcome to the (new)
Women's Legion.[6] But it became apparent that the individual services had
different conceptions of the role of this body. The Air Ministry – perhaps
unsurprisingly – was the most enthusiastic department. It envisaged that
the new legion would train women to undertake specified duties for the
wartime RAF and that a grant would be required from the air force
budget to cover the costs. The War Office was more cautious and contemplated that the organisation would merely register women who would
be ready to serve in the army in an emergency with no call made upon
army funds. As for the Admiralty, it had grave doubts as to whether the

scheme could fulfil any useful purpose for the Royal Navy and questioned the political expediency of endorsing an initiative that could be interpreted as an early public preparation for war.[7] As a result of the impasse, the Marchioness's enterprise began to run into the sand.

Meanwhile, in the summer of 1934 Londonderry approached Dame Helen Gywnne-Vaughan to work under her as chairman of the new legion. Gwynne-Vaughan, Professor of Botany at Birkbeck College, and a former deputy head of the WAAC and head of the WRAF during the First World War, agreed to take on this role. It was, however, an uneasy partnership. According to her biographer, Molly Izzard, the new chairman was not accustomed to running other people's 'shows' and carried with her the professional woman's resentment of prominent society ladies, such as the Marchioness, who received all the plaudits for their patriotic endeavours but seemed to do little of the hard work. She also disliked Londonderry's close friendship with MacDonald, whose anti-war stance during the previous conflict made him a thoroughly discredited figure in her eyes. These irritations, and a lack of worthwhile activity for the new legion, encouraged Gwynne-Vaughan to consider setting up her own organisation.[8]

The immediate consequence was her proposal for an officers' training section within the legion. This would provide a much-needed pool of trained officers ready to lead any women's auxiliary services that might be required in wartime.[9] Early in 1936 she submitted her plans to the War Office and the Air Ministry; the Admiralty was no doubt regarded by this stage as an unlikely participant.[10] In a letter to the Adjutant-General, Lieutenant-General Sir Harry Knox, she envisaged the training of 'daughters of senior officers and so forth – who may have inherited some of their fathers' qualities'.[11] Knox was sympathetic to the proposed scheme, but could not resist a little gentle teasing of the redoubtable Dame Helen: 'You very rightly have a great regard for the qualities of senior officers,' he replied 'but I trust that some of their daughters have not inherited quite all the qualities of some senior officers whom I have known. If they have, it may be a source of trouble to you!'[12]

In the interim the question of the (new) Women's Legion had been referred to a women's reserve subcommittee of the Committee of Imperial Defence (CID). Chaired by Sir William Graham Greene, a former Permanent Secretary of the Admiralty, this reported in the spring of 1936. Having investigated the armed forces' requirements for women in the early stages of an emergency, and contemplated the administrative chaos that was likely to arise by involving an independent, amateur body in the machinery of government, the committee concluded that the creation of a women's reserve organisation was 'not desirable'; that no public money should be made available to any independent scheme that might be set up for this purpose; and that in the event of war the Ministry of Labour was the proper authority to whom the service departments should turn for womanpower.[13] Only the Air Ministry seems to have regretted this verdict. It faced the prospect of immediate air attack on the outbreak of war and believed that Londonderry's enterprise could best provide the categories of trained women that it would require at a few hours' notice. This view remained a minority one.[14]

The CID committee's ruling in effect killed the (new) Women's Legion: later that year it was wound up, the FANY and the (old) Women's Legion continuing as separate entities.[15] A lifeline was, however, offered to Gywnne-Vaughan's officers' training section. It was recommended by the Greene committee that the service departments should have discretion to provide limited assistance to organisations such as hers that might be of value to them in preparing women for duties of a 'supervisory capacity'.[16] As a result, in the summer of 1936 her section was reconstituted as an independent body and renamed the Emergency Service: a title designed to avoid any overtly warlike connotations since indications of belligerence were still regarded as politically undesirable as appeasement unfolded. Dame Helen served as chairman and Viscountess Trenchard, an old friend and wife of the 'father' of the RAF, as vice-chairman. The Duchess of Gloucester agreed to act as patron.[17]

Membership was by personal invitation and Trenchard's daughter, Belinda Boyle, did much of the early recruiting by simply leafing through her address book for likely candidates. Most of those who joined had service connections and the members came to include Lady Olive Newall, whose husband was Chief of the Air Staff, Lady Dorothy Bowhill, who was married to the Air Member for Personnel, and Lady Dorothy Jackson, wife of the General Officer Commanding-in-Chief, Western Command.[18] Among the less judicious enrolments was that of Unity Mitford, the pro-Nazi daughter of Lord Redesdale. Her extreme political views threatened to harm the reputation of the organisation and deter others from participating. When rumours began to circulate that she intended to become a German citizen, Gwynne-Vaughan asked her to leave. Obligingly, Mitford withdrew.[19]

Training of the recruits was soon underway. Evening classes on officership were conducted by members with previous service experience at Regent's Park barracks and the headquarters of 601 Squadron in London, and the War Office and Air Ministry provided lectures on aspects of military administration. An annual camp was also held at Abbot's Hill school in Hemel Hempstead at which the 'cadets' did 'physical jerks', practised drills, took it in turns to give each other orders, and prepared unappetizing meals using the manual of military cookery.[20] 'Most of our friends and relations', recalled Boyle, 'thought us not only mad but bad'.[21] Altogether some 400 women received training as potential officers.[22]

While the Emergency Service was establishing itself, 'Commandant' Mary Allen reappeared on the scene. In the autumn of 1936, she managed to secure an interview with the Minister for Co-Ordination of Defence, Sir Thomas Inskip, to discuss the role of her Women's Reserve in national defence. To assist Inskip, the Home Office compiled a confidential report on Allen's previous activities. It transpired that after the First World War this maverick figure had headed the Women Police Service, an unofficial body intended to train women for the police forces, and in 1921 she had been fined ten shillings for wearing a uniform resembling that of the police. Her organisation had subsequently been renamed the Women's Auxiliary Service and, in connection with women's congresses, she had visited Berlin in 1929 and Rio de Janeiro in 1931, where she had apparently posed as chief of the British women police. This masquerade had led to complaints about her behaviour from the National Council of Women of Great Britain. In 1933 she formed the Women's Reserve and had been roundly condemned in the press by Londonderry for creating an avowedly militarist organisation that would lead to overlap and confusion with other bodies.[23] Most damningly of all, New Scotland Yard confirmed that she was a 'secret adherent' of Sir Oswald Mosley's British Union of Fascists and likely to use her contacts to provide information for this organisation.[24] Predictably, Allen was politely informed that a CID committee had ruled on the issue of a women's reserve and her services were not required.[25]

At this point, Lady Margaret Loch entered the fray. Loch, the wife of Major-General Lord Loch, headed the Women's Legion Flying

Section, a branch of Londonderry's organisation that had been established in the early 1930s to train female pilots and ground crew.[26] In the summer of 1936, she approached the War Office about the possibility of the Women's Legion selecting a small number of 'suitable' women to be trained for 'supervisory work' with the armed forces in time of war. Loch, who had no connection with Gwynne-Vaughan's Emergency Service, was advised to consult the Ministry of Labour. The ministry took the view that her proposal was chiefly a matter for the service departments. In the spring of 1937, she contacted the army authorities again. The War Office was by this stage concerned about the possibility of confusion and overlap between Loch's venture and the Emergency Service. As a result, it was suggested to the Ministry of Labour that there would be administrative advantages if the ministry coordinated the provision of officer personnel in the same way that it had been tasked by the CID committee to oversee the supply of other ranks. The ministry responded that it had in fact interpreted its role as applying to *all* classes of women required by the services and that it would undertake to furnish officers. In order to effect this, it was proposed that on the outbreak of war the ministry would commandeer the membership records of the various women's organisations. These files would indicate which women had the requisite qualifications and training to make suitable officers.[27]

On the basis of these discussions General Knox wrote to Loch and Gwynne-Vaughan in the summer of 1937. He informed them that in a national emergency the War Office would obtain all its female personnel, including the 'supervisory class', from the Ministry of Labour and in order to facilitate this process the ministry intended to take over the records of the women's bodies at an appropriate time. Although reassurances were given that assistance would continue to be provided in the form of military lectures, he bluntly told them that 'we at the War Office shall have no direct dealings with any women's organization in future as regards the supply of personnel'.[28] Loch passed the letter to Londonderry. The Marchioness, still smarting over the recent demise of her (new) Women's Legion at the hands – she was convinced – of the Ministry of Labour, sent a stinging response to the War Office. She complained that the involvement of the ministry would lead to the break-up of trained units such as her Women's Legion motor transport section; that the 'class of person' recruited through labour exchanges would be 'totally unsuitable' for the army;

and that it was 'ridiculous and wasteful' that organisations intended for military service should not have a direct connection with the War Office.[29] Despite her protests, she was told that the matter could not be reopened.[30]

The Auxiliary Territorial Service

Over the winter of 1937–8, the War Office began to reconsider its position in regard to a women's reserve. By this stage, events in Europe were becoming increasingly ominous and the army needed to put itself on a war footing. All possible measures had to be taken to make the most efficient use of its trained manpower.[31] To this end, the Secretary of State for War, Leslie Hore-Belisha suggested that 'There is no reason why women should not be engaged forthwith as part of the Army Reserve, so that on the outbreak of hostilities they can release individuals, and even the bulk of certain units, for inclusion in active formations'.[32] There was also a change of personnel on the Army Council. Knox was replaced as Adjutant-General by Lieutenant-General Sir Clive Liddell, who seemed more receptive to the need for a national pool of trained women.[33] Meanwhile, the well-connected members of the women's bodies relentlessly lobbied service officials to persuade them of the military utility of their organisations. Gwynne-Vaughan and her supporters were tireless in seeking opportunities to press the case for the Emergency Service.[34] Lady Jackson, for example, buttonholed Hore-Belisha when he visited her husband's command.[35] Londonderry and the Countess of Athlone, president of the FANY, were also indefatigable in promoting their respective enterprises. A beleaguered Hore-Belisha reported that the two women were 'always at him about their shows'.[36]

Against this background, the army authorities revisited the issue. Not only did it seem invidious on reflection to rebuff the women's organisations by compelling their well-to-do membership to report to labour exchanges on the outbreak of war, but it also came to be recognised that there were practical weaknesses in the Ministry of Labour scheme. The ministry held no general register of available women and when demands were suddenly received from the service departments for a certain category of personnel, it would be dependent either upon those women who happened to be registered as unemployed at its labour exchanges, or upon volunteers, to meet the demand. Those registered as unemployed varied according to boom and slump conditions in industry and might not be available in sufficient numbers. And while volunteers would no doubt come forward, they might not offer their services quickly enough or be of the 'right class'. It was also evident that a large number of well-qualified women were reluctant to go anywhere near a labour exchange and preferred to deal directly with the War Office.[37] Clearly the system had a number of shortcomings.

As a result, Hore-Belisha – who, it might be noted, had recently joined Londonderry's weekly social circle, the 'Ark', under the animal pseudonym of 'Leslie the Lion'[38] – concluded that the best course of action was for the War Office to rescind the CID's decision and form its own official women's reserve.[39] This would build on the achievements of the existing women's organisations and ensure that on mobilisation the army would have at its disposal a group of enrolled women already allotted to certain posts, who were fully conversant with the duties they were to undertake. In the spring of 1938, a letter was despatched to the CID informing it of the army's decision.[40] The Ministry of Labour representative on the CID's subcommittee on the control of manpower, who had in fact sat on the women's reserve subcommittee two years previously, recorded his strong disapproval of the War Office's executive action on this matter, enacted without any consultation with the relevant authorities. 'This was', he protested, 'a most unusual way of conducting Government business'.[41] But there was little that could be done to halt what was effectively a fait accompli.

During the early summer, the War Office drew up plans for a women's reserve in consultation with Gwynne-Vaughan of the Emergency Service, Londonderry of the Women's Legion and Mary Baxter Ellis, commandant of the FANY.[42] The Air Ministry and the Admiralty were also approached with a view to their inclusion in the scheme. The RAF indicated its desire to participate (with Loch's Women's Legion Flying Section quietly sidelined in the process) but the Royal Navy decided not to become involved.[43] The new organisation, as the Burnett-Hitchcock committee had proposed some twenty years earlier, was to be affiliated to the Territorial Army. The volunteers, who would wear a khaki uniform but remain civilians in the eyes of the law, were to undertake non-combatant duties as cooks, clerks, orderlies, storewomen and motor drivers. They were to be organised as companies on a county basis, under the direction of county commandants. Training evenings would be held in local drill halls and an annual camp organised. The three recognised women's bodies were to form the nucleus, with the Emergency Service serving as an officer training unit and the Women's Legion and FANY supplying drivers. The scheme would be administered in the War Office by the department of the Director-General of the Territorial Army (DGTA). The nomenclature of the enterprise engendered a good deal of discussion. It was originally titled the Women's Auxiliary Defence Service but as no one wished to be known as a 'WAD' this was deemed unacceptable. The name was thus changed to the less offensive Auxiliary Territorial Service (ATS).[44]

In the autumn of 1938, the Munich crisis blew up and war seemed imminent. As public anxiety grew, large numbers of women converged on local authority offices clamouring to undertake some form of national service and the War Office was under increasing pressure to provide an outlet for their endeavours.[45] Moreover, as Viscountess Trenchard pointed out to Hore-Belisha, who at one time had sought to appoint her husband as an unofficial adviser in his dealings with the general staff, if the military authorities did not move quickly to establish the new organisation, then many of the best qualified women would take up other forms of war work.[46] In these circumstances, and before the details of the scheme had even percolated down to many Territorial Army units across the country, the BBC announced the formation of the ATS on 27 September.[47] A new women's auxiliary service thus hurriedly came into being as the anti-aircraft guns were set up on Horse Guards Parade in anticipation of the impending German onslaught.

The early weeks of the ATS were predictably chaotic. The Territorial Army adjutants, who were busy embodying their own male recruits, were often at a loss as to how to deal with the women who descended on the drill halls wishing to join up.[48] Many of the new ATS officers were no wiser about the service. The presidents of the Territorial Army associations were given the task of appointing the county commandants and tended to approach the local 'great lady' to fill this role. The county commandants, in turn, were required to nominate the junior officers and usually plumped for leisured acquaintances who had the spare time to devote to the service, but were often woefully ignorant about their responsibilities.[49] This was a cause of frustration to Emergency Service women who believed that they were much better qualified to take on these posts.[50] Nevertheless, by the outbreak of war, 17,600 women had been enrolled in the ATS and most of the companies were nearing full strength.[51] Some male units quickly accepted the women and gave them what assistance they could in matters of military instruction. But many were unconvinced by their sisters in arms. As one ATS officer, Leslie Whateley (who was later to be head of the service), recalled: 'The regular soldiers, and even the Territorials, were, for the most part, really sceptical as to how much use a woman's army could be to them in wartime. We heard a number of insinuations that our help would be a hindrance.'[52] The War Office admitted that in these early days, 'the Army did not then understand or appreciate the employment of women on a duty which, in peace, had been regarded as essentially a man's job'.[53]

It was not until the spring of 1939 that the army authorities gave serious consideration to the appointment of a female chief for the ATS. Up to this point it was thought that a relatively junior male staff officer in the DGTA's department could oversee the service. It became clear, however, that with the announcement of the doubling of the Territorial Army, the DGTA's branch would be fully occupied with the new male intake. Furthermore, some of the feminine matters with which the hapless DGTA officer had to deal, such as the relative merits of a brassiere and suspender-belt as opposed to a corset in the ATS pattern uniform, did not fall within the competence of the average male staff college graduate.[54] Indeed, Viscountess Trenchard apparently advised Hore-Belisha that the organisation would only be successfully managed once a woman was put in charge.[55] As a result, the War Office began to look into the possibility of appointing a female director to administer the service under the DGTA.

Gwynne-Vaughan, who coveted such a role, canvassed county commandants on the question of a 'head woman'.[56] Her position was that not only were there many 'purely feminine questions' arising out of a women's service that needed to be handled by a senior female figure, but also that such an organisation, however essential, would inevitably be a 'background affair' and that the War Office ought not to divert a valuable male staff officer to running a 'women's show' with which he would have little understanding or empathy. She was also concerned that he would not be taken seriously by his peers: 'other men', she opined, 'don't think very much of a man who is doing a woman's job, whereas they are prepared to like and respect women who can do it'.[57] One commandant, Miss Justina Collins, JP, responded that she was opposed to the appointment of a female head because it would lead to greater self-governance for the ATS and undermine its relationship with the Territorial Army. 'You will perceive', she concluded, 'I am not a feminist'.[58] Gywnne-Vaughan countered that she too would be opposed to any woman who acted independently of higher authority, but that it would be 'a waste' to use a first-class combatant officer to run their organisation: 'So perhaps', she countered, 'I am not a feminist after all in the usually accepted sense!'[59] In the summer of 1939, Gwynne-Vaughan, whose cousin the Earl of Munster had recently joined the War Office as Parliamentary Under-Secretary of State for War, was duly appointed as the director of the ATS (DATS).[60]

Figure 1.2 Dame Helen Gywnne-Vaughan, Director of the ATS 1939–41, inspects members of her force (Fox Photos/Hulton Archive via Getty Images)

The appointment of Gwynne-Vaughan brought to the surface a simmering dispute with the FANY. This body was drawn from what Roy Terry has described as the 'mink and manure set' and considered itself the elite women's organisation. It was determined to retain its distinctive identity within the ATS and tended to hold itself aloof from the new women's service. In particular, it continued to exercise its own informal style of discipline which involved all ranks messing together off-duty and countenanced FANY other rank drivers socializing with male officers at the end of the working day. The drivers, for their part, revelled in their status as 'gentlewoman rankers' and regarded ATS officers – whose role they contemptuously dismissed as 'counting Ats' knickers and making sure they hadn't got nits in their hair' – as little more than trumped-up social workers. The independent behaviour of the FANY was anathema to Gwynne-Vaughan, who embodied the hierarchical disciplinary conventions of the regular army, and on becoming DATS she was determined to bring it into line with other parts of her service. This led to a virtual 'war' with Baxter Ellis, who commanded the FANY motor companies and had been opposed to Gywnne-Vaughan's appointment, and to a great deal of friction between her FANYs and 'interfering' ATS officers. Although it was inevitable that the big battalions of the ATS would eventually assimilate the FANY – with the special concession that they could wear a FANY flash on the shoulder of their ATS uniforms – it was not until the replacement of Gwynne-Vaughan as DATS in 1941 that relations between the parties began to improve.[61]

The Women's Auxiliary Air Force

As part of the Air Ministry's participation in the ATS, it was agreed that separate RAF companies would be formed with their own distinctive badge. The members of these companies, however, soon began to clamour for a much closer association with the RAF than they were able to achieve through their Territorial Army affiliation. At the same time, it became apparent that a shortage of suitable accommodation meant that it was unlikely that the RAF would be able to absorb large numbers of women in the early months of a war. As a result, in late 1938 the Air Ministry decided, in consultation with the War Office, that the RAF companies would be linked to local Auxiliary Air Force units and that they would become officer and NCO (Non-commissioned officer) producing companies. These companies – which the RAF authorities would assume responsibility for – would provide the cadres around which future expansion could take place.[62]

Despite these modifications, the ATS scheme remained unsatisfactory from the Air Ministry's point of view. The RAF companies continued to be subject to army administrative procedures that differed from those of their own service. Moreover, the training requirements of the RAF companies, which were now composed of potential officers and NCOs, were at odds with those of the other ATS companies that were to serve with the army and which catered mainly for other ranks. In these circumstances the Air Ministry concluded in the spring of 1939 that it had no choice but to withdraw its RAF companies from the ATS and set up its own independent women's auxiliary service. The War Office was reconciled to this and on 28 June the Women's Auxiliary Air Force (WAAF) came into being.[63]

The WAAF was to be organised on a county basis. The trainee officers and NCOs in its companies were to wear an air force blue uniform and, like the ATS, would retain their legal status as civilians. They were to undertake mainly administrative training to prepare them to supervise women in similar trades to those of their former service: cooks, clerks, orderlies, equipment assistants and motor drivers (fabric workers being added for companies attached to balloon squadrons). The Air Member for Personnel was to oversee the service in the Air Ministry and a female director of the WAAF (DWAAF) was appointed to advise him. She was Jane Trefusis Forbes, who had served with the Women's Volunteer Reserve (a similar body to the FANY and Women's Legion) during the First World War; built up a successful dog-breeding business during the inter-war years, and then acted as one of Gywnne-Vaughan's stalwarts in the Emergency Service.[64] There were, however, elements within the RAF who plainly had little time for the new airwomen. Air Chief Marshal Sir Philip Joubert, a former Inspector General of the RAF, admitted that 'a very high percentage of the regular RAF officers regarded them as an unmitigated nuisance and gave them no help'.[65]

The first public appearance of the WAAF came at a parade of all the national service organisations in Hyde Park, a few days after its inauguration. One of its NCOs, Felicity Peake, smartly attired in the new blue uniform, was thrilled at the prospect of representing her service at this event: 'My high spirits were soon crushed, however, as I edged my way to a seat on the bus and one of the passengers asked me for a ticket!'[66]

Figure 1.3 Jane Trefusis Forbes, Director of the WAAF 1939–43 (Plt. Off. Stannus/IWM via Getty Images)

The WAAF had little time to bed in before the outbreak of war, as most of its companies were closed down for leave during the months of July and August. This meant that rather than preparing for their impending mobilisation, the 1,700 women enrolled in the fledgling force were instead enjoying their summer holidays.[67]

The Women's Royal Naval Service

The Admiralty's view was that the Ministry of Labour would provide it with womanpower in the event of war and no useful purpose would be served by establishing a peacetime women's reserve. However, it came under increasing pressure to revise its position. During the autumn of 1937, and again in the spring of 1938, Dame Katharine Furse, the head of the WRNS during the First World War, wrote a number of letters to the naval authorities (with similar missives being sent to the Prime Minister's private secretary) enquiring about their policy on the matter. She informed the Admiralty that in view of the deteriorating international situation, former members of the WRNS were eager to serve with the Royal Navy and wished to know what steps were being taken to facilitate this. A series of stalling replies was sent to Furse, explaining that the question was under review and no plans could be drawn up at present, but clearly the naval authorities were now in the firing line on this issue.[68]

In the spring of 1938, the Admiralty decided not to join the War Office and the Air Ministry in the ATS scheme. It was thought desirable, however, to ascertain the likely requirements of the Royal Navy for womanpower in wartime and to prepare the skeleton out- line of a women's organisation. It was also deemed prudent to invite Dame Katharine to offer her advice on such an enterprise. During the summer, the naval commanders-in-chief of the home commands were asked to estimate their requirements for women and, in con- sultation with Furse, discussions began on the structure of a naval service. In the wake of the Munich crisis in the autumn, which added a new sense of urgency, a draft scheme was agreed which established the framework of such a service and acknowledged that some women would have to be recruited and trained in peacetime if they were to be efficient enough to replace naval personnel on the out- break of war.[69]

In the meantime, the CID had recommended that a Ministry of Labour handbook should be issued to the public in which the various forms of national service would be outlined. Government departments were invited to contribute relevant sections. The Admiralty drew up a statement for inclusion in which it was indicated that a limited number of women would be employed for duties in naval establishments in place of male ratings and that further particulars would be available from the Secretary of the Admiralty. The handbook was published early in 1939 and created an avalanche of correspondence in the secretary's office from women eager to join a naval service. Within a few weeks, some 15,000 applications for further particulars had been received and many women who applied believed that they had actually enrolled in the organisation.[70]

Given these circumstances, the naval authorities decided to take the plunge and introduce a peacetime women's auxiliary service. Vera Laughton Mathews, who had served in the WRNS during the First World War and played a prominent role in the Sea Ranger movement in the inter-war years, was appointed as its director. 'I cannot help feeling', Laughton Mathews dryly observed, 'that knowledge of the 15,000 unanswered letters was a spur in urging very busy men to action'. 'What they were looking for', she believed, 'was someone on whom they could dump the whole thing and leave her to get on with it'.[71] The new director obligingly got down to dealing with the vast backlog of applications and finalising the details of the organisation. On

Figure 1.4 Vera Laughton Mathews, Director of the WRNS 1939–46 (© National Portrait Gallery, London)

14 April the Women's Royal Naval Service (WRNS) – the only women's service to revive its First World War title – was announced to the public.[72]

The WRNS was to be based around the major home naval ports. The volunteers (known, as they had been during the previous war, as Wrens) were to sport a navy blue uniform and, like their sister services, retain their legal status as civilians. They were to undertake work as cooks, writers, stewards, motor drivers and communication workers. Regular drills were to be held at local port depots. The head of the Civil Establishment branch in the Admiralty was to assume responsibility for the new service and the director of the WRNS (DWRNS) was to administer it under him.[73] Laughton Mathews's early interactions with naval colleagues were, however, not always easy. While seeking to lay down some rudimentary regulations for her new service, she recalled that 'More than once I was told that I flouted the opinion of an Admiral of thirty-five years' experience. I hung on, miserable but dogged.'[74]

The WRNS did not get off to the most auspicious of public starts. At the national service parade in Hyde Park, the Admiralty, seemingly oblivious to the existence of its new women's service, forgot to include DWRNS among the naval dignitaries to be presented to the King. While Gwynne-Vaughan and Trefusis Forbes were introduced to the monarch as the directors of their respective auxiliary forces, Laughton Mathews was relegated to taking part in the march-past with her Wrens.[75] Nevertheless, despite this oversight, by the outbreak of war, some 1,000 women had been accepted into the organisation and some preliminary training had been carried out at the ports.[76] The three women's services were up and running.

2 ORGANISATION AND RECRUITMENT

The Organisational Framework

On the outbreak of war the peacetime women's services were merged into the organisational structures of their male 'parent' services and adapted to meet wartime requirements. In the WAAF, women served on a 'mixed sex' (or 'component') basis at RAF stations within one of the RAF's functional commands, such as Fighter Command, Bomber Command, Flying Training Command or Maintenance Command. The senior officer of the service was DWAAF. She was a member of the Air Ministry staff, under the Air Member for Personnel, and headed a WAAF directorate within his department. She had limited executive functions and acted mainly as an advisor on WAAF matters. At the RAF stations, RAF commanding officers had overall command of the airwomen (or Waafs) but WAAF officers were responsible for their 'well-being'.[1]

The WRNS was organised differently. Women were incorporated in 'self-contained' female units in one of the Royal Navy's regional home commands, such as Portsmouth Command, Plymouth Command, the Nore Command or Rosyth Command. These WRNS units were employed in naval establishments located within the commands. The senior officer was DWRNS. She headed a WRNS directorate in the Admiralty, operating initially under the Head of the Civil Establishment branch but then in the department of the Director of Personal Services. She enjoyed extensive executive functions in relation to her service. At the naval establishments, the WRNS units came under the overall authority of naval commanding officers but the 'well-being' of the ratings (or Wrens) was again maintained by WRNS officers.[2]

The configuration of the ATS also differed. The peacetime county commandant structure was swept away, with the local 'great ladies' being redeployed to other roles in the service and women mainly embodied in 'self-contained' female units in one of the army's regional home commands, such as Southern Command, Eastern Command, Northern Command and Scottish Command. These ATS units were attached to army establishments within the commands. Women also served in 'mixed sex' units in the army's functional Anti-Aircraft (AA) Command. The senior officer of the service was DATS. She worked originally under the DGTA but was subsequently transferred to the Adjutant General's department in the War Office where she headed the ATS directorate. She too enjoyed a good deal of leeway in relation to the running of her service. Army formation commanders exercised overall control of the ATS personnel in 'self-contained' and 'mixed sex' units, but ATS officers once again looked after the 'well-being' of the auxiliaries.[3]

The organisational structures of the women's services thus varied – the WAAF being more closely assimilated with its 'parent' service than the ATS or the WRNS.[4] The RAF hierarchy justified this close WAAF-RAF relationship on the grounds of avoiding duplication of staff work, increased overheads and the uneconomical use of man and womanpower.[5] It also seemed to chime with the RAF's functionality as one large single 'regiment' and its image as a more modern and less hidebound fighting force than the other two services.[6] But such a fusion could be a source of friction. Air Chief Marshal Sir Philip Joubert observed that there were two conflicting schools of thought on this matter that 'caused a great deal of trouble in the WAAF throughout the war'. On the one hand, he remarked, there were senior airwomen who were 'all in favour of integration with the men from top to bottom'; but on the other there were those 'who considered the administration of the service should be carried out by a hierarchy of females, in the same manner that the senior men ran the men's service'.[7] In illustration of this conundrum, the DWAAF, Jane Trefusis Forbes, was eager that the WAAF should consider itself 'part and parcel' of the RAF,[8] but also complained of being sidelined by her male colleagues, saying that she was 'dead sick of having my views explained by someone else.'[9]

Nonetheless, despite these underlying tensions, what underpinned the administration of all three women's forces was a conviction on the part of the armed forces that while ultimate executive control should rest firmly with the male service establishment, the special feminine nature of these enterprises – what the Air Ministry termed the 'difference of sex'[10] – necessitated that the 'well-being' of servicewomen should remain in the hands of women officers. Indeed, all the women's services incorporated 'administrative' officer branches whose chief military function was to oversee this aspect of their female personnel's lives.[11] These officers, who along with their administrative support staff came to make up some 3 to 4 per cent of the total strength of the women's forces, had no counterpart in the male services and were thus regarded as one of the additional overheads in the deployment of women with the armed forces.[12] Some servicemen dubbed them the women's 'nannies'.[13]

Voluntary Recruitment

In the early period of the war, conscription was not applied to women. The ATS, WRNS and WAAF were forced to rely on voluntary recruitment to meet the growing demands on their forces. (The WAAF had been a pre-war officer and NCO producing organisation prior to the war but began to recruit other ranks on the outbreak of hostilities.) Under wartime recruiting regulations, single or married women were eligible to volunteer. The age limits set by the individual services varied but were generally between the ages of seventeen-and-a-half and forty-three (with parents having to give consent for those under eighteen). Volunteers reported to a recruiting centre affiliated to the service they wished to join. They completed an application form, were interviewed by a recruiting officer, and given a medical examination. If they met the entry requirements and were not prohibited from volunteering under the terms of the schedule of reserved occupations, they were enrolled for the duration of the war. Those who joined up were liable to serve anywhere in the United Kingdom, and subsequently overseas if required, but the WRNS maintained an 'immobile' branch which allowed Wrens to live in their own homes and work in the local naval establishment.[14] In the ATS, enemy aliens (those of enemy nationality living in Britain) accepted for service were at first restricted to domestic duties in special 'Allied Volunteer Platoons', which were akin to the

Figure 2.1 ATS recruitment office, 1941 (Hulton Archive via Getty Images)

army's Pioneer Corps, but were later permitted to serve in almost all trades.[15]

Women volunteered for a variety of reasons. These included a chance to escape an unhappy home life, a desire for companionship, a yearning for a more stimulating job, a wish to emulate relatives and friends who had joined the forces, an attempt to enter a favoured service in advance of conscription, or simply the opportunity to 'swank around in a uniform'.[16] But patriotism was an important motivating factor. There was a widespread desire to serve the country in its hour of need, to do one's bit for the war effort, and contribute to hitting back at the enemy.[17] For some this became a personal quest for vengeance. Margaret Hunt decided to join the ATS as she lay among the ruins of her home after it had received a direct hit during the blitz: 'They're not getting away with that!', she vowed to herself.[18] In 1941 an investigation into public attitudes towards the ATS by the Wartime Social Survey on behalf of the Ministry of Information, which included interviews with some 600 ATS volunteers, revealed that half of the reasons put forward by the auxiliaries for joining up were 'patriotic in nature' or 'allied to patriotism'. By far the most popular 'patriotic' explanation was stated to be 'Because I thought the country needed my services'.[19]

There was a service 'pecking order' among volunteers. The WAAF was the preferred choice for many women. Its association with the heroic exploits of the RAF in the skies over Britain gave it a particularly glamorous allure.[20] The WRNS was also a popular

Figure 2.2 'Free a Man for the Fleet': WRNS recruiting poster (IWM via Getty Images)

preference. It was the smallest service and had a reputation for being highly selective. This endowed it with a distinct social cachet.[21] Both these forces further benefited from what was considered to be a flattering blue uniform.[22] Peggy Erskine-Tulloch admitted to being swayed by navy blue: 'I have to admit that my choice of Service was partly influenced by the fact that khaki would have done very little for mousy hair and a sallow complexion.'[23] On similar grounds, Iris Lambert plumped for air force blue: 'Being a woman, vanity came into it, so I chose the WAAF because brown didn't suit me and I suffered terribly from sea sickness.'[24] The ATS was the least favoured option. As the largest organisation, it was reputed to take the 'odds and ends' left over by the other forces and was generally regarded as the 'Cinderella' service.[25] The Wartime Social Survey found that of those women willing to volunteer for the services, half preferred to join the WAAF, one-third the WRNS and one-fifth the ATS.[26]

For the parents of young volunteers it was not always easy to see them leave the nest. Some refused to give their consent and fought a battle of wills against frustrated teenagers determined to join up.[27] In this regard, pre-war concepts of the 'dutiful daughter' clashed with wartime notions of the independent young woman serving the state.[28] Others insisted that they sit in during interviews at recruiting offices to ensure that the chosen service – like some sort of finishing school – was 'suitable' for their offspring.[29] All that most could do was hope that their daughters settled down in the forces and avoided 'trouble'. Hazel Williams vividly recalled the day she left home to report for duty with the WAAF: 'I shall always remember my Mother, tears streaming down her face, at the door. Then she called me back and said "Don't sit on strange lavatory seats", and pointing to her bosom, "and don't let any man touch you there!"'[30]

Between September 1939 and December 1945, approximately 487,000 volunteers joined the women's services (of whom 79,000 served in the WRNS, 186,000 in the WAAF and 222,000 in the ATS).[31] Voluntary recruitment thus accounted for over three-quarters of the women who entered the wartime forces. This contrasted with the male services in which volunteers made up a third of the total intake.[32] Perhaps the most venerable wartime volunteer was Private Evelyn Wybergh. A woodcarver and former Welsh international hockey player, she lied about her age in order to enter the ATS and was later discovered to be 'not far off 80'. She was often to be seen delivering messages on her bicycle to ATS billets around Chester and was reported to have been 'as wiry as a whippet and right on top of her job'.[33]

The Coming of Conscription

Despite the significant numbers of women who volunteered, compulsion was soon on the government's agenda. By 1941 the competing demands of war industry and the armed forces for limited manpower resources meant that the women's services needed to expand rapidly in order to release male personnel for more active duties. Due to the size of the army the ATS required the greatest intake. It was estimated by the War Office that an additional 100,000 members needed to be recruited for the service by the end of the year in order to counteract the restrictions placed on the allocation of men to the army under the new manpower ceiling set by the government.[34] The ATS volunteering figures fell far short of expectations.

This was due in part to the unwillingness of women to consider joining *any* of the three services. Family commitments prevented many from coming forward to volunteer, whilst others were loath to give up a comfortable civilian job for the communalism and regimentation of service life. Possessive boyfriends, moreover, did not approve of their girlfriends taking the king's shilling. If they were civilians they did not relish strolling out with the equivalent of an able seaman or a leading aircraftsman on their arm, and if they were in the armed forces they did not want their sweethearts 'running the gauntlet' of hundreds of other servicemen in camps across the country.[35] Something more deep-seated might have been at play here too. It was speculated that men had been brought up to believe that war was 'a purely masculine undertaking' and it 'hurt their pride' to think of their womenfolk joining in.[36] Whatever the reasoning, one recruit, Marjorie Hazell, admitted that 'many girls were threatened with broken romances if they dared to join up'.[37] To compound matters, Jenny Nicholson, a WAAF public relations officer, contended that public perceptions of the women's forces had been undermined by 'spinster politics':

> The newspapers were inclined to make the WRNS, ATS, and WAAF sound like the worst kind of domestic service administered by uniformed amazons of gross proportions. The Osbert Lancaster cartoons of this phase of the war were typical. Funny

but vicious was the one showing a large table-legged, monocled woman in uniform, ticking off a fellow-woman-horror for mentioning a man's name in the Mess.[38]

There was, however, a particular 'image' problem with the ATS. Under the ageing Gwynne-Vaughan, the service was not an enticing prospect for a young woman. The drab uniform was a handicap. The khaki colour did not suit the colouring of many women and the cut was shapeless and unfashionable.[39] The spartan living conditions were a further discouragement. The bureaucratic strains imposed by the rapid expansion of the service and the shortage of suitable accommodation meant that life in outlying areas could be harsh.[40] This was exacerbated by Gwynne-Vaughan's insistence that women should endure the same privations as the men. 'It is the only way,' she claimed, 'that I can prove that women can do *anything* they are asked to!'[41] Above all, the reputation of the ATS was undermined by allegations of immorality (as had that of the WAAC during the First World War). Evidently fuelled by the malicious gossip of soldiers, which was said to have its roots in 'male possessiveness', 'professional jealousy' and 'ancient gossip against the WAACs of the last war', lurid rumours began to circulate about the promiscuity of its members.[42] As a result, the Wartime Social Survey reported that 'the nicer type of girl will not look at the ATS'.[43] Parents too began to turn their noses up at the service. Florence Teasdale's mother threw her ATS application form on the fire: 'You're not ending up as some officer's groundsheet', she declared.[44] Occasionally this antipathy spilled over into public contempt. Vera Roberts, who undertook her ATS training in Harrogate, recalled that 'A lot of people had a real down on women like us in uniform ... and the Harrogate ladies gave you a dirty look and just spat in front of you. They thought we were the lowest of the low.'[45]

The War Office did try to improve the 'profile' of the ATS. In the summer of 1941, the increasingly overbearing Gwynne-Vaughan was replaced as director by a much younger and more glamorous officer: Jean Knox. The new DATS, who was promoted over the heads of more senior colleagues, sought to give the service more feminine appeal. The uniform was redesigned to make it smarter. This involved restyling the tunic so that it had a tighter waist and padded shoulders. Efforts were also made to improve the living conditions. These included securing a more generous scale of accommodation furnishings such as curtains,

Figure 2.3 Jean Knox, Director of the ATS 1941–3 (© Imperial War Museum)

bedside mats and divans.[46] This emphasis on appearance and comfort was not welcomed by all ATS officers. When Julia Cowper saw a copy of the *Illustrated* magazine featuring a striking photograph of the new director on the front cover, and an article inside on 'the feminine atmosphere of "ATS Headquarters"', she believed that this put the female officer's role 'on the level of an industrial welfare officer' and took away 'any suggestion of a responsibility to command'.[47] Nevertheless, as Leslie Whateley, who had been made Knox's deputy, recalled: 'When

Jean became Director nothing but the best was good enough for the ATS.'[48] Alongside these initiatives a publicity campaign was launched to stimulate recruiting. This attempted to combat the 'whispering campaign' against the service by providing reassurances about the careful supervision of ATS personnel and the 'high standard of conduct' expected of auxiliaries.[49]

The Ministry of Labour and National Service also put pressure on women to join the ATS. In the spring of 1941, a Registration for Employment Order (REO) was introduced under the Emergency Powers (Defence) Act. This obliged women in selected age groups to register at labour exchanges and provide details of their current employment and family responsibilities. If it was deemed that they were available for work of national importance, they could be 'directed' into war industry. Although the ministry did not have the power to 'direct' registrants into the women's services, it sought to 'persuade' suitable candidates to enrol in the ATS. This involved gently indicating to them that they could be compelled to undertake less congenial work in a munitions factory if they declined to join up.[50]

These measures did not boost ATS volunteering to the required level. By the end of 1941 only 58,000 additional auxiliaries had been recruited. This shortfall had adverse consequences for the army's operational capability. In particular, it seemed likely that mobile units of the field force at home, which formed a vital part of the defences against a German invasion, might have to be sacrificed in order to fill static roles in Anti-Aircraft Command that could be undertaken by women.[51] Against this backdrop, the conscription of women into the services came under serious consideration by the government.

The Minister of Labour and National Service, Ernest Bevin, had been anxious to avoid such a step because, in the words of the author of one of the internal government histories of the women's forces, it 'cut across certain widespread conventional attitudes and would undoubtedly cause a public stir'.[52] But the disappointing ATS volunteering figures (and the possibility that, at a later stage, the WAAF might also not be able to meet its requirements by volunteers alone) forced his hand.[53] Towards the end of 1941, he proposed to the War Cabinet that young women should be compelled to undertake military service. Some of his ministerial colleagues had serious reservations about such a course of action. It was claimed that not all women were suited to a military lifestyle and that male members of the armed forces would 'object strongly' to their womenfolk being forced into uniform.[54] Indeed, Churchill stated that 'he was not at present disposed to favour any form of conscription for the Women's Services'.[55] Bevin, however, was not to be defeated. It was explained that all other practical alternatives to compulsion had been investigated and no other method would suffice. Furthermore, he pointed out that there was 'a widespread feeling in the country that the Government should order the younger women to give their services where they were most needed; and many women were holding back on the basis that when they were wanted, they would be fetched'.[56] After several weeks of fraught negotiation, the War Cabinet eventually agreed in principle to conscription and legislation was drawn up for the approval of parliament.[57]

During the debate in the House of Commons in early December, a number of MPs expressed their anxieties. Agnes Hardie, Labour MP for Glasgow Springburn, contended that the waging of war was a 'man's job' and that 'women have the bearing and rearing of children and should be exempt from war'. 'In spite', she protested, 'of the feminist attitude – and I am as good a feminist as anyone – I say they have no right to conscript women'.[58] George Buchanan, Labour MP for Glasgow Gorbals, was of a similar mind. 'I do not accept the view that women and men are alike', he asserted. 'What is good for a man is not necessarily good for a woman.' He maintained that 'women are not fit subjects to be conscripted into the Armed Forces' and lamented that, as a trade unionist, he never 'thought he would have lived to see the day when a Labour Minister [Bevin] would have been connected with a measure in this House for the conscription of women'.[59] The majority of members, however, were prepared to support the government. Eleanor Rathbone, Independent MP for the Combined English Universities, who had helped to found the Women's Volunteer Reserve during the First World War,[60] regarded the measure as a gratifying opportunity for her female compatriots to serve their nation: 'I believe', she opined, 'that these proposals will be warmly welcomed by the women of the country.'[61] Mavis Tate, Conservative MP for Frome, reasoned that there was no alternative: 'I believe that we are up against such appalling odds that it is idle to maintain that women can keep out of the war.'[62] Henry Brooke, Conservative MP for West Lewisham, agreed: 'We all somewhat dislike the idea of conscription for women into the uniformed services, but it is proved essential.'[63] On

11 December 1941, the legislation was approved and for the first time in British history, women became subject to compulsory military service.[64] One wartime commentator, Margaret Goldsmith, wondered 'whether in times of peace women will now be willing to accept anything but absolute equality with men'.[65]

Under the National Service (No. 2) Act, women in Great Britain between the ages of twenty and thirty were made liable for the military call-up. They were to enjoy the same statutory protection as their male counterparts in relation to postponement on the grounds of exceptional hardship or conscientious objection and as regards their reinstatement in civilian employment on discharge from the forces. But several 'safe-guards' were incorporated in the act's statutes and administrative regulations that differentiated the conscription of women from that of the men. First, married women not living apart from their husbands, or those who had living with them a child of their own under the age of fourteen, were to be exempt from any obligation to serve. Second, those who were eligible to be called-up would have the right to opt for a job in war industry or civil defence if they did not wish to join one of the women's services. And third, no woman would be asked to participate in duties involving the use of lethal weapons (such as helping to operate anti-aircraft guns) unless she signified in writing her willingness to do so. The application of conscription was thus limited in the case of women.[66]

The national service machinery required women of the proclaimed age classes to register at labour exchanges, if they had not already done so under the REO. They then completed form 'NS 196', indicating what type of war work they wished to undertake. Those who opted for the women's services were allowed to express a preference for a particular force, but in order to ensure that the ATS (and in time the WAAF) got the necessary recruits, it was made clear that women would be allocated according to 'the needs of the services'.[67] To help facilitate this process, special entry requirements were laid down for the WRNS (which had a long waiting list for voluntary applicants). These were designed to ensure that a large proportion of optants would be ineligible for the Wrens and included proficiency in German, practical experience of working with boats, or a family connection with the Royal or Merchant Navy.[68] Intakes destined for the women's forces were summoned to a medical examination and interviewed by a service recruiting officer. If they met the basic admission standards, and were not already employed on essential war work or judged to be of 'doubtful character', such as convicted prostitutes, they were posted by the Ministry of Labour and National Service to an individual service in accordance with the womanpower priorities at the time. Those called-up were liable to serve anywhere at home, and later abroad if necessary. In the spring of 1942, the first conscripts reported for duty.[69]

As it turned out, the military conscription of women was to be a relatively short-lived phenomenon. The call-up of new age classes was suspended from early in 1944, as it was thought that volunteers could provide the required intakes in the final stages of the war.[70] Nevertheless, during the conflict, some 125,000 national service personnel were conscripted into the women's forces (17,600 serving in the WRNS, 33,800 in the WAAF and 73,600 in the ATS).[71] Conscripts – or 'army-class' recruits as the Ministry of Labour and National Service preferred to term them, because the choice given to women to undertake civilian war work, rather than military service, was thought to make those who opted for the latter 'tantamount to volunteers'[72] – thus made up less than a quarter of the women who joined the wartime services. The share of conscripts in the total male service intake was two-thirds.[73] Although proportionally few in number, women conscripted into the forces were regarded by some of the early members as a threat to the esprit de corps of their organisations. Jane Macbeth grumbled about the 'bolshie tendencies' of the girls called up for the ATS: 'Now recruits were inclined to demand their rights and did not give all to their country as their duty.' For her, conscription 'gave a blow to the old spirit of volunteering'.[74] Agnes Anderson commented on similar attitudes in the WAAF: 'There was not the same spirit amongst them as we all had, and they used to say to me that they couldn't think how I had stayed in the service all this time.'[75] As Ilana Bet-El has shown, male conscripts during the Great War were regarded in a similarly negative light.[76]

Meanwhile, the Ministry of Information sponsored a film to help improve the image of the ATS and boost recruitment. *The Gentle Sex*, which first appeared in cinemas in the spring of 1943, was written by a young female screenwriter, Moie Charles and directed by Leslie Howard. Filmed at Stoughton barracks in Guildford and featuring real auxiliaries as walk-ons alongside the actresses, it told the story of seven ATS recruits from diverse backgrounds, such as 'Gwen' the cockney waitress, 'Anne' the army officer's daughter, 'Erna' the Czech refugee, and 'Betty' the closeted only child, as they proceeded through basic training and onto service in the ATS.[77] It was intended, in the words of Howard, to demonstrate 'the significance of their work' and 'the magnificent way in which they are doing their duty'.[78] Although the ATS hierarchy was concerned that some of the scenes of auxiliaries under fire during a bombing raid 'were not likely to encourage parents to let their daughters join up',[79] the film did well at the box office and was praised by reviewers. One male critic declared that 'Whenever I pass any member of the ATS in the future I shall feel inclined to raise my hat respectfully ... They perform a hundred tasks which would have astonished their grandmothers.'[80] Jenny Nicholson was also impressed. Although she claimed that none of the actresses suffered the indignities of actual recruits in that they were driven each day from their hotel to the barracks, she nonetheless described it as 'the first truthful and affectionate account of any women's service': 'There was a sturdy tenderness – a health without heartiness – about it which was delightful.'[81] Yet, as Lucy Noakes reminds us, while the film portrayed the new wartime opportunities for women in the ATS, the omniscient closing speech narrated by Howard reasserted 'masculine superiority and power over the female characters':[82]

> 'Well, there they are, the women. Our sweethearts, sisters, mothers, daughters. Let's give in at last and admit that we're really proud of you. You strange, wonderful, incalculable creatures. The world you're helping to shape is going to be a better world because you're helping to shape it. Pray silence gentlemen. I give you a toast. The gentle sex!'[83]

The Markham Report

In order to ease the passage of conscription through parliament, Bevin promised anxious MPs, several of whom had voiced concerns about poor living conditions in the ATS, that a review would be undertaken of the standard of amenities in the women's services.[84] At the end of 1941, he proposed to the military authorities that an interdepartmental committee should investigate the issue. In addition, he suggested that a permanent advisory committee of women should be constituted to guide the service departments over welfare matters. This body would reassure the parents of those called-up and act as an 'invaluable buffer' between the ministries and parliament.[85] Whilst the opportunity for interdepartmental consultation was welcomed by the service chiefs, there was some hostility to the creation of a women's advisory committee.[86] Sir Archibald Sinclair, the Secretary of State for Air, responded that he did not wish to share responsibility for the welfare of the WAAF with such a forum and that his own women officers were capable of giving him better advice than 'a peripatetic committee of ladies who cannot possess the same knowledge of the conditions in the Services'.[87] In the light of these objections, Bevin dropped the idea of a women's body but, early in 1942, an inter-departmental committee was set up to look into the question of ame-nities. This was to be composed of the three male parliamentary secre-taries of the service ministries, together with their counterpart from the Ministry of Labour and National Service and chaired by the Admiralty representative: Sir Victor Warrender.[88]

Concurrently, women's groups began to lobby the government on the matter. The National Council of Women of Great Britain and the Woman Power Committee (the latter being an unofficial group of female MPs and TUC representatives concerned with women's war work) called for an external investigation into the welfare of servicewomen.[89] Irene Ward, Conservative MP for Wallsend-on-Tyne and chairman of the WPC, informed the Lord President of the Council, Sir John Anderson, that 'an internal inquiry by the Departments will be regarded on all sides as prejudiced'. She contended that an 'independent inquiry by women whose names carry weight with the public is the only way of allaying public anxiety'.[90] Despite these representations, the Deputy Prime Minister, Clement Attlee, who was standing in for Churchill at the despatch box, went ahead and announced the forma-tion of the Warrender committee to the House of Commons. His state-ment did not go down well with the MPs present. Not only did this departmental body reek of a 'whitewash' but its all-male composition offended feminist sensibilities. 'Does my right hon. Friend think it would be a good thing', enquired Thelma Cazalet-Keir, National Conservative MP for East Islington and a member of the WPC, 'to set up an all-women committee to inquire into conditions in the male Services?'[91] Outside the house, there was a similarly censorious reaction from interested parties. Attlee received a wave of disapproving letters from such organisations as the National Women Citizens' Association, the London and National Society for Women's Service, St Joan's Social and Political Alliance, and Hampstead Garden Suburb Women's Liberal Association.[92]

By this stage, Churchill had begun to see the vulnerability of the government's position – 'It seemed to me rather odd that the [Warrender] Cte should consist entirely of men', he scrawled on a briefing document[93] – and asked Attlee to meet, on his behalf, a deputation of MPs led by Cazalet-Keir.[94] Having listened to their concerns, and consulted the service ministers, the Deputy Prime Minister recommended that the departmental committee should be superseded by an entirely different body. This would be an independent committee headed by a woman chairman and incorporating a majority of female members.[95] Although Sinclair was said 'to remain unconvinced of the advantage of setting up a [new] Committee',[96] the Prime Minister agreed to its formation.[97] It started work in the spring of 1942.

The committee was chaired by Violet Markham, a prominent public servant who had taken part in a similar inquiry into the WAAC during the previous war, and included Cazalet-Keir; Dr Edith Summerskill, the Labour MP for West Fulham; Mary Stocks, principal of Westfield College, University of London; and Katharine Elliot, chairman of the National Association of Mixed Clubs and Girls' Clubs.[98] Its remit was to report on 'amenities and welfare conditions' in the three women's services. The committee met on thirty-four occasions to consider evidence submitted by the ministries concerned, as well as outside bodies, and visited 123 military camps and stations across the country. Hundreds of letters were also received from concerned parents about the ordeals of their daughters in uniform. These ranged from complaints about the lack of gumboots at muddy camps to accusations that tight-fitting military tunics made women's breasts 'deformed and pendulous'.[99]

In the late summer of 1942, the Markham committee published its report. Much of the findings were concerned with matters affecting the living conditions for servicewomen. It was admitted that during the early period of the war there had been justifiable grounds for complaint and examples were cited of such problems as inadequate accommodation.[100] But the report noted that great efforts had been made to improve the quality of life for female personnel and accommodation now reached 'a reasonable, and sometimes a high, standard'.[101] The committee was keen to stress that gender differences were important in this respect: 'the auxiliaries of to-day are the wives and mothers

Figure 2.4 Violet Markham, 1938, who chaired the committee of inquiry into amenities and welfare conditions in the women's services (© courtesy of Halcyon Palmer)

of the future ... [and] no one desires to apply a wholesale hardening process to the young women who are serving their country'.[102]

The section of the report that grabbed most of the attention, however, was that which addressed the salacious issue of 'service life and morals'.[103] During the course of its inquiry, the committee took the opportunity to investigate the rumours of immorality that had plagued the ATS – which had also begun to sully the reputation of the other women's forces.[104] Summerskill was sceptical about how reliable their findings would be in this regard: 'I never quite understood how, by paying a visit to an officers' mess at lunch-time and making a cursory tour of a camp one bright summer day, one could discover anything adverse about the sex life of the girls.'[105] Nevertheless, while the report recognised that 'standards of sexual behaviour' had changed greatly during the previous generation and that some recruits would bring 'loose habits' acquired in civilian life into the military fold, it was asserted that 'promiscuous conduct in the Women's Services is confined to a small proportion of the whole' – a pattern of behaviour seemingly confirmed by the calculation that the pregnancy rate among unmarried servicewomen was lower than the illegitimate birth rate among the comparable female civilian population. As a consequence, it was contended that 'a vast superstructure of slander has been raised on a small foundation in fact'. This was put down in part to the aphorism that 'virtue has no gossip value', but also to a deep-rooted suspicion of the military profession among the British public, which meant that 'a woman in uniform may rouse a special sense of hostility, conscious and sub-conscious, among certain people who would never give two thoughts to her conduct as a private citizen'.[106] The committee concluded that the reports of scandalous behaviour were thus largely the stuff of fantasy:

> We can find no justification for the vague but sweeping charges of immorality which have disturbed public opinion ... these allegations reflect most unfairly as a generalisation on a body of women, the vast majority of whom are serving their country in a high and self-respecting spirit.[107]

The military authorities were understandably pleased with the report. A statement drawn up for the press declared that the women's services had been 'vindicated' and had 'every reason to feel satisfied'.[108] Leslie Whateley recorded that the 'whispering campaign' against the ATS was largely killed as a result of the inquiry and members of her service could 'now hold their heads high as they went about their work'.[109] The decision of Princess Elizabeth to join the ATS – quite a coup given the royal family's naval connections – seemed to indicate that confidence in the service had been restored.[110]

3 TRAINING AND SELECTION

Training

New recruits to the women's services were posted in the first instance to female basic training centres or depots. The period they spent at these establishments varied over the war years but eventually came to be three weeks for those in the WRNS, four weeks for those in the WAAF and five weeks for those in the ATS.[1] In the WRNS, volunteers were regarded as 'probationers' for the first two weeks of their military careers. This meant they could pack up and leave their training depot at any time during the first fortnight if they decided that life in the Wrens was not for them.[2]

WAAF officer Constance Woodhead described the colourful scenes at her service's training centres when batches of new recruits reported for duty:

> It was interesting to watch the daily arrivals at the recruits' centres; to see the raw material coming in. Women in neat country suits and sensible shoes; girls in shabby frocks, growing too small for them; others in their best finery, dripping with fox furs and pearls and teetering on high-heeled slippers; fancy hats with feathers, simple felts, no hats; silk stockings, cotton stockings, no stockings. Some were eager at once to impress, some merely anxious to efface themselves, some in an agony of shyness, others as bold as brass, some intelligently interested, some

already quivering with dislike at the herding together; all terribly anxious to do the right thing in this strange new world . . .

Sometimes mother or auntie came too, just to make sure that everything was all right; once two small infants were brought along by a would-be recruit in the touching faith that a grateful country would take care of them whilst mother cooked for the RAF. Once or twice an indignant husband turned up in an attempt to claim a wife who had slipped off without his knowledge to join the WAAF.[3]

One of the first experiences for recruits of this 'strange new world' was an assignment to sleeping quarters. The starkness of a barrack could come as quite a surprise to those who were accustomed to more comfortable surroundings. Roxane Houston of the WRNS compared her quarters to those of a nineteenth-century workhouse: 'Narrow little iron beds with only a narrow strip of dingy carpeting and a narrow locker dividing each from its neighbour. Everything narrow, meagre, impersonal, small worlds of isolation.'[4] The issuing of clothing, personal equipment and 'necessaries' was another rite of passage. In the ATS, for example, this included such items as steel helmet, ground sheet, respirator, eating irons, enamel mug, identity discs, mending kit, hair brush, greatcoat, peaked cap, skirt and jacket, shirt and tie, brassiere, corset, rayon knickers, lisle stockings, lace-up shoes, and – as a special concession to women – winceyette pyjamas.[5] Some of these garments were looked upon with disbelief by those of a fashion-conscious disposition. Winifred Lane recounted that 'the famous khaki knickers, of silky-feeling rayon with elastic at the legs as well as the waist, were greeted with incredulous laughter'.[6] Others were less amused by their new apparel. 'I'll never forget the loathing of seeing my legs clad in khaki lisle stockings', groaned Iris Bryce. 'I felt like my Gran.'[7] A medical inspection was a further initiation. This often involved women stripping off, forming up like a chorus line and being poked and prodded by a medical officer looking for hidden ailments and conditions ('bugs, scabies and babies' quipped one WAAF examinee[8]). For the more bashful recruits, this proved to be something of an ordeal. 'We were very modest in those days', recalled Shirley Aston of the ATS. 'Having to parade naked appalled us.'[9] An introductory pep talk was an additional formality. Eileen Smith and her fellow WAAF recruits were assembled in a hangar and addressed by their female commanding officer: 'She told

Figure 3.1 WAAF recruits being issued with service shoes, 1941 (Watford/ Mirrorpix via Getty Images)

us what was expected of us, how to behave, how to dress and then proceeded to tell us that there were American soldiers in the village nearby, saying "Now gals, I want no necking down the lane."[10]

During their initial training, female personnel underwent a programme of rudimentary military instruction designed to assimilate them into the forces. The syllabi came to resemble that of their male counterparts, with an emphasis on 'spit and polish', drill, route marches, PT (physical training) and lectures on service procedures. Women were not, however, expected to undertake weapons' training.[11] Much of the instruction was carried out by the female staff, but male NCOs took part in the conduct of drill.[12] Eileen McMurdo of the ATS indicated that these servicemen found the task of drilling women exasperating at times:

> Our initiation into the complexities of squad drill were [sic] conducted by the Regimental Sergeant Major who was 'on loan' from one of the regiments of Guards. He was not the gentlest of

creatures on the parade ground but then he had a tougher job than most sergeant majors. It must have required nerves of steel and the patience of a saint to teach us 'rookies' the basic difference between a right and a left turn to say nothing of coping with the odd female who, after a half an hour or so of trying to master the fundamentals of moving to the right in threes, would dissolve into tears declaring that she'd never been shouted at like that in her whole life and who did the RSM think he was anyway?![13]

Yet they also derived a certain satisfaction when 'their' recruits reached the required standard. Pat Sparks of the WAAF reminisced that her regular flight sergeant could not conceal his delight when his trainees mastered their drill movements: 'E Squadron,' he proudly exclaimed, 'you're marvellous!'[14]

For many women, their basic training proved to be a considerable culture shock. A number were bewildered by the military timetable. Hilda Mason confessed to being so confused during her first few days in the ATS that she never knew where she should be or what she should be doing at any given time. She thus 'paraded with whichever section was nearest'.[15] Some were disconcerted by the depersonalisation of the training regime. 'Like prisoners hearing the gate shut and the key turned,' reflected Muriel Gane Pushman on her induction into the WAAF, 'we were locked into a system where we were numbers and did as we were told; our human likes, dislikes, fads, or even temperaments were not a matter for consideration.'[16] Others were flummoxed by service terminology. Houston found the naval lexicon of the WRNS – in which a floor was a 'deck', a wall was a 'bulkhead', a dining room was a 'mess' and a trip out of camp in a ten-ton lorry was 'going ashore' on a 'liberty boat' – to be mystifying: 'I began to feel I was living in a sort of looking-glass world, and wondered if I'd ever fit in.'[17] A few were picked on if they were perceived to display airs and graces. Mary Lee Settle, an American WAAF volunteer, was thrown into a puddle of mud by spiteful airwomen in her hut: 'That'll teach the fuckin' toffy nose', the ringleader proclaimed.[18] A handful soon fell foul of military regulations. Bryce, still reeling from the frumpiness of her ATS wardrobe, was placed on a charge of misappropriating the King's uniform after her first kit inspection:

> We'd been shown how to lay out the kit, everything folded in a certain way and placed strategically on top of your bed, and

we standing to attention by the side of the bed. Sgt. [Sergeant] Watson slowly walked from bed to bed, followed by Cpl. [Corporal] Lacey. A brief nod if all was well, or a shake of the head and the offending garment wrenched up and thrust against the trembling khaki clad individual who had dared to place a shirt too near the pyjamas. My turn next. She stopped, looked at the bed, her eyebrows disappeared beneath her cap peak, she swivelled round on me, then eyes widened as she looked at the bed once more. The Cpl. was trembling now, but I just stood, puzzled. What was wrong? I'd watched my neighbours and oh so carefully folded and placed everything in the right order. 'Where's the rest of it?' Sgt's voice thundered the length of the hut. Heads turned to look at me, then quickly straightened front as Cpl. glared up and down. I looked at my kit and realised what she meant. I smiled and sighed in relief 'Oh, you mean the bras and corsets, I couldn't wear those, especially the corsets, all those bones. No, I've got my own roll-ons. I've sent the others to my Gran for her jumble sale.'

Sgt's face turned pink, then sweat glistened around her nose and her eyes bulged, she seemed to choke, but managed to blurt out to the Cpl. 'Put her on a charge NOW.' She resumed the rest of the inspection and I was marched out of the hut to sit and wait my fate [confined to barracks for forty-eight hours].[19]

Inevitably, there was a good deal of heartache among new recruits. Gabrielle Reilly discovered that soon after arriving at her WAAF training camp 'all the glamour of joining up and doing one's bit had well and truly vanished. One was just left with a painful feeling in the pit of one's stomach and a sense of loneliness.'[20] Vee Robinson found her early weeks in the ATS equally trying: 'There were muffled sobs sometimes after Lights Out and I have to admit that some were mine.'[21] The conscripts were said to have found it particularly difficult to adjust. Joan Cowey recorded that 'the girls [in the ATS] who were drafted had a hard time accepting it. I remember girls getting really hysterical in the barrack rooms – they couldn't cope.'[22] Some unfortunate women became so traumatised that they broke down completely and were quietly removed from the new intakes. Bryce wrote of one such case:

Poor little Marian touched all our hearts. An only child from 'a nice part of Neasden' she'd worked as a filing clerk in a local printers 'only at the end of the High Street, Mum was pleased as I could still go home for dinner'. After a life of gentle coddling she now found herself being shouted out, wearing uncomfortable ill fitting clothes, getting soaking wet doing PE on the barrack square and no Mum ... By the end of the third week as we all groped our way out of the Gas Hut [after being exposed to gas as part of anti-gas training] she just broke down and cried and cried and cried. No one could stop her. Cpl. slapped her face, then we laid her on her bed, and finally she saw the MO [medical officer] and went into Sick Quarters. A week later her kit was collected and we never saw her again. I sat on my bed that night and felt an ache deep inside me – oh lucky, lucky Marian. How I wished I could be back in civvy street again.[23]

In order to ease their transition into the WAAF, Jane Trefusis Forbes concluded that female intakes to her service needed to be managed with greater sensitivity than their male counterparts if they were to be prepared for the rigours of service life:

Although in broad principle there is no reason to treat women substantially differently to men, it appears that owing to the

Figure 3.2 Waafs on parade at a RAF Fighter Command station, 1940 (Saidman/ Popperfoto via Getty Images)

greater difference between normal civilian life and Service life in the case of a woman compared with man, there occurs a slightly greater shock and change to a woman coming into the Service.

For these reasons it is important that recruits should be handled with every possible care and consideration.[24]

Yet despite any initial anguish, most 'rookies' gradually adjusted to their new surroundings. Pushman observed that she and her fellow recruits found themselves 'accepting orders and rules, at first in a spirit of resignation, then with growing enthusiasm, and finally with a determination to match ourselves individually and collectively to the challenge'.[25] In similar terms, Bryce recognised that by the time the '"square bashing" was almost over I realised that I had accepted the, to me, artificial, unnatural programme of my new life'.[26] At the end of her training, McMurdo 'felt that I could have accepted any challenge to fight the entire Nazi horde unaided, and, if necessary, to the death'.[27]

Augmenting these tendencies was a growing affinity with their male 'parent' services. For Angela Mack of the WRNS, such a bond was sealed by a lecture given to the trainee Wrens by a 'fierce' naval officer:

He made it very clear that it was our duty to defend our country to the nth degree, if necessary to our last breath. We were exhorted to give one hundred and twenty per cent of our best every moment of every day to live up to the great tradition of the Royal Navy. Much was made of the fact that we would be *part* of the Navy and not an auxiliary service as were the ATS and WAAF. Whatever happened we must not let the Navy down which had so generously – perhaps this particular officer secretly considered *unwisely* – allowed women to share their duties and responsibilities. Although I appreciated his unspoken reservation, it did not detract from the patriotic fervour all these talks had brought out in us. It was the 'England Expects ... ' message and, I imagine, as one woman, we all gave our hearts to the Royal Navy from that moment.[28]

Joan Wyndham's heart was captured more fancifully. She reported that the 'grand finale' of her WAAF basic training was a talk on 'esprit de corps': 'We rather liked this one. The main theme seemed to be keeping the pilots happy and off the booze, giving them a home atmosphere and so on. We all felt we could do this rather well.'[29]

Figure 3.3 Wrens learning morse code at HMS *Mercury*, the Royal Navy's signal training establishment, 1943 (Keystone Features via Getty Images)

In any event, Rebecca Barnett discovered that before long, in true RAF style, she and the other WAAF recruits 'shouted "wakey-wakey!" in the mornings, talked of a "pukka lot" or of things being a "wizard prang" and everybody was simply a "bod"'.[30] Likewise, Mary Lee Settle related that on a first excursion from their initial training unit into nearby Hereford, the trainee Waafs 'called out the Forces' insult they had just learned, to civilians, out of the bus windows, "Ah, you dirty civvie, get some in!" – the "some" being time in the service, of which they had had about three weeks'.[31]

Once women had completed their basic training, those who required further instruction for the roles they were to perform in their service were transferred to more specialist training units. The length of the courses varied from two weeks for less skilled jobs, such as an ATS mess orderly, to six months for the more complex duties women came to undertake, such as a WAAF flight mechanic.[32] A good deal of this training came to be conducted at the male 'parent' service's technical training schools and the pattern of instruction generally conformed to that of the servicemen. A number of the courses, however, had to be lengthened because of a perceived lack of scientific knowledge on the part of female recruits.[33] It was found, for example, that it took at least a month longer to train a WAAF electrician than her RAF equivalent. 'Few women, unless they had taken a course on electricity in the home,' it was observed, 'had a clear idea of a volt or an amp.'[34] The advent of mixed-sex trade training did arouse some hostility in male service circles. There was, for instance, some resistance in the RAF towards airwomen being taught alongside airmen. But, according to the Air Ministry, 'this opposition gradually died down as the success of co-operative training was proved'.[35] Meanwhile, when Dorothy Calvert of the ATS discovered that most of the instructors at her radar training course were male, she was delighted: 'That was a plus for a start, for if I had got to learn anything, I would rather it was a man doing the teaching, as I always found women bitchy, or they were with me.'[36]

For those earmarked as potential officers, female officer cadet training units were established. The time they spent at these institutions fluctuated during the conflict, with the duration of the basic syllabi finally settling at four weeks for those in the WRNS and eight weeks for those in the WAAF and ATS.[37] The curricula mirrored those of their male equivalents, with instruction in such matters as service administration, military law, the conduct of ceremonial parades and 'woman-management', but the trainees did not study battle tactics.[38] Jenny Nicholson provided a flavour of her WAAF officer cadet lectures:

> Shuffle into separate huts … Just like school. 60 desks. Blackboard. Lecture desk at top and on rostrum. Find desk marked 81 and move in. Schoolgirl rabble. Crashing of desk-tops. Filling of fountain pens and borrowing of blotting-paper. Expect any moment to hear '*Quis*?' 'Ego' of school days …
>
> … lecture on 'Discipline and Morale.' Had impressed upon us hundred vital points. Discipline defined as 'habit of Law and Order.' Morale defined as 'Inner condition' – maintained by

Good Leadership, Personal Interest, Loyalty, Efficiency, Initiative, Ingenuity, Complete Fairness. Whole matter gone into thoroughly. Completely absorbed . . .

Lecture on 'Etiquette and Customs.' When passing troops with uncased colours you will salute the colours. You don't salute when riding a bicycle (for security reasons). Don't chat at breakfast in the Mess. Great detail on how you pass port. Not done to apply for leave the moment you arrive on new station . . .

Lecture on 'Anti-Gas.' Morbid reference to hot sweet tea, to removing patient's dentures, and disarming the depressed . . .

Lecture after tea, 'Organization on an RAF Station.' Assistant Adjutant is responsible for the destruction of rats . . .

. . . lecture on 'Women in HM Forces.' Instructive. Learn that Swiss cross reversed became Red Cross at International Convention at Geneva, 1864. WAACs were in Army of Occupation, 1919. WRNS have trade [of] 'Hall Porter.' . . .

Hungry by end of 'Messing' lecture. Buy two doughnuts and number of biscuits at Break. 'Never give airwomen on night shift unattractive sandwiches.' . . .

Get 'Arrest and Custody' lecture from only man lecturer. Kind, grey Squadron Leader. Difficult to absorb. Open and close arrest. Who can arrest you for what, and who suffers. Hold a mock court martial to illustrate how it works. Good performance from fellow-students picked to take part. They make entrance through outside door that opens on to playing fields. Storm breaks in middle of trial. Very wet second witness.[39]

Implicit in their training was an expectation that fledgling officers should learn to conduct themselves as 'gentlewomen'. During her WRNS officer cadet course, Ann Tomlinson believed that she and her fellow trainees were closely monitored at mealtimes for signs of uncouth behaviour:

I remember sitting at one of those long tables, being very much aware of the high table which was raised on steps at the far end of the room under this magnificent arch, where the senior members of staff of the [Royal Naval] College sat, and we all knew – how we knew, I do not know, but we did know, all of

us – that we were being watched throughout every meal, and
that our manners were being taken note of. The way we con-
versed with people and the way we behaved ourselves, our
whole demeanour was being watched and noted. And we
would say to each other, 'Now that is not becoming to an officer
and a gentlewoman'.[40]

At Barbara Littlejohn's ATS officer training unit, the cadets were
required to attend a 'sort of social hour' with their instructors and
engage with them in 'cocktail chit-chat'. As one of the youngest trainees,
and unaccustomed to small talk, she found this 'one of the most difficult
things that we had to do at OCTU'.[41]

Some women regarded their officer training as akin to life in
a rather claustrophobic girls' boarding school. 'The whole thing was so
strained', complained Josephine Peyman of the ATS. 'A mass of females
all living under the shadow of dismissal, all trying to outshine each
other, all trying to talk louder and so draw attention to themselves.'[42]

Figure 3.4 The Duchess of Kent, Commandant of the WRNS, inspects WRNS
officer cadets at the Royal Naval College, Greenwich, London, 1941 (© Imperial
War Museum)

Yet most managed to survive the ordeal and assume their new officer status within units. A few felt uncomfortable initially in the more rarefied surroundings. Daphne Coyne recalled that

> At dinner on my first evening at the Wren officers' quarters [in Newcastle] I'd had a very perfunctory welcome from the other officers and it had gone on from there. I had been depressed to see that I was the only young one at the table. To my twenty-one years, almost all the others were in their thirties and forties and unmarried. Here was a hot bed of bitchiness, jealousy and knitting patterns. I had landed among some very embittered women and they made it clear that I was not welcome.[43]

Others relished their enhanced military status. Joan Wyndham found her new life as a WAAF officer to be 'absolutely the cat's whiskers':

> I nearly died of shock when I first walked into the Mess [at RAF Bentley Priory, the headquarters of Fighter Command] – all chintz sofas and blazing log fires – and a suave blonde walked up to me and said, 'Hello, Wyndham, how about a gin and lime?' The food is wonderful and booze flows in abundance. Our private sitting-room is called the ante-room, large and sunny with a piano and a radiogram.
>
> All my fellow officers are fairly glamorous and a gay, wild lot, always talking about the Savoy or the Berkeley, and the night-clubs they've been to. They are mad about swing and play hot jazz all day.
>
> The Wrens, who share our Mess, are sniffy and stuffy, read-ing good books in one corner of the ante-room while the WAAFs go trucking madly around the gramophone singing 'Bounce Me Brother with a Solid Four'.
>
> ... I feel I am living in some wonderful dream.[44]

Training courses were also organised for commissioned officers.[45] These were generally designed to update and improve their administra-tive knowledge. At the ATS junior officers' school, which ran a four-week programme along these lines, the women were appraised on their performance and, in conformity with standard army practice, were shown any adverse comments in their course reports. The school assess-ment procedure had to be reviewed, however, after it was found that it upset the students. In contrast to male officers, many of whom regarded a disparaging report – 'a stinker' – as almost a badge of honour, female officers who were criticised apparently returned to their units 'in a very depressed state' and, as a result of spreading 'alarming reports' about the school, created a wave of 'hysteria' among other officers ordered to attend the course, which in turn inhibited their ability to benefit from it.[46] According to Leslie Whateley, this episode demonstrated to the ATS authorities that they had to take careful account of the 'peculiar psychology of women'.[47]

Selection

During the early period of the war, a woman was usually earmarked for a particular employment within her service on the basis of a brief interview with an officer at a recruiting centre or basic training centre, who sought to ascertain a recruit's qualifications and preferences.[48] This rather arbitrary method, however, began to prove problematic as the range of trades open to women expanded – many of which did not have a civilian equivalent – and conscription brought recruits from a wider variety of educational, occupational and social backgrounds into the forces.[49] Chief Commander Edith Mercer, a psychologist who acted as the technical advisor on personnel selection matters in the ATS, summed up the challenge:

> Clearly, if efficient use was to be made of the human material available, a selection problem of considerable magnitude existed and one which involved not only accurate information of the existing attainments and experience of these recruits but also an assessment of their potentialities for training on new lines.[50]

To remedy this, in 1942, the ATS instituted a more 'scientific' selection system that utilised psychological tests to help allocate auxiliaries to specific jobs.[51] The WAAF and WRNS also adopted such tests to varying degrees in order to assist in the selection of its personnel.[52]

The new selection system developed in the ATS ran on parallel lines to that in operation in the army.[53] At recruiting centres, women were required to complete the Progressive Matrices test of general intelligence. This was designed to screen out those whose low scores indicated that they were unlikely to perform any useful military function. Some 6 per cent of candidates fell into this category and were not admitted to the service.[54] Those who proceeded to basic training then completed a further battery of aptitude tests. This included a clerical instructions test, a spelling test, an arithmetic test, a spatial awareness test and a mechanical comprehension test.[55] These tests were broadly the same as those taken by male soldiers, but some modifications were made for auxiliaries.[56] The arithmetic test, for example, was thought to be too difficult for women – 'the average female adult', contended wartime service psychologist Philip Vernon, 'cannot even manage decimals' – and a simpler version was substituted.[57] The mechanical comprehension test was also adapted so that the questions were, in the words of Vernon, based on 'cooking, clothes, motor cars and other things of which women might be expected to have had experience'.[58]

After completing the tests, recruits were interviewed by a specially trained female personnel selection officer (PSO) who assessed a woman's educational attainment, civilian experience, physical characteristics and personal interests. The PSO then recommended a recruit for suitable employment within the service. In making this judgement, she took into account the test scores and other selection criteria laid down for each trade in the detailed job analyses drawn up by ATS psychologists, as well as the fluctuating demands for different categories of employment. Auxiliaries were subsequently posted for specialist training on the basis of this recommendation.[59]

Some recruits were sceptical of the newfangled ATS selection methods: 'These [aptitude] tests, we heard on good authority, had been devised for the sole purpose of fitting the maximum number of square pegs into round holes', quipped Eileen McMurdo.[60] But there was evidence to suggest that the revised procedures helped to ensure women were allocated to the most suitable employment within the service. A follow-up study was conducted to test the validity of the PSOs' recommendations and this revealed that of the 39,000 auxiliaries who proceeded to specialised training between October 1942 and October 1943, 94 per cent of trainees were successful in reaching the standard required to warrant posting to their respective employments. An opportunity was also taken to compare the performance of those who had undergone the full selection process with those who had been sent to specialist training without having been evaluated by a PSO. It was found, for example, that while the training failure rates for clerks and drivers selected under the modified system was 4% and 14% respectively, it was 11% and 30% for the others.[61] 'Where the evidence was available', noted Senior Commander Mary Wickham, one of the ATS psychologists who conducted this research, 'wastage was at least halved by the use of selection methods.'[62]

As for officers, after the outbreak of war, they were mainly drawn from the ranks and selected for officer training after a short interview with boards of senior officers who sought to assess their leadership potential.[63] Margaret Egerton recounted her nervous appearance before one such ATS panel. The fifth daughter of the Earl of Ellesmere, she had spent the early months of the conflict undertaking clerical duties at various headquarters in Scottish Command but, by her own admission, could only type with two fingers and was hopelessly confused by the numerous War Office acronyms:[64]

> We were told we were to become officers and we were sent up in front of Dame Helen Gwynne-Vaughan, who was about a mile high, with straight grey hair and gaiters – really, she was a man and very terrifying. Another on the panel was Lady Maud Baillie, very smart in kilt and uniform jacket.
>
> ... I marched in. 'Sit Down, Egerton. Do you play hockey?' 'No, ma'am.' Did you go to school?' 'No, ma'am.' Are you a Girl Guide?' 'No, ma'am.' They were absurd questions but I found myself answering 'No' to all of them and thinking: Please let me say 'Yes' to *something*.
>
> 'Well, what are you? Are you a clerk?' 'Before the war, no, ma'am. I find clerk work very difficult. I spend the whole morning typing and the whole afternoon rubbing it out.' They roared with laughter.[65]

Egerton passed the board, but this largely subjective selection method became increasingly anachronistic as the demand for offi-cers grew and candidates came to be drawn from outside the traditional officer class.[66] Unsurprisingly, the members of these panels also gained a reputation for allowing social class prejudices to colour their judgements: 'They look out for dirty nails, holes in stockings and try to find out if your mother was a char', reckoned Joan Wyndham.[67] Although the WAAF and the WRNS persevered with these interview boards, the ATS opted to moder-nise its officer selection procedure and in 1943 extended the use of psychological testing to those recommended for commissioned rank.[68]

Under the new ATS officer selection system, which closely resembled that developed in the army, those who were considered to be officer material were sent to a female War Office Selection Board (WOSB) for forty-eight hours. At these establishments the candidates, who were known only by numbers, undertook various intelligence, personality and group tests in order to evaluate their leadership potential. These included the 'leaderless' group test, during which batches of candidates were observed as they completed practical tasks. Attendees might also be interviewed by a psychiatrist in order to detect any unrecognised qualities or underlying instability. It was found that most of the testing procedures employed at the male WOSBs could be adapted for women. But those designed merely to measure powers of endurance and physical courage were deemed to be 'unsuitable' for female personnel, who would not be expected to lead their women into action, and were thus omitted from the programme.[69] Other refinements were also advocated for the ATS selection boards. It was suggested that since the average age of auxiliaries was 'markedly lower' than soldiers, and that many of the former had come directly into the forces from home, female candidates needed to be capable of exerting a 'mother' style of leadership ('a woman who is essentially interested in each of her auxiliaries as an individual and whose outstanding quality is kindly understanding'). Likewise, given the fact that those ATS officers without operational duties tended to undertake more administrative work than the average army officer, so bureaucratic competence was considered to be of enhanced significance. Moreover, it was contended that female officers needed to be able to get on better with the other sex than their male colleagues:

> The majority of ATS officers have to work directly or indirectly in co-operation with male officers, while in the Army, a comparatively small proportion of the officers will need to co-operate with women officers. It is, therefore, important to select women as officers who will be able to work happily with men, and who will not err either on the side of being too shy and distant, too emotional or too dictatorial. Suspicion that a candidate would have difficulty in maintaining such a friendly relation with men should make the ATS Board hesitate about passing her.[70]

During 1943, some 4,800 auxiliaries went through this new selection process, of whom a third were sent on to officer training.[71] The selection process was an uncomfortable experience for many. Olivia Scovell acknowledged that 'The WOSB was an ordeal. For forty-eight hours we had to do things pretty well non-stop, and everything we did was watched and noted.'[72] In her case, this included a practical group exercise, which involved constructing an overnight shelter from items of farmyard rubbish, during which she was 'fully aware that my insular activity was not really showing the right Girl Guide spirit', and the completion of 'an appalling paper which asked us to give a description of ourselves as seen, first, through the eyes of our best friend, and then, through the eyes of our worst enemy. It was like baring one's soul.'[73] Scovell (who failed to make the grade and returned to the ranks) was also surprised to find a curious emphasis on the candidates' future role as homemakers. She recalled that at the end of her selection period they were all called together for a farewell speech from the female president of the board:

> It was a talk which she must have learnt by heart, and the same message was obviously given on dozens of these partings. All those who attended WOSBs could almost quote it. It blended condolences with congratulations, and finished off on the lines, 'For those of you who have passed, I know that you will make splendid officers. For those who have not passed, I know that you will continue to do your duty. For all of you, however, I know that some day you will get your heart's wish and become wonderful wives and mothers!'
>
> As we left shortly afterwards I heard several mutterings of 'What on earth a WOSB has to do with wives and mothers I can't imagine!'[74]

4 WORK

The Expansion of Roles

On the eve of war, the range of jobs undertaken by the women's services was very limited in scope. As we have seen, in the WAAF, women were employed in six categories of work: as cooks, clerks, orderlies, equipment assistants, motor drivers and balloon fabric workers.[1] In the ATS, they were utilised in five categories: as cooks, clerks, orderlies, storewomen and motor drivers.[2] And in the WRNS, they were also deployed in five categories: as cooks, writers, stewards, motor drivers and communication workers.[3] All of these duties were non-combatant roles that, in the words of one naval commander, could be categorised as 'conventionally applicable to women'.[4]

Once hostilities commenced, new job opportunities soon opened up. Manpower shortages compelled the military authorities to broaden the span of employments in order to release servicemen for combatant duties.[5] Moreover, as women proved themselves proficient in their new military roles, so the male service establishment became more sanguine about extending their functions further.[6] The three service departments tended to decide these matters on a case-by-case basis.[7] In the Air Ministry, for example, a standing committee was established in the autumn of 1940 to assess the practicability of substituting Waafs for airmen in RAF employments not previously open to the WAAF. This substitution committee, which was composed of senior RAF officers from relevant directorates, together with DWAAF, met on seventy-one occasions during the war. It was guided by the principle that 'no work should be done by a man which could be done efficiently by a woman'.[8] This involved an analysis of such factors as the degree of physical strength required, the location and working conditions of certain RAF stations, the operational risks involved in high training failure rates and whether employing women on the maintenance of aircraft would have 'the psychological effect on aircrew of giving them unnecessary worries'.[9] On occasions, such evaluations resulted in a stark reassessment of traditional gender assumptions. In the spring of 1941, the committee considered the possibility of employing Waafs in the more technical RAF trades. The initial view was that this was not feasible because 'women had not an inherent mechanical instinct and consequently could not be trained to reach the degree of skill required'.[10] However, after experiments in certain trades proved 'highly successful', the committee revised its opinion and by the summer of 1943 Waafs were employed across all RAF trade groups.[11] Constance Woodhead summarised this change of perception:

> the mental picture conjured up by the sceptics of a girl gazing in bewilderment at a large aircraft engine and weeping because of the grease on her hands and face, gradually faded. It changed to an actual picture of a brisk, capable young woman in overalls, hair tucked under a beret, scrambling over an aircraft, almost to the manner born.[12]

When all army establishments were formally specified as comprising 'military "and/or ATS" personnel', Leslie Whateley saw it as a sign that the army had come to regard the ATS as 'in substitution for' soldiers, rather than merely as an 'encumbrance or addition'.[13]

Over the course of the war there was a dramatic expansion in the variety of jobs open to servicewomen – many of which were customarily 'masculine' in nature. In the WAAF, women came to be engaged in approximately eighty categories of work. These included such duties as an acetyelne welder, flight mechanic, air frame fitter, electrician, instrument repairer and barrage balloon operator. In the WRNS, women were placed in some ninety categories. These comprised such tasks as a ship mechanic, torpedowoman, despatch rider, bomb range marker, boats' crew and boom defence Wren. In the ATS, women were assimilated into roughly 130 categories. These encompassed such occupations as a sheet metal worker, carpenter, vehicle mechanic, armourer,

Figure 4.1 WAAF flight mechanics and armourers service a RAF Hawker
Hurricane, 1943 (Rider-Rider/IWM via Getty Images)

searchlight operator and instrument number in an anti-aircraft
battery.[14] One contemporary commentator on the participation of
women in the war effort, Vera Douie, remarked that these were functions 'quite undreamt of in earlier times.'[15]

    Some of these roles came close to being combatant in character.
WRNS boom defence Wrens – 'boom defence' having little to do with
the true nature of their activities – despatched free-flying latex balloons
with incendiary devices and trailing steel wires across the North Sea on

Figure 4.2 Wrens move a torpedo in readiness for loading onto a submarine, 1943 (Lt. J. A. Hampton/IWM via Getty Images)

the prevailing winds, with the intention of igniting forest fires and damaging overhead power lines in Germany.[16] WAAF barrage balloon operators fitted explosive charges to the cables of the balloons to help bring down enemy aircraft that flew too close to their blimps.[17] ATS operational numbers in anti-aircraft batteries worked the fire-control apparatus that located targets and directed the gunfire.[18] The Adjutant-General, General Sir Ronald Adam, acknowledged that the non-combatant status of these female 'gunners' was decidedly ambiguous: 'it must be admitted that in the case of AA batteries the distinction was rather "thin"'.[19]

Occupational hierarchies soon began to develop within the women's services. In the ATS, auxiliaries undertaking jobs that were deemed 'manly' and close to the 'frontline', such as those working on anti-aircraft gun sites, tended to enjoy the highest prestige.[20] In the WAAF, it might have been expected that those employed on barrage balloon sites would have been held in similar esteem. Yet they were looked down on by others in their service. Instead, it was the aircraft plotters in the operations rooms at the RAF bomber and

Figure 4.3 Waafs learning how to handle a barrage balloon (© Imperial War Museum)

fighter stations who were regarded – and were prone to regard themselves – as the superior beings. Tessa Stone has suggested that this was partly due to class distinctions – the 'rougher' types of women were said to man the barrage balloons, whilst the more genteel gravitated towards the plotting tables – but it was mainly a result of their closer proximity to combat flying operations and thus their more tangible contribution to the RAF war effort.[21] Hazel Williams admitted that her fellow plotters 'were very snooty and considered that they were to the other WAAF trades what RAF Air Crew were to ground trades'.[22] Rebecca Barnett confirmed that, as a WAAF teleprinter operator, the plotters she came into contact with 'often had noticeable upper-crust accents and the sort of manner that went with it ... On the other hand, we, the signals lot, put ourselves above some trades too.'[23] It is arguably the genteel image of WAAF plotters tracking the movement of aircraft around plotting tables like croupiers at a roulette table that has become one of the dominant motifs in representations of women's wartime military service.[24]

Figure 4.4 WAAF plotters at work in the Operations Room at the headquarters of the RAF's No. 11 Group, 1942 (© Imperial War Museum)

Such was the allure of 'ops' that a few plucky airwomen managed to smuggle themselves onto RAF missions. Rosemary Britten, a WAAF intelligence officer at RAF Earls Colne, clandestinely joined the crew of a Halifax bomber in 296 Squadron as it towed a Horsa glider full of troops across to Germany during Operation Varsity: the airborne crossing of the Rhine in the spring of 1945. She refrained from applying her usual powder and lipstick 'because I wanted to look like a German girl in case of bailing out' and the crew carried her parachute and 'Mae West' (life jacket) to the aircraft 'so that I merely looked like a love-sick Waff officer bidding a fond farewell to the brave unto the very last moment'. Badly damaged by anti-aircraft fire over the landing zone, the Halifax was forced down on an airfield in France. On returning to the UK, Britten, who was thought to have been killed when other crews mistakenly reported that the aircraft had been destroyed, was carpeted by a female superior over her illicit flight: 'I had an hour's lecture and was threatened with the AOC [Air Officer Commanding] and dire consequences if anyone let it out. Awful tales of questions asked in the House. As a matter of a fact I think she was jealous.'[25]

Figure 4.5 An ATS cook stirs a cauldron of stew at an army cookhouse, 1942 (Sgt. Wooldridge/IWM via Getty Images)

Despite the great expansion of roles during the war years, there were limits to this process. The majority of servicewomen continued to be utilised in 'feminine' jobs. By the final stages of the conflict, roughly two thirds of those across the three women's services were engaged in catering, domestic, clerical or communications work.[26] In the ATS, for example, 11% of its total strength at the start of 1945 were employed in catering, 15% in communications, 16% in domestic, and 28% in clerical posts.[27] What was more, even those undertaking more 'masculine' duties could find themselves performing 'housekeeping' chores for their male colleagues. Norma Lodge and her fellow ATS radio location mechanics dubbed themselves the 'Charminster Chars' when they were required to clean and polish the workshops on top of their

Figure 4.6 An ATS teleprinter operator at a London HQ, 1942 (© Imperial War Museum)

technical work.'[28] Likewise, WAAF aircraft electrician, Joan Bulpitt, was not given any 'proper' electrical work to do at RAF Keevil and was simply ordered to 'keep the stove stoked up, and fetch tea and cakes from the Naafi! I became very good at crosswords.'[29]

In addition, servicewomen were never fully interchangeable with men across a number of jobs. The long hours and physical strength required for certain functions meant that male counterparts were not always replaced on a one-for-one basis. In the ATS, 44 per cent of its personnel in early 1945 were deployed on duties with a more generous five-for-four or three-for-two replacement ratio.[30] Moreover, within the nominally one-for-one posts, women were sometimes restricted as to what tasks they could perform. In the WAAF, air frame fitters were not allowed to work outdoors at night; motor mechanics were forbidden to hand start heavy engines from cold; armament assistants were not permitted to fire guns; and tailoresses were proscribed from fitting airmen's clothes.[31] Indeed, in the autumn of 1942, an Air Council letter specified that while RAF personnel were required to work a minimum of sixty hours per week, Waafs were limited to forty-eight hours, except in cases where they were working side by side with the men and which made different hours impractical.[32]

Furthermore, there were a range of jobs from which servicewomen were excluded. Whilst Wrens, for instance, were employed as submarine attack teachers, which involved operating a simulator that trained submarine captains in the latest tactics for attacking enemy ships,[33] there was resistance to Waafs serving as flight simulator instructors. Airmen, it was believed, 'might not take kindly to having their faults corrected by women'.[34] In similar terms, although civilian women pilots in the Air Transport Auxiliary were utilised to ferry RAF aircraft between factories, storage depots and operational air bases, Waafs did not undertake comparable flying duties.[35] Air Chief Marshal Sir Trafford Leigh-Mallory, Commander-in-Chief of the Allied Expeditionary Air Force, found it 'astounding' that the WAAF should not share in the RAF's essential function of flying, especially since members of the ATS helped to man AA batteries, and that this 'pedestrian, Safety First policy' put the service at a grave disadvantage in recruiting 'the best and most adventurous type of woman'.[36] Most notably, however, servicewomen remained firmly barred from undertaking direct combatant roles in the forces. These included acting as aircrew in RAF squadrons, as seamen on Royal Navy warships and as soldiers in frontline fighting units of the army.[37] As one early ATS recruiting poster starkly put it: 'The men will do the fighting, you must do the rest.'[38]

This denial of combatant status extended to the use of firearms. As Corinna Peniston-Bird has demonstrated, there were 'fuzzy' gender boundaries in operation here since those serving as armourers repaired rifles, pistols and machine guns, whilst others visited weapons ranges to learn to shoot. ATS officer Lavinia Orde nonchalantly recalled volunteering for instruction in firing a Tommy gun, a Bren gun and a PIAT anti-tank weapon whilst attached to General Montgomery's headquarters in South Eastern Command.[39] Nevertheless, servicewomen were technically prohibited from personally using lethal weapons as part of their duties.[40] This led to a good deal of uncertainty as to what 'defensive role' they should play if they found themselves in the presence of the enemy at close quarters. In the different orders of battles for local defence schemes, members of the ATS, for example, were variously required 'to take shelter with the civilian population'; 'render First Aid, assist with communications, or carry out other non-fighting duties'; and 'use Arms in defence of their HQ, or in self-defence in the last resort'.[41] Precisely which instructions were given was said to be dependent on the 'imaginative ability' of male commanders and 'their opinion on the usefulness of women as a whole'.[42]

This institutional aversion to female combat and the bearing of arms seems to have been largely driven by deep-seated gender conventions. Edith Summerskill, who mounted a vigorous but unsuccessful campaign to convince the War Office to permit women to serve as combatant members of the Home Guard, suggested that the underlying cause was a 'nineteenth-century conception of womanhood' which determined that 'women are still weak, gentle creatures who must be protected'.[43] Penny Summerfield speculates that there might have been deeper psychological concerns lurking in the male service mind, that associated the gun with the phallus and gave rise to fears of 'collective emasculation'.[44] Yet a distaste for female combat was not an exclusively male phenomenon. Vera Laughton Mathews opined that while she would not forbid female personnel using lethal weapons – and 'boom defence' Wrens apparently received some weapons training to defend their launch site – women were simply not designed for killing:

> As one who believes that the similarities between men and women are much more marked than their differences, I would say that one of those differences lies in the taking of human life. The women's part in producing life is so infinitely greater than the man's, that one feels she must do violence to her nature in deliberately destroying life.[45]

Jean Knox seems to have held similar views:

> Women have won a merited place in the active army, but they cannot be trained to kill. I don't believe women can take life as men can. I know nothing of Russia [where women were fulfilling combat roles in the wartime armed forces], but I know

women. Women give life. They are not designed to take life, even in total war.[46]

Jane Trefusis Forbes offered a different perspective. She regarded her force as an integral part of the RAF's 'fighting chain' and thus the question of killing was more one of semantics than conceptions about 'the womanliness of women'.[47] Nonetheless, from a post-war perspective, the DATS, Mary Tyrwhitt, believed that the 'defensive role' of auxiliaries in the face of the enemy had been left unresolved: 'I feel that during the 1939/45 war we managed to skim over this fact by reason of the essential "temporariness" of the ATS and of the crying need of the Army for additional pairs of hands'.[48]

ATS in Anti-Aircraft Command

The servicewomen who perhaps came closest to challenging the combat taboo were the ATS 'gunners' in Anti-Aircraft Command. Before the outbreak of war, Major-General Sir Frederick Pile, the unblimpish AA chief, had begun to consider the possibility of employing women in an operational role. In 1938 he invited a leading female engineer, Caroline Haslett, to advise him on their capacity to operate the fire-control instruments in anti-aircraft batteries. After a series of weekend visits to gun sites in the Surrey hills, suitably armed with mackintosh and umbrella, she assured him that they could perform this function if called upon to do so.[49]

Shortly after hostilities broke out, Pile wrote to the War Office floating the idea of utilising the ATS operationally in his command.[50] The response was predictably frosty: 'there can be no question of the employment of members of the ATS on operational duties of a combatant nature', pronounced the Director of Military Operations and Plans, ' ... unless and until the man-power position becomes acute'.[51] By the end of 1940, with the Blitz in full swing, this scenario had arisen. AA Command was nearly 18,000 under strength and Pile, who was already deploying many members of the ATS non-operationally as cooks, clerks, drivers and orderlies, approached the army authorities again over the matter. He proposed that the ATS be allowed to replace some male fire-control operators in anti-aircraft batteries in order to help alleviate the manpower shortfall.[52]

The prospect of women going into action alongside Royal Artillery gunners on gun sites was anathema to some within the military establishment – what the author of AA Command's internal wartime history described as 'fluttering the dovecotes with a vengeance'.[53] But Pile received timely backing from a War Office committee, under Air Marshal Sir Philip Joubert (at this time an assistant chief of the Air Staff), which had been set up to inquire into the organisation of his command in light of the manpower shortages. It supported Pile's proposal as a means of economising on personnel and concluded that 'any objections would nowadays appear to be sentimental rather than practical.'[54] The endorsement of the Joubert committee swung the matter. Although Sir James Grigg, the Permanent Under-Secretary of State for War, dubbed Pile's proposal 'breath-taking and revolutionary', in the spring of 1941 the Army Council gave its consent.[55] The War Cabinet added its own blessing shortly thereafter.[56] Pile wrote of 'outraged cries of horror from the diehards. But it was pure mathematics that forced everybody's hand'.[57]

In the early summer, the mixed-sex anti-aircraft batteries began to take shape.[58] The ATS would operate the fire-control instruments that located the targets and directed the gunfire, but Royal Artillery personnel would *fire* the guns. This ostensibly protected the women's non-combatant status, yet entailed a degree of sophistry. It was a matter of debate, for example, whether there was a significant difference between manning a predictor machine, which fed information to the gun crews about the predicted course of hostile aircraft, and pulling the firing lever of a 3.7 inch gun: both were essential to bringing down the German bombers.[59] 'There was a good deal of muddled thinking', commented Pile, 'which was prepared to allow women to do anything to kill the enemy except actually press the trigger'.[60] It was also the case that ATS 'gunners' continued to rely on their male colleagues for armed protection against enemy parachutists or saboteurs attacking gun sites. The ban on servicewomen using firearms led to the bizarre situation of women undertaking guard duties equipped only with a stick and a whistle.[61]

These new mixed batteries were first deployed towards the end of the summer.[62] Inevitably there were teething troubles. On some of the early gun sites, the soldiers and auxiliaries were naturally wary of one another and had difficulties in gelling as a unit. Kina Manton, the senior ATS officer of one of the first mixed AA regiments based near

Figure 4.7 ATS personnel serving at a 3.7-inch anti-aircraft gun site, Wormwood Scrubs, London, 1941 (Lt. Puttnam/IWM via Getty Images)

Edinburgh, recalled that 'for the first week or 10 days it was difficult to get the sexes even to speak to each other except when driven to it by virtue of their work'.[63] In tandem with this, there were concerns about a male loss of face and a suspicion that the auxiliaries would get more favourable treatment. One male 'gunner' officer in AA Command admitted that 'the AT "invasion" is felt as a humiliation' and that there were fears 'the men will have to do all the dirty work ... while the women do all the soft jobs'.[64] Beyond the confines of the AA camps, these strange new military phenomena were greeted by the public with a mixture of inquisitiveness and suspicion. ATS 'gunner', Mari Hopkins, remarked that when a mixed battery arrived on an AA site 'its perimeter was haunted for the first few days by local people staring at the female curiosities and hoping, perhaps, to catch a glimpse of a pair of khaki bloomers dangling from the barrel of an ack-ack gun'.[65] Some looked upon these units with deep moral concern. Manton, for example, was accused by locals of being in effect the 'madam' of an army brothel.[66] Gradually, however, a camaraderie developed in the batteries and public attention waned as the novelty wore off.[67] The commanding officer of one of the first mixed batteries confessed that he had 'loathed' the idea of such a role, but there was 'practically no difference at all between the running of a mixed or any other battery'. He recorded that there had developed 'a really fine spirit of mutual help between the sexes' and that in their first action 'everybody stood up to the ordeal extremely well'.[68] By 1943, approximately 30,000 auxiliaries were manning the fire-control apparatuses on AA sites and Pile pronounced the mixed units 'a triumphant success'.[69] 'The experiment', he declared, 'had exceeded even my more sanguine hopes.'[70]

There were occasional cases of female 'gunners' breaking down under the noise of the gunfire and being removed,[71] but most seem to have relished their 'frontline' duties. ATS staff officer Mary Thomson recalled that when a mixed battery near Weymouth shot down a German plane and the pilot parachuted into the sea, the women were so fired up by the thrill of battle that after spotting the airman attempting to get to the shore they shouted out to the rescue team: 'Don't save him, don't save him!'[72] They also displayed a good deal of courage. When Private Nora Caveney, an eighteen-year-old predictor operator from Walsden in Lancashire serving with 148 (M) Heavy Anti-Aircraft Regiment, was mortally wounded by a bomb splinter as she tracked an enemy aircraft over the south coast in April 1942 – the first member of the ATS to be killed in action – her place was immediately taken by a female colleague, Private Gladys Keel, who ensured that the guns were able to keep firing without interruption.[73] Another predictor operator who showed great calmness in action was Private Violette Szabo (later to be posthumously awarded the George Cross for her heroism as a secret agent with the Special Operations Executive in occupied France).[74] It was said that 'Her jesting at moments of stress, without a sign of fluster or concern, happily proved infectious and helped to allay the misgivings of the battery commander as to the girls' ability to face up to real danger.'[75] For many auxiliaries it became a matter of pride to perform as well as their male comrades when the alarm sounded. 'We were determined', reminisced Betty Holbrook, 'to shine gloriously in any raid that might take place'.[76] Elizabeth Hunter confided that she was prouder of having served with an AA battery than any other role she performed in the service: 'We thought we were terrific, we were the only girls actually fighting.'[77]

Meanwhile, despite their 'manly' employment, the auxiliaries did not abandon their femininity on the gun sites. Manton reported that

> Many, both male and female, had expressed a fear that the life would make the women of a mixed unit 'unfeminine'. They would have felt re-assured if they could have heard the comments of the male officers when knitting and embroidery made an appearance in the command post. Instinctively it was forbidden, but the hours when nothing happened were long and gradually the men were persuaded to see that neither activity interfered with immediate readiness or efficiency and much fancy work was done in unpromising surroundings.[78]

Dorothy Calvert, a radar operator in a mixed battery, corroborated these feminine tendencies. Although she dressed like a male gunner and learnt to swear, sing bawdy songs, drink beer and smoke – 'no longer the little village girl, but a bit of a ruffian'[79] – she confessed to a periodic female 'weep in':

> A real feminine act, sitting on our beds, the Sgt. too, all howling at once, very funny I suppose, but women were women, in uniform or civvies, and no one could fathom the way the female mind works or acts. We, after a good weep, would tidy up, giggle, feel a lot better and get on with the work in hand.[80]

She also recalled that on Christmas Day in her battery the male gunner officers dressed up as the ATS, 'make-up and all', and served dinner to the auxiliaries.[81]

The employment of women in the mixed batteries raised the issue of whether the ATS should be more closely integrated into the army. Pile was in favour of greater assimilation and pressed for his auxiliaries to be enlisted in the Royal Artillery: 'I could not see why, if a woman was to play exactly the same part in a battery as a man, she should be controlled by a women's organization such as the ATS.'[82] But the female hierarchy firmly opposed this and saw in it the seeds of the break-up of their institution. 'The ATS were very jealous of their position', continued Pile. 'They were a woman's service – run by women. No male officer should have any authority over them – nor was his advice heeded. They were there to help the Army, but only as they thought fit.'[83]

Figure 4.8 Winston Churchill; his daughter, ATS officer Mary Churchill; and General Sir Frederick Pile, Commander-in-Chief of Anti-Aircraft Command, watch a demonstration of measures used to combat flying bombs over the south of England, 1944 (Capt. Horton/IWM via Getty Images)

This attitude was illustrated by an outburst from Jean Knox whilst chairing a meeting of senior women officers at the War Office shortly after the establishment of the mixed batteries. Manton attended the meeting and was subjected to a vituperative attack from the head of her service when she suggested that her auxiliaries' allegiances tended to lie with their batteries rather than with the ATS:

> After a harangue from the chair on the importance of being loyal to our own Service, separateness, building a fine body of women and the undesirability of the Army having anything to

do with us, we were asked our opinions individually as to whether the ATS rank and file should be loyal first to their regiments or to the ATS ... When my turn came, with my usual tact I said winning the war mattered most of all and that the ATS were in fact loyal to their units first last and all the time and that this was a 'good thing'. The ATS was too vast for them to visualise as a living entity anyway and women would serve what was personal and near at hand. The result startled me – Jean Knox called me a lot of things, sacked me out of hand, burst into tears and rushed from the room![84]

In fact, Manton – who, it should be noted, was quickly reinstated by Knox's deputy, Leslie Whateley – went as far as to claim that 'our own ATS higher command did not believe in us, did not understand what we were aiming at and even perhaps hoped we would not succeed'.[85]

The ATS authorities won this particular battle and, with the support of Adam, who maintained that the women's conditions of service would be better safeguarded under the existing arrangements, the female 'gunners' were not subsumed into the Royal Artillery.[86] Pile concluded that 'in this laudable ambition of getting the girls equal status ... I was more of a feminist than the members of the ATS Directorate'.[87] Nevertheless, as Shelford Bidwell points out, 'some sensible concessions were made to regimental feeling, without impugning the loyalty owed to the Service'.[88] Women serving with the batteries were permitted to wear the RA grenade badge on their blouses, the AA Command formation sign on their sleeves and the white gunner lanyard on their shoulders. On the gun sites, female 'corporals' were addressed as 'bombardier' and female 'privates' as 'gunner'.[89] In the meantime, Knox, whose relations with the army authorities became increasingly strained, resigned 'for reasons of health' in the autumn of 1943 and was replaced by Whateley.[90]

In addition to their service in the mixed gun batteries, members of the ATS were also employed on searchlight duties in AA Command. These entailed illuminating enemy aircraft in the powerful beams, in order to aid the anti-aircraft gun crews. Despite some concerns within the War Office about whether women would be 'temperamentally or physically capable of enduring the hardship, the night watches and the tedium of searchlight manning',[91] in 1942, ATS detachments were deployed to Royal Artillery searchlight units and, uniquely, an 'all-

Figure 4.9 Leslie Whateley, Director of the ATS 1943–6 (Popperfoto via Getty Images)

female' ATS searchlight regiment – the 93rd – was formed.[92] In the initial stages, the regiment did receive some surreptitious male assistance with the heavy mechanical tasks on its small, isolated searchlight sites. Pile confided that

> We had to keep very dark about the fact that on most of these sites, in the early days of the experiment, there lived in a tent a solitary and carefully chosen gunner. It can be imagined what play could have been made by the more prurient sections of the

Press with the fact that among these unchaperoned young women lurked a solitary male soldier. His duty was to swing the heavy Diesel generator, in the days before this equipment was fitted with a self-starter. We never had any trouble from these solitary gunners, and as the matter never reached the ears of the politicians all was well.[93]

The regiment was also handicapped by its inability to defend itself against enemy aircraft. One of the tactics the German pilots adopted was to fly down the beams of these units in order to shoot out the searchlights and a particular complaint of the 93rd was that its auxiliaries were not permitted, like their male counterparts, to protect their sites with machine guns. Manton, who came to know the regiment well when it was serving in her AA brigade near London, observed that 'all they wanted was the chance to hit back, instead of having to behave like sitting ducks'.[94] Nonetheless, Pile stated that

all in all, the experiment was every bit as great a success as it had been in the case of the Heavy AA regiments ... Every time I visited such a site, and it was much easier to go there than to get away, I wondered why we were ever such fools as to doubt that the thing would work.

And work it did. The girls lived like men, fought their lights like men, and, alas, some of them died like men. Unarmed, they often showed great personal bravery.[95]

One former member of the 93rd, Elizabeth Oldham, found the experience of serving with the regiment exhilarating: 'We spent long hours awake, waiting – but when we got something in our sights it was fantastic.' She also enjoyed the esteem of belonging to such a distinctive operational unit: 'We were unique, and when I first went home my father walked me all round Stockport, he was so proud.'[96]

Workmates

Inevitably, there was a good deal of suspicion on the part of servicemen across the armed forces to the prospect of working alongside women. WAAF flight mechanic, Dorothy Hobson, recalled, for example, that 'the airmen in our hangar didn't seem very happy to see us and the Flt/Sgt didn't seem to know what to do with us'.[97] WRNS boats' crew, Pamela Burningham, recollected that the reaction of her chief petty officer was 'girls in the Navy, whatever next? Flighty young things, can't expect them to do a man's job properly.'[98] Indeed, a number of senior officers tried to avoid employing women at all. Constance Woodhead admitted that 'it was years before some commanding officers could be induced to accept a WAAF section on their stations'.[99] In similar vein, Vera Laughton Mathews observed that 'there were naval officers who declared that they would fight against having WRNS to the last ditch'.[100]

The female personnel could be given a tough time at work by their male colleagues. There were schoolboy jokes at the women's expense. Working in a naval store, Wren Jean Rawson was asked for such items as 'tartan paint' and 'left-handed hammers'.[101] There was a reluctance to help women struggling with their jobs. When WAAF driver, Peggy Wells, approached an airman to help crank up her tractor delivering bombs to aircraft he refused: 'You joined up to replace a man so get on with it.'[102] Sometimes women were deliberately snubbed. ATS officer K. T. Mannock recalled that when she was posted to a staff role at the War Office, her male superior officer 'totally ignored my presence and made no effort to give me any work to do. He was, I suppose, one of the old school who thought the little woman's place was in the home'.[103] In turn, some servicemen could be teased by their male colleagues if they worked closely with female personnel. Burningham recounted that her male coxswain, Nobby Clarke, who had survived a torpedoing whilst on a Russia-bound convoy and been given an 'easy' job while he recovered, was referred to as 'Wren Clarke' by the sailors.[104]

There were also instances of sexual harassment. This could take various forms. WAAF photographic assistant, Pamela Brisley-Wilson, recalled one RAF NCO, 'an ageing, ugly, bumptious, dirty, old man', who would gather together groups of young airwomen and tell them 'quite disgusting jokes. Half of them I was quite sure didn't understand them.'[105] WAAF waitress, Morfydd Brooks, recollected that in the sergeants' mess at RAF Scampton the air would be blue with sexual innuendos:

> The doors would burst open and the Aircrews would swarm in shouting boisterously. As we served their food we young Waafs had to endure a barrage of good natured banter. 'How about

a date Darling?', 'How is your Sex life?', 'I dreamt about you last night', 'Would you like to sleep with me?', 'Please serve us in the nude'. Then someone would shout, what is the collective noun for Waafs? They would answer, the collective noun for Waafs is 'A Mattress of Waafs'. They would all then erupt into hilarity.[106]

Sometimes such 'banter' would spill over into attempted sexual assault. ATS clerk, Lois Goossens, was forced to make a dash past a table of 'rough and ready' Black Watch soldiers during mealtimes in her mess hall in order to avoid being molested: 'if their Sgt. Major caught them making a grab for us, he walloped them with his baton'.[107] Likewise, middle-aged male officers could use their privileged position in the military hierarchy to harass young servicewomen. WRNS typist Penny Martin had to manoeuvre herself out of the unwelcome clutches of her naval officer boss: 'He had tried to get more than somewhat familiar late one night when we were alone in his office (on business) and I was shocked out of my socks . . . I made it quite clear that the whole idea was repulsive.'[108] At their naval base, WRNS signaller, Edith Dixon, and her female colleagues were required to work in pairs at night on the switchboard to safeguard them from the male ratings.[109]

Some brave servicewomen decided they were simply not going to put up with this treatment and complained to the military authorities. One such woman was Mary Thomson (then Mary Dixon). She had a particularly harrowing experience whilst serving at the headquarters of an anti-aircraft division in Newcastle. The 'revolting' male major-general, she remembered, began to take an unhealthy interest in her. He would encourage her to sit next to him at meal times; he asked his batman to visit her billet with a view, she believed, to reconnoitring the entrances; he would caress her bare arms when in shirt-sleeve order; and he attempted to grope her under a rug on the back seat of his official car during a visit to a RAF base. The denouement came when he asked her into his office one morning, locked the door, and literally chased her around his desk and settee before she somehow managed to escape from the room. The shock of the incident was such that she was unable to recall how she evaded his grasp, but 'I can remember the horror of it and thinking how is this going to end'. Thomson, however, was now convinced that this man was a serious menace and as the daughter of an archdeacon and god-daughter of a field marshal she was certainly not intimidated by the trappings of rank. She thus made an official complaint to her military superiors, was interviewed by the relevant Anti-Aircraft Corps commander in Edinburgh, and told him that she was quite prepared if necessary to repeat the allegations in front of the Army Council. The offending general – who, it was rumoured, had already been posted away from a previous appointment because of 'trouble' with an ATS driver – was removed. Nevertheless, despite this victory, she could not escape a pang of guilt: 'I really felt awful because he was a sick man.'[110]

The proprieties to be observed between senior male officers and their female subordinates could lead on occasion to friction with the women's services. When Admiral Sir Bruce Fraser, the Commander-in-Chief of the Home Fleet, discovered that his WRNS chauffeur, Wren Cockerham, had never been on board a warship, he invited her and two other Wrens to be shown around HMS *Duke of York* in Scapa Flow and take tea on his flagship. This, however, contravened WRNS regulations

Figure 4.10 ATS officer Mary Thomson (then Mary Dixon), c. 1945, who served as a staff officer in Anti-Aircraft Command. She ended the war with the rank of Controller (Colonel), later becoming Deputy Director, ATS, Middle East Land Forces (courtesy of Richard Thomson)

which laid down that Wrens were only allowed on board ships in organised groups and on specified days. A bitter row blew up between Fraser and the WRNS hierarchy in Orkney.[111] WRNS Chief Officer Macpherson at Lyness contended that such a flagrant breach of the rules would undermine discipline, lead to jealousy and resentment on the part of Wrens who did not receive such an invitation, and imperil the 'moral reputation' of her service.[112] For his part, Fraser was indignant at the attitude of the local WRNS officers and, as commander-in-chief, believed that if he wanted to show his appreciation to those who worked for him, his wishes should be complied with.[113] Such was the strength of feeling on the part of the WRNS officers over this issue that Macpherson and two of her female colleagues requested to be discharged from the service.[114] In the end, the dispute was defused after Vera Laughton Mathews visited Fraser in Orkney and bluntly told him that the rules had been made because 'they had been found necessary', that unofficial visits were 'liable to misunderstanding', and that he should 'show the way to the Fleet'. The Admiral promised to toe the line but, given Macpherson's 'uncompromising attitude' and 'present frame of mind', her discharge from the WRNS was arranged.[115]

Such conventions could sometimes inhibit the appointment of servicewomen to personal assistant posts within the military hierarchy. In what has been described as a 'hitherto unheard-of step', Lieutenant-General Sir Andrew Thorne, the Commander-in-Chief of Scottish Command, invited Mary MacDonald, a subaltern in the ATS, to join his staff as a second aide-de-camp, partly in response, she suspected, to Russian criticism that the western allies were not making full use of women. Yet he was subsequently forced to cancel the appointment of this highly-efficient officer (later to become a lecturer in politics and fellow of Somerville College, Oxford) when, according to MacDonald, 'higher authority' hinted that it was not 'proper' for the army commander to travel round his command with an unmarried woman: 'The driver was insufficient chaperone.'[116]

Despite these tensions, as time went on, male-female working relations seem to have settled down. Dorothy Hobson recorded that after the frosty reception she received from airmen, the competence she displayed at her job eventually secured her their approval. One night she took her usual place at the WAAF table in the cookhouse but was called over by one of her male colleagues. '"Come and sit with us," he said to her, "if you're good enough to work with – you're good enough to eat with." I picked up my plate and mug of tea and went to sit with them. At long last, I felt that they had accepted me as a fellow mechanic.'[117] Likewise, Pamela Burningham remembered one day overhearing a private conversation between her hard-bitten chief petty officer and another chief in the bosun's stores. '"Don't you criticise them girls", she heard the former say. "Better than your lads in many ways. Do their jobs well, they do." So we knew he was an old softie really.'[118]

Some formerly sceptical senior officers became effusive in their praise of female personnel. 'When I was told that I should have to take a large number of ATS', admitted the army commandant of a Royal Army Ordnance Corps depot, 'I was horrified at the thought. I did not like it at all. Within six months I had completely changed my views. They were magnificent.'[119] The Royal Navy commander of a submarine depot wrote in similar terms of his Wrens: 'I say quite frankly that I didn't like their presence .... However it wasn't long before I became completely converted. The Wrens behaved splendidly.'[120] These sentiments were shared by a RAF group captain: 'When the first little trickle of Waafs drifted into my station I was inwardly rather resentful .... How wrong I was ... thank Goodness that this country could produce such a race of women as the Waafs on my station.'[121] 'In the end, curiously enough,' remarked Constance Woodhead, 'some of the most persistent antagonists of women in the service became among the most ardent in their admiration and support of the WAAF.'[122]

For their part, many women came to identify strongly with units of their 'parent' service. Not only did this apply, as we have seen, to the auxiliaries in the mixed AA batteries, but was also a particular hallmark of the Waafs who worked at the operational air bases. They tended to develop a close affinity with the RAF aircrew flying combat missions. Radio-telephone operator Pip Beck recorded 'the relief if all the aircraft returned safely; or the sad, empty feeling if someone was missing'.[123] Special Duties Clerk Patricia Thom remembered that 'we were always watching and waiting for them to come back, hoping they'd all make it'.[124] After many of Morfydd Brooks's flyers failed to return from the Dambusters' raid in 1943, she and her fellow waitresses 'burst into tears' at the sight of the empty tables in the mess the following day. Over the next few weeks they were posted away to work with different squadrons: 'the Higher Ups thought that we Waafs had become too involved with the Aircrews to function efficiently and therefore we must be separated. I think they were right.'[125]

Airwomen also took on unofficial 'maternal' roles for flyers. While some darned socks and sewed wings on RAF uniforms for their male colleagues,[126] others became part of a psychological support network. Edna Skeen, the WAAF 'map queen' at RAF Scampton, became a lucky charm for superstitious airmen: 'After each briefing, each would touch me on the shoulder and say, "See you tonight." This became a ritual and they considered it bad luck if they went out without touching my shoulder.'[127] Grace Archer, a WAAF intelligence officer at RAF Mildenhall, was asked by her station medical officer to keep a look out for flyers suffering from nervous exhaustion: 'I felt it to be a tribute to his faith in me that he asked me to let him know if I thought any aircrew member needed his help, as I saw more of them than he did.'[128] Another WAAF intelligence officer, Edith Kup, recollected that she and other airwomen at RAF Pocklington often found themselves comforting anxious and distressed aircrew. She remembered consoling a navigator trembling with nerves:

> He was in a dreadful state, he'd had some pretty rough trips and was shaking like a leaf. It all came out and he had a good cry on my shoulder. I talked to him rather like one of my horses frightened by rough handling .... Eventually he felt better and off he went to bed. I am pleased to say he survived the war. He wasn't the only one and I'm sure the other girls had similar experiences, though no one ever mentioned it. These things were sacrosanct, and the boys knew they could trust us.[129]

Jenny Nicholson confirmed that the bonds with the aircrews were especially strong among the Waafs directly involved in 'ops':

> What most impressed me was how completely the women who were closely connected with the planning and carrying out of operations had adopted the characteristic behaviour of the men who were compelled to live and die in an atmosphere of superlatives and habitual tragedies. I was in an Ops room immediately before a bombing operation. The crew came in to the Cypher officer to empty their pockets. A morbid enough performance at any time. A sergeant pilot placed the items of his pocket-collection on the desk one by one. String, letters, money, a lump of sugar pinched from the Mess, a diary and two toffees.

The WAAF Code and Cypher Officer checked the assortment, tied it up into a neat little bundle and locked it in a safe. 'Tell Mum I died happy,' joked the Sergeant Pilot. 'Only the good die young,' she reminded him. 'Good show – then I'll live to tell the tale.' Actually he didn't.[130]

Airwomen in these operational roles were sometimes first-hand witnesses to the agonies of flyers in combat. Aileen Clayton, an intelligence officer at RAF West Kingsdown during the Battle of Britain, recounted that the female staff intercepting Luftwaffe radio traffic were able to listen into German formation leaders ordering their aircraft to dive onto unwitting RAF fighter pilots below but, to their frustration, had no means of warning them in time: 'I would often hear one of the WAAF operators murmuring: "Oh God, ... oh God, ... please, ... *please* look up ... ", and I knew how helpless she felt.'[131] They also facilitated 'kills'. On one occasion at RAF Hawkinge, Clayton and her team were instructed to call in No. 11 Fighter Group when they detected a familiar German reconnaissance pilot, who usually chatted away in English over the airwaves on the assumption that he was being

Figure 4.11 Bomber Command aircrew being interviewed by a WAAF intelligence officer at RAF Lakenheath, after returning from a mine-laying operation on the enemy coastline (© Imperial War Museum)

monitored, operating on his regular beat. She heard him shot down in flames by a flight of Spitfires and regarded herself in part as 'his executioner':

> He was unable to get out and we listened to him as he screamed and screamed for his mother and cursed the Fuehrer. I found myself praying: 'Get out, bale out – oh, please dear God, get him out.' But it was no use, he could not make it. We heard him the whole way down until he fell below reception range. I went outside and was sick.[132]

Meanwhile, workplace relations between servicewomen and their female officers in the women's forces could be variable.[133] Wendy Ferguson of the WRNS recounted that 'some women made marvellous officers, but others thought they were the Queen!'[134] In similar fashion, Amy O'Connor of the ATS recorded that 'some of the women officers were good and some weren't. I think they were always frightened of losing their dignity ... it always seemed to me as if they daren't let go'.[135] In the WAAF, the 'administrative' (or 'G') officers oversaw the 'well-being' of airwomen on RAF stations and they were described as 'the backbone of the service':

> Their days were filled with endless pettifogging details, lists and charts and records, visits to working sites, to quarters, trips down to Equipment, to see about so-and-so for the women ... Evenings and weekends would be just as busy, with classes for one thing or another, sessions of 'non-specialist training', discussion groups, entertainments, games and matches.[136]

Yet there was social class antagonism towards them on the part of some airwomen. 'Such officers were chosen not for specific skills,' opined Mary Lee Settle, 'but for a mystic hangover from a distant peacetime – a quality called Officer-material, which usually meant that one's voice was careful, one's bearing "genteel", that one was, at least in form, a "lady".'[137] Others in the WAAF remarked on the high-handedness that could accompany the granting of commissioned rank. Madeau Stewart maintained that 'On the whole women officers were tolerable. But it has to be said that some women who acquire power over other women become tyrannical and, in the end, absurd.'[138]

There were, moreover, fissures within the female officer corps. Constance Woodhead reported that there was a rift between the WAAF 'administrative' officers and the WAAF 'substitution' officers (who directly replaced RAF officers in specialist technical roles and were thus less inclined to concern themselves with the administration of air-women) since the latter regarded themselves as 'making a bigger contribution to the war effort than any administrative officer could possibly be doing'.[139] There were also, according to WAAF officer Muriel Gane Pushman, generational divides:

> Most of the women in the higher echelons of command were older. Many were spinsters who had found in the war something which at last gave purpose to their lives. To me it seemed their own position, and the general pecking order was so important to them that a plethora of petty jealousies frequently distorted their judgement. There seemed to be resentment against young officers coming up, particularly if they happened to be pretty. It was as though they regarded the privileges of rank almost as compensation for having missed out in other directions. On this basis, they could, I suppose, have seen it as somehow unfair that girls who already had the advantages of youth and good looks should also receive officer status. Yet it was true that the only sort of girl this type of officer seemed to be able to tolerate was either the bespectacled little mouse or the strident anti-man feminist.[140]

David Morgan and Mary Evans have suggested that the military caste system prohibited gender solidarity across the ranks in the women's forces: 'What female officers did not encourage was any sense of solidarity amongst women.'[141]

Performance

During the course of the war, there were many acts of bravery performed by female personnel. Among them, WAAF telephone operator, Elspeth Henderson, was awarded the Military Medal for her 'courage and example of a high order' after the operations' room in which she was working at RAF Biggin Hill received a direct hit during an air raid in 1940. Despite being knocked over in the blast, she continued to maintain contact with Fighter Command headquarters until the building caught fire and she was ordered to leave through a broken window.[142] WRNS despatch rider, Pamela McGeorge, received the British Empire Medal (BEM) for her 'great gallantry and complete disregard of danger' whilst delivering urgent despatches to the naval commander-in-chief in Plymouth in the midst of an air raid in 1941. An explosion blew her off her motorcycle and damaged the machine beyond repair, but she ran half-a-mile through the falling bombs to deliver the documents to Admiralty House before volunteering to go out again into the maelstrom.[143] ATS 'gunner', Grace Golland, earned the BEM for her 'courageous behaviour in danger and complete and unsparing devotion to duty' on a gun site during a raid in 1944. Engulfed in smoke and flames from fifty incendiary bombs that landed nearby, she ensured her predictor team remained in action and through her coolness enabled the guns to carry on firing at enemy aircraft for nearly an hour.[144]

There were also examples of exceptional skill and intuition. In illustration of this, WAAF photographic interpreter, Constance Babington Smith, is credited with making the first identification of a German V-1 flying bomb at Peenemünde in late 1943. As head of the section at the Allied Central Interpretation Unit at RAF Medmenham, which was responsible for the interpretation of aerial reconnaissance photographs of enemy aircraft and aircraft factories, she and her team were briefed to look out for 'anything queer' at this German experimental facility on the Baltic coast and, whilst pouring over a poor-quality image taken by the pilot of a RAF Mosquito, spotted a ramp holding a small cruciform shape at the lower end of inclined rails. This eagle-eyed discovery, combined with the examination of other photographs of possible launch sites and storage facilities in France, indicated that a flying bomb attack from across the Channel was imminent. As a result, the allied air forces demolished these sites under Operation Crossbow.[145] She was later described as 'the outstanding Allied authority on the interpretation of photographs of aircraft'.[146]

Servicewomen came to play an important role in the secret war. As the Battle of the Atlantic intensified, a team of WRNS officers and ratings, for instance, helped to design and play out anti-submarine war games with the naval officers of escort groups at the Royal Navy's Western Approaches Tactical Unit in Liverpool.[147] One of the Navy's leading U-boat hunters recalled that 'These girls became so experienced in the tactics of convoy battle that they were able to save many a salt-crusted sea-dog from making the errors which would inevitably lead to disaster to their convoys of model ships.'[148] Female personnel were also well represented at Bletchley Park in Buckinghamshire, the wartime home of the Government Code and Cypher School, which penetrated the signal communications of the Axis powers. Some 2,600 members of the WRNS, 1,100 of the WAAF and 400 of the ATS came to be based at Bletchley and various outstations,[149] and they were employed in a variety of duties related to the cracking of the enemy codes. These included operating the 'bombes', electro-mechanical machines used by cryptologists to help decipher messages sent from the German enigma machines, which incorporated a series of rotating drums and plug boards to replicate the workings of enigma. The job involved painstakingly adjusting the bombes' settings in line with carefully worked out 'menus', provided by the code breakers, in order to turn encrypted messages into 'plain' text. One such Wren bombe operator, Diana Payne, recounted that this 'soul-destroying' work entailed long and varying shift patterns, noisy conditions, great meticulousness and considerable psychological strain:

> All the Wrens took the job very seriously, and we felt the weight of responsibility that any mistake or time wasted could mean lives lost. An example of this tension was when I took a Wren out to visit some relatives. In the middle of tea she turned white and left the room, taking me with her. She thought she had made an error whilst on duty. We worked it out on paper and decided all was well. Panic followed while we wondered how to dispose of the secret piece of paper, which we burnt in a tiny bowl in the kitchen. My cousins, alarmed by the smell, thought we had gone quite mad.[150]

'To keep our morale up,' Payne continued, 'we were told that Winston Churchill was constantly on the line to his "most secret source", and that our work was absolutely vital.'[151] But over time the strain began to tell:

> Many of us developed digestive troubles with the constant change of hours. My friend collapsed unconscious, suffering from overstrain, and was invalided out of the Service. Another had nightmares, and woke up one night clutching a phantom drum. There were cases of girls going berserk on duty.[152]

These pressures were compounded by the fact that they were unable to disclose to anyone – not even to close family – the nature of the duties they were undertaking:

> We had no category badges, and were supposed to say, if asked, that we were just 'Writers' [clerks]. Sometimes it was very difficult

having so little to say about one's life, and this explanation did not always satisfy relatives and friends, so my wartime activities were considered unimportant and something of a failure.[153]

It was not until the 1970s, following the publication of Frederick Winterbotham's *The Ultra Secret*,[154] that the key wartime role of Bletchley Park, and those who worked there, began to emerge. Although the more senior positions in the establishment were dominated by men,[155] it has been said that servicewomen, along with their civilian female colleagues, made up 'the back-bone of Bletchley's code-breaking organisation'.[156] Such secretive work, together with the many other highly-confidential wartime duties that women in the forces came to perform, was credited with helping to explode certain long-standing gender myths. Vera Laughton Mathews commented that one of these was that '"Women can't keep a secret!" Well, the war has shown beyond any doubt that they can keep secrets.'[157]

But what of the ordinary rank and file? Early in 1945, the three service departments were asked by the Royal Commission on Equal Pay to assess the quality of women's work in the forces compared to that of the men. The Admiralty reported that on the basis of a like-for-like comparison in terms of educational background and general intelligence, the 'WRNS personnel are at least the equal of, and are frequently superior to, RN personnel in jobs which require manual dexterity, neatness or accuracy'. It was, however, recorded that 'outside this field, with a few exceptions, their efficiency is estimated to be less than that of men by up to as much as 25%'. According to the naval authorities:

> The general inferiority attributed to women is ascribed to a variety of causes such as lack of physical strength and inability to stand up to so much prolonged strain, notably on watchkeeping . . . ; inferior mechanical aptitude, except in simple processes; lower capacity for the application of knowledge to practical use; inclination to get flustered in emergency and more easily discouraged when up against difficulties; lack of capacity for improvisation; unwillingness to accept responsibility and inability to exercise authority.[158]

The War Office evaluation was similar in tone. Its assessment was that 'the work of women is equal to, or better than, that of men' in functions 'where routine manipulative skill is required' and 'where routine detail and repetitive work is involved'. But it was stated that 'the percentage of men who are capable of reaching a high standard is considerably greater than the percentage of women, due particularly to lack of ambition, lack of willingness to accept responsibility, lack of background and lack of experience on the part of the women.' As for the auxiliaries who helped to man the guns in the mixed AA batteries:

> Women employed as instrument numbers, operators, fire control, and plotters compare very favourably in these duties with men. But in camp duties and fatigues they are generally unsuitable, particularly where physical strength is required. Generally speaking, women are found easier to train, absorb knowledge more quickly and tend to show more initial enthusiasm than men; but men on similar duties maintain a higher rate of efficiency over a long period and are less likely to lose enthusiasm.[159]

The Air Ministry response echoed that of the other services. Its view was that 'in work of a routine or sedentary nature women produce better work than men; it is more accurate and interest in it is sustained for longer periods than in the case of men'. Yet it was noted that 'for work requiring the exercise of initiative, responsibility and drive, men produce the better work', and that 'men are generally superior to women in the ranks of sergeant and above'.[160] Among the individual categories of work assessed, WAAF telephonists, general duties clerks and waitresses were said to be 'superior to men'; radar operators, wireless operators and high-speed telegraphists 'equal to men'; and balloon operators, armament assistants and motor transport mechanics 'not equal to men'. Air frame fitters, instrument repairers and electricians were considered to be 'equal to men on routine repetition work [but] inferior to men in fault finding improvisation, handling strange equipment, initiative in over-coming difficulties, and in heavy work in aircraft'. In similar terms, flight mechanics were 'equal to men on repetition work but not equal in work requiring detailed mechanical knowledge or improvisation'.[161]

Such gender-laden judgements did not, however, go unchallenged. The DWAAF, Lady Mary Welsh, the wife of the recent head of the RAF delegation in Washington, who had taken over from Trefusis Forbes in the autumn of 1943,[162] was asked to comment on a draft of the Air Ministry's submission and thought it was 'a little discouraging' and 'likely to give a misleading impression'. She believed that it did not take sufficient account of such factors as the rapid expansion of the WAAF,

Figure 4.12 Lady Mary Welsh, Director of the WAAF 1943–6 (Popperfoto via Getty Images)

the relative youth of its personnel compared to that of the RAF (in 1945, 70 per cent of airwomen were twenty-five or under, but only 45 per cent of airmen) and their limited training experiences in civilian life. In relation to the assertion that the work of airwomen could only compare to airmen in the lower ranks, she contended that the senior NCOs among the RAF ground staff were still mainly regulars and 'there is a natural prejudice on the part of these men against admitting women and helping to train them to take these higher posts'.[163] There were also some unease in male circles about the generalisations made in the submission. The Permanent Under-Secretary of State for Air, Sir Arthur Street, remarked that

> I cannot help feeling that here we stray inevitably from solid facts to the realm of conjecture and opinion. In matters such as these on which there is controversy between feminists and anti-feminists, it is only too easy to be prejudiced or to give the appearance of being prejudiced.[164]

Despite these concerns, the RAF authorities lodged their appraisal with the royal commission and DWAAF's views were not incorporated in the final document. On finding out, she registered a 'strong protest'.[165]

5 STATUS AND DISCIPLINE

Change in Status for the ATS and WAAF

At the start of the war, members of the ATS, WAAF and WRNS were still technically civilians. They were enrolled under a form of contract to their respective auxiliary services, rather than being enlisted or commissioned into the armed forces and were not subject to the full panoply of military law, as incorporated in the Army Act, Air Force Act or the Naval Discipline Act. The penalties that could be meted out by women officers to their subordinates were limited to such minor punishments as extra duties, stoppages of leave, restrictions of privileges and 'admonition'.[1] When it was suggested in the War Office that on the outbreak of hostilities ATS personnel might be designated as members of the armed forces and brought more extensively under the Army Act, such a step was firmly opposed by the army authorities: 'there are no grounds on which we should be justified in taking the revolutionary step of giving women the status of officers and soldiers'.[2] They remained in effect 'camp followers'.[3]

By the spring of 1940, it had become apparent that modifications needed to be made to the disciplinary code of the women's services. First and foremost, there was no legal sanction to prevent women leaving the forces if they wished to do so. As a result, some of them simply walked out from their posts as the mood took them. This caused considerable disruption to the work of their units and represented a lamentable waste of training resources. There were also concerns about the threat to the country's security since a number had access to secret military information. General Pile's personal ATS clerk, for example, up sticks and left one day, taking with her a shorthand notebook full of the AA chief's confidential correspondence. Between January and May 1940, some 2,500 members of the ATS were discharged, which equated to a loss of about 10 per cent of the total strength of the service over these months and a significant proportion of these cases were in effect 'walkings out'.[4]

In addition to this, female officers had difficulties in controlling the more delinquent women who remained. Not only did these officers occupy their positions on a courtesy basis, and thus could not strictly issue lawful commands, but also the scale of punishments was regarded as inadequate to deal with more serious offences and dismissal was obviously not a sanction that could be widely used in wartime.[5] One WAAF officer, Barbara Whittingham-Jones, commented that 'the triviality of allowable punishment of WAAF personnel tends to expose the whole fabric of WAAF discipline to ridicule in the eyes of the male personnel'.[6] Furthermore, if discipline cases were referred to male commanding officers, they sometimes found it difficult to follow the same procedures for servicewomen that applied to the men. 'I had to point out', recalled Felicity Peake, now officer in command of the WAAF section at Biggin Hill, 'that it did not help discipline, or please the airmen if an airwoman, who was marched in before the CO on a charge, was invited by him to be seated and offered a cigarette!'[7]

In the summer of 1940, the three service departments jointly approached the War Cabinet's Home Policy committee with a view to resolving some of these disciplinary issues. In view of the recent Emergency Powers (Defence) Act of 1940, which permitted the issuing of defence regulations requiring persons to place their services at the disposal of the King, and of Defence Regulation 29B, which compelled police constables and firemen to remain in their posts, it was proposed that a similar regulation should be issued obliging members of the women's forces to continue to serve unless released by the relevant authorities. Contraventions would be punishable by the civil courts with fines of up to £100, or three months imprisonment. It was further suggested that women officers be given the power to dock pay for 'absence without leave'; 'refusal or neglect to perform duties'; and 'loss or destruction of, or damage to, official property'. These deductions would not exceed £1 for each offence.[8]

The Home Policy committee was doubtful about the proposals. There was a general feeling that it would be difficult to persuade parliament to support a regulation that made female 'deserters' liable to trial by a civil court – with all the stigma attached to an ordinary criminal charge and the likelihood of widely divergent verdicts depending on the outlook of different civilian justices – when their male counterparts were tried by a military court martial. It was thus recommended that the service departments explore whether the women's forces could be brought more fully under military law in order 'to avoid differentiation of treatment in this respect as between men and women serving in the Forces'.[9]

After several months of contemplation, the War Office came to the conclusion that its ATS personnel should become members of the armed forces and appropriate sections of the Army Act extended to them accordingly. This was thought necessary in order to strengthen the hand of women officers in matters of discipline and help reduce the 'desertion' rate. It was also hoped that such a recategorisation would increase the prestige of the ATS and encourage greater levels of recruitment. What brought matters to a head, however, was the recommendation of the Joubert committee that women should be employed operationally in AA Command. If members of the ATS were to man the fire control instruments on gun sites then it was imperative that they should not be permitted to leave the service at will. What was more, the position of the women's forces in relation to the Hague Rules on the laws and customs of war was not entirely clear. If the country was overrun by an invading force, and ATS women were found to be undertaking 'practically combatant duties' with the gun batteries, it was contended that as civilians 'they become liable to be shot if taken prisoner'.[10]

In the spring of 1941, the army authorities approached the War Cabinet with a view to giving the ATS fuller military status. It consented to this and gave the other service departments the opportunity to opt in. The Air Ministry agreed to do so, but the Admiralty declined.[11] On 25 April, the Defence (Women's Forces) Regulations were promulgated. Under these, all women enrolled in the ATS and WAAF, whether their enrolment dated from before or after the making of these regulations, were declared to be 'members of the armed forces of the Crown' and the Army Act and Air Force Act applied to them by the Army Council and Air Council 'to such extent and subject to such adaptations and modifications as may be specified'.[12] The DATS at the time, Helen Gwynne-Vaughan, regarded these reforms as entirely appropriate for the new generation of women who were 'accustomed to be on level terms with men' and likened them to entering her 'promised land'.[13]

In the wake of the 'militarisation' of the ATS and WAAF, their female officers were granted the king's commission. Although they maintained different rank titles – an ATS 'second subaltern', for example, was the equivalent of an army 'second lieutenant', and a WAAF 'squadron officer' that of a RAF 'squadron leader' – the badges of rank were the same as those worn by male officers of equal status.[14] Furthermore, in certain circumstances, these women officers were authorised to issue orders to soldiers and airmen. In the ATS regulations, it was stated that 'when they are normally employed on those duties for which they have been detailed to serve with troops, officers of the ATS have power of command over such military officers and soldiers as may be specially placed under their orders from time to time by any superior military authority'.[15] Likewise, an Air Ministry Order confirmed that 'Officers and airmen of the Royal Air Force may be placed under the orders of officers or non-commissioned officers of the Women's Auxiliary Air Force if of higher relative rank'.[16] Jenny Nicholson recorded, however, that there was some institutional reticence to acknowledge this subversion of gender roles:

> There was an inclination to shy at admitting that men were ever put in the position of having to take orders from women. But they often were. In the RAF, towards the end of 1943, I ran across a WAAF officer with RAF officers serving under her in undeniable command of a small RAF formation.[17]

Decisions were also made as to which disciplinary sections of the relevant service acts should be applied to the women's forces. The ATS became subject to sections 15 and 40 of the Army Act. These dealt with such offences as 'absence from duty without leave' and 'conduct to the prejudice of good order and discipline'. The WAAF was covered by sections 9, 10, 14, 15, 16, 24, 28, 39A and 40 of the Air Force Act. These included the same offences that applied to the ATS, but also incorporated such transgressions as 'injury to equipment' and 'damage to aircraft'. As for the scale of penalties for female other ranks, designated ATS and WAAF officers, as well as RAF commanding officers or army area or district commanders, could impose summary punishments such as admonition, extra duties, confinement to camp for up to fourteen days, or forfeiture of pay for the same period. Other ranks could be tried by court-martial, but it was only possible to remand them for trial if they so elected and the only additional sanction available to such a tribunal was the forfeiture of twenty-eight, rather than fourteen, days pay. Sterner punishments such as detention could not be imposed.[18]

Some doubts, however, emerged as to the position of service-women overseas. It was apparent that the Defence (Women's Forces) Regulations did not legally extend to all places outside the United Kingdom and that in some parts of the world members of the women's forces could only be dealt with under military law as 'camp followers'. In order to clarify matters, an amendment was made to the Army and Air Force Acts in 1943 which ensured that those disciplinary sections of the acts already applied at home by the Army and Air Councils could be given effect abroad.[19]

The Exclusion of the WRNS

The Admiralty had put its name to the interdepartmental sub-mission to the Home Policy committee in 1940. Although it regarded the disciplinary problem as largely an issue for the ATS and the WAAF – 'the WRNS', commented the Head of the Civil Establishment Branch, 'seem to get along all right by a combination of good officers, esprit de corps, and bluff'[20] – there was a willingness to go along with the War Office and the Air Ministry on this occasion for the sake of uniformity.[21] But the question of making Wrens members of the armed forces and extending the Naval Discipline Act to women was a much more contentious issue for the naval authorities.

Vera Laughton Mathews was firmly in favour of the WRNS coming into line with the other women's services on this question. She contended that it was undesirable for highly trained Wrens, or those engaged in secret work, to be able to 'resign at will' from their posts; that a number of the duties they carried out could be regarded as coming within the 'combatant sphere'; and that as female personnel worked side by side with naval ratings so they should be subject to the same punish-ment for similar offences. Indeed, she believed that the prestige attached to such a change of status would give a welcome boost to her service: 'To be recognised as part of the Navy will certainly be good for morale and esprit de corps and will therefore ensure a higher standard of efficiency.'[22]

The Admiralty consulted the naval commanders-in-chief at home over what it termed this 'revolutionary' change and they were hostile to any such reform. 'This is not the proper place to enter into biological or psychological reflections on the varying capacities and capabilities of the two sexes', contended the Commander-in-Chief, Portsmouth, Admiral Sir William James. '[But] we should never forget that women are women and that Acts of Parliament designed many years ago for the purpose of controlling men combatants cannot be suitably applied to women engaged in modern warfare.'[23] In the light of the opposition, the naval authorities decided this was not a path they wished to pursue. It was pointed out that the 'desertion' rate in the WRNS was very low, amounting to thirty-seven cases out of a force of some 11,000 between December 1940 and March 1941 and therefore its disciplinary record did not necessitate such a step. It was further noted that the legal advice obtained by the Admiralty indicated that if Wrens undertook combatant roles they were fully protected under international law by the Hague Rules and the Geneva Convention. It was calculated, moreover, that there would be particular problems in applying naval law to the WRNS since nearly half of its personnel were living in their own homes as 'immobiles' and thus outside the control of the service unless they were on duty.[24] Underpinning this was a reluctance on the part of the Royal Navy hierarchy to see young women paraded in front of a naval court. According to Laughton Mathews:

> The shadow of the court-martial loomed large in the minds of the tender-hearted naval officers who shrank from the painful thought of a little Wren in the dock, though women pass through the civil courts every day despised and degraded, with never a sigh nor a thought from the gold-braided.[25]

Although an Admiralty Fleet Order in 1942 recognised that, in certain situations, naval ratings could be required to work under the direction of WRNS officers or higher ratings – Laughton Mathews related examples of male ratings training as parachute packers under leading Wrens, while other ratings in the accountant branch worked in pay offices under WRNS officers – members of the WRNS remained technically civilians and were not subject to the Naval Discipline Act.[26]

Ongoing Disciplinary Issues for the ATS and WAAF

Despite the change of status for the WAAF and ATS, there continued to be concerns over their disciplinary codes. The Air Ministry, for example, soon received representations from RAF home commands and groups about the shortcomings of the new WAAF regulations. Not only did the stipulation that prevented other ranks from being tried by court martial without their consent mean that recourse to such a tribunal was virtually impossible, but also the penalties available were deemed ineffective in dealing with recalcitrant airwomen. Those awarded extra duties sometimes refused to perform them; confinement to camp was difficult to enforce on those who were determined to break out or those living in billets outside a base; and forfeiture of pay made little difference to those who were not dependent on this source of income. These problems were compounded by the arrival of a number of female 'conscripts' who found it difficult to adapt to service discipline, as well as the reluctance of the civil courts to deal with military offences. A recommendation for discharge was often the only option.[27] 'The scale of punishments at present authorised', complained the Air Officer Commanding No. 24 Group, 'is entirely inadequate either for punitive or for deterrent purposes.'[28]

The disciplinary challenges that confronted some WAAF officers were vividly illustrated in a report submitted to the commanding officer of RAF Tangmere on 27 May 1942 by Flight Officer Whittome, the officer in charge of the WAAF section. In her report she described the antics of one of her airwomen:

> ACW [Aircraftwoman] Silvie arrived at Westerton Camp Orderley Room at approximately 22.25 hours on the 26th instant. She came in shouting, waving her arms about and walking round and round calling out 'The bloody Richmond Arms is closed'. The duty Corporal and Sgt. Cooper (Admin) endeavoured to persuade her to go to her room and to bed. This she refused to do. She burst into the Cooks' Room, where many of them were sleeping, shouting at the top of her voice. She flung out of their room and into the Boiler Room, pulling down all the soiled sheets which were stacked ready for the laundry, and threw them all on the floor; as fast as NCOs picked them up she pulled them down again. She endeavoured to throw an

airwoman's overcoat, which was hanging up to dry, into the Boiler, but was prevented by Sgt. Cooper. She then emptied a coke bucket all over the floor, threw paper and any odd article she could find across the room, then made for the Salvage bin which Sgt. Cooper was standing in front of. She remarked 'I don't want to fight you because you've got three bloody stripes, but I'm going to empty that bin.' And empty it she did. After this she went into the Nissen hut, where a number of girls were sleeping, shouting and screaming. She emptied a vase of flowers on to the floor, then rushed back to the Officer's office, where she stripped the Notice Board of some dozen or more notices, emptied the officer's desk, drawers and cupboards, emptied files full of DROs and PORs and other documents on to the floor. Next she went into the Telephonists' bedroom and by now had wakened and disturbed nearly fifty airwomen.

The redoubtable Silvie was eventually put to bed with the assistance of two male RAF police corporals, but the frustrations of Whittome were plain:

> We have . . . had nearly six months of these periodical outbursts and outrageous scenes, and I feel the NCOs think that I am letting them down in allowing an airwoman so obviously unsuitable for the Service to remain in the unit, and in asking them to cope again and again with these hysterical and nerve-wracking episodes.
>
> Silvie has a shocking influence in many ways in the unit. The timid girls and some of the NCOs are terrified of her and think that she can do anything she likes without being punished, simply because were she charged for offences as other girls are, she would never be off a charge – the difficult girls rejoice in her exhibitionist acts and praise her for her courage in standing up against authority . . . .
>
> I would like to stress the harm this girl is doing and has done to the WAAF both inside and outside the Service.[29]

Air Chief Marshal Sir Philip Joubert shared the disciplinary concerns. He opined that at the outset of the war 'the WAAF were mostly of a type that had a sense of responsibility and enthusiasm for their work' but when conscription was applied 'the picture changed in a radical

Figure 5.1 An ATS military policewoman on patrol, 1943 (Eric Harlow/Keystone Features via Getty Images)

manner'. Whilst visiting RAF stations as Inspector General in 1943, he deplored the presence of what he termed 'Borstal girls, trollops and thieves amongst a mass of decent women' and lamented that 'the women officers did their best, but not many of them had the training and none the authority that would have helped them to control their unruly flock'. What complicated matters, he added, was that the Judge Advocate General, Sir Henry MacGeagh, had 'thrown a very large spanner in the works' by maintaining the narrow legal opinion that the Air Force Act could not be held to apply, from a disciplinary point of view, to airwomen.[30] MacGeagh's view was that women, through their gender, were technically disqualified from becoming members of the air force through the Air Force (Constitution) Act of 1917 and the Sex Disqualification Act of 1919.[31] 'This', observed Joubert, 'threw the whole system of punishment for bad behaviour into complete confusion.'[32]

The ATS faced many of the same disciplinary dilemmas as the WAAF. Julia Cowper, author of the War Office's internal history of the ATS, highlighted in particular the trouble it had in controlling its more incorrigible miscreants when no custodial punishments were available:

> ATS unit commanders used many devices to hold their defaulters, but they escaped from camps and barracks clothed in shirts and knickers and without their shoes; they squeezed through lavatory windows which appeared small enough to preclude the passage of anything bigger than a cat; they scaled walls and dodged guards. Those who preferred to remain with their units where they were housed, fed and paid, were sometimes greater problems than those who escaped. They destroyed beds and black-outs and any other Government property on which they could lay their hands, refused to obey orders and were subversive to the discipline of the whole unit. Three recruits made history when, amongst other exploits, and clad only in pyjamas, they mobbed a male RSM [Regimental Sergeant Major] on parade, after which they were, contrary to all orders, placed under lock and key. Authority was obtained for their discharge that afternoon but not before they had torn down the walls separating the three cells, partitions which had proved strong enough to restrain generations of male offenders.[33]

To try and mitigate the position in the WAAF, various RAF commanders pressed the Air Ministry to introduce some form of military detention for habitual offenders.[34] It was, however, reluctant to do this on the grounds that this would entail the setting up of an extensive network of WAAF detention barracks staffed by female guards and informed the lobbyists that, in its view, the existing scale of penalties was adequate:

> The [Air] Council consider that the discipline of the WAAF should, in general, be based upon inculcating in the individual the desire to do the right thing in the right way, rather than upon the threat and fear of punishment. They consider that tactful and sympathetic handling of recalcitrant airwomen should do

much to avoid difficulty and to foster in them the growth of a correct attitude of mind.[35]

Meanwhile, over the summer of 1942, the Markham committee was looking into this matter as part of its inquiry into amenities and welfare conditions in the three women's services and on the basis of complaints it received from female officers recommended that 'further disciplinary powers are required'.[36] In the light of this, the Air Ministry revisited the issue and, with the support of Jane Trefusis Forbes, devised a series of proposed amendments to the WAAF code of discipline. These included the stipulations that other ranks should be remanded for trial by court martial without their consent and that this tribunal be permitted to award a sentence of confinement to camp for up to twenty-eight days, with or without forfeiture of pay for the same period. Furthermore, it was suggested that a court martial should have the power to award sentences of up to six months imprisonment in a civil prison for offences such as stealing from other airwomen or repeated absences without leave.[37]

In order for the Air Ministry to proceed with these modifications, the War Office needed to adjust ATS regulations along corresponding lines if, as the Markham committee wished, the women's services were to remain in step. In the summer of 1943, the executive committee of the Army Council approved in principle similar changes to the ATS code of discipline.[38] But the Secretary of State for War, now Sir James Grigg, vetoed these modifications. He remained unconvinced that there was any compelling need to introduce a more draconian scale of punishments and was particularly opposed to the prospect of locking up servicewomen in civil prisons, with all the stigma that this entailed, while their male counterparts served their sentences in military detention barracks. This, Grigg believed, would give rise to 'political controversy'.[39] 'I am quite ready to face a row if there is real need for it,' he stated, 'but in the present case I am not convinced that there is.'[40] The proposed amendments to the ATS disciplinary regulations were thus dropped.

Grigg's intransigence put the Air Ministry in a quandry.[41] Its first inclination was to forge ahead with its suggested revisions to the WAAF code of discipline. This was justified on the grounds that both RAF and WAAF opinion was strongly in favour of stiffer penalties; that flagrant disciplinary lapses by airwomen which went inadequately punished were said to have an especially demoralising effect on RAF personnel – a state of affairs which did not apply to the same extent in the army and Royal Navy as the ATS and WRNS were not so closely assimilated with their 'parent' services; and that civilian women employed in factories under the Essential Works Order of 1941 could be imprisoned for certain misdemeanours, such as habitual absenteeism, for up to three months.[42] However, the concerns of the new DWAAF, Mary Welsh, and a number of RAF commanders, about the stigmatisation of airwomen sent to civil prisons, as well as their uneasiness over the principle of handing offenders over to the civil power for service offences, persuaded the Air Ministry to look again at the idea of introducing some form of military detention.[43] At the end of 1943, the advice of Violet Markham was sought on the matter and it was recommended that WAAF 'detention huts' should be set up at selected RAF stations where offenders could be sent summarily by their commanding officers for between fourteen and twenty-eight days, or by a court martial for periods up to forty-two days. These detention facilities, it was

Figure 5.2 WAAF police take part in a demonstration court martial at the RAF police school (© Imperial War Museum)

envisaged, would provide 'corrective training' that would 'aim at cap-
turing the airwoman as an individual and awakening her to a proper
sense of self respect and pride in the WAAF'.[44]

In the spring of 1944, the Air Council withdrew the right of
WAAF other ranks to refuse to be tried by court martial and empowered
this tribunal to award a sentence of confinement to camp for up to
twenty-eight days, in addition to forfeiture of pay for the same period.
It also agreed in principle to the introduction of detention.[45] A fact-
finding visit was subsequently paid by Air Ministry officials to Fort
Darland military detention barracks at Chatham and a set of draft
regulations for WAAF detention rooms drawn up in consultation with
Molly Mellanby, a women's prison commissioner and former governor
of Aylesbury Borstal.[46] In devising these rules, it was recognised that
powers had to be available to control those in detention who were not
amenable to normal codes of behaviour; otherwise the Air Ministry
might be placed in the invidious position of having to release detainees
prematurely because it had no authority to subdue them – a predicament
that would 'bring ridicule on the scheme'. As a result, the regulations
included the right to restrain a violent airwoman by placing her temporarily in solitary confinement and removing all of her personal
possessions.[47]

Welsh, however, objected to these procedures. Although she had
been party to the decision to recommend detention, she anticipated 'the
most lenient form' and the rules 'went a good deal further than she had
envisaged or was now prepared to approve'. She had thus come to the
view that the introduction of detention at this late point in the war would
evoke public criticism and give the erroneous impression that the WAAF
was an undisciplined force which required stronger disciplinary measures
than the other women's services.[48] 'The fact that DWAAF now feels that
she cannot support a scheme for detention for airwomen', minuted one
Air Ministry official, 'has rather thrown us back on our heels.'[49]

In the summer of 1944, the matter was reconsidered by the Air
Council.[50] There was some frustration over the change of heart. 'At the
earlier stage', observed the Chief of the Air Staff, Air Chief Marshal Sir
Charles Portal, 'the criticism had been that there was too little deterrent
effect. Now we are running away from detention because there might be
criticism that it was too harsh.'[51] He was in favour of pressing ahead on
the grounds that the absence of this punishment was by all accounts 'a
real handicap to successful WAAF administration' and the Air Ministry

was 'only seeking to apply to the WAAF the same rules as were applied to airmen'. Yet the Secretary of State for Air, Sir Archibald Sinclair, took a more cautious line. He noted that the service had managed to get by without detention since the beginning of the war and was of the opinion that to institute it now 'would give rise to a great deal of parliamentary and public criticism' and 'react adversely on the prestige of the WAAF', especially since there was little prospect of Sir James Grigg agreeing to extend it to the ATS. He thus recommended it should not be pursued at this time; a decision supported by the WAAF hierarchy.[52] Although there was some discussion of alternatives over the following months, such as the possibility of longer sentences of confinement to camp being served at specially selected RAF stations where the exits were carefully controlled, no further wartime changes were made to the WAAF code of discipline.[53] During the final period of the conflict, it was estimated by Fighter Command that the lack of a serious deterrent for persistent absentees resulted in nearly double the number of airwomen to airmen being absent without leave from its bases.[54] Constance Woodhead concluded that the WAAF disciplinary code was so inadequate that 'officers sometimes felt that they were running the service mainly by bluff':

> Serious and responsible members of the WAAF always felt that for the service not be completely subject to the Air Force Act in the same manner (or as nearly as possible in the same manner) as the RAF was both illogical and undesirable.[55]

In the meantime, WAAF officers continued to deal with the day-to-day transgressions of their airwomen as best they could. Felicity Ashbee recounted the case of Leading Aircraftwoman Watkins who worked in the cookhouse at RAF Stenigot but had apparently refused to scrub the floor properly and then 'cut up rough'. Charged with insubordination, she was brought before the RAF commanding officer. Propelled into the room by two WAAF guards, a hatless but turbaned Watkins – she wore curlers encased in a turban under her WAAF cap – stood defiantly in front of the station commander and Ashbee while the lengthy charge was read out:

> 'Now Watkins,' said the CO, looking up from the charge sheet. 'Have you anything to say?'
> 'Yessir, I have, Sir!'

'Well, what is it, Watkins?'

'It's my veins, Sir!'

'Your *what?*' said the CO, genuinely startled.

'Veins, Sir, my *veins*!'

And with an unexpectedly acrobatic movement, the solid Watkins heaved one leg up onto the CO's desk with a crash. The crash was the greater because cookhouse personnel still wore old-fashioned, wooden-soled clogs to preserve their feet from floors chronically sodden with water or grease.

It was true. The leg in question was a fine specimen of knotted varicose veins, displayed by an equally dexterous tug to the lisle stocking and the clog which, had the idea occurred to Watkins, was a weapon capable of doing quite a bit of damage. But discretion being the better part of valour when the charge was insubordination, the CO merely drew back an inch or two from the proffered evidence and allowed the culprit to tell her tale in full.

'I've always done my work properly, Sir … It's just these dratted veins … They don't half draw. My other leg's just as bad. I can show you.'

'All right Watkins, I'll take your word for it,' the CO said hurriedly . . . .

'Is that all, Watkins?'

'Yessir.'

'Right, you may remove the evidence.'

'Sir?'

'Put your leg down, Watkins.'

'Yessir!'

Leg and clog were withdrawn from the table, nearly sweeping the CO's wire in-tray off at the same time. I caught it with one hand and with the other proffered him Watkins's docs. He glanced at them, then looked again at the bulging lumpish form . . .

'Watkins,' he said.

'Sir?'

'I'm going to dismiss this charge, but, now listen carefully. That cookhouse floor has got to be spotless … and that means *whenever* I think to come in and take a look at it. Understood?'

The unbeautiful, middle-aged face relaxed with a disbelieving smile. 'You bet, Sir! Bless you Sir!'[56]

The WRNS Remains Excluded

In the wake of the Markham report, which recommended that 'equal disciplinary powers and punishments should obtain for the three Services',[57] the Admiralty was forced to look again at the question of Wrens becoming members of the armed forces and the application of the Naval Discipline Act to them. During the autumn of 1942, Laughton Mathews took this opportunity to renew her efforts to bring the WRNS into step with the other women's forces. Not only did she continue to argue that it was wrong for a woman to 'just walk out of the Service', often to go to a better paid job, but also drew attention to a number of developments that had taken place since the spring of 1941, which she believed should make the naval authorities revise their previous judgment. These included the great expansion of the WRNS, along with the fact that over a third of the new recruits each month were now 'conscripts', which threatened the 'real volunteer spirit' of her force; the significant increase in the categories of work, a number of which were connected to the use of lethal weapons; and the growing number of women serving overseas within appreciable distance of the front line. Difficulties had also arisen at some bases where small groups of Wrens were required to work under WAAF officers who had no more authority over them than they had over civilians. It had become apparent, moreover, that because WRNS personnel were not regarded by the Admiralty as an 'an integral part of the Naval Forces', they were unable to qualify for some benefits available to other members of the women's forces, such as the remission of death duties for those who died of disease contracted on active service. 'It would appear', the Head of Naval Law was reported by the DWRNS to have remarked, 'that there is some advantage in dying a member of the ATS rather than a member of the WRNS.'[58]

Laughton Mathews was supported by the Director of Personal Services at the Admiralty, Rear Admiral Harold Walker. He agreed that 'the standard and keenness of recruits is bound to fall with the increased entries largely drawn from the conscripted age groups, and as "war weariness" increases'. The psychological effect of altering the legal basis of the WRNS, he contended, would be considerable, especially on 'would-be deserters', and it would be better to act before pressure of circumstances forced the hand of the naval authorities.[59]

Other Admiralty officials, however, were opposed to any change. The view was held that there was no real need to alter the disciplinary basis of the WRNS since the number of 'deserters' was still comparatively small, totalling 158 cases out of an average force of 30,000 during 1942, and the future 'walking out' rate a matter of conjecture. Wrens involved in combatant duties were considered to be adequately protected under international law and, given the Defence (Women's Forces) Regulations did not extend outside the UK at this time, those stationed abroad were deemed to be in the same legal position as members of the ATS and WAAF. Members of the WRNS working under the command of officers from another women's service, it was observed, were akin to Royal Navy personnel serving in allied ships and if they offended should be dealt with by officers from their own force. As for any loss of benefits suffered by Wrens as a result of their different status, it was surmised that this could be remedied by routine administrative action, rather than by altering the nature of the service.[60]

The Admiralty Board considered that the arguments were evenly balanced and requested the views of the naval commanders-in-chief at home.[61] The latter maintained that a change of status was neither necessary nor desirable and pointed in particular to the difficulties of applying naval law to 'immobile' Wrens who still made up a quarter of the organisation.[62] The Commander-in-Chief, Plymouth, Admiral Sir Charles Forbes, believed that any alteration to the legal standing of the WRNS risked demotivating female personnel: 'I am very doubtful whether they can be driven with satisfactory results by the enforcement of a disciplinary code designed for men. The attempt to do so might well damp that enthusiasm and pride in service to their country which are the chief motive power behind the Women's Royal Naval Service.'[63] In the summer of 1943, the Board decided against any alteration of status.[64]

The matter was not, however, laid to rest. Early in 1944 Laughton Mathews pressed it again. She reported that the number of 'desertions' was increasing, running to 325 cases out of an average force of 54,000 during 1943, and one of the commonest reasons for 'walking out' was pressure brought to bear on Wrens by husbands who were themselves in the Royal Navy. 'Recently', the DWRNS disclosed, 'a Commander RN rang up [the] WRNS Officers Appointments Section and announced that his wife, a Third Officer, was not returning to duty and said: "What can you do about it? I know you can do nothing."' It was also contended that new entrants over the past year had brought about a deterioration in 'manners and morals' and that the psychological effect of being under naval discipline would help combat cases of insubordination. A further consideration was the increasing number of WRNS officers holding technical positions of responsibility and it was asserted that if these officers were 'legally part of the Navy', their hands would be strengthened in dealing with naval personnel working under them. The Chancellor of the Exchequer, moreover, had now confirmed that Wrens were not entitled to a remission of death duties due to the fact that they remained civilians in the eyes of the law and it was feared that at the end of hostilities Wrens might be refused HM forces' benefits on similar grounds.[65] The 'immobile problem', it was added, was much reduced due to the fact that only 14 per cent of the WRNS now fell into this category.[66]

Concurrently, the naval commanders-in-chief had begun to have second thoughts on the matter. In the spring of 1944, the Commander-in-Chief, the Nore, Admiral Sir 'Jack' Tovey, who had taken up this appointment the previous summer, declared that his views were at variance with those of his predecessor and he was in favour of bringing the WRNS under the Naval Discipline Act. He argued that much of the antagonism shown by senior naval officers in his command to a change in status was due to 'ignorance of altering circumstances' and pursued 'even in obstinate disregard of well-informed counsel'. He drew particular attention to concerns about 'mass desertion' during the demobilisation period, when many Wrens might want to return to civilian life in advance of their release date, and to the increasing anxiety of female personnel about the possibility of being denied post-war benefits.[67] Tovey's opinions were taken on board by a number of his counterparts. 'I concur reluctantly', commented the Commander-in-Chief, Rosyth, Admiral Sir Wilbraham Ford, 'that the time has now arrived to place the WRNS under the Naval Discipline Act.'[68]

Admiralty officials were not, however, convinced by this belated groundswell of opinion in favour of reform. Not only was it pointed out that there would be many legislative complications in amending the Naval Discipline Act to allow a modified version of it to be applied to Wrens, but also that any effective deterrent to desertion would be impossible without the introduction of detention, which neither the War Office nor Air Ministry had seen fit to adopt. Only a very few women, it was indicated, were affected by the ineligibility for death duty concessions and there was no reason to believe that members of the WRNS would be treated inequitably in any future government schemes. In the summer of 1944, the naval authorities ruled once more that there would be no change in status, but an Admiralty Fleet Order was issued warning naval officers that encouraging their WRNS spouses to desert was 'a most objectionable and reprehensible dereliction of duty'.[69]

For Laughton Mathews, the failure to bring her service under naval law – an aspiration which, according to one of her senior officers, 'has come to be looked on as the real test as to whether we are, or are not, accepted into full partnership as an integral part of the Navy'[70] – was a source of regret. She believed that the opinions of the naval commanders-in-chief should not have held such sway, 'especially in a matter concerning the status of women where so many men have personal prejudices', and it was wrong for the members of her force 'to be legally civilians': 'I think this was the only major matter of policy for the WRNS on which the Admiralty did not take my advice and I must confess that I live up to the old adage in regard to convincing a woman against her will.'[71]

6 NECESSITIES OF LIFE

Uniform

The basic uniform of the women's services was similar in style to that of their male 'parent' forces.[1] Members of the ATS wore a khaki jacket, shirt, tie and peaked cap; their counterparts in the WAAF an air force blue jacket, pale blue shirt, black tie and air force blue peaked cap; and those in the WRNS a navy blue jacket, white shirt, black tie and, from 1942, a navy blue sailor hat (with a tricorne hat for officers and petty officers). But servicewomen were provided with skirts, rather than trousers, as well as a number of other feminine accoutrements such as rayon knickers, boned corsets and lisle stockings.[2] And, unlike their male counterparts, they were expected to make do and mend. Marjorie Hazell recalled WAAF clothing parades at which the officers were reluctant to exchange worn items for new ones on the grounds that they could be repaired by their female owners: 'This used to annoy the WAAFs in particular, as they were naturally expected to darn their stockings and mend their shirts, whereas an airman would often be excused this.'[3]

As the war went on, and the range of jobs expanded, so the working clothing of servicewomen became more 'masculine'. ATS 'gunners', for example, put on battledress at their gun sites, WAAF flight mechanics donned overalls in their hangers and WRNS boats' crews sported bell bottoms on their harbour launches.[4] But this propensity to adopt male clothing did not always go uncontested, as the protracted discussions in the Air Ministry over the issue of trousers for airwomen testifies. Towards the end of 1939, Jane Trefusis Forbes pressed for the provision of 'dark blue slacks'. She pointed out that due to the rapid expansion of her service many recruits were still without a regulation WAAF jacket and skirt and that trousers would provide additional warmth as the winter approached.[5] Yet some of her senior male collea- gues were unconvinced. The view was put forward that 'this form of dress has not yet been universally accepted by women in this country', that it 'might lead to humorous comment or ridicule' and that it 'would take some years for the WAAF to live down'.[6] DWAAF, however, was determined to pursue the matter. Not only did she contend that it was important that women's lower limbs should be kept warm so as to prevent 'liver and bladder complaints' and 'feminine disorders', but also that many women working in the civil defence services and industry wore trousers.[7] It was agreed that slacks would be made available as a temporary measure pending the provision of full uniform to Waafs.[8]

Although the Air Ministry intended that these trousers should eventually be withdrawn, the air attacks on RAF stations during 1940 brought about a rethink. The raids meant that airwomen were often required to rush during the night from their sleeping quarters into protective trenches and spend long periods out in the cold.[9] In these circumstances, Trefusis Forbes called for the existing slacks to be retained, and further pairs made available for new WAAF intakes, as these could be quickly slipped into during an alert and would provide the necessary warmth whilst women took shelter.[10] The finance branch, however, raised objections. It was doubted whether the time saved in dressing, and the extra comfort of the wearer, warranted the £10,000 cost of this extra item of clothing. If trousers were considered necessary, it was suggested that they could be issued in place of skirts with little or no overall additional financial outlay.[11] DWAAF stood her ground. She asserted that her Waafs working on aerodromes were squarely in the target zone and it would 'seem unfortunate' to begrudge the extra expenditure when their lives might depend on the speed with which they could get to whatever cover was available. As for the notion that WAAF skirts could be replaced by trousers, she dismissed this masculi- nisation as 'absurd'. 'It is unlikely', she commented, 'that anyone would care to contemplate a force of women marching about in caps, tunics and slacks.'[12] Trefusis Forbes won the day, but the Treasury then intervened in the matter. It was of the opinion that a stock of trousers should only be made available at selected RAF stations and that these should be handed out temporarily to personnel at these bases, who would then return them when posted elsewhere.[13] The Air Ministry responded that all its stations were considered likely targets of enemy bombers and to retain this clothing for communal use would be both impractical and uneconomic.[14] Eventually, in 1941, official approval was given for an issue of 'slacks, blue' to all airwomen who were not entitled to working suits as part of their trade, but the RAF authorities laid down that these trousers were to be worn 'only when it is necessary to take shelter from air raids'.[15] After instances came to light of Waafs wearing them on 'unauthorised occasions', an order was sent out the following year reminding them of this air-raid stipulation.[16]

Some female personnel embellished and adapted their uniforms to their own tastes. As Tessa Stone has argued, this was partly to emphasise their individuality within the conformity of military life.[17] In the WAAF, for example, junior officers serving with Fighter Command would – in the manner of the raffish RAF aircrew who adopted their own characteristic modes of dress – stroll around with coloured scarfs around their necks. When pulled up by their seniors for infringing uniform regulations they would casually reply 'oh, those rules don't apply to us, ma'am; you see, we're "operational!"'[18] But it was also about retaining a sense of femininity. Thus some servicewomen padded the shoulders of their jackets with government-issue sanitary towels in order to create a more alluring silhouette; others surreptitiously shortened their skirts so that they conformed to a fashionable length; and a number substituted daintier briefs for their voluminous service knickers.[19] Mary Thomson wore a string of pearls under her ATS shirt because she wanted to adorn herself with 'something that was feminine' while Constance Babington Smith splashed on lavish quantities of *L'Heure Bleue* perfume by Guerlain 'on the theory that the masculinity of WAAF uniform needed a little counteracting'.[20] 'On the surface we might all look the same,' confided WAAF officer Muriel Gane Pushman, 'but underneath – ah, underneath – we were individual, female, and our souls were satin and lace.'[21]

On one occasion a concern for an attractive look seems to have had tragic consequences. Early in 1944, Leading Wren Ann Walker was working at a radial drilling machine in a maintenance shed at Port Edgar. She was wearing a regulation blue bandanna distributed to WRNS machine operators as a protective head covering. But, as was the fashion of the day, she had left a portion of hair showing at the front where the bandanna was tied in a bow. It appears that as Walker was leaning over her machine to change the size of the drill, some of her hair and head gear got caught in the vertical driving shaft which was still in motion and, according to the board of inquiry set up to investigate the incident, she suffered 'a complete avulsion of ¾' of the scalp, the whole thickness being removed to the bone'.[22] As a result of this horrific accident, it was laid down that WRNS personnel working on machines with moving parts would be issued with 'peaked safety caps' and that care was to be taken 'to ensure that no loose ends of hair are visible when the cap is worn.'[23]

The standard uniform of the WRNS was generally regarded as the most stylish of the three women's services.[24] According to Anne de Courcy, the blue-black design was chic, slimming and well-suited to youthful British complexions. In her view, the dark tones, with their subliminal references to policemen, exuded an air of 'sophisticated authority': 'To see a Wren officer in full fig was to view an attractive woman with just that hint of the dominatrix that seems to appeal to so many Englishmen, especially those from a public-school background.'[25]

Accommodation

A range of segregated living accommodation was provided for the women's forces. This included hutted camps, barrack blocks and billets in private or requisitioned houses. The standard of quartering in the WRNS was generally better than in the ATS or WAAF because of its smaller size, its concentration around established naval ports, and the fact that its 'immobile' branch lived in their own homes. But conditions could be tough for servicewomen in the hastily constructed military bases that sprung up across the country. It was not unusual, for example, for female personnel to find themselves living alongside a dozen or more women in a drafty, prefabricated Nissen hut with a walk of several hundred yards across a frozen field to the nearest ablution block.[26] Grace Houghton of the ATS recalled that at one anti-aircraft camp the female latrines were enclosed from view by sacking hanging from four posts staked in the ground: 'When the sun shone your shadow could be seen, and one morning the wind was so rough a post fell down and left one of the Ats sat on the throne. What a cheer went up from the gunners!'[27]

Figure 6.1 ATS recruits at a hutted camp, 1941 (Keystone/Hulton Archive via Getty Images)

The military authorities did, however, seek to ease the plight of servicewomen where they could. Members of the women's services were entitled to more generous accommodation scales than their male counterparts. Not only were they granted extra washing and toilet facilities, but also additional sleeping space. In the ATS, each auxiliary was permitted 45 square feet of space compared to 30 square feet for a soldier; in the WRNS the equivalent figure was 40 square feet for a Wren and 30 square feet for a naval rating; and in the WAAF it was 38 square feet for an airwoman and 32 square feet for an airman.[28] 'We have tried where possible', explained the DWAAF, Mary Welsh, 'to keep rather better living conditions generally for the airwomen because we are sincerely anxious not to allow the airwomen to become brutalised by service conditions.'[29] In the army it was the job of the Royal Engineers to lay on the additional amenities for the ATS and the enhanced sanitary arrangements were said to have been a particular 'headache' to them.[30] Auxiliaries, for example, required more water than soldiers, due in part to their frequent washing of underwear and use of WCs rather than urinals. They also got through considerably more toilet paper. In 1942 an allowance of three times the male rate was agreed.[31]

For their part, female personnel sought to make their living space as homely as possible. This could involve repainting the walls, hanging civilian curtains, or rearranging beds and wardrobes in order create more privacy.[32] 'To complete the homely effect', wrote Olivia Scovell of her ATS quarters, 'many of the beds were adorned with mascots of various kinds and in various stages of wear. Some of these mascots had been taken to boarding schools at a tender age and dragged through all the vicissitudes of a long school life before arriving in an army hut.'[33] Constance Woodhead observed that 'the instinct for home-making never died in many of the service women.'[34] Meanwhile, some women officers were determined to feminise the living quarters of their charges. Barbara Cartland, who served as an honorary ATS welfare officer in Bedfordshire, recalled a titled ATS officer who asked for

> 'pretty pink satin cushions for the dear girls' in a new camp, but forgot, when passing the plans, to indent for gas rings in the billets, so that when the place was completed it was found that the girls had to walk a mile and a half for a cup of hot tea![35]

If standards of 'housekeeping' fell below acceptable levels, the culprits might be brought to book. WAAF officer, Felicity Hill, admitted giving her airwomen a stern telling off when she discovered that they had gone on duty, leaving their hut in a chaotic state: 'it infuriated me that attractive girls could be so sluttish. What, I asked, would your fiancés and boyfriends think if they could see in what unfeminine squalor you choose to live?'[36] This domestic primness also extended to displays of male 'pin-ups'. While few batted an eyelid at soldiers' lockers adorned with alluring pictures of Jane Russell, in many ATS barracks, images of Tyrone Power, Errol Flynn or Clark Gable were banned by female commanding officers because they were considered bad for discipline.[37]

In certain circumstances, women were required to live temporarily under canvas. During the flying bomb attacks in 1944, mixed anti-aircraft units were hurriedly deployed to makeshift gun sites on the East Anglian coast. Here, members of the ATS had to 'rough it' in leaky tents that gave little protection from the mud and damp that pervaded the marshy coastal areas. After a visit to one of the units, Tom Driberg, the Independent MP for Maldon and former Beaverbrook press journalist, 'exposed' the primitive living conditions and the matter was raised in the House of Commons. Most of the women, however, seem to have been perfectly willing to face these hardships. The commander of a mixed anti-aircraft brigade at Burnham assembled 1,000 auxiliaries serving with his formation and offered to post any of them away within twenty-four hours if they felt they could not put up with the privations. He received just nine applications – all from female clerks.[38] According to General Pile, 'not one operational girl wished to do otherwise than to stay and fight the battle'.[39]

Food

Servicewomen were also provided with their meals. Female personnel were allotted approximately four-fifths of the male ration entitlement in the expectation that they would require less to eat than their male counterparts.[40] In the ATS, this worked out at roughly 2,800 calories a day for each auxiliary.[41] Adjustments were, however, made for those who undertook more active duties than other women. Female 'gunners', for example, were put on the same ration scale as the men.[42] The necessity of sharing kitchen and dining facilities with 'parent services' also helped to equalize matters. In the WAAF, strains on accommodation, shortages of manpower and the need for stringent fuel economy, meant that many airwomen had to abandon their own dining halls and eat in the big RAF station messes where they were served the same rations as the men.[43]

The services were said to have received more and better food than the heavily rationed civilian population.[44] 'Compared to civilian rations,' opined Marjorie Hazell, 'we lived in luxury.'[45] But the standard of fare was variable. Barbara Littlejohn recalled that at her ATS signals training camp the staple diet of boiled potatoes, gritty cabbage, fried spam and a suet pudding known as a 'depth charge' 'would have gone over alright in a Dickensian workhouse no doubt, but ... did nothing for our morale': 'Our big treat in the evening was to go down into the town and eat baked beans on toast at the Salvation Army canteen.'[46] Waaf Mary Palmer complained that the meals at her RAF base were so unappetising that 'on entering the cook-house the smell put us off before we got to the food .... The bins for pig-swill were chock-a-block with our leftovers.'[47] Eileen McMurdo of the ATS was

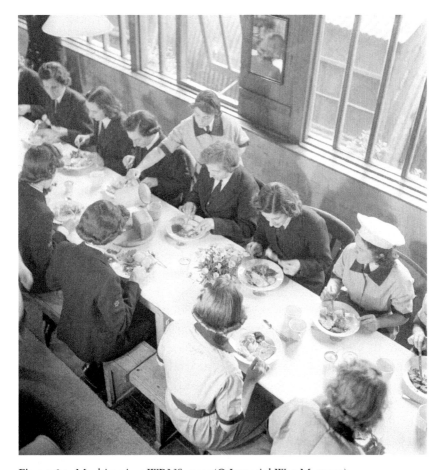

Figure 6.2 Mealtime in a WRNS mess (© Imperial War Museum)

stationed at a combined operations headquarters at Fort Southwick, near Portsmouth, and recorded that the naval cuisine there was little better:

> One thing which all three services had in common was the often appalling standard of the food and the naval cooks did their best to keep up the tradition of mediocrity.
>
> At Southwick one of the 'cook's special' dishes was a small, round rissole which looked and tasted like india-rubber. I once heard them being described in the mess hall by a burly, naval rating using the sort of picturesque vulgarity at which the lower mess deck excels.

'Gawd strewth' he exclaimed, 'I see they're serving up the
Captain's balls again!'[48]

Moreover, if women brought their culinary grumbles to the attention of
superiors, they usually received short shrift. Waaf Mary Winter
recounted that 'one day one girl, braver than the rest, answered back
when the WAAF officer came round and asked if there were "any
complaints?" "Ask the fish, Ma'am," said Biddy. "It speaks for itself."
Needless to say, she got jankers.'[49]

Pay

The level of servicewomen's pay was determined by the government shortly before the outbreak of war, on the premise that the pay
commonly drawn by women in civilian employment was less than men,
with an average difference of about one-third. Members of the women's
forces, like their sisters working in the civil defence services, thus generally received two-thirds of the pay of their male colleagues of comparable rank and trade in their 'parent services'. This was a principle
described by the Treasury as 'fair relativity'. However, since
a proportion of the remuneration of the armed forces was provided in
kind, through such items as clothing, accommodation and food, the
overall ratio was said to have been higher than two thirds.[50] At the end
of 1941, a private in the ATS with six months service earned 14s a week
in basic pay, but when these other elements were factored in, the total
emoluments rose to 50s 6d. This was nearer four-fifths of the emoluments of an equivalent unmarried male private.[51]

The inequalities in service pay did not go unquestioned within
the military establishment. General Pile advocated that if ATS 'gunners'
took over identical jobs from soldiers on the gun sites it was only right
that they should receive the same rates of pay as their male
counterparts.[52] In similar terms, Admiral Sir 'Jack' Tovey questioned
why the remuneration of WRNS officers was so much lower than shore-
based male Royal Naval Volunteer Reserve officers when they held
appointments of equal responsibility.[53] The disparities were starkly
exposed when women proved more capable than the men they worked
alongside. 'There were undoubtedly cases here and there', admitted
Constance Woodhead', 'where an officer or airwoman was "carrying"
an RAF officer or airman and being paid two thirds of his rate, possibly

even holding a rank junior to his while she did the best part of his work.'[54] Nevertheless, the women's forces seem to have accepted the inequity with comparatively little complaint.[55] Helen Gwynne-Vaughan conceded that although she had spent her entire professional civilian life fighting for equal pay, it was difficult to justify the same level of remuneration for servicewomen, since in many cases they did not replace men on a head-for-head basis and, ultimately, would not be called upon to fight as combatants. 'In view of the fact that the State is prepared to employ women only in the background and of their consequent lesser utility,' she acknowledged, 'it is fair that their pay should be less than that of soldiers who are liable to be sent forward.'[56] Vera Laughton Mathews shared these sentiments. She had been hesitant to support the two-thirds pay formula on the grounds of equality, but came to the conclusion that it was vindicated by the greater dangers faced by servicemen:

> I realised that in the Services there was some justification for less pay for women. Although, in fact, there were men at shore bases doing precisely the same work as women and no better, even men precluded by health from going to sea, yet in the main, men in the armed forces were recruited for a life of hardship and danger and sacrifice beyond all comparison with what was demanded of women. One could not measure such sacrifice in terms of pay, but nor could one with any conscience attempt to argue for equal pay for those who were allowed to give so much less.[57]

In 1943, the Woman Power Committee sponsored a debate in the House of Commons on 'women in national service' during which the issue of equal pay for servicewomen was raised. Edith Summerskill, one of the members of the WPC, declared that when the matter had been aired in parliament earlier in the war, it had been explained that woman in the forces could not receive the same pay as their male counterparts because many of them did not substitute for men on a one-for-one basis. This, she maintained, was no longer the position as women were replacing men head-for-head. Furthermore, she contended, if servicewomen were paid less than men on the basis that they were non-combatants, not only did this have dubious validity in the case of ATS 'gunners', but also begged the question as to why soldiers serving in the non-combatant branches of the army, such as the Pioneer Corps, were paid at the same rate as those in the fighting arms.[58] If the level of danger determined pay, she surmised, 'we must argue that a private in the front line in Sicily should be paid more than a general in Whitehall'.[59]

The Minister Without Portfolio, Sir William Jowitt, responded for the government after having been briefed by the service departments.[60] Whilst he agreed that there were many jobs being undertaken by women on a one-for-one basis, it was pointed out that there were still a significant number of roles that required a three-for-two substitution ratio. He asserted, moreover, that *all* soldiers, including those in the Pioneer Corps, could be called to perform 'combatant duties' in an emergency, whilst no servicewomen, even those on the gun sites, would be required to do so.[61] 'The question arises,' he observed, 'as to how far these jobs done by women and men can really be said to be comparable.'[62] The government position thus remained unchanged.

As for the amount of money they were paid, some young servicewomen found themselves with more disposable income in the forces than they had in civilian life. Grace Houghton had handed over most of

Figure 6.3 Wrens receiving their pay, 1942 (© Imperial War Museum)

the wages from her job in a carpet factory to her mother, so when she joined the ATS 'I thought I was rich'.[63] Others, however, tended to find themselves running short before the weekly pay parade came around. Eileen Hazell discovered that her ATS pay 'did not go very far. One had to be an expert to juggle all the little bits and pieces one needed.'[64] A number continued to make financial contributions to their families after entering the services. Waaf Mary Mackenzie arranged for part of her earnings to be sent home to help support her disabled father and 'hard-pressed' mother, who had lost both their house and their cooked meat business in Brighton during a bombing raid. As a result, she never received more than half of her pay whilst in the forces.[65]

7 MEDICAL MATTERS

Medical Arrangements

At the start of the war, servicewomen who required medical attention were generally treated by male medical officers of their 'parent' services in the same way that women patients in civilian life were often looked after by male practitioners. But as the women's forces expanded, so female medical officers were appointed to camps and bases where there were significant concentrations of female personnel.[1] This was timely. In the army it was reported that there was a curious reluctance on the part of some male regimental medical officers to undertake the care of members of the ATS and one senior Royal Army Medical Corps (RAMC) staff officer announced that his subordinates could not possibly examine them 'below the chest'.[2]

The status of women doctors in the wartime armed forces became, however, a matter of controversy. Before the outbreak of hostilities, the Medical Women's Federation (MWF) had approached the War Office in anticipation of female medical practitioners being recruited into the services and pressed for them to be employed in the army on the same terms and conditions as their male counterparts.[3] Yet although they were granted equal pay, the army authorities decided that they would not be commissioned into the RAMC. Instead, they were to be 'attached' to the corps and given relative rank.[4] The position of women doctors serving with the RAF's medical branch was similar.[5] This anomalous status could on occasions leave female medical officers in an invidious position with regard to other medical staff, particularly in view of the fact that they were invariably called upon to treat male personnel in the medical facilities in which they worked.[6]

In 1941, officers in the ATS and WAAF were granted the king's commission after the promulgation of the Defence (Women's Forces) Regulations. As a result, female doctors serving with the army were offered commissions in the ATS.[7] This reignited the debate over their status. In the autumn, the MWF wrote to the War Office calling upon it to commission female medical officers into the RAMC:

> The proposal to segregate medical women in the Women's Forces, so that they serve with and not in the RAMC appears to us seriously to contravene the recognised principle of professional equality between men and women practitioners, and is therefore unacceptable to medical women. Women doctors volunteer to serve with the Army as <u>doctors</u> and not as women, and they consider that any arrangement which places them in a separate category from their professional colleagues infringes this fundamental principle.[8]

The army authorities were unmoved. Not only was it argued that there was no legal authority to grant women commissions in the male 'land forces of the crown', but also that circumstances could arise in which RAMC officers, like those in other technical corps, were required to exercise command over soldiers in their capacity as fighting men and that this obligation could not be properly carried out by women. Furthermore, the fact that some 80 per cent of female medical officers accepted commissions in the ATS, with the rest opting to remain under their existing contracts, seemed to vindicate the War Office position.[9]

The MWF did not let the matter rest. In the spring of 1942, a letter from its president, Dr Clara Stewart, was published in the *British Medical Journal* in which she asserted that the different status of women doctors serving with the army and RAF – the Royal Navy chose to commission its female medical officers into the Royal Naval Volunteer Reserve – violated 'the long-established and well-proved principle of complete equality between medical men and women'.[10] She contended that there was no insuperable difficulty to commissioning female doctors into, if necessary, temporary womens' sections of the army and RAF medical services and that in the event of a military emergency 'medical women would be expected to rise to the occasion just as

medical men would do, and in such circumstances it would unquestionably be easier for all concerned if they had well-defined rank and status.'
In the meantime, she advised women doctors not to accept commissions
in the women forces.[11]

The War Office held firm in the face of this ultimatum and the
MWF was informed that female medical officers would in future be
required to accept commissions in the women's services. This in effect
closed the matter.[12] Reflecting on the episode, the official historian of
the Army Medical Services, Professor Francis Crew, could not disguise
the departmental exasperation over an issue

> which, having its origin in a praiseworthy endeavour to secure
> the adjustment of patent anomalies, developed into something
> of an agitation concerned primarily with the furthering of social
> principles which at this time seemed to have no place in military
> affairs. Certainly the women medical officers serving in the
> Army were far less interested in the theoretical considerations
> pertaining to their status than were their official champions.[13]

For its part, the MWF continued to sit indignantly on the sidelines. 'It is
difficult to understand', remarked the writer of one internal memorandum, 'the grudging and reactionary attitude of the Whitehall
authorities.'[14] Nevertheless, it did what it could to assist medical
recruiting for the forces and had to admit that 'women doctors in the
Services had very little to complain of'.[15] At their peak numbers, some
600 female medical officers were serving with the army, 117 with the
RAF and 25 with the Royal Navy.[16]

Servicewomen underwent regular medical inspections ('free
from infection' or 'FFIs' as they were invariably known) and arrangements were made for those who were unwell to report sick. Minor
ailments were normally treated in designated sick quarters in the units
or camps to which they were attached (or at home in the case of Wren
'immobiles'). In the ATS, such accommodation was allotted on the basis
of 2 per cent of strength, double the rate for male soldiers, with a similar
level of provision in the WAAF. More serious cases were admitted to
female wards in military hospitals, or civilian Emergency Medical
Service (EMS) hospitals, depending on local circumstances. Those
with mental illnesses could be sent to specialist institutions such as the
Neurosis Centre at Mill Hill or St Andrew's psychiatric hospital in
Northampton.[17] Leslie Whateley commented that if soldiers were

hospitalised their fathers did not expect regular reports from commanding officers on their sons' conditions, unless dangerously ill, but mothers of her auxiliaries 'presumed this their right in the case of daughters'.[18] Indeed, when Clementine Churchill was informed that a woman in Mary Churchill's ATS barrack room had contracted meningitis, she arrived unannounced at the camp within twenty-four hours to check up on her daughter. 'The authorities', recounted an embarrassed Mary, 'were annoyed by her turning up in such an irregular fashion.'[19]

Convalescent facilities were extended to women in the services who required rehabilitation before returning to their duties. These were generally run by the British Red Cross Society and the Order of St. John on behalf of the EMS, and were usually situated in large country houses.[20] They did not, however, offer much in the way of reorientation to the rigours of service life and, as Julie Anderson has shown, the female patients were reported to 'sit about over the fire and on the lawns and on their return to their units are found to be unfit for a full day's work'.[21] To help improve matters, in 1943 an ATS Reconditioning Centre (a title widely derided) was established at Hatchford Park, near Cobham in Surrey. This took on the role of a convalescent depot, similar to those provided for soldiers, as well as a general physical development establishment for undersized women recruits. Under the command of a female medical officer, the 'trainees' (they were not to be called 'patients') participated in an intensive three-to-five-week programme of physical exercise and educational activities.[22]

Some rudimentary health education was given to women on joining up and this included instruction in matters of personal hygiene.[23] In the WAAF, a lecture on VD and pregnancy was part of the syllabus, but this was not always very enlightening.[24] Mary Lee Settle recalled that such a talk was delivered to her intake by a stern, Eton-cropped, female officer wielding a swagger-stick who told them 'about crabs, warned about toilet seats, skipped over prophylactics, urged antiseptics, pictured tertiary paralysis'. 'She looked as if the only sex she had experienced,' observed Settle, 'was a flipped towel in a locker room.'[25] Another Waaf, Jean Wallace, lamented the lack of meaningful sex education for those who were inexperienced in such matters. 'There certainly were no contraceptives made available to the girls,' she reminisced, 'so our fate was in the hands of our men. All we had were myths and old wives' stories which we had brought into the forces with us, like the popular one that if you had sex standing up, you could not get pregnant. No consideration was shown for the private dilemmas which we faced.'[26]

In the WRNS, there was some pressure to issue contraceptives to female personnel. Vera Laughton Mathew recounted that a senior Admiral sought to convince her service's medical superintendent, Dr Genevieve Rewcastle, to make prophylactics available to the Wrens, in the same way that they were issued to their naval counterparts, but he was told that 'there was no indication that such a policy was necessary'. On another occasion, a naval medical officer approached a senior WRNS officer along similar lines, arguing that 'They're going to do these things and we may as well accept the fact'. But Laughton Mathews was having none of it. 'We did not accept it', she insisted. 'We expected a very high standard of conduct and the Wrens knew it.'[27]

The Health of Servicewomen

The fact that servicewomen were predominantly young and fit ensured that their health was generally good.[28] But the incidence of minor sickness in the women's forces was found to be higher than in the male services. In the WRNS, it was at least 40 per cent above that in the Royal Navy.[29] In the ATS, it was roughly double that in the army.[30] These different rates were put down to the fact that female personnel were encouraged to report sick at an early stage and were confined to bed for complaints which a serviceman might have been told to ignore.[31]

The picture was not, however, uniform. The level of minor sickness in the WAAF was twice that in the RAF during the first two years of the war, but from 1942 the female rate came more into line with that of the male.[32] This realignment was thought to be connected to the changing social class profile of the airwomen. During the early period of the conflict, the WAAF was still a volunteer force and a significant number of its recruits were said to be drawn from the middle and upper-middle classes. These Waafs, it was claimed, had been sheltered as children from many of the commoner ailments and thus had less immunity to them. Furthermore, it was opined that their upbringing had conditioned them to be very health conscious and to seek immediate medical advice, even for the most minor of complaints. Yet with the military conscription of women from late 1941, the social background of the WAAF intakes widened and, according to the official history of the RAF medical services: 'more familiar with physical discomfort and its occasional medical consequences, these recruits were much less concerned by it and regarded such things as colds, coughs and minor skin disorders as part of the general pattern of everyday life to be endured without surprise or complaint'.[33]

There were further occupational variations. In the WRNS, an inquiry at one 'northerly' naval air station in 1944 found that the rate of minor sickness among cooks was four times greater than among mechanics and seventeen times greater than among writers. It was thought that this was primarily the result of the cooks working a three-watch system that did not allow them enough time for rest and relaxation.[34] In the WAAF, the airwomen serving in Bomber Command were discovered to have appreciably lower annual rates of sickness than those in other RAF commands. This was puzzling since many of the bomber stations were located in 'bleak cold areas' near the east coast and the amenities during the expansion of these bases had often been primitive. It was surmised that in such an active operational command the Waafs 'found themselves too busy to be ill'.[35]

In relation to their mental health, the rate of discharges due to mental 'disorders' was generally higher for servicewomen than for men.[36] In the WAAF, where invalidings on the grounds of psycho-neuroses peaked at almost three times the male rate, this was put down to the particular problems young, sheltered female personnel faced in adjusting to military life:

> This difference was almost certainly due to the greater difficulty women experienced in adapting themselves to Service conditions. A considerable proportion of these women had never had a civilian job and tended to break down rapidly under conditions of community regimentation. They were usually solitary, shy individuals with few external interests and dependent on maternal decisions. They had a tendency to form strong emotional attachments.[37]

As Hazel Croft has shown, male service psychiatrists made a number of gendered observations about the suitability of female personnel for the armed forces in their assessments of servicewomen who suffered breakdowns.[38] They drew attention, among other factors, to women joining up 'impulsively for glamour and excitement'; to the fact that they were 'not so accustomed to discipline in daily life'; to women being 'very prone to hysterical reactions under service conditions'; and to 'the psycho-biological significance of service in the armed forces, implying as it does the subordination of traditional female values and primary biological functions in the compulsory interruption of the reproductive career at its optimum period'.[39]

As the war went on, particular physical health issues relating to servicewomen were highlighted by the military authorities. One such matter was foot deformities. It was reported, for example, that over half of ATS recruits had some anomaly of the feet. The problem was said to be partly the result of wearing poorly designed, high-heeled civilian shoes. Recruits were thus invariably left hobbling about uncomfortably in their stout, new, flatter-heeled service shoes after a day's drilling. As a result, special care was taken to ensure that military footwear was properly fitted, instruction was given in the care of the feet and chiropodists provided treatment in more serious cases.[40]

Another concern was head infestation. An investigation at ATS training centres in 1941, revealed that a quarter of intakes were infested

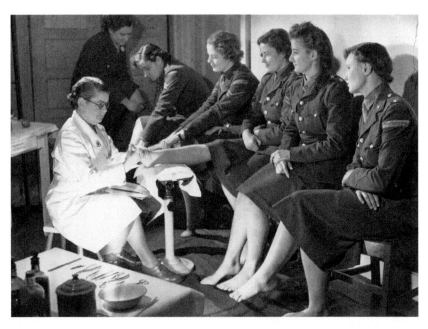

Figure 7.1 Members of the ATS have their feet examined by a nurse, 1941 (© Imperial War Museum)

with *pediculosis capitis* (head lice). A similar proportion was found to be affected among WAAF entrants in 1942. The rates of infestation, however, varied according to the regions from which recruits were drawn, with the figures for the North and Midlands being higher than those for the South and the highest levels identified among those from Northern Ireland (among whom a considerable proportion hailed from Eire).[41] The affliction was thought to be related to poor and over-crowded civilian living conditions, but also to the reluctance of women to wash their hair after expensive hair treatments.[42] The disin-festation of such large numbers of female trainees presented consider-able difficulties and some of the accepted remedies, such as the application of vinegar, paraffin or sassafras to the scalp, were found to be of doubtful effectiveness. Trials were therefore carried out of new preparations and a thiocyanate known as 'lethane 384 special' was adopted which proved very effective. Alongside treatment, service-women were encouraged to wear their hair short, wash it regularly and comb it thoroughly. It was recorded that by the time airwomen were posted away from WAAF training depots the infestation rate had fallen to under 2 per cent, while the rate among trained ATS auxiliaries was less than 1 per cent.[43]

A further issue was menstrual disorders. In 1945, a survey of the ATS revealed that approximately a quarter of its personnel had experi-enced some form of menstrual disturbance – mainly amenorrhoea or delayed menstruation – on entry into the service. This was regarded as common among women who had undergone a major disruption to their way of life, like that entailed on joining up.[44] In 1944, a study of the military occupations of those in the WAAF who had suffered from amenorrhoea showed that the highest incidences were to be found among airwomen in sedentary jobs, such as clerks, whilst the lowest rates were among those in more strenuous roles, such as flight mechanics. It was thus concluded that the more active the work, the better the menstrual health.[45] The vast majority of servicewomen were reported to have corrected themselves within six months without med-ical intervention, but a small number who continued without menstru-ating, in some cases for up to fifteen months, required endocrine treatment.[46] Women in the forces also suffered from varying degrees of dysmenorrhoea (pain during menstruation).[47] In the ATS, it was advised that the attitude of those in authority should be 'tactful and sympathetic, neither too spartan nor too coddling'. It was recommended that auxiliaries in discomfort be permitted to lie down for a couple of hours, with a cup of tea and a hot water bottle on the abdomen, but that they should be encouraged to return to work as soon as possible.[48] An additional complication was menorrhagia (abnormally heavy or prolonged menstruation).[49] Since it was believed that this condition could be triggered by the vibration of tracked vehicles, such as Bren gun carriers, members of the ATS were forbidden to drive this type of transport.[50]

Fears about sterility surfaced too. Shortly after the mixed anti-aircraft batteries were formed in 1941, rumours began to circulate in the ATS that those operating the radar sets used for gun laying would be rendered infertile. These stories appeared to have some credibility since the cathode ray tubes used with the radar apparatus had some similarities to x-ray tubes, the radiation from which was known to have deleterious effects on reproductive functions. The Medical Research Council was asked to investigate and found that no hazardous rays were emitted from the radar equipment. The rumours, however, kept reoccurring and were never completely scotched.[51] Brigadier John Rawlings Rees, the consulting psychiatrist to the British army, put these down to cases of transient amenorrhoea among female 'gunners' combined with anxieties about the hardening and defeminising effects of such operational duties.[52]

Meanwhile, the sanitary habits of some female military personnel raised a few eyebrows. Sanitary towels (STs) were issued free of charge.[53] Yet not only did some of the more naive recruits have little understanding of the purpose of these products, continuing to employ rags which they then rinsed out in readiness for their next period,[54] but others put them to rather unorthodox use. In the WAAF, this included polishing buttons, removing make-up, straining ground coffee, muffling the noise of banging doors and being worn across the eyes (with the loops fitted neatly around the ears) when trying to sleep after night duty.[55] Moreover, when STs were utilised for their intended purpose, their disposal frequently left something to be desired. Although special waste disposal bins were provided, many flushed their used articles down the lavatory. This invariably blocked the drains. More worryingly, there was a tendency on the part of some to shove the offending items (often unwrapped) into odd corners, such as the back of cupboards or behind pipes, or even to leave them lying on the floor or on window sills.[56] Corporal Vera Cole of the ATS recalled that a woman in an adjacent room to hers was discovered to have stuffed soiled STs (or 'bunnies' as they were nicknamed in the service[57]) under her mattress. This rotted the fabric and created such an odour that the bedding had to be taken way and burnt by two male orderlies. 'It was not a very pleasant job', admitted Cole, 'and made the rest of us feel ashamed'.[58] Female officers and NCOs could only maintain constant vigilance and exhort their charges to act hygienically.[59]

For their part, some servicemen were not above a bit of gentle ribbing of their female colleagues with regard to their monthly periods. Dorothy Calvert and her fellow auxiliaries had to collect their STs from the medical inspection room in their mixed battery, where they were required to sign for them (in order, she reckoned, to demonstrate to the medical officer that they were 'not in the pudding club'). She was then forced to carry hers back to her hut in a plain cardboard box to avoid being spotted by the soldiers. 'In those days', Calvert reminisced, 'girls were very self conscious of being female. We hated the men to know what we were doing, as they would strike up singing, "The Red Flag," or "Red Sails in the Sunset," or something equally apt.'[60]

Venereal Disease

The military authorities had long experience of coping with VD among servicemen, but its occurrence among servicewomen brought new dimensions to the problem. It was a difficult disease to diagnose in females since there were often no overt symptoms, as was usually the case with males.[61] Also, the social stigma attached to it was greater for women than for men and associated with the 'moral laxity' of the 'good-time girl' or the 'amateur prostitute'.[62] Jane Trefusis Forbes opined that 'if a man has v.d. it is taken for granted, but if a woman has it she is a disgrace to the country'.[63]

Careful provision thus had to be made for dealing with VD in the women's forces. To help identify the condition in the ATS, which the routine medical inspections could not hope to pick up, a number of camp sick quarters were designated as 'gynaecological centres', where experienced women medical officers could examine those who were suspected of having the disease. Auxiliaries were not forced to undergo examination, but if they refused, and there were strong grounds to believe that they were infected, they could be discharged 'services no longer required'. For those members of the ATS requiring hospitalisation, the treatment of VD came to be concentrated in three general army hospitals: Shenley (from 1941), Netley (from 1942) and Chester (from 1943). It was hoped that by incorporating these patients in establishments that catered for auxiliaries with other ailments, the ignominy of the specialist VD hospital might be avoided.[64] This was not, however, always successful. An American venereologist visited Shenley and reported that when the weekly trainload of female VD cases arrived they were ostracised by the staff, who viewed them as 'moral lepers'.[65] At this time VD was still regarded by the army as a type of self-inflicted wound and, like soldiers, auxiliaries admitted to hospital with it had part of their pay docked while undergoing treatment. But this, it was contended by medical officers, tended simply to deter those with VD from declaring their condition. In 1944, it was decided that both men and women should incur no stoppages from their pay for the first thirty days of treatment (which covered most cases).[66]

In the WAAF, those who were found to be suffering from VD were originally sent to the London Lock hospital: a long-standing civilian VD clinic. It came to be regarded, however, as undesirable for airwomen to be associated with such an institution and cared for alongside non-service women of 'doubtful character'. From 1942, VD cases were transferred to the RAF general hospital at Evesham. This, it was calculated, would better preserve the confidentiality of the patients and thus reduce the notoriety of their condition.[67] After treatment, an airwoman was to be posted to a new RAF station in order 'to give her a fresh start in life'.[68] In the WRNS, arrangements were made by the naval authorities for Wrens with VD to be admitted to hospitals willing to take them, but it was reported that the disease 'presented no problem' in this smaller and 'carefully selected' force.[69]

The incidence of VD among servicewomen varied over the war. In the ATS, the rate peaked at 5.3 cases per 1,000 women in 1942. Thereafter, it declined to less than 1.0 per 1,000 for the rest of the war.[70] The same broad pattern emerged in the WAAF. The rate was 1.15 cases per 1,000 in 1940; it reached a high of 3.88 per 1,000 in 1942; and then fell to 2.11 per 1,000 by 1945 (see Table 2 in appendix). These figures were considerably lower than those for soldiers and airmen. The average annual rate for the army in the United Kingdom was over 10.0 cases per 1,000, while the equivalent rate for the RAF was nearly 9.0 per 1,000.[71]

The VD levels in the WAAF were closely scrutinised in the Air Ministry. The fluctuations were difficult to explain, but it was thought that the comparatively low rates early in the war might have been the result of missed cases, while the decline after 1942 was related to a gradual decrease in the younger age groups among the WAAF intakes – the highest rates tended to be among the eighteen to twenty-one-year-olds – and the cumulative effects of anti-VD lectures and propaganda. Another influence on the variations was the degree of undetected pre-service infection. In 1942, for example, 1.4 per 1,000 of the new recruits were said to have contracted VD before entry.[72] Analysis of the levels of VD across WAAF trades in 1942 revealed that the highest incidence occurred among airwomen in less skilled jobs, such as waitresses, while the lowest rates were among those in higher skilled roles, such as radio, radar and teleprinter operators.[73] The reduced levels among radar operators, for instance, was put down to the fact that 'the standard of girls attracted to this trade was high' and that they 'maintained higher social and moral standards' than those in other types of work.[74] Members of the RAF were – perhaps unsurprisingly in view of their close interaction with the WAAF – alleged to be the chief source of VD infection among airwomen. In 1942, they were held responsible for nearly half of cases, with British soldiers and civilians blamed for most of the rest. A shift, however, took place in 1944. Whilst a third of infections were still attributed to the RAF, the allied and dominion forces were now deemed to account for a similar proportion (see Table 3 in appendix). It was presumed that this was the result of the increased numbers of overseas military personnel in the UK 'far removed from their home environment and family ties'.[75] The rates among Waafs serving in Bomber Command were reported to be consistently higher than those in Fighter Command. This was believed to reflect the similarly differing levels of disease among the airmen in these two commands.[76]

Pregnancy

Pregnancy among servicewomen presented a further set of challenges to the military authorities. Carrying a child was not thought compatible with efficient military service and pregnant women were released from the forces. In the ATS and WAAF, it was intended that this should normally be three months after conception. In the WRNS, expectant Wrens were permitted to stay on as long as circumstances permitted, provided that this was 'not likely to cause physical strain' or was an 'inconvenience to fellow workers'. Most were discharged after six months.[77]

In order to be released, women had to have a medical certificate confirming their pregnancy.[78] For those in the ATS who suspected they might be in this condition, the camp gynaecological centres were able to assist in providing a diagnosis. Arrangements were also made for pregnancy tests to be carried out when necessary at the University of Edinburgh's Pregnancy Diagnosis Laboratory (which had been established by Francis Crew in the inter-war years and was attached to the university's Institute of Animal Genetics). The Aschheim-Zondek test utilised in this process involved injecting the urine of auxiliaries into female mice and if the woman was pregnant the urine induced changes in the ovaries of the mice. The supply of suitable rodents was, however, severely curtailed by the destruction of the stocks of one of the country's largest breeders by enemy bombing and a shortage of animal feedstuffs. As a result, the frequency of the test had to be restricted and the onus put back on unit medical officers.[79] WAAF personnel were also subject to the Aschheim-Zondek procedure but those in the WRNS were assessed using the *Xenopus laevis* test. Instead of mice, this employed South African claw-toed frogs, which, despite the difficulties of importing, the Royal Navy managed to source.[80]

Reliable statistics on pregnancy rates among servicewomen were not available until some time into the war, partly because releases on these grounds tended to be lumped together with other compassionate discharges,[81] but the figures indicate a steady increase. In the WAAF, the level rose from 46.2 cases per 1,000 in 1942, to 89.7 per 1,000 in 1944. In the ATS, it grew over the same period from 55.23 per 1,000, to 89.87 per 1,000 (see Table 4 in appendix). A breakdown of the ATS figures for the period from July 1943 to December 1944 revealed that 409 per 1,000 of the married strength, and 28 per 1,000 of the unmarried strength, were discharged pregnant (see Table 5 in appendix). This meant that nearly half of all married auxiliaries – married women making up approximately one-seventh of the overall strength in early 1944[82] – were lost to the service due to pregnancy during this period. This was described in the official history of the Army Medical Services as a 'remarkable figure'.[83]

Unmarried pregnancies were, however, a more problematic issue within the women's forces – not least in the harm it did to their reputation.[84] There were a few women who deliberately sought impregnation with the intention of securing release. In the ATS, expectant auxiliaries were discharged under paragraph eleven of the relevant appendix of the service's regulations and this administrative clause became a code word for 'in the family way'. Anne Varley recalled that 'one of my mates was so determined that she crept to the men's quarters and shouted "Para 11" under the windows. She was hauled in within seconds and later obtained her discharge and an illegal abortion.'[85] Yet most seem to have fallen pregnant unintentionally and had to come to terms with their predicament as best they could. Some were so ashamed and fearful that they tried to harm themselves. Olive Noble caught one of her fellow Waafs downing a bottle of aspirins in the toilet and grabbed it off her: 'When I enquired why on earth she was taking such drastic action, her reply was that she was "Pregnant" and was desperate . . . . I told her nothing was worth giving up your own "life" for.'[86] Others sought to conceal their condition for as long as possible, often in the hope of a miscarriage. This was a problem for medical staff since the regular health inspections could not identify all cases, especially as it was possible for women to absent themselves during these check-ups and it was not always easy for female officers to notice the expanding figures of their subordinates hidden beneath service jackets. Even if they were suspected of being pregnant, they could not be forced to undergo an examination to determine this.[87] As a result, a number of babies were born in military camps and bases. According to Felicity Hill, one airwoman, who was discovered to be in the early stages of labour, had her baby girl delivered in the sick quarters of RAF Benson. The male station commander was said to have doted on the child, fellow Waafs knitted bootees, and when the mother left the service and went home to her parents, she announced that she intended to name her daughter 'Bensonia'.[88] But there were more tragic tales. Sylvia Drake-Brockman recounted that at RAF Silverstone the remains of a five-month-old foetus were found in a lavatory pan: 'Needless to say the expectant mother was never discovered'.[89]

Considerable thought was given to the welfare of unmarried pregnant personnel. 'An illegitimate child's life', emphasised Trefusis Forbes, 'is of the same value as a legitimate child' and the women's forces put in place a good deal of support for these expectant mothers.[90]

It was recognised that they were likely to be under 'great mental strain' and required 'especially sympathetic handling'. Advice was to be provided on such matters as ante-natal services, places of confinement, maternity benefits and affiliation orders. The servicewomen were encouraged to take their families into their confidence and return home to be cared for. Those, however, who did not wish to disclose their condition to relatives (the ATS chose not to inform parents unless requested by an auxiliary, whilst the WAAF and WRNS reserved the right to notify them if a woman was under twenty-one years of age), or whose relations were unwilling, or unable, to look after them, could be put in touch with such voluntary organisations as the Church of England Moral Welfare Council that could make maternity arrangements on their behalf and facilitate their admission to an appropriate moral welfare hostel. To smooth the transition to civilian life, in 1942 the ATS established a Special Discharge Depot at Whittington Hall, near Worcester, where unmarried auxiliaries could be accommodated whilst assistance for them was being put in place in advance of release. Servicewomen who wished to return to the forces were permitted to do so six months after giving birth, if they were regarded as being suitable for re-enrolment.[91] Edith Summerskill praised the 'humane and moral approach' of the services and opined that 'the harsh realities of war help people to see this age-old problem in its proper perspective'.[92] Barbara Cartland expressed similar – if more forthright – views:

> The Services did their best for those girls . . .
>
> They needed an encouraging word, a helping hand, not sermons or fingers pointed in scorn.
>
> It was always the plain, withered virgins who had never been tempted and never had the opportunity of going wrong who had the most to say about it.[93]

In fact, some single airwomen admitted that they joined the WAAF knowing they were pregnant because of the support they would receive inside the force once their condition became known.[94]

As the war went on, it became clear that additional facilities were required for unmarried expectant mothers who could not be cared for by their families. Not only did it prove increasingly difficult for voluntary organisations to make adequate maternity arrangements for all those who needed them, given the wartime increase in illegitimate births on the home front, but there was also reluctance on the part of some servicewomen to enter moral welfare hostels because of their strict rules and regulations. As a result, a number were forced into poor law institutions to have their babies. Although they had no official obligation towards their former personnel after they had left the women's forces, the military authorities were naturally anxious about this state of affairs and lobbied the Ministry of Health to develop a maternity scheme for unmarried servicewomen – a process expedited by the Markham report which recommended that the ministry should give urgent attention to the needs of expectant mothers. From 1943, servicewomen were thus entitled to apply for admission to government maternity hostels if they could not obtain assistance from other agencies. The Soldiers', Sailors' and Airmen's Help Society sifted the cases and acted as a link between the services and the ministry.[95] By the spring of 1945, over 900 applications had been received from members of the women's services for places in these hostels.[96]

For some in the forces, this was not enough. In the autumn of 1944, the Commander-in-Chief of Bomber Command, Air Chief Marshal Sir Arthur Harris, took time from overseeing the strategic bombing of Germany to write a strong letter to the Air Ministry about the issue of unmarried pregnant airwomen in his command. He argued that the policy for the disposal of these personnel was inadequate because the concealment of pregnancies until a late stage made it difficult for proper arrangements to be made by the voluntary organisations or the Ministry of Health. Not only did he suggest that many single airwomen were reluctant to report their condition because of the perceived disgrace of having to return home, discharged and disowned by the WAAF, but also that the problem was aggravated by the Air Ministry's practice of informing the parents of those under twenty-one. This made them even more determined to hide their pregnancies, particularly those from 'a good home background'. Furthermore, he contended that the RAF authorities had a strong moral obligation to care for these airwomen since service conditions were partly responsible for their situation:

> The conscription of minors into its ranks, the youth of the WAAF as a whole and of many of its administrative Officers in particular, must surely be accounted as contributory causes in the rise of the illegitimate pregnancy rate, whilst the opportunity and temptations offered by the enforced propinquity of

communal Service life, must be regarded as additional factors in the increase of laxity.[97]

He therefore proposed that the Air Ministry should no longer force out pregnant unmarried airwomen who were unable to make private arrangements. Instead, they would be retained as unpaid, civilian-clothed members of the service and accommodated in a special WAAF maternity hostel right up until the time of confinement. This hostel would offer pre-natal care and instruction in 'mothercraft'. The provision of such an establishment, asserted Harris, would not only mitigate some of the practical problems of disposal, but also 'indicate a fuller appreciation of the moral issues at stake, and reflect greater credit upon the Service than does the present policy of disassociation and discharge'.[98]

The Air Ministry, however, was not inclined to agree with Harris. The views of the WAAF hierarchy were sought – one of whose staff officers dismissed Bomber Command's suggestions as 'guided more by sentiment than by practical common sense'[99] – and his proposals were rejected. It was maintained that the Ministry of Health was the body responsible for the care of pregnant women and that the RAF medical service should not take over this function; that the problems facing unmarried mothers were better handled by experienced civilian welfare workers; and that such a hostel would inevitably bring opprobrium on the WAAF and 'lay the Services open to the accusation that they are making illegitimacy attractive and easy and encouraging immorality'. It was considered that the policy in place was sound and that 'the remedy of disclosing her condition lies in the airwoman's own hands'.[100] Harris was forced to accept this ruling but retorted that 'I much regret that the change of policy which I proposed . . . is regarded as unacceptable.'[101]

8 OFF DUTY

Recreational Activities

In the ATS and the WAAF, servicewomen not on duty were normally required to spend one evening each week in their camps or billets. This was known as a 'barrack night' or a 'domestic night' and was generally used for such chores as cleaning quarters, washing underwear, sewing stockings, pressing skirts and polishing shoes.[1] Some female personnel resented this intrusion on their free time and wondered why their male counterparts seemed to escape such an inconvenience.[2] Nevertheless, these evenings could become lively affairs. Eileen McMurdo recalled that the 'characters' in her ATS billet would oblige the auxiliaries with a 'turn or two' as they huddled over their darning needles or queued up for the temperamental electric iron:

> One of these was Vicki who would entertain us with her 'raw recruit act.' Dressed in an assortment of our uniforms, overlarge jacket and skimpy skirt, army issue bloomer legs hanging well down below her knees and with a hat rammed down over her eyes she would proceed to 'take the mickey' out of everything the ATS held sacred in the broad accent of her native Plymouth.[3]

To members of the RAF, the WAAF 'domestic night' took on the mystique of a curious female ritual. One male officer wrote of 'that evening on which the WAAF are kept in barracks and foregather for reasons which, other than the mending of "smalls", are wrapped in mystery more profound than freemasonry'. The RAF corporal on gate duty at his base termed it the women's 'confinement night'.[4]

When they were not engaged in these domestic tasks, service-women participated in a wide range of leisure activities in their off-duty hours. Some whiled away the time simply reading, writing letters, knitting, or chatting to friends in the forces.[5] For Dorothy Calvert, these casual interactions with her ATS hut mates demonstrated both the diversity and solidarity of the group:

> I found it very fascinating, that in such a small Island we could all speak some kind of English, and yet all sound so different. I always liked to listen to the girls who came from wealthy parents, speaking in their Eton collar and top hat way, and yet they were the same as the rest of us, only when they swore, or sang bawdy songs, it sounded a lot more daft. Then perhaps we English would have to gang up against the Scots, when they were having a 'We hate England' day. We would say 'Sod off back to Scotland then, we can manage without you.' These spates [sic] would last a few minutes, then the Welsh girl would say something in her own tongue, which could have been anything, and we would forget the spate and fall about laughing ... Taking all in all, we really got on famously, not Angelic, just normal.[6]

Others were more active in their leisure time. A number, for example, participated in education schemes laid on for the services. According to one participant at RAF Ternhill, these could inspire some animated discussions:

> Let me take you along to the Education Block at 2015 hours one Thursday to have a peep at the Group in Session. The subject for tonight is 'AREN'T MEN BEASTS' and LACW [Leading Aircraftswoman] Prince, BEM, who is of the opinion that they are, is going to try and bring the Group round to her way of thinking. Diffidently she mounts the rostrum, for it is her first appearance, and puts forward a reasonable, sound argument in support of her case. Many hardened 'discussers' are seen taking copious notes which will form the basis of the many arrows they

are going to sling at her later. The very able Group Leader then declares the subject open for discussion and the fun begins ...

'Women's place is in the home' declares one speaker.

'Not at all' replies another, hard on his heels. 'Let her work outside if she wants to.'

Back and forth the ball is flung from airmen to airwomen, from officer to NCO ...

At 2300 hours, the Group Leader has to bring the meeting to a close as the lights are liable to go off at any moment. Reluctantly we drag ourselves away from the Discussion Group and wend our way to our various messes, still arguing hotly.[7]

On other occasions these events needed different billing. It was reported that when one civilian lecturer spoke to an ATS audience on the topic of 'Prospects for Poland' the talk 'failed dismally'. Yet when the same lecture was advertised to another ATS unit under the title of 'Would you marry a Pole?' the ensuing discussion was said to have been 'lively in the extreme'.[8] Female personnel also took part in various sports.[9] Lois Goossens of the ATS played in a mixed hockey match against the soldiers, but the referee had to curtail it as 'the men played dirty by bashing us with their sticks and tripping us up'.[10] In contrast, Edith Kup of the WAAF participated in a corresponding game against the airmen and 'since they were too gentlemanly to play too hard, we beat them hollow'.[11] Amateur theatricals were another pastime. Janet Sykes of the ATS took to the stage in a review for her mixed searchlight battery and sang 'The Last Time I Saw Paris' so badly that 'the memory embarrasses me still'.[12] More daringly, Claire Lowry of the WRNS performed a high-kicking 'Tiller Girls' routine at a naval concert that was 'much appreciated by the matelots'.[13] The cinema was an additional attraction. During the weekly film shows at Lilian Bader's RAF station 'whenever the hero embraced his loved one there would be loud Donald Duck sounds from the men and indignant shushes from us girls'.[14]

Dances were a further recreation for servicewomen. In Doris Hatcher's mess dining room a notice would be posted up asking for quotas of Wrens to sign up for dances at nearby British military bases: 'Trucks used to come from different army camps and pick us up – "passion trucks", as they were called.'[15] On occasion, complications of rank and gender might arise. Molly Gale, a regimental sergeant major in the ATS, was regularly asked onto the dance floor by

Figure 8.1 Waafs watch their colleagues competing at a RAF sports meeting, 1941 (George W. Hales/Hulton Archive via Getty Images)

male other ranks during the Saturday-night dances at her Royal Artillery training camp: 'I knew when it had been a bet by the whistles from his mates as we circled the floor. I usually asked if I shared the bet.'[16] If civilian women were present, feminine rivalries could surface. 'We are not allowed to wear "civvies" on the camp', complained airwoman Josette Demey, 'and we feel very much at our disadvantage towards those civilian factory girls who come to dance with "our" RAF boys.'[17] Indeed, when female personnel were authorised to attend dances out of uniform there was invariably a desire to don something more glamorous. Whilst stationed at Wilton House near Salisbury, Eileen McMurdo's ATS signallers were invited to a dance in the local town hall at which fancy dress was to be permitted as a 'special treat':

> The one stipulation made by our commanding officer was that we would wear either a bona-fide fancy dress or our uniforms but that dance or party dresses would not be allowed. Nothing daunted, many of the girls sent home for their evening finery

and there was much wracking of brains as they tried to think of some effective way of converting them into fancy dress.

On the night of the dance the majority of us played it safe and stuck to our uniforms but a few of the hardier element turned up at the Town Hall looking very chic and attractive even if it wasn't easy to tell where the evening dress ended and fancy dress began . . . .

The most blatantly thin 'disguise' of all was a long, flowing white gown worn by one of the signal office staff which appeared without any extra adornment at all. The only slight concession the wearer made to the occasion was a small wreath of artificial laurel leaves nestling precariously and practically invisibly amongst her upswept hair. She announced that she had come as 'Peace in our time.'[18]

When the US forces arrived in Britain, invitations to dances at their bases tended to be especially sought after. Not only was the dancing lively – Waaf Joyce Taylor was 'shaken and shocked but nevertheless pleasurably excited' by her American dance partner's jitterbug[19] – but also the abundant food provided for the female guests seemed like manna from heaven in heavily-rationed wartime Britain.[20]

Drinking in pubs and bars was an added means of relaxation for women in the forces.[21] For some, this was a novel – if somewhat disconcerting – experience. Joan Zeepvat entered a public house for the first time on a night out in Wrexham with an ATS colleague and two sappers and was cajoled into imbibing a pint of Welsh lager: 'I don't know how I managed to swallow it. It tasted like the Bitter Alloes that the teacher used to have on her desk to stop us biting our nails.' Thoroughly tipsy, she travelled back to her camp recumbent in the overhead luggage rack of a train: 'Not a drop of Welsh Lager has ever passed my lips again.'[22] Others took to alcohol rather better. WAAF officer Frances Stone was persuaded to participate in a 'schooner race' between RAF officers at her air base and discovered, much to her surprise, that she was able to drain a tankard of beer in double quick time: 'I could only imagine that the fact that I had had my tonsils removed when I was at College made me able to drink so quickly.' Thereafter, she was regularly asked to challenge male new-comers to down a pint in the mess bar: 'I was never beaten, but much later an RAF officer in Fighter Command produced a dead heat.'[23]

A few participated in more unruly behaviour. 'Those ATS girls are a disgrace', thundered one member of the public in Chester. 'They come into this pub at night and line up against that wall. Soldiers give them drinks and then when they're blind drunk they carry them out into the street. And we're paying public money for them too.'[24] Elsewhere, Joan Wyndham described the alcohol-fuelled revelries she enjoyed with her fellow WAAF plotters at a RAF station near Preston:

> The highspots of our social life are pub parties given by the girls in our Mess, which usually turn out to be Babylonian orgies. Pandora, Oscar [ine] and I are not very good at these affairs where everybody kisses everybody else, no matter how repulsive. We eat and drink our way steadily through the 1/6d. worth we put into the kitty and look neither to right nor left. Gussy is a much better mixer, and she can also play piano – 'Love's Old Sweet Song' on piano keys awash with beer. After the party the scene at the bus stop usually beggars description, WAAFs collapsing and being sick in the road, airmen peeing against the wall, couples rolling in the grass. Last time Pandora was sick all night from the pork pies.[25]

The military authorities were sensitive to the off-duty activities of servicewomen and on occasion intervened in order to protect what Gerard DeGroot has termed their 'feminine virtue'.[26] In the WAAF, for instance, there were concerns about excessive consumption of alcohol among airwomen and, whilst heavy drinking was common among RAF aircrew and even indulged by senior commanders,[27] guidance on this issue was circulated to female officers:

> The habitual taking of alcohol should be discouraged. While it should be appreciated that many women in the Service have been accustomed in the past to temperate indulgence in alcohol without undesirable repercussions, a danger arises in the case of the young recruit who is a stranger to alcohol, but who may be led astray by older and more sophisticated companions. The officer should be on the lookout for this and can often, by changing hours of work and barrack huts, break up undesirable associations.[28]

In the ATS, there was a particular anxiety about the 'bad impression' created by auxiliaries smoking in public places. In the view of the DATS, Leslie Whateley, 'such habits looked unattractive and unfeminine in civilian clothes, and in uniform worse'. Her first impulse was to deal with the matter informally by word of mouth. However, she allowed herself to be overruled by her senior officers and, in the spring of 1944, issued a written instruction that auxiliaries must not smoke in public when in uniform.[29] This prohibition included whilst walking on the streets, travelling on buses, queuing for the cinema or browsing in shops.[30] The order soon came to the attention of MPs who raised it in the House of Commons. Emanuel Shinwell, the Labour MP for Easington, wondered why there should be 'discrimination between men and women in the Forces as regards smoking' and enquired whether it would not be better for the government to 'get on with the war, instead of indulging in these pettifogging regulations?' The Secretary of State for War, Sir James Grigg, sought to explain the rationale behind the directive, but was clearly discomforted by the predicament he had been put in. He argued that this order – which in fact amplified a 'no-smoking on the streets' clause in the 1941 ATS regulations that had obviously fallen into abeyance – sought to ensure that 'the appearance of the auxiliaries did credit to their Service', yet acknowledged that 'whether this object can best be secured by detailed instructions, or by relying on the good sense of the auxiliaries is a matter of opinion'.[31] Although Whateley's order continued to stand, she was contrite: 'I certainly learnt my lesson never to go back on my first inclination.'[32] Penny Tinkler has suggested that this no-smoking episode was redolent of the fragile 'respectability' of women in uniform.[33]

The question of contact between white servicewomen and black American servicemen also arose. As David Reynolds has related, the War Office preferred not to put much in writing on this subject because of its sensitivity, but indicated that members of the ATS should have minimal interaction with black GIs.[34] Yet this did not prevent local army commanders from issuing their own instructions. One senior officer in Southern Command advised that 'white women should not associate with coloured men' and should not 'walk out, dance, or drink with them'.[35] Likewise, Mary Lee Settle recollected that during her WAAF basic training the new recruits were told by the female 'admin' officer that she 'absolutely forbid' them to be seen talking to black American soldiers. But this did not go down well with all those present.

'She's not fucking well going to tell *me* oo to see!', Settle overheard one Waaf mutter to another.[36] This wartime hostility to interracial relationships was an aspect of what Wendy Webster has termed 'sexual patriotism'.[37]

Meanwhile, higher authority could find itself drawn into efforts at damage control in regard to women's off-duty activities. In the summer of 1942, an article appeared in *The New York Times*, under the headline 'US Soldier Spanks Mary Churchill as Retort to Jest Over His Big Feet', which recounted the events at an ATS party in London at which the Prime Minister's daughter, who had just been promoted to sergeant, was said to have been put over the knee of Private Bill 'Feets' Adams of Grand Rapids, Michigan, who 'paddled' her for making fun of his size 14EE service shoes (the largest issued by the US army: 'a shade smaller than Clipper Pontoons'). The assailant, it was reported, 'did not think of the incident as a matter of applied democracy – it just seemed a natural thing to do at the time'.[38] Downing Street officials got wind of the story and the Ministry of Information was consulted as to whether steps should be taken to prevent its publication in the British newspapers, in order to forestall the episode having 'a discouraging effect on mothers of possible recruits for the ATS'. It was, however, considered that any such action might simply draw attention to the story, which apparently had not been widely circulated, and the matter was allowed to rest.[39]

Beauty Rituals

Regardless of their roles with the armed forces, many servicewomen spent part of their spare time undertaking beauty rituals of one type or another. Regulations were drawn up to govern their appearance when in uniform. They included the stipulations that hair was to be 'neat' and worn 'off the collar', that make-up, if used, should be 'discreet' and that nail varnish must not be 'highly coloured'.[40] But these did not prevent female personnel from going to considerable lengths to enhance their looks. As Pat Kirkham has commented, 'women in uniform took beauty and duty just as seriously as their civilian sisters'.[41]

There were, for example, night-time beauty rituals. In Kathleen Cove's WAAF hut, the scene before lights out was invariably of 'girls in varying stages of undress, sitting on their beds putting their hair in curlers'.[42] One of Joan Zeepvat's ATS room-mates inserted so many hairpins that they covered her head 'like a metal bonnet'.[43] There were also morning rituals. Pamela Brisley-Wilson's regular wake-up routine in the WAAF was to 'freshen my face with cotton wool and a mixture of rose water and witch hazel and then apply my face cream and lipstick and rouge'.[44] Barbara Rhodes found that her WRNS navy blue uniform was prone to smudging with make-up and face powder whilst dressing for duty so 'we nearly all left our skirts and jackets off until we had attended to our hair and complexions'.[45] In preparation for social events, the beauty process intensified. 'Like all girls,' reported one Waaf, 'there's a tremendous pride in appearance. When we went to a dance last week, some girls spent the entire afternoon titivating themselves.'[46] If for some reason beauty accessories were in short supply, this could cause a tremor in the ranks. 'Undoubtedly, the worst thing of all,' admitted Marjorie Hazell after her kitbag and those of her fellow Waafs had been mislaid among the baggage of a Guards regiment during a train journey to a new RAF camp, 'was the loss of our hair curlers and make-up.'[47] It was reported by one airwoman that 'all told,

Figure 8.2 Members of the ATS apply make-up, 1941 (Hulton-Deutsch Collection/ Corbis Historical via Getty Images)

more make up is used in, than out of the WAAF'.[48] A wartime observer, Peggy Scott, put this enhanced concern for appearance in the services down to 'a different femininity': 'It is not merely to attract men but because they think more of themselves. Doing men's work and being treated as mates by the men has given the girls a better sense of their own value.'[49]

Inevitably, some stepped over the boundaries of what was considered decorous. Claire Lowry's unruly 'wavy bob' and penchant for brilliant lipstick and bright nail varnish resulted in regular trouble with her WRNS officers: 'Called to the Office, suitably immaculately attired, with my hair rolled up around my head, and wearing the minimum of make-up, I would stand on the square of carpet, to be thoroughly told off.'[50] Yet in other regards, the military authorities seemed willing to collaborate in these beauty endeavours. In the ATS and WAAF, hairdressing salons were established at bases where there were large concentrations of servicewomen.[51] In the WRNS, a lecture was given to Wrens by a former employee of Elizabeth Arden on 'the correct way to wear makeup with uniform'.[52] And in the ATS, a sleek khaki shoulder bag was issued to auxiliaries that they used as a receptacle for their cosmetics when off duty (gas mask cases having previously fulfilled this purpose).[53] In fact, Martin Francis has suggested that there was a belief that the presence of attractive airwomen at RAF stations could give a positive lift to the spirits of hard-pressed male aircrew.[54] One Czech Spitfire pilot, Miroslav Liskutin, was so captivated by the WAAF parachute packers at RAF Catterick that he wondered if someone had handpicked 'a team of beauty queens, to help with the morale'.[55]

Romances with Servicemen

Military life invariably offered unattached servicewomen (and, no doubt, some attached as well) plenty of opportunities for romantic interludes with male colleagues during their off-duty hours. At Christian Lamb's naval fort 'we were all longing to fall in love'.[56] In Edna Smith's mixed anti-aircraft battery 'there were lots of romances … it was natural'.[57] At Marjorie Hazell's aircraft maintenance unit 'everybody paired off … There were no spare girls.'[58] 'In the forces', confirmed Waaf Joan Arkwright, 'a boyfriend seems to be one of the necessities of life.'[59]

Female personnel could, however, be discriminating in their choice of men, especially when there were plenty of eligible ones to choose from. This was well illustrated in a report drawn up for Mass Observation on the love life of Waafs. Compiled by Aircraftswoman Nina Masel (who before joining up had been a paid investigator for MO), and entitled 'The Great Digby Man-Chase', it provided a candid commentary on the attributes that she and her fellow plotters at RAF Digby looked for in their service boyfriends, as well as the ruthlessness of the 'hunt':

> The main consequence of a lot of women living together seems to be that, since everyone realizes that everyone else's emotions, aims and actions are similar to their own – conventional barriers and restraint are torn down, and conversation gets down to bedrock.
>
> The presence of both sexes always imposes restraint in conversation. The soldier's fumbling excuse for hard swearing is always: 'Oh, well, when a lot of us lads get together ... ' Similarly, when women are together in our circumstances, we use words which we wouldn't think of 'bringing out in public'.
>
> Not only in choice of words, but also in choice of topic and depth of discussion, is this new candour created. Even at women's tea-parties, where the other sex is excluded, women are on their guard against each other, and don't admit their basic feelings ... But here, we've got to know each other well; we're all in the same boat and we're all after the same thing. So why kid each other?
>
> And what is this thing we're all after? Obviously, a man. Preferably an officer or a sergeant-pilot. I should say that 85% of our conversation is about men, dances (where we meet men), etc, etc; 15% about domestic and shop matters; and a negligible percentage on other matters.
>
> But to get a man is not sufficient. It's easy to get a man; in fact it's difficult not to. Competitive factors in the Great Man-Chase are under the following headings ...
>
> 1. Quality: The decisive qualities are rank; wings; looks; money; youth; in that order.
>
> Rank is unbelievably important. There's a Wing-Commander here whose only redeeming features is that he's young. He isn't

good-looking; he's owned to be a great bore; and he's extremely 'fast' – (which is <u>not</u> a recommendation, see later). Yet he could go out with any woman on the station he cared to ask; no one would refuse. And all this rests purely on his 3 rings and wings.

'My dear', Dorothy, his favourite confided in me, 'he's a dreadful bore – you chat away and all he says is 'yes' or 'no' and you're left wondering what to say next. And honestly, to be quite frank – although it's a dreadful thing to say – I honestly wouldn't dream of going out with him if he wasn't a Wing-Co.'

The height of sex-rank is commission plus wings (higher commission the better). Sergeant-pilots and ground-commissions tie for second place. This includes army officers. Ground stripes come a poor third. For the rest, as far as most Ops. girls are concerned, there is little hunting-value.

In the term 'looks', I include charm, personality, etc. This counts only as a narrow comparison, viz: P/O [Pilot Officer] A is better than P/O B, because he is more charming, but we'd rather go out with P/O B, who is not charming, than with Sergeant C who <u>is</u> (and he's good looking, too).

Members of the army without commissions don't get a look in at all . . .

2. <u>Quantity</u>: Naturally, the more men one can fasten to one's train, the more prestige one gains in the Chase.

3. <u>Intensity</u>: A deliberately vague term, embodying length of affair, seriousness of affair, extent of ardour, and its manifestations.

Of course, the longer you can keep your man, the higher up you are in the competition. It's better if he's madly in love with you. He shouldn't be seen in public with other women. And telegrams, chocolates, cigarettes, and really 'classy' evenings out all put you a step higher on the ladder.

As far as physical manifestations are concerned, the average operations girl admittedly likes a man who can kiss well, eyes 'wandering' with suspicion, and definitely abstains from actual immorality. Technique in kissing is of first importance.

Thus:

'Norman's a dear, but so inexperienced. When he kisses me, nine times out of ten he misfires.'

Or,

'There's one thing about Allen. He does know how to kiss.'

Or,

'I felt really hurt. He saw me all the way back to the billet, and then just shook hands with me.'

Further than kissing is not eyed favourably:

'I <u>like</u> Bill, and he <u>is</u> a Squadron-Leader and all that, but I simply can't face the coping I have to do every evening.' ('Coping' having become the accepted term for dealing with unwanted passion.)

So the most eligible men are those who kiss well, but 'know when to stop'.

In summary, the best position to be in is to have lots of winged officers of high rank, young, with plenty of money, sending telegrams and cigarettes regularly, falling violently in love with you for a long time, preferably good-looking and amusing.

What is all this for?

It seems to me that practically the entire object of this Chase is a matter of vanity and prestige. It is nice to find that so many desirable men are attentive to one. It is even nicer to prove this to others, by appearing with various escorts at all public functions.

Becoming, of necessity, subjective: – I allowed myself to drift into this Chase for the past few months and have discovered:

(a) that I am happiest when I am conducting two or three successful affairs with eligibles as above,

(b) that I am second happiest when I am <u>pretending to other girls</u> that they are successful affairs as above,

(c) that the moment I'd 'hooked my man', it gave me great pleasure to appear at dances with him, in front of my friends, particularly if <u>they</u> were unescorted,

(d) that one of the most triumphant moments of my life occurred when a telegram arrived for me, in the mess, from a very high rank officer. My immediate reaction was: 'Thank God this arrived in the mess, in front of them all, and not in the billet. That <u>would</u> have been a waste!'

I have reason to believe that these reactions are fairly typical ...

A girl on our control had been trying very hard to get a date with a new officer. She was sitting next to him in the Ops. Room, one day, full of concentration in her conversation, when suddenly she smiled, looked across at me, and mouthed the words: 'Got him!'[60]

The attraction of officer-aircrew was corroborated by other Waafs. Joan Wyndham admitted that at station dances 'everyone [was] hoping to get off with a pilot':

The sergeants' Mess Hall was hung with balloons and streamers left over from Christmas and a rather ropy band was playing on the platform. As we strolled in to the strains of 'Deep Purple' it seemed that all the men were about five feet tall. Soon we were whirling around the room clasped to the amorous bosoms of these pint-sized Romeos, dreaming all the time of our ideal, a mythical character whom we have christened Squadron Leader the Hon. Anthony Ashley-Dukes. Any minute now, we felt, he would swan in, so weighted with 'gongs' that he could hardly stand up, and sweep us off our feet. Meanwhile we have to put up with the sweaty embraces of these 'wingless wonders'. The very worst thing about being at a Filter Command is that there are no pilots! I can't describe the effect wings have on a WAAF. Our theme song should really be 'If I Only Had Wings'.[61]

Elsewhere, the romantic impulses of servicewomen could lead to more speculative assignations. Eileen McMurdo recalled that on slack Sunday mornings she and her fellow ATS other ranks would sometimes engage in telephone flirting whilst manning the army switchboards:

It was during one of those quiet Sunday shifts that Mollie, a newcomer to Southern Command, got into conversation with Captain Casey. He had one of those attractive 'dark brown' voices and most of us had at some time or other passed a Sunday morning in conversation with him. Mollie was obviously quite captivated and was having a long, cosy chat as the rest of us sat reading our papers but gradually as she began making arrangements to meet him that evening, we put down our papers and gave her side of the conversation our full and undivided attention. When she had twittered her final 'goodbye' she turned to find us watching her, grinning delightedly.

'Well, well, <u>well</u>!' someone remarked. 'What do you know! – She's got a date with our Captain Casey! What have <u>you</u> got that we lesser beings lack?!'

Mollie was a small pert blonde from London and although she hadn't been with us for long we had gathered that there wasn't a lot she didn't know about most things. She took our ribbing and friendly interest with amused tolerance wanting to know as much as possible about Captain Casey. As she hadn't yet actually met him 'in the flesh' as it were, we willingly supplied a few details.

Mollie and I bunked in the same room so I was on hand that evening as she was getting ready for her dinner engagement at the 'White Hart'.

'I told him what I'd be wearing so that he'd spot me right away,' she said, pouring herself into a tightly fitting red corduroy suit. I agreed that in that outfit he'd spot her without any trouble at all, asking if she didn't think it just a bit risky making a 'blind date.' By this time several other members of the shift had drifted into our room and were sitting around watching her preparations.

'Risky?' she asked. 'After what you crowd told me about him this morning? And that <u>gorgeous</u> voice too! Come off it girls – Cut out the sour grapes!' and with one final approving glance at her reflection in the mirror, she was off.

Although Mollie had started first, she'd had to make one or two detours around the area of the billets giving the officers quarters and company office a wide berth to avoid the risk of being seen leaving in forbidden civilian dress. We had already reached the 'White Hart' and were sitting at various strategic points around the lounge as she made her entrance.

She swept through the revolving doors and stood poised, short musquash jacket draped casually around her shoulders as she looked about her with a faintly eager and speculative eye.

The tall lean figure of Captain Casey unfolded itself from one of the armchairs and he strode across to meet her, hand outstretched.

We had told Mollie quite a bit about Captain Casey that morning. We had told her about his large country house in Surrey and of his leisurely pre-war life as a country squire, shooting and riding to hounds, etc. What we had omitted to mention was the fact that his fame as a 'wolf' was renowned amongst the ATS of Southern Command, that he was fast approaching sixty, was as bald as an egg and the unfortunate possessor of a set of the whitest of white, ill-fitting porcelain dentures which 'clicked' very distinctly at intervals as he talked. We had also forgotten to mention that he was known throughout command either as 'Old baldy' or 'Castanets Casey,' in honour of his teeth.

As we watched, they crossed to the bar for a pre-dinner drink and Mollie managed to tear her fascinated gaze away from the flashing porcelain for just long enough to cast us a venomous look as we sat innocently sipping our drinks.

We were waiting in a body for her at the billets when she sneaked in at the back door to change into uniform before signing in.

She used one or two choice London expressions as she told us precisely what she thought of us and our mean, lowdown tricks. At last, running out of steam, she finished indignantly, 'I can imagine what any of you would have felt if you had been confronted by that dream of delight!'

There was a yell of laughter at this and it was some time before we could compose ourselves sufficiently to explain our hilarity.

Firstly, we apologised for not telling her all the fascinating details about Captain Casey but that we just couldn't resist the temptation.

'We felt we were entitled to see the fun in a way,' someone concluded. 'No one can ever resist that gorgeous voice of his and, when we were new to "Command," most of us made a blind date to meet 'old baldy' in the lounge at the White Hart!'

I think she felt a little better about the whole episode after we had welcomed her to the 'Casey Club', but we noticed that it was a long time before she could face answering his extension when he called, particularly on a nice, lazy Sunday shift.[62]

Sometimes female desire went unrequited. Dorothy Calvert related that on her anti-aircraft gun site one other rank was so smitten with a young male officer that she followed him around like a love-sick puppy and 'when he came near her on duty, she would pass out'. He, however, wanted nothing to do with her and 'no matter what anyone said to her, she just did not grasp the fact'. Eventually, she had to be posted away 'before someone did something desperate'.[63]

The romantic entanglements of service life did raise issues for the military authorities. The question of female other ranks and male officers having relationships with one another was one such matter. In the armed forces it was not regarded as conducive to good military discipline for commissioned and non-commissioned ranks to cavort together off-duty, so inter-rank affairs tended to be frowned upon.[64] This did not, however, as we have seen, prevent couples from pursuing such romances. Janet Sykes of the ATS would, for example, cycle miles out into the countryside to meet her troop commander boyfriend to avoid being seen together publicly: 'it was a strange courtship'.[65] Joyce Greaves's officer-pilot lover would dress himself up as a sergeant in order to accompany her to WAAF dances: 'you did all kind of crazy things like that and got away with it'.[66] Frances Annett and her companions in the WRNS were regularly smuggled into a nearby dockyard by their naval officer beaus on the floors of taxis: 'I had many a dinner and evening on board a destroyer this way.'[67] Indeed, it seems that Wrens, of whatever rank, often adorned parties in the officers' wardrooms whilst ships were in port. Anne de Courcy stated that 'a good-looking Wren was always welcome, whether lower deck or officer'.[68]

These inter-rank relationships become the subject of discussion in the Air Ministry. Complaints were made from within the RAF that some of its commanders were more liberal than others with regard to their attitudes towards off-duty relationships between RAF officers and WAAF other ranks and that the divergence of practice was leading to discontent. This included 'suspected favouritism by RAF officers, and consequent jealousy among airwomen'; 'resentment among airmen that airwomen of corresponding rank should be treated differently to themselves'; 'familiarity of airwomen with RAF officers undermining the authority of the WAAF officers and NCO's'; 'cases of airwomen who do not wish to go out with RAF officers but are doubtful of the consequences of refusal'; and 'difficulties which arise when an RAF officer and airman both entertain similar sentiments towards the same airwoman'.[69]

When Air Ministry officials looked into this matter in 1943, the War Office view was said to be 'to let sleeping dogs lie', while the Admiralty – by virtue of the fact that the WRNS was not subject to the Naval Discipline Act and allowed its Wrens greater discretion to wear civilian clothes off duty, which tended to camouflage the problem – was thought not to 'keep a dog at all'. Nevertheless, since male and female personnel were so closely integrated on RAF stations, it was resolved that the Air Ministry position ought to be clarified.[70] This included the circulation of a letter to RAF commanders which laid down that, while the 'question of social intercourse' between RAF and WAAF personnel should be largely determined by 'the edicts of common sense and good taste', male officers on a station should exhibit 'the same attitude and relationship towards airwomen as has always existed between officers and airmen' and that

> association off the station between Royal Air Force officers and airwomen who belong to the same station should in normal circumstances be avoided, particularly in the immediate vicinity of the station and, where considered necessary in the interests of the Service, should be prohibited.[71]

Despite these impediments, RAF romances continued to bloom across the ranks. As Eric Taylor observed, 'most sweethearts found ways round the regulations, and "sleeping dogs" were allowed to rest undisturbed'.[72]

Another concern was the sexual behaviour of women in the forces with their service boyfriends (of whatever rank). Some female personnel undoubtedly exploited the abundance of available men to satisfy their desires. WAAF officer Edith Kup, for example, recorded disapprovingly that at her RAF station 'the sigs [signals] girl was vastly oversexed and a menace to the boys, who used to come to us for protection from her. We called her "Any Old Iron" amongst ourselves and found her blatant behaviour very undignified to say the least.'[73] In similar terms, Dorothy Calvert wrote disparagingly of an ATS 'gunner' who 'had the morals of an alley cat, she literally took on anyone. She was the sort that gave our service a bad name'.[74] But many seem to have practiced a good deal of self-restraint. 'The Great Man Chase', for instance, while highlighting the romantic rapaciousness of plotter airwomen, also indicated that there were limits to the physical intimacy they permitted within their relationships. This was corroborated by others. 'I had lots of boyfriends', reminisced ATS officer Judy Impie, 'and I knew that if one of them wanted to go farther than the usual kiss and cuddle, particularly below the belt, instinct said no.'[75] 'There were those who did, and those who didn't', recorded Joyce Sears of the WRNS. ' ... Most of the girls I knew were in the second category. There was a tendency to close ranks against the others, when identified.'[76] WAAF officer Felicity Ashbee confirmed that 'the fear of pregnancy kept a lot of girls on the "straight and narrow"' and that 'a great many of them too had been brought up to believe you should wait for "Mr Right"'.[77] Calvert recalled that 'narrow minded people thought that gun sites were glorified "Knocking shops," but they could not have been more wrong': 'I for one had "kept my hand on my halfpenny," as the old saying goes, for twenty years, so I was hardly going to start flashing it around, as soon as I left home and put on a uniform.'[78]

The service authorities, however, did their best to keep their women on the 'straight and narrow'. The members of Lois Goossens's ATS unit were escorted to one local dance by a Corporal Trodd who 'would have made an ideal prison wardress'. At the end of the evening, she formed the auxiliaries up on the dance floor and marched them back to their barracks like errant school girls: 'We were furious and dreadfully embarrassed in front of all the men we had been dancing with.'[79] Outside Nancy Walton's WAAF billet, a line was painted around the building which airmen were not permitted to step over when accompanying Waafs back to their quarters after a night out: 'We would both have been on a charge if we had crossed the line, as the WAAF NCOs were very alert to the possibility.'[80] At Vera Cole's army camp, her ATS officer would search the buildings by torchlight after dances to ensure that 'none of us were doing anything likely to result in our being dismissed from the Services under Para [11]'.[81] In the WRNS, highly-sexed Wrens could find themselves under threat of expulsion from the force. Although Vera Laughton Mathews admitted that 'the day has gone by when chastity was regarded as the only important virtue in a woman', she nevertheless believed that 'the girl had to go out who frankly thought nothing of promiscuity, and who when caught out avowed that she had done no more than anyone else would have done'. Her view was that

> However much one believes in an equal standard of responsi-
> bility in sex matters between men and women, I cannot see how
> it is possible to enforce equality of treatment in a Service, espe-
> cially in war-time, when the results [possible pregnancy] are so
> different.[82]

These temptations of the flesh also came to feature on the Air Ministry
agenda. In 1943, as a result of anxiety about the incidence of VD and
illegitimate pregnancies among airwomen, particularly the eighteen to
twenty-year-olds, the WAAF hierarchy reflected on the moral probity of
their charges. It was contended that these lapses were by no means
confined to women in the forces and were 'a national problem' brought
on by the circumstances of war. Nevertheless, it was surmised that the
'emotional strain' of working on operational airfields, the consumption
of alcohol which led to 'a certain amount of horse play' and upset the
women's 'judgement', and a lack of guidance from female officers and
NCOs for 'these young and high spirited girls who have left home at an
earlier age than is normal', were contributory factors in cases of immorality in the service.[83] It was further recognised that different codes of
propriety had to be applied to airwomen and airmen. In this regard,
there was an acknowledgment that even though 'the standard of sexual
behaviour has altered greatly in the last generation, the fact remains that
loose behaviour in a woman is regarded more seriously than in a man'. It
was thus concluded that 'while there should not normally be discrimination between men and women in the Service, in this particular question it is essential that the women in the Service should be judged by
a different standard from the men'.[84]

Steps were taken to stiffen the moral resolve of young airwomen. These included the provision of a lecture on 'moral behaviour'
to WAAF officer cadets and NCOs at their training schools and the
delivery of a similar talk to other ranks by 'specially chosen' female
officers.[85] Yet, as the WAAF authorities discovered, it was not always
easy to uphold high moral standards when the RAF itself was reluctant
to delve too closely into the private affairs of its airmen and airwomen.
As Constance Woodhead pointedly observed:

> Although it was recognized early in the war that the WAAF was
> an integral part of the RAF, the male service was curiously
> hesitant to accept any responsibility for the moral relationship
> between the two services. It is true that, here and there, station

commanders accepted so much responsibility that they defeated their own ends, since they tried to set barbed wire between the men and women and prevent them meeting at all. In the main, the onus for the maintenance of a high moral standard seemed to be borne by the WAAF officer, nor did she always receive as much support in her efforts, from the RAF, as might have been expected. A sincere, conscientious officer, trying to look after her airwomen, was sometimes even openly sneered at as an interfering Mrs Grundy by RAF officers who should have known better.[86]

A similar point was made by Vera Laughton Mathews in relation to the frivolous attitude of some naval officers towards the WRNS:

In overwhelming numbers and often in very difficult conditions ... [the Wrens] lived up to the high name and reputation which they had themselves built for the Service.

It is not surprising that some fell by the wayside and the path was not made easier by those senior naval officers, happily only few, who insisted on regarding the Wrens as borne for amusement purposes.[87]

Affairs with commanding officers created particular complications. Felicity Ashbee participated in a court of inquiry when it came to light that the male CO of a remote RAF radar station in North Wales had been 'fancying around' with his WAAF personnel. She admitted, however, to being mildly amused when taking evidence from the airwomen concerned since they 'had to describe what their Station Commander had been getting up to, while at the same time avoiding giving the impression that they were "ladies of easy virtue"'.[88] She was less amused to discover that her own station commander at RAF Stenigot had casually dismissed a case of absence without leave which she had remanded to him – a WAAF corporal who had been missing from camp one night and refused to provide any explanation – since he was involved in an extra-marital relationship with the accused. After failing to take on board heavy hints from another of her female NCOs not to remand the case, she cursed her naivety since 'only two days ago, he was assuring me he'd never been unfaithful to his wife'. All she could do was hope that 'the CO will restrain himself a bit more in future'.[89]

A further issue that came to light was a tendency on the part of the parents of servicewomen to interfere in the latter's military love life. On occasion, this intervention could come from a parent within the forces. Ursie Barclay's mother was also her ATS company commander and she kept a close watch on her daughter's affections when Barclay worked as a waitress in an army sergeants' mess:

> One day she found me sitting down having tea with the sergeants instead of waiting on them so she took me away quick – she must have thought: 'She's obviously going to fall in love with a sergeant', and she wasn't having *that*. So I was made clerk to one of the officers.[90]

More often, however, it came in the form of external approaches from concerned parents. Despite a War Office ruling that if 'the happenings of private life did not bring discredit on the Service, they were of no concern to the military authorities', Leslie Whateley recalled that, as Deputy Director of the ATS, she regularly received requests from mothers and fathers for interviews with her about their daughters' unsuitable boyfriends:

> Once again I came up against an instance of how a women's service differs from a male organization. It would be exceptional for parents to approach the War Office about a son's romance, but I can remember many instances of distraught parents visiting me and begging me to get some male member of the forces (not necessarily of the Army) moved from the same station as their daughter. On some occasions, when I was really convinced that the case warranted it, I did re-post a daughter to another unit. Only once in all these cases did I succeed in getting the male authorities to take action from their side.[91]

Inevitably, a number of service romances resulted in marriage. Arrangements were made, whenever possible, for married servicewomen to take periods of leave at the same time as their military spouses,[92] but the question also arose as to whether husbands and wives should serve alongside each other in the forces. With regard to the ATS, it was decreed that auxiliaries should not serve with their spouses in the same unit, largely due to 'difficulties in the exercise of command'.[93] In the WAAF, however, it was decided that airwomen should be permitted to serve at the same base as their husbands, except in cases where one was an officer and the other in the ranks.[94] This was also the position in the WRNS, with the proviso that there should not be too big a disparity in rank between married naval and Wren officers.[95] Some mischievous couples were able to exploit these rather cumbersome protocols for their own amusement. Airwoman Jean Edge, a waitress at RAF Drem, was married to a senior officer at nearby RAF Grangemouth and, without divulging that they were man and wife, would wait on her husband Paul in the officers' mess at Drem when he visited on official business:

> I was lucky in having a husband with a great sense of humour, who did not mind in the least that I was 'other ranks' . . .
>
> He was now a wing commander and frequently flew to Drem and dined with the station commander, Sir Archibald Hope, known as 'Sir Bald' because he was. It was fun serving them with their meals. On one occasion I could not resist putting a glass of Guinness in front of Paul. This puzzled Sir Bald, and Paul had to think quickly to explain its appearance without revealing that I was his wife and knew what he liked to drink.[96]

Meanwhile, as a result of clothes rationing and a meagre allowance of clothing coupons, many women in the forces were unable to get married in traditional white dresses and often there was no alternative but to walk down the aisle in their uniforms. This was said to be a constant source of disappointment to them. In order to alleviate this, in 1944 the ATS introduced a wedding dress service. Under this scheme, dresses were donated to the War Office by various philanthropic organisations and public-spirited individuals – Barbara Cartland contributed over seventy which she purchased through placing advertisements in such society magazines as *The Lady* – and auxiliaries could arrange to borrow a garment for their wedding day from a central pool. This enterprise was subsequently extended to the other women's services and some fifty dresses came to be in constant circulation.[97]

With service romances came heartbreak when a boyfriend or husband was killed on active service. WRNS officer, Betty Hodges, was given the unenviable task of informing a fellow female officer that her husband had perished with his submarine crew: 'It was such a dreadful shock that at first she thought I was playing some terrible trick on her. "But Bobby can't be dead, he can't he can't." It was terrible to see, and there was absolutely nothing I could do about it.'[98] When one of Eileen

Figure 8.3 Staff Sergeant-Major Twist of the ATS embraces her husband, Lance Bombardier Twist, 1941 (Lt. Bainbridge/IWM via Getty Images)

McMurdo's ATS corporals, who was pregnant and shortly to be discharged, was told that her paratrooper husband, 'Dear, quiet Bob', had been killed in Normandy, such was his wife's distress that she was taken by ambulance to the sick bay and suffered a miscarriage: 'What adequate words are there to comfort a woman who had not only lost her husband but also the baby to whom they had both been looking forward to with such joy?'[99] At Pip Beck's RAF Bomber Command base, the Waafs who were romantically attached to aircrew lived under the constant shadow of tragedy:

There was another marriage – a girl in my billet. This was Jean, who lived downstairs. Eighteen years old, 5 ft. nothing, with a cloud of dark hair and dark eyes, a pale face and a sweet, husky little voice. Her favourite song-of-the-moment was 'Not a Cloud in the Sky', and we loved to hear her sing. Sitting by the fire in her room, one or other of us would beg her to sing it, and if she shyly demurred we would cry, 'Oh, go on!' She usually gave in, thinking no doubt of her Peter, as she crooned the romantic words – [Sergeant] Peter Rix, a Rhodesian in P/O [Pilot Officer] Hackney's crew.

After she returned from the short honeymoon leave they'd had, two of us from the billet sat talking to her, and one, unforgivably, asked, 'What was it like, Jean – you know!' Just as bad, I listened, all ears. 'Oh … ' said Jean, embarrassed, 'Well – I – I don't know … I didn't like it very much … ' We didn't press for further details. Poor Jean – and poor Peter. In less than two months she had lost him. Flying with F/Sgt. [Flight Sergeant] Tetley, he didn't come back from a trip to Dusseldorf. She was paler still, with dark rings around her eyes, and stunned. We never saw her cry. Neither did we hear her sing again.[100]

Such tragedies could lead to superstition. In the RAF, Waafs who had been romantically linked to a succession of dead flyers became known as 'chop girls' and tended to be shunned by other airmen as bringing bad luck.[101] A wartime RAF medical officer, Dr David Stafford-Clark, observed the harmful effects this could have on the airwomen concerned:

A young WAAF officer who had lost two men friends in succession, both on operations, developed an acute depression with considerable feelings of guilt in response to the rapidly accepted verdict among the rest of the squadron that she was a jinx and carried 'the kiss of death'. This was not a grim joke; it was an even grimmer belief, sincerely held; one Captain of Aircraft, a Flight Lieutenant with DFC and bar, going so far as to forbid any member of his crew to take her out, on pain of expulsion from the crew. There was no point in adding to the risks, he said.[102]

Eileen Smith recalled the silent anguish of one such 'jinxed' airwoman:

> On more than one occasion she became engaged to a crew member and the engagement ended sadly when her fiancé was killed on a raid. On her bedside she had a few large studio photos of these men and I would see the dim red glow of a cigarette as she smoked into the early hours of the morning trying to come to grips with the tragedies of war.[103]

Yet an airfield romance might help to heal a damaged airman. Colin 'Hoppy' Hodgkinson, a RAF Spitfire pilot based at RAF Coltishall who had lost his legs in a flying accident shortly before the war but (like Douglas Bader) had overcome his handicap to become an accomplished wartime flyer, had an intense, passing relationship with 'Claire', a 'goddess ... thinly disguised as a WAAF officer'. For Hodgkinson, who had flown almost a hundred operational sorties and was beginning to feel the psychological strain, 'it was flattering for my ailing pride to be the recognized cavalier of this pretty, witty, much sought-after woman'. And, as he candidly admitted, 'her acceptance of me as a companion enormously helped to restore the masculine confidence my disability had undermined'.[104]

'Anybody's Meat'

Sexual harassment in the workplace spilled over into off-duty hours. ATS officer Margaret Egerton recounted that the army officers in one of her wartime messes, whom she termed 'absolute shits', would 'say filthy things to embarrass me ... [and] resented me largely because I was a female ... and because I wouldn't respond to a pass'.[105] At one military base, some of the airwomen took to concealing hatpins in their uniform lapels in order to fend off sexual assaults by servicemen in the darkness of the camp cinema. 'I had occasion to use mine', recollected a forearmed Waaf. 'The lights came on when the airman screamed and clutched his bottom. Everyone stared at me. After that I was known as "the pin up girl".'[106] If the opportunity presented itself, prurient servicemen could adopt more voyeuristic methods of harassing their female comrades. Barbara Littlejohn of the ATS recorded that a signalmen at her intercept station at Kedleston Hall in Derbyshire, whose job it was to stoke the boiler that served the auxiliaries' bathroom, was discovered to have rigged up a set of mirrors in the boiler room that allowed him to spy on the women bathers: 'He must have had an eyeful of every girl in the camp before he was found out.'[107] On other occasions, they would leer at them suggestively on the streets. One male Royal Army Medical Corps private admitted that

> Whenever a girl, or a group of girls in uniform pass a group of soldiers, the same actions can be observed, and the same words can be overheard. All look at the approaching girls' faces, smile, look at the legs as they pass, end up by watching their behinds waggle under the tight khaki skirts and generally pass the following jovial comments: 'Not bad.. eh!' 'Nice bit of stuff mate.' 'Not arf a bitch..' 'Look at her fucking arse!' 'Christ she's a bit of all right ain't she?' 'Blood lousy' ... The comments vary with the prettiness of the girls. Often there are shouts, and laughter.[108]

American servicemen could also pose a sexual threat to members of the women's services. Social events at their military bases were invariably lavish occasions, but sometimes there was a price to be paid. Bettine Rose remembered one ATS dance she attended at a US aerodrome:

> Most of the time was spent dodging the more undesirable types of Yanks who were offering cartons of 'Camels' or silk stockings in exchange for a visit to their quarters. There seemed to be no discipline from their officers at all.[109]

Indeed, in May 1944, the MP for Grantham, Denis Kendall, complained in the House of Commons that in his constituency women could not walk unescorted through the town because of the inability of the US military authorities to deal with the 'improper behaviour of the American forces and the complete failure to prevent unconcealed immorality and to give proper protection to women'.[110]

The military authorities did take some preventative action to protect servicewomen. The 'Wrennery' of Joan Dunhill and her fellow landing craft maintenance Wrens was surrounded by barbed wire and patrolled by a naval guard to secure it from an adjacent camp of sailors and marines.[111] WAAF clerk, Nancy Walton, and her female comrades were given a course in self-defence at their camp in order to fend off potential attackers.[112] On the rare occasions that men and women were forced to sleep in close proximity, special steps might be taken to prevent any sexual assault. WAAF stenographer Olive Noble reminisced that after having missed a train connection to the RAF Burns Unit at Rauceby in Lincolnshire, and been left stranded at Grantham station, she was taken in by a nearby army unit and given a bed for the night in the all-male sergeants' mess. She protested this was not the 'done thing' but an officer re-assured her that a sentry would be posted beside her bunk all night to ensure there was 'no funny business': 'The Guard was still standing there next morning when I awoke wondering where on earth I was!'[113]

Yet it seems that in many cases servicewomen were simply left to handle unwanted sexual advances as best they could. Some female personnel became adept at fending off predatory servicemen. ATS driver, Win Dowd, utilised a number of psychological ploys when pestered by US servicemen she encountered whilst walking home to her billet in East Anglia:

> My first plot was the schoolmarm approach. They usually opened with 'Carry your bag, mam?' 'Why, thank you, young man,' I would reply, and hand over the case. That was one hand accounted for. 'And how are you liking England? We do so appreciate your help over here.' This often got rid of them at the first turning. 'Have to turn off here, mam. Nice to meet you, mam.' When one fellow came on a bit strong I tearfully told him that I had promised my sailor boyfriend that I would wait for him. The GI tried persuasion, telling me that with a war on we all had to take our fun where and when it came. I still kept on about the boy away at sea and our plans for when he came home. Eventually he went very quiet, and when we reached the door of my billet I found that he was in tears. He shook my hand in both of his, lifted it to his lips and kissed it, spluttering: 'I have a girl at home and I would like to believe that she is acting just like you.' He didn't know just how much I *was* acting.[114]

Sometimes more forceful action was required. ATS radar operator Dorothy Calvert experienced several molestations whilst in the service and fought back with considerable venom:

> When we started from London the carriage was full, and we were all having a very friendly chin wag, but as always had to happen on long journeys, the carriages gradually emptied as

each person reached his destination. This happened on this journey, which left one soldier, and me. As we had all been so pally, I thought the rest of the journey would be uneventful; we would just sit in a matey silence. I picked up my book and began to read. Then suddenly this bloke, who was sitting opposite leapt at me, pushing his hands up my skirt. I was absolutely taken aback, but only for a moment. The lecherous little bugger, he had been waiting to get me alone from the moment we got on the train, getting more and more worked up.

Once again my fighting blood was up, for as he bent over me I hit him in the throat as hard as I could with the side of my hand, and with my knees I knocked him right in the middle stump, which was ready for a knock down. Well that stopped his wind, and his gallop, as I shoved him on to his seat, groaning and gasping. Then I got to my full five feet and stood over him, and told him that if he so much as moved or blinked, that I would bloody well kill him, and believe me I would have had a jolly good try, but the brave lad sat without moving for the rest of the journey.

These assaults left her with a strong sense of sexual treason:

The sad thing was, out of all the times that I was molested, it was always one of our own servicemen. I often wondered who my enemies were, and it filled me with anger and disgust that our own men held us so low, just because we were in uniform. Did they think that we were anybody's meat, just for their enjoyment? One thing was very certain, to get through one's service stint 'Virgo Intacta' or in the same way as when you first joined up was almost impossible, and quite a challenge, but I suppose that it was just another risk we had to run in war-time.[115]

'A Special Problem'

For lesbian women, wartime military service offered opportunities to seek out others in the forces who shared their attraction to members of the same sex. Vick Robson was posted to train as a WAAF electrician at RAF Usworth and discovered a group of fellow lesbians at the base: 'I got in with some girls stationed there, and they said "Are you like us?" So it started off again and I thought "Oh, I'm back on Cloud Nine again".[116] For heterosexual women, however, the exposure to same-sex relationships in the services could come as something of a shock. Margaret Herterich was left bewildered by an incident she witnessed during her ATS anti-aircraft training at Oswestry camp:

> The only quarrel I heard the whole time that I was in the forces happened here and was very strange and upsetting at the time. It happened in the ablutions when all of a sudden one girl started to scream and attack another girl. We all turned round and heard the attacker screaming out, 'Don't touch her, she's mine, she's mine. I love her.' Two military police came in and took her away. I was completely mystified until someone explained that she was 'a boy-girl', and going to be discharged. I still wasn't much wiser![117]

There were also cases of unwanted sexual advances from female colleagues. Eileen McMurdo described such an occurrence early in her ATS career whilst living in a billet at Cosham near Fort Southwick:

> As I turned over in my sleep I became drowsily aware that someone was in bed beside me. It didn't take many moments for me to become very wide awake indeed to the realisation that Barney was stretched out by my side, stark naked. I lay for a moment stiff with shock as what I had at first thought to be a bad dream suddenly became reality. As my senses came fully together I let out a yell as I leapt out of bed and headed for the door. Before I could reach it, the door opened and standing on the threshold was Amy, one of the shift corporals, who had the room next to ours ...
>
> I stood shaking like a leaf; Amy put her arm around my shoulders, calming me until gradually the shaking subsided. Barney was sitting bolt upright in my bed with the blankets pulled up under her chin as if to protect herself from my look of shocked disbelief.
>
> Amy glared across the room at her.
>
> 'You! Get up! Get yourself into my room and wait there. I'll deal with you later!' she snapped.

When Barney left the room I told Amy what had happened. Still feeling sick with shock I whispered.

'Her hands were like filthy black beetles crawling all over me. I couldn't believe it. I just couldn't believe it. Not of Barney'.

Amy took me by the shoulders and gently shaking me she said: 'Poor little 'un! They just don't come any greener than you, do they?! I've had my suspicions for some time that she's ... [a lesbian] but I couldn't say anything as I wasn't one hundred per cent sure. Anyway, I'll make damned certain that she doesn't bother you again, you can be sure of that!'

She was true to her word. When I returned from duty at the Fort a couple of days later Barney's effects had been removed from our room and shortly afterwards Barney left our Company at Cosham: I presumed that she had been posted elsewhere but I never could bring myself to enquire too closely.[118]

ATS officer Margaret Egerton described a similar episode in the Orkneys, in terms redolent of the stereotype of the manly lesbian:

Off the boat got this ... *man*, with nicotine round her mouth, kitbag over her shoulder and an Eton crop. You had to censor letters in Orkney and it was obvious from hers that she was a ... [lesbian]. As a corporal, she messed with the three male sergeants and would drink them under the table every night.

Our lights went out at 11.00 pm and then you had a Tilley lamp if needed. It was so cold I had eleven army blankets on my bed. That night, through my dreams, I heard the distant sound of revelry and it seemed to be getting nearer.

It stopped outside my door. In my half-asleep state I heard the door being opened. It was this corporal, drunk as a coot. It was pitch dark and I heard heavy breathing getting nearer, until she bent over me. She stank of whisky.

'It's your turrrn tonight, ma'am,' she growled. 'It's your turrrn tonight ... '

Then I came to. I said: 'Get the hell out of here, Staff!,' and she went, leaving me thinking: What do I do in the morning? But it was never referred to again. When I rang up our Commanding Officer next day to say that I'd had a lesbian assault she sounded puzzled and said: 'What's that?'[119]

For other women, however, participation in the forces gave them the opportunity to re-evaluate their sexual orientation. Sarah Allan's military service was a 'God-send' as she was liberated from her restrictive home life and a 'stifling network of boyfriends in whom she had very little interest'. She discovered a small band of lesbian women in her ATS unit and, empowered by this, experienced 'her first physical relationship with a woman'. This, it was said, 'helped her to recognize and label her sexuality'.[120]

Although lesbianism, unlike male homosexuality, was not an offence under English law, the military authorities were concerned about its impact on discipline in the women's services and the malicious gossip and scandal that might arise.[121] In 1941, the chief woman medical adviser to the ATS, Dr Letitia Fairfield, drew up a memorandum on same-sex relationships, entitled 'A Special Problem', which, although never generally issued to ATS officers, was available to those who needed guidance on this matter. In the memorandum, Fairfield drew a distinction between an 'emotional crush' and a 'sexual attraction akin to falling in love', and contended that 'consciously homosexual friendships between women are usually kept entirely or almost entirely on a mental plane' while 'perverted physical practices (i.e. unnatural variations of the physical intimacies which would be natural between persons of opposite sexes) are fortunately rare': 'Where this occurs it is either among women of a depraved type or among the self-conscious intelligentsia, who are probably more actuated by craving for excitement than by real desire.' Her advice to female officers in cases of suspected lesbianism was 'to act only on definitive evidence' as 'allegations of homosexuality are highly libellous'; to explore the 'innocent explanation for incidents before accepting a sinister one', such as women sleeping together in beds 'for warmth' or because they had slept with their sisters 'all their lives and think it is a natural thing to do'; to bear in mind that lesbian behaviour was 'not necessarily associated with masculine physique or with the adoption of male clothing or pursuits'; and that any action taken 'should vary with circumstances'. Fairfield argued that 'homosexuality is essentially the persistence of an immature mental and emotional phase. This gives hope that the foolish adolescent, or even the middle-aged woman who had slipped into childish sentimentality, will grow out of an unhealthy craze.' But as practical measures she recommended that couples sharing an excessive attachment should be separated by reposting one of them if they cannot be diverted by other interests ... For the fortunately rare cases of perverted practice or attempted corruption of other women by talk or example, discharge from the service would be the only course.[122]

In 1941, Jane Trefusis Forbes also offered some guidelines for dealing with members of the WAAF who displayed 'lesbian tendencies'. Describing them as 'misfits', she recommended that a woman suspected of lesbianism should be told that her 'behaviour is that of a schoolgirl and that these sentimental attachments are not what we expect from airwomen who must necessarily always set a good example to others.' 'Unless she does pull herself together after a talk or two', she continued, 'it is obvious that we would have to dispense with her services.'[123]

The association between lesbianism and the 'foolish adolescent' was, as Emma Vickers has indicated, consistent with prevailing notions of the 'schoolgirl crush' and 'boarding school desire' that featured in the sexological typologies of the period.[124] Moreover, as she points out, 'queerness had yet to make the full transition from an act to an identity'.[125] Nonetheless, the women's forces seem to have adopted a pragmatic response to the presence of lesbian women given the overriding need to retain trained personnel.[126] Dr Albertine Winner, who served as a woman doctor with the Royal Army Medical Corps, reported that in the ATS most cases of lesbianism were 'dealt with by judicious posting' and 'only some half-dozen women had to be discharged on these grounds out of nearly a quarter of a million who passed through our hands'. She described this as 'a very remarkable record'.[127] It was also possible for lesbian women quietly to pre-empt the military authorities. WAAF conscript, Pat James, missed her civilian female lover in London and 'happened to hear that people were getting out of the WAAFs by being lesbians. So I thought that I would.' She thus arranged an appointment with a service psychiatrist: 'He just asked about how I felt when I saw a woman, about my reaction. I told him, and I was out very quickly.'[128]

9 OVERSEAS SERVICE

Deployment

During the course of the war, members of the three women's services were deployed with their male 'parent' forces all around the world. In the spring of 1940, a party from the ATS arrived in France to serve with the British Expeditionary Force (BEF) and as the conflict progressed servicewomen were posted to such places as the United States, Canada, the West Indies, Egypt, Palestine, Algeria, Kenya, South Africa, Italy, Gibraltar, Malta, Australia, India, Ceylon and north-west Europe.[1] By the end of the conflict, approximately 31,000 female personnel were based overseas. These included some 18,000 from the ATS, 7,000 from the WAAF and 6,000 from the WRNS.[2]

The decision to employ the women's forces abroad was not taken lightly by the military authorities. For example, while the Air Ministry gave its consent to a contingent of WAAF code and cypher officers being sent to the Middle East in the summer of 1941,[3] it was unwilling to send other airwomen to this theatre. The Air Member for Personnel, Air Marshal Philip Babington, judged that it would be problematic to provide suitable accommodation for a large number of Waafs in the region and that it was not safe for women to venture out at night in some areas. In addition, it would be difficult to bring them home if they fell pregnant and the presence of female personnel would complicate matters if the armed forces had to be evacuated in a military emergency.[4] It was not until early in 1944 that the RAF authorities consented to a more general posting of airwomen to the Middle East. This was largely due to the pressing demands on RAF manpower, as well as the improved military position in the theatre, but it was also hoped that it would enhance the prestige of, and pride in, the WAAF.[5] It was apparent, moreover, that the arrival of Waafs at foreign bases invariably boosted the spirits of their male colleagues stationed there. Constance Woodhead wrote that 'due attention was given to the repeated plea that the presence of officers and airwomen would raise the morale of the RAF in certain places'.[6]

Meanwhile, various safeguards were built into the deployment of servicewomen overseas. There were provisos regarding age. In the ATS, the minimum age for volunteers to serve abroad was set at twenty and in the WAAF twenty-one. In the WRNS, women over twenty-one were eligible to volunteer, with parental consent needed for those under that age.[7] There were limitations on the duration of tours of duty: in the ATS, the period was fixed at three years, whilst in the WRNS it was between two and two-and-a-half years and in the WAAF it was two years.[8] And there were restrictions on certain types of work. In the Middle East, for instance, airwomen were not permitted to serve as drivers 'owing to the risk of a breakdown in native areas, where a woman might be at a disadvantage'.[9]

There were also more general stipulations drawn up regarding the utilisation of female personnel in overseas theatres of war. During the so-called 'great flap' in the summer of 1942, when Rommel's Panzerarmee Afrika advanced deep into Egypt, the Mediterranean fleet, along with its WRNS units, was temporarily evacuated from Alexandria and Wrens based at the port were hurriedly packed into railway cattle trucks and transported overnight to Ismailia.[10] In the wake of these events, the Admiralty laid down some ground rules for the deployment of the WRNS abroad. These specified that Wrens should not normally be deployed in 'forward areas' where they could fall into the hands of the enemy, but that 'the efficiency of the Service must be the first consideration' and in the event of an emergency those engaged in 'important operational duties', such as cyphering, would be expected to remain at their posts with their male colleagues.[11]

The War Office developed its own guidelines. In the summer of 1943, with preparations for the invasion of France underway, discussions began among the army authorities on the employment of the ATS on the continent of Europe. General Sir Bernard Paget, the new

Figure 9.1 WRNS officers in Alexandria, Egypt, 1942 (© Imperial War Museum)

Commander-in-Chief of 21st Army Group – the Anglo-Canadian formation earmarked for the landings in France which included auxiliaries
among its headquarters' staff – suggested that a clear policy needed to be
drawn up on this issue and proposed that members of the ATS should be
utilised at rear headquarters, base installations and along the lines of
communication. He contended that they had 'by their discipline, efficiency and esprit-de-corps' earned the right to serve with the army in this
theatre; that they would 'free more men for the forward areas'; and that
while they would not be deliberately exposed to the dangers of enemy
action, there was 'no reason why they should not take the same risks
overseas as they do under war conditions at home'. It was also reported
from North Africa that the presence of Queen Alexandra's Imperial

Military Nursing Service (QAIMNS) near the front line had had 'a most beneficial effect on the morale of the troops'.[12] The ATS hierarchy endorsed this deployment on the continent. Senior female officers cautioned that auxiliaries should not proceed abroad too early in a campaign, in case they proved to be 'a liability rather than an asset' and that in contrast to the presence of the QAIMNS in forward areas, which conveyed 'a sense of security' to troops, the employment of the ATS close to the front 'might give rise to a sense of obligation and responsibility on the part of commanders and soldiers'. Nevertheless, the view was held that members of their force should serve in any theatre of war required by the army other than those involving Japan.[13]

There was, however, some wavering on the part of War Office officials about the deployment of the ATS in Europe.[14] Concerns were raised about the political risks of sending auxiliaries into an active theatre of war, where there was the danger of a military reverse. There were also doubts about whether adequate accommodation and other facilities could be provided for women in devastated areas. In such adverse circumstances, it was cautioned that they 'might well be an encumbrance'.[15] Yet with a decision about the despatch of female personnel to Italy pending, in late 1943 Sir James Grigg agreed to a set of principles for the employment of the ATS overseas. These specified that no auxiliaries were to enter theatres of war where there was the 'slightest prospect' of invasion by the Japanese, but that in other theatres discretion was to be left to British commanders-in-chief. They were to make their judgements on the bases that women should only be employed when 'the military situation is so stabilised as to give a reasonable assurance that our hold on the territory is secure' and when 'our penetration of the territory is sufficiently deep geographically to ensure adequate living conditions and amenities for British women employed in the back areas'.[16]

These War Office criteria were rather more protective of servicewomen than those drawn up by the Admiralty, in that they made no mention of 'the efficiency of the service' as being the first priority in a deployment and drew no distinction between those engaged in 'important operational duties' and others.[17] In view of this, and given the desirability of uniform inter-service practices in this matter, the naval authorities were reluctantly obliged to come into line with those of their army counterparts. The Air Ministry also adopted these general principles.[18] There were, however, members of the ATS who bridled at the restraints put on their employment abroad, since there were occasions when they were prohibited from working in areas in which civilian women from such organisations as the British Red Cross Society and the Council of Voluntary War Work were operating. One post-war report recorded that this anomaly was 'strongly resented by the ATS and justifiably so'.[19]

The despatch of sizeable numbers of servicewomen overseas brought to the fore the question of trooping arrangements for the women's services. As the war went on there had been complaints from parents, and from servicewomen themselves, about the conditions on troopships and in early 1944 representatives from the three women's forces met with the relevant military and civilian authorities to 'thrash out the difficulties'. 'Thrash is the correct word,' recounted Leslie Whateley, 'for I had the feeling the whole time that the Chairman of the Committee (a major-general) wished all my sex at the bottom of the sea, rather than on it in ships.'[20] Despite this animus, it was agreed that a special scale of troopship accommodation should be provided for female personnel. This included the provisos that no more than 250 servicewomen would normally be embarked on any ship; that 20 square feet of sleeping space was to be allocated to each woman on troop decks during journeys west of Suez, with cabins provided for them east of Suez whenever possible; that a minimum of eight lavatories per hundred women were to be provided adjacent to their quarters; and that when necessary a twenty-four-hour guard was to be mounted on the women's accommodation to ensure their privacy.[21]

Some servicewomen were transported to foreign postings in Royal Navy warships. In the summer of 1941, an entire WRNS party of twelve cypher officers and ten wireless telegraphists perished en route to Gibraltar when their small, slow-moving merchant ship, SS *Aguila*, was sunk by a German U-boat 500 miles west of Land's End.[22] This loss came as a great shock to the WRNS. Vera Laughton Mathews regarded it as 'one of the worst blows our Service suffered' and a salutary lesson for those who might have imagined that servicewomen would somehow remain inviolate to the tragedies of war:

> I think their death brought home to many for the first time the
> realization that these young women were not joining up to wear
> a smart uniform or to have a good time, that they accepted

willingly a share in the hardship, the responsibility and the perils of Service life.[23]

As a consequence, it was agreed that Wrens would henceforth be permitted to travel in fighting ships whilst proceeding overseas.[24] Yet this was not always popular with the sailors. Mary Pratt, sailing from Kenya to Ceylon on HMS *Chitral* in late 1943, recalled that their presence caused 'widespread dissent':

> Two days out from Mombasa, a German U-Boat was sighted in the distance – normally a fast destroyer would give chase and engage the enemy, but, because of females on board, we turned tail for harbour again, to await a safe passage – our names were mud, though most of us would have relished a good scrap at sea![25]

Where practical, efforts were made to recruit locally for the women's forces. Early in 1942, for example, an ATS training depot was established at Sarafand in Palestine and, after appropriate screening to ensure that the Axis powers or extremist groups did not infiltrate the British forces, local women were enlisted for service in the Middle East (with some also later serving in Italy and Austria). The vast majority of the recruits were Jewish volunteers from Mandatory Palestine – including recent refugees from Europe who had strong personal reasons to help defeat the Nazis – but there were also contingents of Greeks, Czechs and Cypriots, as well as some Arab women.[26] The creation of this Palestinian branch of the ATS was not without its difficulties for the British female commanders on the spot. Not only were a number of the recruits unable to speak English so ATS officers had to work through interpreters,[27] but also some of them were deemed difficult to handle: 'The UK contingent soon learned to be surprised at nothing ... ', commented Tryce Taylor. 'A newly arrived English Sgt. Major was surprised that no one took any notice when a Private hit her smartly on the head with a file tray. Pte N. was just in one of her "moods".'[28] Furthermore, there were political tensions arising from the fact that such bodies as the Jewish Council of Women's Organisations in Palestine seemed intent on trying to ensure that the service became a vehicle for the Zionist ambitions of the Yishuv. Indeed, much to the infuriation of the local ATS chief, recruiting posters appeared embellished with the Star of David, which suggested that the enterprise was to be exclusively Jewish.[29] Nonetheless, the ATS authorities seemed to have welded this disparate group into a credible force.[30] At their peak, some 5,000 ATS personnel were based in the Middle East, of whom 4,000 had been raised locally.[31] After the war Jewish women from Palestine who had served in the ATS helped to establish the women's corps of the Israel Defence Forces but, as Anat Granit-Hacohen has observed, their wartime service with the British forces sat uncomfortably alongside the active resistance of the Yishuv to the British mandatory regime in the Zionist narrative.[32]

Elsewhere the enlistment of local women led to bureaucratic wrangling in Whitehall. In 1942 there were demands for additional ATS personnel to serve in Washington DC, but with growing pressures on the force in the UK it was difficult to spare more auxiliaries for the USA. In response, it was decided to recruit women from the West Indies for service with the Washington-based ATS.[33] This initiative, as Ben Bousquet and Colin Douglas have demonstrated, resulted in an inter-departmental dispute over the racial make-up of the recruits. The position of the War Office, some of whose officials displayed a barely disguised racism towards those not of 'pure European descent', was that only white Caribbean women should be appointed to jobs in Washington.[34] Any other course of action, it was claimed, 'might well cause embarrassment to the American authorities'.[35] The view of the Colonial Office, however, was that to operate such a colour bar would create resentment among black West Indians and, mindful of the political unrest in the Caribbean in the 1930s, threaten imperial stability.[36] In the end, the War Office got its way and 200 white West Indian women served with the ATS in the USA. But the Colonial Office insisted that black West Indian women should be deployed with the ATS in the UK.[37] As a result, despite the best efforts of the War Office to prevent such a step – 'I don't at all like your West Indian ATS ideas', sniped Sir James Grigg to his opposite number at the Colonial Office, Oliver Stanley, when he was pressed on the matter in the spring of 1943[38] – a racially-mixed group of 100 women came to serve in Britain. In the meantime, a further 300 West Indian women were employed with the ATS in the Caribbean itself.[39] These auxiliaries were said to have been eager to aid the 'mother country'. 'We felt that we were British', remembered Ena Collymore-Woodstock. 'I was defiantly British, I felt that way.'[40] But they inevitably encountered racial prejudice. In the Caribbean, ATS officers stationed there were alleged to have blocked the award of a British Empire Medal to Connie Mark, a black Jamaican auxiliary employed to undertake secretarial duties, because she refused to clean their houses for them like a colonial servant.[41] Peter Fryer cites the following examples of racism in the UK:

> A West Indian girl in the ATS was refused a new issue of shoes by her officer, who added: 'At home you don't wear shoes anyway.' An Army Officer to a West Indian ATS: 'If I can't get white women I'll something well do without.'[42]

A related issue was a desire on the part of the military authorities to protect the racial superiority of British servicewomen in overseas stations. In India, for instance, Constance Woodhead recorded that the administration of WAAF personnel was complicated by the requirement that 'the prestige of white women had to be safeguarded'. Airwomen in Bombay were reported to have been unwilling to travel to their work in the same lorries as 'natives of the sweeper class' and alternative transport arrangements had to be made for them. This was, she remarked, 'a natural and correct objection but tiresome for authority'. Woodhead further observed that the interactions between the Waafs and the locally recruited Indian women whom they worked alongside were

Figure 9.2 West Indian ATS recruits in the UK, 1943 (Central Press/Hulton Archive via Getty Images)

'harmonious but quaint. The airwomen regarded the others with a tolerant good-humour that did not admit of equality.'[43]

Compulsion

In the early years of the war, the overseas service of members of the women's forces was conducted on a voluntary basis. The Admiralty, however, found it increasingly difficult to meet the growing demand for Wrens abroad from volunteers alone. In 1943 it thus placed a liability for compulsory service overseas on 'mobile' WRNS officers and ratings over the age of twenty-one, except in cases where this would cause 'undue hardship'. Those already enrolled at the time of this new liability were permitted to claim exemption from the obligation and some 11,500 female personnel did so.[44] The Air Ministry chose not to follow this path. There was some concern as to whether overseas commitments could continue to be fulfilled by volunteer airwomen and, as a result, the age at which they could volunteer to work abroad was lowered to twenty if older Waafs were not forthcoming. Nevertheless, it was calculated that requirements could be met without compulsion.[45]

The War Office was also faced with the prospect of compelling members of the ATS to serve overseas if required. In order to increase the number of auxiliaries eligible for posting abroad, in the spring of 1944 the army authorities lowered the minimum age at which they could volunteer for such service to nineteen.[46] There continued, however, to be a worrying shortfall of volunteers. This was largely put down to parental disapproval. 'There are many girls who would like to volunteer,' recorded General Adam, 'but who have pressure put on them by their parents not to do so.'[47] As a result, and given the political sensitivities involved, in the late autumn Sir James Grigg approached the War Cabinet for permission to institute the compulsory drafting of the ATS overseas. It was estimated that there would soon be a net deficiency of 3,500 auxiliaries for commitments abroad if there continued to be a reliance on volunteering.[48] 'The demands for ATS from overseas commands', argued Grigg, 'now far exceed the number of volunteers and, in this respect, the position is likely to become progressively worse.' It was also pointed out that under the present arrangements the periods of foreign duty for auxiliaries would inevitably get longer: 'it will become increasingly difficult to restrict the overseas tour for ATS to the present maximum of three years if we are unable to provide the necessary replacements from home'.[49]

The War Cabinet was hesitant. Ernest Bevin, for example, was concerned about the wisdom of applying compulsion at a time when munitions workers were beginning to be released from government service and wondered if all possible avenues to increase the number of volunteers had been explored. It was also questioned why the WAAF had apparently managed to secure the necessary volunteers when the ATS had not.[50] Grigg continued to press the War Office's case. It was contended that all reasonable steps had been taken to stimulate volunteering within the ATS, including tours of home commands by senior female officers to elicit suitable candidates, and that the WAAF was not faced with the same difficulties in obtaining sufficient numbers of volunteers as the ATS. The former, it was explained, incorporated a higher proportion of Waafs to airmen than that existing between auxiliaries and soldiers, and whilst the RAF deployed less than half its personnel overseas, the army had to utilise two-thirds of its strength abroad. Furthermore, it was re-iterated that not only was there an urgent need to send auxiliaries overseas to make up for shortfalls in male personnel, especially signallers and clerks, but it was also stressed that their presence would hearten the troops in foreign parts, particularly in occupied Germany where a policy of non-fraternisation would be put in place.[51] 'Another very important reason why it is desirable to have as many British women overseas', Grigg thus stated, 'is the effect this will have in maintaining the morale of the soldier.'[52]

The War Cabinet revisited the issue and, subject to various safeguards, agreed to the War Office's request.[53] In the meantime, the Prime Minister sounded out his daughter, Mary, on the subject. She had asked the auxiliaries in her mixed anti-aircraft battery about whether they wished to proceed overseas. 'The almost universal reply', noted Churchill, 'was "Not half"!'[54] At the end of 1944, it was announced by Grigg in the House of Commons that while volunteers for foreign service would continue to be sought, and given priority in assembling drafts, members of the ATS would become liable for compulsory posting abroad. Yet this obligation would only apply to auxiliaries who were over the age of twenty-one (the equivalent age for soldiers at this time was eighteen-and-a-half), unmarried and deemed medically fit for such a posting. Additionally, it was stipulated that auxiliaries sent overseas to serve with mixed batteries would be strictly confined to volunteers, that female personnel would not be deployed in India except as volunteers and that they would not be despatched to Burma or West Africa either compulsorily or as volunteers.[55]

Before this policy could be activated, MPs insisted that the matter should be debated in the House, much to the frustration of Leslie Whateley, who believed that 'the whole object of the Service would be defeated if a political faction dictated how and where we could post auxiliaries'.[56] During the debate in early 1945, a number of members voiced their anxieties. Spearheaded by the Labour MP for East Edinburgh, Frederick Pethick-Lawrence – who, it was pointed out with a certain irony, as a former leading light of the Women's Social and Political Union was 'the man who went to gaol to get women votes' but was now 'against sending our daughters abroad'[57] – various concerns were expressed. These included the military necessity of drafting auxiliaries overseas, the home ties of those sent abroad, the conditions for women in theatres of war, the dangers to them of enemy action and the threats to their morals from the 'licentious soldier'.[58] 'Certain restraints which prevail at home under normal conditions', warned Pethick-Lawrence, 'are somewhat relaxed when we get into foreign countries.'[59] Grigg and the supporters of the proposals, however, won the day. It was emphasised that whilst every effort had been made to comb out soldiers for frontline duties, the number of ATS volunteers for service overseas was still far below what was required in order to help maintain the fighting troops. It was also pointed out that members of the WRNS were already liable for compulsory posting abroad, a decision that no one had questioned. Furthermore, reassurances were given that the family responsibilities of auxiliaries would be taken into consideration when posting overseas and drafts would not be sent until senior ATS officers were satisfied that adequate amenities were in place. It was affirmed, moreover, that auxiliaries would be mainly confined to rear areas and, given the recent V-weapon attacks, would probably be safer abroad than in the south of England.[60] As for the moral perils, these were considered to be overplayed. 'Women's standards of morals are not determined by geographical boundaries', asserted Edith Summerskill. 'The weak and irresponsible girl will get into trouble in London, Bristol, Manchester or Wigan. If she is going to get into trouble, she will not wait until she gets to the other side of the Channel.'[61] In April 1945, as the war in Europe was drawing to a close, the new scheme was promulgated in an Army Council

Instruction, with the added provisos that members of the ATS would not be compulsorily posted overseas if there were sufficient volunteers in an auxiliary's trade, if they were the only child of one remaining parent, or if there were compassionate reasons for keeping them close to home. The opportunity was also taken to reduce the ATS tour of duty overseas to two years, with postings to India and Ceylon (which was to be treated as a single theatre), as well as to Washington DC, cut to eighteen months.[62]

In order to reassure her auxiliaries, Whateley wrote to them to explain the need for compulsion. In her letter not only did she attempt to counter those who might claim there were still young, fit men at home who could be employed with the army abroad by stressing that 'all is not gold that glitters' and 'you cannot use a weakling as a Battle-school instructor', but she also argued that even if additional manpower could be found, it would be wrong to prolong the war to train it when a body of trained women was already available to answer the calls of Field Marshals Montgomery and Alexander.[63] She further appealed to the benevolence of the future wives and mothers in the ATS:

> Many of you will marry and bring children into the world, and we are not going to have it laid at our door that for want of a little more unselfishness on our part now our children or our husbands might have to go through the horrors of another war, which with modern science will be far worse than even this one. Selfishness has brought us into this war and only unselfishness on the part of us all can bring a lasting peace.[64]

This was not the end of the matter. As Jane Rosenzweig has shown, following notification of the War Office's intentions in regard to the issue of compulsory postings overseas, many letters of complaint from agitated parents, worried about the prospect of their daughters being dispatched abroad, arrived in Whitehall.[65] One indignant father claimed that 'rumour has it these girls are about to be sent overseas to satisfy the sexual impulses of our men and to make it unnecessary for them to fraternise with foreign women'.[66] To put official minds at rest, in May 1945, Violet Markham and Mary Stocks (who had served together on the 1942 Markham committee) undertook a fact-finding visit to ATS units in France, Belgium, Holland and Germany on behalf of the army authorities. They reported 'bitter complaints' from auxiliaries about the innuendos circulating in the popular press at home 'on the comforts to the troops theme' and concluded that

> We could find, during our visit, no grounds for stories detrimental to the character and morale of the ATS . . . .
>
> From all we saw and heard we feel that we could reassure the most anxious of parents as to the general surroundings in which their daughters are working and the measures taken to ensure their welfare.[67]

General Adam was understandably cheered by these findings: 'I need hardly tell you', he informed Markham, 'that the general tone of your report . . . makes very reassuring reading to me. Indeed, I always felt that this was the story you would bring back from any visit to the ATS overseas.'[68]

Meanwhile, the ATS hierarchy did what it could to monitor the well-being of its auxiliaries abroad. On a tour of inspection of Italy in the summer of 1945, Whateley discovered that the ATS signallers in Bari had been housed by the army in a 'third-rate' hotel sandwiched between a brothel and a prophylactic station: 'I was extremely angry with those who had selected such a billet for these women . . . [and] made up my mind that they must be moved.'[69] She also took the opportunity to request more ironing facilities for members of her force in Italy as they 'felt acutely about the fact that . . . they had to appear in crumpled drill skirts, while the American Servicewomen, beside whom they worked and lived, had all the means available to be perfectly turned out'.[70]

Service Life Overseas

Members of the women's forces performed a wide variety of occupational roles overseas. These included such employments as cooks, clerks, switchboard operators, storewomen, nursing orderlies, convoy drivers, radar operators, electricians, air mechanics and meteorologists.[71] In addition, WRNS code and cypher personnel were deployed aboard large troopship passenger liners (known as 'monsters') to handle the signals traffic and were part of the communications staff that accompanied Churchill to the wartime allied conferences in Washington, Casablanca, Quebec, Tehran and Yalta.[72] Joan Schwarz was one of the Prime Minister's personal WRNS cypher officers at Yalta in early 1945 and recalled that such was the delight of the British naval delegation from Moscow at meeting a contingent from her service at the conference, that a belated New Year's Eve party 'ended up with them drinking champagne out of WRNS shoes'.[73]

Working conditions abroad could be challenging. WAAF tele-printer operator, Rebecca Barnett, found herself performing her duties in a sweltering RAF palm hut in Ceylon.[74] ATS clerk, Daphne Smith, plied her trade in a sodden, shrapnel-holed army tent in Normandy.[75] WRNS wireless telegraphist, Joan Dinwoodie, toiled away in a bat-infested naval watch-room in Kenya.[76] An assignment to the RAF's Telecommunications Centre Middle East (TME) was a particularly onerous posting. Built underground in the desert near Heliopolis on the outskirts of Cairo to house the signals and cypher sections of the main RAF headquarters, the constant noise of the communications machinery, combined with the stifling heat, pervasive dust and lack of fresh air, invariably left the airwomen physically and mentally drained.[77] For one WAAF code and cypher officer, Ailsa Donald, who suffered from bronchial asthma, this environment (nicknamed 'the hole') was especially difficult to function in: 'even now the initials TME make my blood run cold ... It was hell'.[78]

Despite the best intentions of the military authorities, there were occasions when servicewomen were sucked into combat zones. During the campaign in France in 1940, members of the ATS got caught up in the chaos of the BEF's retreat. Ambulance driver Doreen Atkinson vividly remembered running for cover from Luftwaffe dive-bombers, when her convoy of vehicles was held up by a battery of Royal Artillery guns:

> The front plane seemed to waggle its wings, and then it banked over and came screaming straight down towards me ... I buried my chin and nose as far into the soft earth as I could and lay petrified. It was awful; a succession of sharp explosions, flashes, cries, showers of clods, sods, stones and powdered earth landing all round. And in the midst of all that came the scream of the next dive-bomber, more earth-shuddering bangs, cries and showers of debris, and then the next, and the next, and the next. And then it was over. Silence, except for the far-away drone of the departing Stukas.
>
> Three gunner stretcher-bearers carried their bloody, motion-less loads into the first two ambulances, and then we edged our way past the guns, glad to be clear of such a target.[79]

The ATS contingents were successfully evacuated across the Channel, but some of them got away very late in the day. A party of bilingual ATS telephonists working at an exchange in Paris was among the last Allied troops to escape from the capital before the Germans arrived. They were said to have driven out of the capital with their male Royal Signals colleagues as the enemy entered the city from the other side. The women eventually arrived in Britain on 16 June, having embarked on an old Channel steamer at Saint-Malo.[80]

In the Middle East, female personnel were drawn into forward areas. At the time of the 'great flap' in 1942, 502 Motor Ambulance Company, ATS, was based in Alexandria, sixty miles from the front line, but sometimes its duties took it closer to the fighting. Pat Hall, a sergeant in the unit, recounted that this could be an exhilarating, if somewhat unnerving, experience for the female drivers:

> An occasional highly coveted job took an ambulance westwards on the desert road where a daunting sign glared at a new-comer 'Are you prepared for an ambush?' Jane [one of 502's drivers] was the first to encounter this and wondered momentarily if she should stop and apply some powder and lipstick. There seemed otherwise little preparation she could make.[81]

Elsewhere in the theatre, the proximity of the enemy led to steps being taken to enable servicewomen to defend themselves. Elizabeth Watkins was a WAAF code and cypher officer based at the Hotel Metropole in Cairo, decrypting vital military messages from the battlefronts, and with the Germans threatening to break through to the city she was taught how to handle a gun at close quarters in case her unit was overrun:

> Of course women were not meant to carry fire arms, but that very week we had been taken to the roof of the hotel and shown how to use them. Anyone who had one (mine had been liberated from an Italian) was permitted to carry it. Tactfully, it had been made plain that it was preferable for women cypher officers not to be taken prisoners, and we were shown how to shoot ourselves should it become necessary.[82]

In Italy, members of the women's services could be found close to the front. ATS clerk, Angela Cummins, was assigned to Allied intelligence and in the immediate aftermath of the battle of Monte Cassino in 1944 she and her colleagues picked over the battlefield for enemy documents:

As we were climbing to the top, all the way we saw Polish soldiers, clearing up after the battle, collecting bodies. I saw a bayonet sticking out from behind a rock and decided to have it for a souvenir. I went over and gave it a tug, and out rolled a German body. I was shocked, I can tell you! I didn't take the bayonet, after all, as you can imagine.[83]

One intrepid ATS officer, Junior Commander Goggin, even apprehended a senior enemy commander in Italy. This servicewoman was appointed to run a civil affairs unit, whose task it was to administer newly-liberated territories until civil government was restored, and in 1945 the team was assigned to the province of Cremona. Although the area had still to be cleared of Germans and there continued to be sporadic fighting between them and the Italian resistance, Goggin persuaded the US army to ferry her unarmed party across the River Po to the city of Cremona where, in tandem with a female refugee Hungarian doctor, she set to work on reorganising the systems of public health, welfare and education amidst periodic shooting. Three days later, the German officer in charge of the garrison emerged from his hiding place and personally surrendered to Goggin rather than face the wrath of the partisans.[84]

In north-west Europe, ATS 'gunners' were utilised in the anti-aircraft firing line during the winter of 1944–5 to help combat the V-weapons directed against newly-liberated Belgium.[85] Joan Cowey and forty female comrades were despatched to a gun site defending the key port of Antwerp and, on arrival in Belgium, they were met by trucks to take them to the anti-aircraft camp. The army drivers expressed their anxiety about female personnel being deployed to such a target area: 'Antwerp was really getting it bad. They said they didn't know who was responsible for sending us, but they felt bad about women being sent into it.'[86] As feared, the day after they arrived the camp received a direct hit from a V-2 and a number of the ATS contingent were wounded while they unpacked in their Nissen huts. 'We just sort of crawled out and nothing much was said', recollected Cowey. 'We wanted to be tough so we wouldn't let the men down.'[87] Despite such setbacks, mixed anti-aircraft batteries in Belgium were said to have destroyed nineteen V-weapons.[88] 'We had certainly travelled a long way from the days when it had been doubtful whether women were capable of taking an operational role', observed Major-General Sir Frederick Pile of these units.[89]

The presence of female personnel in the vicinity of the battlefield could, however, leave servicemen in rear areas feeling emasculated. Pat Hall's husband was an officer in the Royal Artillery based in Beirut – where 'only one shot had been fired in anger, at an unidentified felucca'[90] – and when she visited him while on leave after months of pressurised work near the front in Egypt, a tension was apparent between them:

> there was no denying that the reversal of the normal wartime marital roles created a bit of a strain, especially on John. Instead of the warrior returning from the wars to lay his spoils at his lady's feet, it was the lady returning from an active service zone – luckily without spoils – to bring up-to-the-minute news from the front to his brother officers.[91]

A perception of male disempowerment could also be found among servicemen working alongside their female colleagues overseas. Joan Cowey discerned that some of the male gunners on her Belgian gun site were uncomfortable about the arrival of the ATS:

> I think at this point a lot of the men felt badly about having women stationed with them. You can understand that. There were some veterans of Middle East campaigns, of big battles, and it must have been a real comedown for them to be serving with women. They never said anything, though. It's just what I thought.[92]

This male unease was corroborated by WAAF wireless operator Mary Winter. She was assigned to work with the mobile signals unit of the 2nd Tactical Air Force in Belgium, which had been in theatre since shortly after D-Day, and it was apparent that the integration of airwomen into this male-dominated detachment was tantamount to 'stealing all their thunder': 'One even said he was writing home to tell his wife what danger he was in ... and how she wouldn't believe him if there were WOMEN out here!'[93]

Off duty, servicewomen overseas were able to sample the delights of parts of the world that few would have had the opportunity to visit in civilian life. During her deployment in South Asia, Prim Taylor of the WRNS was lavishly entertained on the estates of tea planters in Ceylon, learnt to surf in the Indian Ocean and visited the Taj Mahal in Agra.[94] In the Middle East, Eileen Shaw of the WAAF rode a camel around the pyramids at Giza, devoured ice cream at Groppi's cafe in Cairo and sang with a choir in the Bethlehem grotto during midnight mass (despite the organ breaking down).[95] In North America, Elizabeth Dunkley of the WRNS explored an old whaling station at Siasconset on Nantucket Island off Cape Cod, went black duck shooting on the St. Lawrence River in Quebec and participated in a squaw dance around a bonfire on a Navajo Indian reservation in Arizona: 'One Christmas in Tennessee I tried to learn poker but too much Bourbon whisky defeated me!'[96] There was also room for more illicit escapades. Elizabeth Watkins was regularly smuggled aboard test flights by a friendly RAF pilot at the Heliopolis maintenance unit when he put a bomber through its paces. These flights involved Watkins borrowing a parachute from one of the airmen and hitching up her skirt in order to pass the straps of the harness between her legs:

> Once I saw everyone smirking as I went out to the plane and wondered what was wrong; was I showing too much leg? Only when I took the parachute off did I see the owner's name, 'Virgin', stamped right across it.[97]

British female personnel tended to be much in demand as off-duty companions for servicemen abroad. In Ceylon, the social whirl around Colombo was, according to Wren Dorothy Smith, 'incredibly heady stuff for girls of our age ... As there were literally about 1,000 men to one girl, and many of the lads had not seen a white girl for months or years, you can imagine how spoilt we were. We loved it!'[98] The same was true in Egypt. Jean Wright described the excitement generated by the arrival of her party of Waafs at Ismailia on the Suez Canal: 'The men, as you can imagine, were absolutely delighted to see so many English girls in their midst. Overwhelmed by all the flattery we were able to pick and choose our escorts.'[99] Wren Penny Martin experienced a similar level of male attention in Alexandria and Cairo:

> To be young and reasonably attractive in Egypt at that time meant, honestly, that one just had to put one's foot down and determine to stay home at least <u>one</u> evening out of the month but even that was sometimes difficult. It is no exaggeration or lack of modesty to say that one had half a dozen invitations for every one that there was <u>time</u> to accept.[100]

In Algiers, the arrival of a contingent of ATS officers was keenly awaited by their male colleagues but, as K. P. Mannock self-deprecatingly confessed, she and her female comrades did not quite live up to their expectations: 'As a group, I'd say we were very lacking in glamour and I felt very self-conscious at being dragged off to parties, where no doubt there was the expectation of a truck full of young lovelies.' Nevertheless, the men seemed delighted to see them: 'Our hosts were too polite to show any disappointment and it was made known that just to talk to an English woman was sufficient compensation for the efforts which they made to entertain us.'[101]

The heavy social demands on servicewomen overseas could be draining. There were instances of 'party fatigue'. Third Officer Todd of the WRNS was based at Kilindini in Kenya and reported that one of the drawbacks of such a posting was 'too much gaiety ... there were very few women and they were always in demand. Most of them found after six months they had to abandon the entertainments and expeditions and could only cope with their work.'[102] There was also the risk of excessive flattery. Before departing abroad, ATS officer Ursie Barclay and her

Figure 9.3 Waafs and airmen dancing at the Lady Rosalinde Tedder Club in Cairo, Egypt, 1944–5 (© Imperial War Museum)

colleagues were warned not to have their heads turned by the barrage of compliments they were likely to receive in foreign parts. 'If you get asked out to dinner by twelve young men on the same night when you get wherever you are going,' the women were reminded, 'it's not because you are popular. It's because you're scarce.'[103] As part of their preparations for embarkation, Betty Platts and her fellow Wrens were given a pep talk on the dark arts of carousing in the tropics. 'Remember,' they were told, 'that men's passions are easily roused in hot climates, and beware of slap and tickle parties, and also a long drink called a Tom Collins, that has a hidden kick.'[104]

The dearth of female companionship for servicemen overseas could make British female personnel particularly prone to sexual harassment. ATS officer, Lavinia Orde, described a wearisome predictability to the social functions she attended in the male officers' clubs and rest villas in Naples:

> All seemed to talk about what they had been doing in the war, about their squadron leader or commanding officer, what was likely to happen in the war in the future ... Once I would have been thrilled to hear such talk but it ... [was] beginning to pall ... As time went on these parties always seemed to end in the same way as Jack or Bill or Ralph or whoever who had taken one got lit up on the very cheap wine and made less and less sense and got more and more amorous.[105]

In such circumstances, servicewomen became adroit at repelling unwelcome advances. WAAF teleprinter operator, Rebecca Barnett, was stationed at Koggala in Ceylon and a RAF sergeant there was strongly attracted to her:

> It came to a head one night, when he was in charge of a truck that was to take a crowd of us to some occasion. The truck was already fairly full when I arrived. Then, just as I was about to climb into its rear, 'Determined' (I used to sometimes call him) waylaid me and physically pulled me to the front beside the driving compartment. In my embarrassment I hardly liked to shout out my objections in front of a whole truck-load of girls, so I spent easily five minutes dissuading my amorous Sergeant with urgent whisperings, 'No, no, no,' I kept repeating. I didn't want to be wooed, or anything else, he tried to suggest. It must

have looked like shots from a silent movie as I stood there rejecting him while trying to remain a lady at the same time. In the end he released me and I crawled onto the form amidst muffled giggles and accusing 'Ohs' and 'Ahs', but, of course, the girls understood really. We were all prone to such advances where men are desperate for women. On reflection, I feel that we were a very able lot of WAAFs to come through such a time with so little damage to ourselves.[106]

On occasion, senior women officers were forced to intervene in order to safeguard female personnel. WRNS officer Betty Hodges recalled that at her headquarters at Minden in occupied Germany

> Quite frequently I would have Wren ratings requesting to see me on personal matters with regards some of the rather more unpleasant RNVR Officers' conduct towards them. These men would have made passes at them which were in no way reciprocated. Would I please help them as they were very embarrassed 'particularly as he is an <u>Officer</u>!' That meant that I would have to go to see the Commander of the Barracks, hoping that he would resolve the situation.[107]

If servicewomen struck up relationships with local men they could face official disapproval. In 1944, a Wren Waddell employed in Egypt was reported to have been seen in 'out of bounds' areas of Alexandria with 'an Egyptian, whose morals left a lot to be desired' and it transpired that she was pregnant with his child. Waddell was persuaded by her WRNS superiors to return to the UK, rather than marrying the man and 'throwing away her birthright for ... an infatuation'. But the female officer dealing with her case in the Middle East could not disguise her racial disgust at the behaviour of the Wren in question: 'The details are extremely sordid, and having seen the man, I feel quite nauseated, and wonder why white women do these things.'[108] In 1945, the Admiralty issued instructions that if a Wren overseas proposed to marry 'a coloured person or a Maltese' then efforts should be made to persuade her not to take this step and, if necessary, transfer her to another station in order to 'reconsider the matter under different conditions'.[109]

A posting abroad also afforded fresh opportunities for female personnel to indulge their femininity. In South Africa, Daisy Baldwin of the WRNS created satin underwear made from fabric obtained in Durban's Indian bazaar.[110] In Egypt, Jean Wright of the WAAF sported the latest in black strap handbags available from the leather goods shops of Alexandria.[111] In France, Fanny Gore Browne of the WRNS sampled the rich fragrances stocked by the perfumiers on the Rue du Faubourg Saint-Honoré in Paris.[112] In Italy, K. P. Mannock and her ATS colleagues had stylish civilian dresses made up for them in Rome to wear on evenings out in the city. Although these 'little numbers' (as they were known) were popular with their female owners and much admired by the servicemen – 'our men friends were delighted to see us in other than khaki'[113] – their senior ATS officer objected to this flouting of the uniform rules and ordered that civilian clothes could only be worn whilst on leave at least fifty miles away from their headquarters. 'Nevertheless,' snorted Mannock, 'it took more than an order to quell our enthusiasm for turning ourselves into women after hours and to defy it became the game of the moment.'[114] Thus, the determined frock wearers camouflaged their 'little numbers' and devised a system of lookouts to check that the coast was clear before making a dash out of their quarters:

> Sometimes I felt that the world had indeed gone crazy when I, a woman of nearly fifty, would cram a khaki skirt and shirt over a civilian dress and rush downstairs to a waiting car, where the offending uniform would be whipped off and rolled into a bundle.[115]

In some places the male service establishment aided and abetted these feminine tendencies. In Malta, for instance, the naval authorities relaxed the uniform regulations to allow WRNS personnel to don civilian clothing in public on certain occasions whilst off duty. 'Dances are the most elaborate affairs ... ', wrote one Wren officer on the island. 'All the Naval officers from VAM [Vice-Admiral Malta] down are most insistent that one wears evening dress.'[116] When, in the spring of 1944, such practices were brought to the attention of Vera Laughton Mathews she regarded them as 'most undesirable'.[117] It was important for the prestige of the WRNS that members of her service should 'take pride in their uniform and be seen about in it' and she argued that it acted as 'a definite protection to young girls in many Stations overseas which are filled with troops of various nationalities'. She maintained, moreover, that the wearing of uniform was an important aid to 'lessening class differences':[118]

> there may be some awkward questions asked if it becomes known that service in the WRNS overseas involves a heavy expenditure on clothes, or alternatively, the working class Wren being completely put in the shade by her more well to do colleagues.[119]

Yet when Laughton Mathews tried to enforce stricter uniform protocols overseas this was met with considerable naval opposition.[120] The Commander-in-Chief in the Mediterranean, Admiral Sir John Cunningham, was opposed to such measures.[121] He opined that giving Wrens opportunities to wear civilian clothes occasionally when off duty should not be seen as diminishing the uniform but rather as a welcome chance for them to demonstrate their womanly charms:

> I am confident that all members of the WRNS serving under my command are extremely proud of their uniform, and that they should take a feminine delight in wearing a dress of a different colour and material on gala occasions cannot be regarded as an indication that they look with disfavour on their uniform, rather does it serve to confirm one's hopes that Service life has not robbed the women of Britain of their natural feminine instincts.[122]

The Commander-in-Chief of the Eastern Fleet, Admiral Sir James Somerville, was also resistant to any tightening of the conventions. Not only did he contend that such a step would be very unpopular with the Wrens in Ceylon, but also that donning uniform in public around the island actually undermined the prestige of the WRNS:

> The fact that women are wearing uniform suggests to the natives that these white women have to work, and the fact that they have to work suggests immediately that they are of lower class than the white women residents who they regard as 'Masters" wives or daughters, and therefore persons whom it is necessary they should treat with respect in order to avoid the anger of the masters.
>
> ... if proof were needed it could be shown by the fact that Wrens in uniform are treated with far less respect by native

Figure 9.4 Admiral Sir James Somerville, the Commander-in-Chief of the Eastern Fleet, inspects Wrens serving in Colombo, Ceylon, 1944 (© Imperial War Museum)

servants, rickshaw coolies, taxi drivers and shop assistants than when they are dressed in plain clothes.[123]

He further asserted that there was a tendency for off-duty uniformed Wrens in port areas to be harassed by sailors of the 'lower deck':

> Whilst it is desirable to cultivate good relations between the WRNS and the Lower Deck, it must be appreciated that in a crowded port with many libertymen ashore who have not seen a white woman for some time, it becomes a matter of embarrassment to be continually addressed by sailors and, not to put it too strongly, to be pestered by requests to accompany them, or to make an appointment for some future date … it must be admitted that a considerable percentage of Wren ratings, who are daughters of officers, or of a different social status to men of the Lower Deck, find it most embarrassing to be continually addressed by sailors and even more embarrassing to disengage themselves, without causing offence, from such

well meaning attempts at making acquaintance. On the other hand, respectable women in plain clothes are rarely addressed by sailors thanks to the natural politeness of the lower deck.[124]

Eventually some compromise was arrived at whereby WRNS personnel abroad were officially permitted to wear civilian clothing once a week in public whilst off duty.[125] But it seems that these instructions did not reach all overseas commands. In the spring of 1945, it was reported that Wrens serving with the British Pacific Fleet were allowed to don plain clothes on a daily basis when off base during their leisure hours.[126]

On occasion, members of the WRNS conspired with their sisters in the other women's services to subvert the latter's dress codes. Betty Hodges recollected that the Wrens employed with the Allied occupation force at Minden after the end of the war in Europe were given permission by the local naval authorities to attend parties out of uniform. This, however, caused friction with servicewomen from the ATS and WAAF: 'when our Wrens went to their parties in dresses, they had all the men at their feet rather than the poor uniformed girls'. Hodges tried to persuade her female opposite numbers in the other women's forces – 'both rather elderly and seemingly weighed down with responsibility' – to loosen the rules and allow their charges to attend these functions in civilian garb, but they were concerned that 'some girls would have more dresses than others . . . [and] who knows (darkly) what a poor girl would do to get another dress?' To ease matters, Hodges suggested that if party-going members of the other services were not allowed out of their barracks in plain clothes, they could change into their frocks in the naval quarters – 'which, of course they did, with the greatest delight' – and then, before returning home, slip back into uniform again: 'How very childish!', she remarked of this charade.[127]

Some discretion seems to have been exercised over the deployment of servicewomen in a defeated and resentful Germany. For example, eighteen-year-old WRNS teleprinter operator Laura Mountney (who later became Laura Ashley, the prominent dress designer and interior decorator) was among the first waves of Wrens to land in France after D-Day and when she moved inland from Normandy to her new quarters in a chateau near Paris, which had previously been occupied by German officers, she had gleefully torn down the many pictures of Hitler that adorned the walls and made a triumphant bonfire of them. Yet when she was due to be transferred to Germany with her naval unit after VJ day,

Figure 9.5 ATS telephonists, Minden, Germany, 1945 (© Imperial War Museum)

her father, who had been badly shell shocked in the trenches during the First World War, objected and she was posted back to the UK instead.[128] Those who did serve in Germany in the aftermath of the conflict displayed a mixture of emotions. There was suspicion of the civilians with whom they came into contact. Eileen McMurdo of the ATS sensed an 'almost palpable hatred which emanated from the majority of Germans towards the members of the forces of occupation'.[129] There was pity for the malnourished children. Dorothy Dixon, also of the ATS, admitted that 'I could feel little compassion for the German men and women, but the sight of near starving children appalled me and I broke many Army orders by giving them food.'[130] And there was defiance. Angela Mack of the WRNS visited the Reich Chancellery in Berlin and, amid the ruins of Hitler's office, 'gave a silent "up yours" to the macabre Adolf'.[131] When

Figure 9.6 Waafs survey the damaged Hall of Mosaics in the Reich Chancellery after the fall of Berlin (© Imperial War Museum)

discussions took place in the Admiralty about the participation of the WRNS in the demobilisation of its German navy counterpart, the Marine Helferinnen, one of the arguments used was that Wrens would bring 'a soupçon of hard-heartedness to stiffen a male disbandment organisation which otherwise might be too tender-hearted to the German Women's Naval Service'.[132]

10 DEMOBILISATION AND THE CREATION OF THE PERMANENT WOMEN'S SERVICES

Demobilisation

As early as 1941 the government began to plan for demobilisation and following lengthy discussions between the Ministry of Labour, the three service departments and other relevant government agencies, a release scheme for the armed forces was announced in the autumn of 1944.[1] This was to come into effect at the end of hostilities in Europe. Like their male counterparts, the bulk of servicewomen were to be released in groups determined by a combination of age and length of war service (known as category A release) with the oldest and longest serving generally being demobilised before the rest. According to this formula, two months of service was to be treated as the equivalent of one additional year of age. Therefore, a woman of twenty-four with five years of service would be in the same release group as a woman of thirty with four years of service. In line with their male equivalents, provision was also made for a small number of servicewomen with special skills to be released regardless of age and length of service, in order to undertake urgent reconstruction work (known as category B release). Underpinning these arrangements, the Reinstatement in Civil Employment Act of 1944 obliged employers to offer both servicemen and women the civilian jobs they had occupied immediately before their war service on terms and conditions no less favourable to them than if they had not joined the forces. If this was not possible, employers were required to provide the next best alternative.[2]

There were, however, differences between the male and female release schemes. Whilst married servicemen, for example, were to have no priority of release over their single male comrades, married servicewomen were to be granted precedence over single female colleagues, if they so desired, in order to return to their marital homes as quickly as possible. Furthermore, rather than being issued with a civilian 'demob' suit on release, as was the intention for servicemen, servicewomen were to be provided with a cash grant and clothing coupons in order to purchase a civilian outfit to suit their individual tastes.[3] What these variations indicated were not only assumptions about the importance of members of the women's forces to the revival of family life in post-war Britain but also about the desirability of enabling them to dress fashionably and elegantly on their return to civvy street. Penny Summerfield remarks that 'the message concerning servicewomen was consistent with the return to gender norms expected of all women'.[4]

Such gender norms were also incorporated in various educational schemes that helped to prepare female personnel for civilian life. As Patricia Allatt has shown, the ground was prepared to some degree by the booklets compiled by the War Office to inform the regular current affairs discussions that ATS officers, like their male opposite numbers in the army, were expected to conduct with their subordinates during the war.[5] One booklet about women's roles in the post-war world, written by William Emrys Williams, the Director of the Army Bureau of Current Affairs, and issued to officers in early 1944, offered pointed advice on how to counteract the arguments of feminists if they appeared to be gaining the upper hand in a debate on this topic:

> In most discussions about women there comes a point at which someone tosses a hand-grenade into the debate. The well-worn phrase 'Women's place is the home', for example, can be depended upon to make the argument really explosive, for it develops extremism on both sides. On the one hand it makes the Grand Turk positively livid in his affirmation that he is the superior sex and that women's role is subordinate to his. On the other hand it goads the Ultra-Feminist into the preposterous proposition that women have a right to do everything that men do . . . .

If you find that 'Women's place is the home' is rousing a one-sided opposition you might find it salutary to balance things up by taking a familiar feminist slogan to pieces.

'A Woman Has a Right to a Career'

This slogan is usually repeated by upper-class feminists whose women-friends practise the more elegant professions – novelists, actresses, staff-managers and so on. It ignores the grim fact that most women who work are inevitably employed on rather wearisome jobs – such as filling bottles in factories. The feminist extremists always overlook this fact and consequently glamourise the whole discussion. Is there really anything more attractive to a woman in the prospect of a job of her own than in the prospect of a home of her own? Is this alleged 'right to a career', moreover, to apply in a competitive or sex-combative way? What reasonable ground may there be, for instance, for the fear so many married soldiers express that they will come back to find women entrenched in their jobs?

What about biological differences and social responsibilities? How do you equate women's role as mothers with their role as wage-earners?[6]

While Williams acknowledged that 'from the experiences and experiments of wartime we may expect certain new trends to appear in the post-war employment of women', he suggested that 'whatever else we look forward to after the war we must put first of all the principle that as many women as possible should marry and have babies'.[7]

The gender conventions were, however, most evident in the resettlement training courses organised for servicewomen in the run up to their release. In the autumn of 1944, the directors of the women's forces were invited to give their views on the types of classes that would be most beneficial to their female personnel and they 'stressed very strongly the need for the provision of home management courses':

A considerable number of the younger members of the Women's Services who were looking forward to the early establishment of a home had received no training and had missed the normal opportunities for learning the art of home-making. It was therefore of the greatest importance that full provision should be made as far as resources allowed.[8]

Instruction in domestic subjects was prominent in the offerings for servicewomen. An ATS 'Home Training and Handicraft Centre', for example, was established at the Royal Ordnance Corps depot at Donnington where the auxiliaries were able to acquire a knowledge of 'cookery', 'housewifery', 'laundry' and 'dress-making'.[9] 'Efficient housewives and mothers', it was observed, 'are a better war memorial than so much carved stone.'[10] Elsewhere, WRNS 'Housecraft' vans, fitted with modern kitchens and household appliances, toured home naval units to tutor Wrens in similar household tasks.[11] Civilian bodies, such as local education authorities and women's institutes, were also involved in these activities. It was reported that over a six-month period in 1945, 654 'single lectures or demonstrations', 184 'short courses' and 190 'classes' were arranged by various external organisations for the women's services on 'mothercraft', 'housecraft' and 'domestic science'.[12] Those serving overseas were not forgotten either. The WAAF, for instance, ran two-week courses on 'home management' for airwomen in Palestine using a bungalow at Ramleh equipped as a contemporary home.[13]

There were sometimes waiting lists for such classes and most seemed to have appreciated the opportunities to learn basic domestic skills.[14] Elizabeth Watkins signed up for a week-long WAAF 'brides course' at a seaside villa in Margate, where the students were given 'imaginary families' composed of two young children and a husband working nine hours a day on the national weekly average wage of £5 and were taught how to manage a household budget and attend to the domestic chores. 'It was a good course,' she recalled, 'stressing that budgeting time is as important as budgeting money. The immediate benefits were that I could now cook a meal, clean a house, and had made myself a fetching dress in a deep pink angora wool.'[15] The *Royal Air Force Quarterly* commented that the attendance at the classes provided for Waafs revealed that they were 'deeply interested in the domestic spheres of cookery, homecraft and mothercraft'.[16] A few, however, were sceptical of these offerings. Before her mixed anti-aircraft battery was disbanded, Marian Mills attended a series of lectures for the ATS on 'home management', incorporating 'shopping', 'dusting', 'home nursing' and 'mangling', which she regarded as 'prehistoric'. They were, in her estimation, 'a hurried attempt to reorient our minds towards women's traditional role and away from dangerous ideas of infiltrating male preserves in the workplace'.[17]

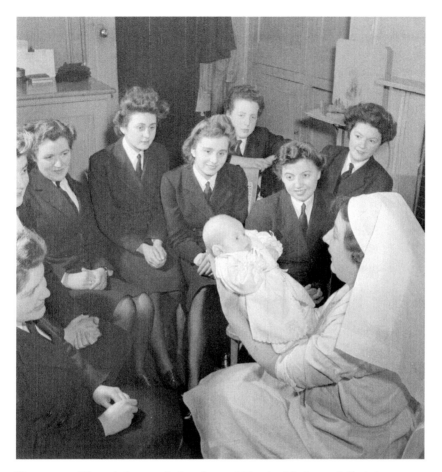

Figure 10.1 Wrens being taught 'mothercraft' by the Mothercraft Training Society (© Imperial War Museum)

In June 1945, the release scheme commenced and female personnel eligible for demobilisation were, as a general rule, discharged from the forces after the appropriate documentation and other administrative procedures had been completed at dispersal centres or other designated service establishments in the UK.[18] The release process was not without its stresses and strains. There were complaints from servicewomen about delays in bringing them home from overseas. Such frustration led to a 'sit-down strike' by a contingent of WAAF clerks at a RAF base in Egypt, during the summer of 1945, over the non-appearance of troopships to repatriate the airwomen. This dispute was only resolved after Felicity Peake, who was now the senior WAAF staff officer at RAF headquarters in Cairo, had obtained an official explanation from the Air Ministry about the shortage of suitable shipping and an assurance that a vessel would soon be on its way to embark them.[19] 'They were understandably fed up', empathised Peake, 'at being constantly "fobbed off" with excuses.'[20]

There was also some criticism of the priority given to married servicewomen in the release schedule. Such a preference, explained Constance Woodhead in regard to the WAAF, proved particularly irksome when married personnel exploited their marital status for their own advantage:

> As it turned out, some selfish young wives claimed their priority without the slightest intention of setting up house with their husbands; this caused great heartburning among the older spinsters, who were anxious to get a good start in the race for civilian jobs and whose releases were thereby delayed.[21]

Similar grievances surfaced in connection with the ATS. Major-General Alan Pigott, the Director of Recruiting and Demobilisation at the War Office, outlined the dilemma facing the military authorities:

> it was argued that it was both unnecessary and unfair that those married women who had not lived with their husbands for years and had no intention of doing so again should receive any priority. The contention was perfectly true; some married women obtained a priority for which there was no justification. But in practice there were no means of discovering these undeserving cases. It was not practicable to expect an ATS commanding officer to ask each of the married women under her command whether she intended to live with her husband, nor was it likely that those who did not so intend would give a truthful reply if they wanted an early release. In fact the concession was inevitable, whether logical or not. Public opinion had never tolerated the call-up of married women, and during the war much criticism was aroused by the refusal of the Services to grant discharge to a woman on marriage. The married men in the Services would certainly expect that their wives should be released at once, if they wished, to prepare their home for their return. Love, which proverbially laughs at locksmiths,

would doubtless have laughed at any regulation which attempted to retain married women until their group fell due for release; and it is better that regulations should not be laughed at.[22]

Another gripe was the value of the clothing grant given to demobilised servicewomen. After hard negotiations with the Treasury, whose female representative was convinced that a suitable outfit could be obtained for £8 15s, a sum of £12 10s was settled on. This was based on the estimated cost of certain utility-style items, including hat, scarf, raincoat, shoes, stockings, blouse or jumper and 'costume', together with an alterations allowance. There was, however, much grumbling that this grant was insufficient to equip women adequately for civilian life and did not appear to be equal in value to the suit of clothing provided for servicemen.[23] Leslie Whateley reported that among members of the ATS 'dissatisfaction was so general that I gave permission – and even encouraged them – to write to me if after demobilization they had proof that the grant was insufficient. There was no question about the fact that they had my sympathy'.[24] The sum was subsequently raised to £13 16s.[25]

A further irritation that came to light was the disparity in the war gratuity paid to servicemen and women on leaving the forces. Female personnel were to be entitled to two thirds of the gratuity (a payment in reward for war service) of the corresponding male ranks.[26] According to Woodhead

> some bitterness was felt at the apparent inequality of these benefits as between RAF and WAAF; but DWAAF [Mary Welsh] refused to ask for a gratuity at the same rate as the RAF, pointing out that it was illogical to accept two-thirds of the RAF rate of pay for six years and then to demand an equal rate of gratuity, since the latter was based on the accepted rank and rate of pay.[27]

Meanwhile, pressure was exerted by parents for the early release of the women. Whateley received pleading letters, as well as personal visits, requesting the premature discharge of daughters from the ATS, but was determined to hold firm in the face of such lobbying – especially from those who thought that rank or position would earn them preferential treatment. 'Both those in the Service and their parents', she insisted, 'had to be made to realize that if the rate of demobilization was speeded up for the women, it could be only at the expense of those men who had been serving overseas for so many years.'[28]

Despite these difficulties, the release arrangements seem to have operated reasonably smoothly.[29] By the end of 1946, approximately 350,000 female personnel had been discharged from the women's services under category A release and 4,000 under category B. The latter were earmarked for such industries as clothing, textiles and shoe manufacturing.[30] 'The demobilization scheme', concluded Pigott, 'was, beyond question, successful in achieving a very difficult operation without major trouble.'[31]

The anticipation of a return to civvy street generated a range of impulses. Many were attracted by the prospect of wedlock and domesticity.[32] Lady Violet Apsley estimated that on the basis of her experience as an honorary ATS welfare officer in Gloucestershire, 'probably about 75 per cent of the women in the Forces are looking forward in the future to marriage and a home of their own'.[33] Yet wartime service also spawned a desire for travel and adventure that appeared to challenge the notion of a conventional domestic existence. A Mass Observation report in 1944, entitled *The Journey Home*, recorded that '*wanderlust* is very widespread in the women's Services. The uppermost feeling seems to be a negative one: 'I'll never be able to settle down again.'[34] This cross current was said to be partly a result of the women's services comprising a higher proportion of female personnel from relatively affluent backgrounds, compared to those in industry, who could afford to indulge more stimulating post-war lifestyles. But it was also put down to a number of 'deeper' explanations:

1. The life of the Service girl has been completely changed by the war, more so than any other section of the community. Life after the war has become simply a subject for imaginative speculation.

2. Because her life is entirely devoted to the war, as one of our observers in the WAAF remarks, 'The war is an object in itself, not a transitory period during which everything stops.'

3. The Service girl is often very young, many coming straight from school. The future was vague before the war, and has only become vaguer in the interval. She has no ready-made life to which to return.

4. The Service girl is almost entirely cut off from civilian life. Whereas the woman in industry returns home in the evening

and takes up the thread of home affairs, the Service woman has only her periods of leave in which to find a contact with her old life.

5. The routines, uniforms, uniformities of Service life, necessarily more rigid than anything civilians know, built up the urge to step out into new independences, individualities.

All these factors contribute to make the Service girl readier than her counterpart in the factory, to take a leap forward into the unknown.[35]

This sense of restlessness was corroborated by Joan Wyndham: 'Five years of regimentation – not to mention those ten years at the convent – have left me with a lust for liberty that has to be satisfied', she confessed during the autumn of 1945, when contemplating her release from the WAAF, 'and all I really want now with all my heart is to be let off the leash – to be gloriously, totally and dangerously free.'[36]

Whatever their hopes for the future, the experience of demobilisation could be an unsettling one for servicewomen. There was a sense of isolation after the close comradeship of the forces. Phyllis Smart completed her discharge from the WAAF with a solemn handshake from a female officer and a brisk 'Thank you for coming': 'I was out! I have never felt so forsaken in my life. After being part of a huge family for so long, I was on my own. I lay in bed that night and cried.'[37] There were strains in readjusting to life in the parental home. After her departure from the WRNS, Joan Dunhill's family 'seemed to find it hard to accept that you were no longer just a young girl, but a mature and changed adult who had learned to stand on her own feet and make her own decisions'.[38] And there were anxieties about resuming married life. As J. Myler poignantly recounted, she and her spouse were virtual strangers after lengthy war service apart:

> There was also the knowledge that my husband was on his way back to me. Knowledge that made me glow and tingle from head to foot, but at the same time I was apprehensive. So many years had passed since our wedding day and those few short hours we were together and I knew his life must have been so different in Burma, the extent of which I only discovered much later and I realised that he would have changed, but how much and in what way? I knew I had changed since he went away and I wondered if he would be able to accept those changes and feel the same about me.

> Right now I had to face the fact that from this moment my life would be very different, just as it was so different when I joined the WAAF. Whether or not my husband and I would be able to cope with so much that would not only be strange, but perhaps difficult and certainly unknown was something that only time would tell. One thing I did without doubt know, and that was that I was going to have a damned good try.[39]

Furthermore, there were frustrations for those who returned to comparatively mundane civilian jobs. Liz Sealey, formerly of the WRNS, noticed that 'those who had been there all during the war did pay a great deal of attention to such trivia as to how many paper clips one had used, and such like. It did, for a little while, seem rather petty after Service life'.[40] Mary Palmer, recently of the WAAF, found herself 'bored stiff after nearly four years of intense work and everything happening round me'.[41] Angela Mack was surprised at the extent of 'prejudice against women from men' in the workplace following her stint with the Wrens:

> this was very strange at first to us, who had worked in the services alongside men and had got used to it, felt quite relaxed about it and had developed a good working rapport. Our first thought was that a lot of men in the business world were weird, neolithic creatures whose attitudes were scandalously out of date. We hoped they would soon wake up to reality.[42]

Some renegotiated their working identities. Marjorie Hazell related that her close comrade Rene, an ex-WAAF driver, stuck to her pre-war trade as a dressmaker for only a short period after release: 'She missed the outdoor life, and the freedom of the MT [motor transport] Section, and looked around for a more mobile job. She found it on the platform of a London bus.'[43] In contrast, Dinny Law, an ex-WRNS ship mechanic (landing craft), emphatically rejected her wartime incarnation: 'After the war, I decided never ever to do a man's job again and found the most feminine job I could at Cyclax of London. I learned to massage faces and make them up.'[44]

Whatever their individual experiences, Helen Forrester commented ruefully on a lack of public recognition for the returning servicewomen:

> For years afterwards, one would come across brick walls with *Welcome Home Joey* or *George* or *Henry*, splashed across it, in drippy, faded whitewash.

I never saw such a message painted for the Marys, Margarets, Dorothys and Ellens, who also served. It was still a popular idea that women did not need things. They could make do. They could manage without, even without welcomes.[45]

Figure 10.2 A mother welcomes home her daughter, demobbed from the WAAF, 1945 (Fox Photos/Hulton Archive via Getty Images)

The Creation of the Permanent Women's Services: The Assheton Report

Discussions over the long-term future of the women's forces began in earnest in 1943. Early that year Violet Markham and Thelma Cazalet-Keir (the latter having served on the 1942 Markham committee) visited the Deputy Prime Minister, Clement Attlee, to ascertain what consideration was being given to section nineteen of the Markham report which raised the issue of the continuation of the women's services after the war: 'are the auxiliaries to vanish from the scene and be lost in the shadows of demobilisation?', the authors had enquired in their report. In response, Attlee suggested that an ad hoc committee, incorporating representatives from the various departments concerned, be set up to look into the matter and this was approved by the War Cabinet.[46]

In the spring of 1943, such a committee was duly established under the chairmanship of Ralph Assheton, the financial secretary to the Treasury. It was asked to make recommendations on the future of the three women's auxiliary services. In order to arrive at its judgements, the committee sought the preliminary views of the respective service ministries. All three departments acknowledged that in any new major war women's forces would once again have to be mobilised on a large scale and that both they and the Ministry of Labour wished to avoid the 'delays and difficulties' that had been encountered at the start of the present conflict. Yet there were varying departmental perspectives on the organisation of these services in peacetime. If circumstances permitted, the Air Ministry was in favour of retaining a slimmed down WAAF on a regular footing, supplemented by a reserve organisation, which would continue to carry out duties with the RAF. In contrast, the War Office wished to maintain the nucleus of a permanent ATS, together with a reserve force, but the former would fulfil a purely administrative, training and mobilisation role. The Admiralty was less enthusiastic. Its stance was that while it would be advantageous to operate a reserve of women to be called up for naval service as required, probably overseen by a permanent skeleton headquarters' staff, there would be 'no room' for any regular women's organisation comparable to the WRNS. The reasons for this, it was claimed, were due to the 'special circumstances' of the Royal Navy. These included the necessity of maintaining a constant flow of naval personnel between the three types of service that sailors were required to undertake in peacetime (home shore, home sea and foreign) and ensuring that their service was evenly divided between these three categories. A sizeable WRNS would decrease the number of shore jobs available at home and thus 'conflict with this essential feature of the Naval Service'. It was also contended that for every Wren employed, one fewer active service male rating would be available for the fleet in wartime.[47]

The heads of the three women's forces at the time were also consulted. Jane Trefusis Forbes strongly supported the notion of a regular WAAF. She proposed that its establishment should be a fixed percentage of the RAF establishment and that it be employed largely in the more skilled roles for which advanced technical training was required. To support her case, she pointed out that since a significant number of airwomen served side by side with airmen on operational stations, it would be inefficient to organise a peacetime WAAF except on the basis of a permanent enterprise. She also argued that such a force would allow parents to become 'habituated to the idea of their daughters belonging to a service' and that it would 'maintain the necessary sense of trust amongst the members of the RAF in the capacity of women to undertake work of a technical nature with the Air Force'. 'The need to create this trust', she added, 'had been a hampering feature in the present war at the beginning.'[48] Jean Knox stated that in her view the 'minimum requirement' after the war would be to retain the nucleus of a regular ATS. Without such a body of trained women, she stressed, 'the strain imposed on those who would suddenly become responsible for creating a service from nothing would be excessive'.[49] As for Vera Laughton Mathews, she suggested – perhaps at variance with her naval colleagues – that a small regular WRNS was necessary in order 'to keep the Service as a living organisation' and that it need not disrupt the rotations of the Royal Navy if it undertook jobs in peacetime naval establishments which would normally be filled by civilian women.[50] All three senior officers agreed that a 'high proportion' of female personnel hoped that the women's services would remain in place after the end of hostilities and 'provide them with an opportunity for a permanent career'.[51] Markham herself was sounded out too. She recognised that there were many factors to be taken into account when considering whether the women's forces should continue in peacetime, but that there was 'positive advantage' in employing women in such military capacities as they had a 'humanising influence' and 'for certain work were more suitable than men'.[52]

During the course of their deliberations, the representatives of the service departments on the Assheton committee understandably endorsed the positions of their respective ministries. The non-service members, it was recorded, drew attention to arguments in favour of regular women's services. These included the 'number of spheres in the Services for which women have a special aptitude', the belief that 'the presence of Service women in Service Establishments is advantageous from the point of view of morale', and the 'continuous educative effect on Service and public opinion' which, however efficient a system of reserves might be, would 'better ensure an adequate supply of trained women to be mobilised for the enlarged Women's Services which would be needed in time of war'.[53]

In its report, completed during the summer of 1943, the committee acknowledged that it was difficult to formulate detailed plans for the peacetime women's services until the configuration of the post-war armed forces had been decided and the budgetary position was clearer. Nevertheless, it made some tentative recommendations. These largely followed the lead of the individual service ministries and entailed a permanent, if smaller, WAAF to undertake RAF duties along existing lines; a permanent ATS nucleus to perform administrative, training and mobilisation functions, together with a reserve force; and, whilst it was accepted that there were practical objections to a regular WRNS on 'an active footing', a permanent WRNS headquarters, augmented by a reserve organisation.[54] The War Cabinet approved these proposals, but a statement was made by Churchill in the House of Commons that the future of the women's services after demobilisation could not be determined separately from the armed forces as a whole and that the time had not yet arrived to decide policy on this matter. Reassurances were given, however, that the women's organisations would be required for some time after the conclusion of hostilities.[55]

Deliberations within the Air Ministry

Towards the end of 1944, the RAF authorities examined in more detail the likelihood of a regular WAAF as envisaged in the Assheton report. With the end of the war in sight, an Air Ministry committee tasked with looking into the manning of the post-war RAF revisited the merits of the case. The committee's starting point was that in a future major conflict manpower considerations would make it 'imperative' to utilise women in the armed forces to the 'maximum extent possible' and it was thus vital to maintain a women's reserve. Yet the prospect of operating a regular WAAF, as well as a reserve, was regarded as more problematic.

A number of arguments were set out in favour of such a standing force. It was asserted, for example, that as far as possible, the RAF should be organised along the same pattern in peacetime as it would be in wartime and that women should thus be closely assimilated into its post-war structure. Besides, only by retaining a permanent WAAF could it be ensured that the necessary continuous experience was acquired to enable women to be allotted to the most appropriate air force trades and that the standards of discipline and efficiency necessary in an expanded wartime service could be nurtured. In addition, if a large RAF was required after the end of hostilities and it was not possible to recruit male personnel of the right quality, women might be needed to supplement the available manpower, particularly given they were 'unquestionably better than men on certain duties'. Furthermore, not only was it desirable that the public should be 'educated and accustomed to the continued employment of women in the Services' but also if there was to be 'full and cordial co-operation' between the genders, the latter needed to come to view the former's employment with the RAF as routine: 'Only so will it be possible to avoid the difficulties which have arisen in the past as a result of antagonism and prejudice in the Service against the introduction of women.' Women, moreover, had 'played their part' in the wartime RAF and would 'expect to take their share in the post-war regular forces'. They might well resent being forced into a non-regular service and this could limit recruitment for a reserve. In any case, it would be problematic to organise and train a women's reserve if there were no WAAF schools or similar units staffed by female personnel on a permanent basis.

Various grounds against a standing service were also laid out. The incorporation of women in a regular WAAF, it was claimed, would give rise to 'problems of administration, training and accommodation', the overhead costs of which would be far greater than the benefits obtained from their employment. In particular, the marriage wastage rate alone would make them 'wholly uneconomical'. The Registrar General's reports indicated, for example, that if the average age at entry was nineteen, the annual wastage from marriage would be 7.4 per cent. When this was added to the higher wastage rates than men from other causes, along with the increased incidence of sickness, it was calculated that it would be necessary to enlist annually about three times as many women as men to fill the equivalent number of posts. Likewise, experience had shown that women were unable, in many cases, to fulfil all the tasks associated with the jobs they were under-taking, such as station defence duties, and further costs would be incurred because of the need to employ more male personnel at RAF establishments. What was more, the deployment of women overseas would be limited by climatic and other factors, such as the non-availability of appropriate amenities, and this would lead to a 'lack of flexibility and mobility'. To aggravate matters, whilst the command of men by women had been 'accepted to a limited extent in war time, it might be resented as a general rule under peace conditions and so lead to friction and discontent'. As for the women themselves, although they might have been 'willing and anxious' to do all they could to aid the war effort and would have expected appropriate roles to be made available to them for this purpose, 'these arguments would not hold good in peace time'. It was thus likely that many would not be prepared to sign up for full-time employment in a regular WAAF. This could make it hard to secure suitable officers and NCOs.[56]

The preference of the DWAAF, now Mary Welsh, was for a regular service, covering a wide spectrum of RAF duties, supported by a reserve. The manning committee was, however, divided on the best way forward and unable to give a clear lead.[57] In early 1945, the matter was referred to the Air Ministry's post-war planning committee. This came down in favour of proceeding on the basis that there should be a peacetime reserve but no regular WAAF. The planning committee was swayed in particular by the costs of maintaining a standing organisa-tion, the problems in obtaining competent female officers and NCOs to run it, and the fact that it would inevitably displace trained men who would be urgently needed as the core of an expanded RAF in wartime.[58]

Yet when this decision came to the attention of the new air member for personnel, Air Marshal Sir John Slessor, he was doubtful it was the correct one. He studied the reasoning for and against a regular WAAF, as formulated by the manning committee, and found the case against to be not of 'much substance' whilst the case in favour to be 'unanswerable' in several respects. In his opinion, the clinching argument was that in a future war the RAF would need to draw on significant numbers of women – 'which no-one contests' – and therefore a regular WAAF was a sine-qua-non of a credible women's service in the opening phases of such a conflict, since a reserve was unlikely to be fit enough to play an immediate part on its own: 'Few will deny that the WAAF was very largely ineffective during the first year of war because it had no foundation of experience, organisation or training.' Slessor asked the Air Council to reverse the verdict of the post-war planning committee and give its consent to a post-war regular WAAF, supplemented by a reserve.[59]

In the Air Council's discussion of this matter in the summer of 1945, there was some hesitancy about the Air Ministry acting unilaterally. The view was expressed that this question should be considered in relation to the intentions of the other two service departments and that there were 'important political implications' which would have to be evaluated. 'Women might claim', it was suggested, 'that, having proved their fitness in war, they should have access to the three Services like other members of the community despite possible objections on the score of economy.' It was agreed that a draft cabinet paper be drawn up.[60]

This paper, which was drafted in August 1945, explained that while there was a general consensus that reserve organisations should be maintained in peacetime, the embodiment of regular forces was a more complex affair. This involved questions of whether there were 'sound Defence reasons' for such institutions; whether the costs would be 'worth while'; and whether there would be public pressure for women to be allowed to have a career in a military service, as did those in the civil service, on the grounds that 'they have amply proved their fitness for a wide range of Service duties'. It was proposed that a new interdepartmental committee be set up to devise a common policy for the three armed forces.[61]

Deliberations within the War Office

The army authorities had been reassessing their own position in the aftermath of the Assheton report. Over the course of 1944, the War Office post-war army problems committee had mulled over the question of a regular ATS and not only recommended that a small standing service be retained in peacetime, supplemented by a reserve, but also suggested that its female personnel might perform certain military duties in addition to the administrative, training and mobilisation roles envisaged at the time of the Assheton inquiry. Yet in early 1945 the executive committee of the Army Council had cast doubt on these aspirations by questioning if the costs of such a force would be justified given the likely available funds. The matter was referred back to the post-war problems committee for further reflection.[62]

During this committee's reconsideration of this matter, which involved the participation of Leslie Whateley, who was much in favour of a regular ATS, compelling arguments were made in support of a standing force. It was agreed that the 'real case' rested on the conviction that the manpower situation in the future 'will not permit of mobilization for a national war without the use of women in the Services'. Linked to this was the admission that the ATS had 'undoubtedly suffered from having been born late'. Its senior officers and NCOs, for example, now had only six years of service experience behind them, rather than the twenty-five to thirty years of their male counterparts. Furthermore, in the early period of the conflict, the ATS had been 'seriously handicapped because of the fact that the Army did not then understand or appreciate the employment of women on a duty which, in peace, had been regarded as essentially a man's job'. Overall, it was estimated that as a result of the 'lack of preparation' for war, the rapidly expanding ATS had lost the equivalent of approximately 50 per cent of its strength through 'inefficiency' during the period between 1939 and 1941. A regular force was thus required, since there was a great deal of difference between 'expansion from a germ and building up a complete organisation from nothing'. It was reckoned, moreover, that if the peacetime regular army had recruiting difficulties, a standing ATS could usefully make up for a shortage of regulars and that 'there are certain duties which are more efficiently done by women than by men'.[63]

In the summer of 1945, the post-war army problems committee reported back to the executive committee of the Army Council. There were, it was stated, two separate but interconnected aspects to the question: the need to ensure the 'full and early use' of women in an expanded wartime army; and the possibility of utilising women in the smaller peacetime 'active army' as a means of increasing its effective embodied strength. The first aspect was believed to be uncontroversial. Shortages of manpower had made it necessary to employ significant numbers of women across the armed forces in two world wars. Not only was it considered axiomatic that women would once again be required for service in a large future conflict but it was also evident that one of the chief hurdles encountered by the ATS in the early phase of the present war had been the difficulties of rapidly expanding the service without the existence of a permanent nucleus on which to build: 'Our endeavour to do so was, for a long period, most wasteful both in personnel and in loss of efficiency'. It was thus recommended that a small regular ATS, supported by a reserve, be maintained in order to expedite this anticipated expansion. Some of this force would be involved in 'staff, administration, training, recruiting' with the rest undertaking selected military duties with the army.

The second aspect was considered more contentious. If the principal constraining factor in the size of the 'active army' was a shortage of manpower, then there was a strong case for a larger regular ATS to augment it. If, however, the chief constraining factor was finance, then the justification for a more substantial ATS would be diminished. Special accommodation and additional overheads required for such a women's service would make it costly to maintain, regardless of the savings in lower pay. In addition, from the viewpoint of 'all-round usefulness' in an army mainly needed for overseas service, they would be 'individual for individual, of less value than men'.[64]

The executive committee of the Army Council gave its approval to a small regular ATS, together with a reserve, but was reluctant to make a judgement on a larger standing service because it was not yet possible to predict the financial limitations under which the post-war armed forces would operate.[65] Shortly after this, the War Office was asked to associate itself with the Air Ministry's draft cabinet paper and join a new inter-departmental committee to consider the question of permanent women's services. The army authorities declined on the grounds that their planning was already at an advanced stage and their involvement in such a forum would achieve little. Yet they were willing to discuss the matter at the inter-service consultative body on post-war organisational and administrative problems (known as PICB), a committee that operated under the aegis of the War Office.[66]

Deliberations Within the Admiralty

The naval authorities also reviewed their policy as outlined in the Assheton report. In the summer of 1945, the Admiralty's naval personnel reconstruction committee, which had been tasked with re-examining the merits of a permanent WRNS, reported that it could find no grounds to depart from the position as laid out in 1943. A large regular WRNS, it was opined, would greatly diminish the number of 'home shore billets' available for male ratings and would 'certainly be resented by the Lower Deck'. As for a small regular WRNS, other than a headquarters staff, it was doubted that this would 'prove of any value as a basis for expansion'. It was thus concluded that unless it was found impossible to recruit enough men for the peacetime Royal Navy, a post-war women's naval service would only continue as a reserve organisation.[67]

In tandem with this, there was a belief within the Admiralty, as outlined in its submission to the Royal Commission on Equal Pay in 1945, that from the 'limited experience' of utilising women under war conditions, it was not possible to draw any 'sound conclusions' about the extent to which they could be successfully employed in a permanent peacetime WRNS across the variety of roles normally undertaken by men:

> It is of course clear from the very fact that women are not employed in ships of war at sea, that in the Naval Service women cannot be regarded as carrying out the full range of duties that fall to men. Apart from this, accurate comparison is made impossible by factors such as the complete absence of any objective analysis or statistical survey of the results achieved by women, the policy of utilising men on the physically arduous tasks (except for ships cooks), the training of women in the limited field of the duties of a rating on which they are likely to be employed contrasted with the wider training necessarily given to a man even in war time, because he is likely to be sent to a ship, and the relative educational and mental quality of men and women recruited into the Naval Service in war. The last factor is of special importance. The popularity of the WRNS combined with the small numbers required has enabled the WRNS recruiting authorities to pick and choose, with the result that speaking generally the WRNS comprises women of good education and bright intellect of a standard that is definitely higher than the average war-entered man who remains a rating . . . . There is no doubt, in the Admiralty view, that the

success which has attended the employment of Wrens in certain technical posts previously confined to men is in part due to the exceptionally high quality of the girls recruited for the WRNS.[68]

Meanwhile, the naval authorities received the Air Ministry's draft cabinet paper with its call for inter-service consultations. The DWRNS, Laughton Mathews, urged her department to participate and also took the opportunity to sound a dissenting note. Although she admitted that the matter was 'rather outside DWRNS' sphere', she nonetheless argued that if women's services were to be required in a future conflict, the retention of small, active regular forces, combined with reserves, were the most efficient means of securing their swift involvement after the outbreak of hostilities. She also posited that 'permanent Women's Services should exercise a very good effect on the morale of the Forces in peace-time especially for those stationed in isolated places'.[69] The naval authorities agreed that it would be beneficial to engage in discussions with the other armed forces.[70]

Joint Proposals to the Defence Committee

In the autumn of 1945, the three service departments began joint consultations at PICB.[71] At this stage, the War Office had settled on a small regular peacetime ATS, the Admiralty was ill-disposed towards an equivalent WRNS and the Air Ministry was still undecided on the shape of a future WAAF. During the course of these discussions, Air Marshal Slessor went back to the Air Council early in 1946 in the hope of persuading it to make a firm decision on a regular post-war WAAF, so that agreed inter-service proposals could be put to the cabinet. He argued that without such a women's force its members would be consenting to a RAF shorn of an essential wartime component which could not be recreated in under a period of eighteen months to two years. What was more, they might well be condemning the RAF to a deficit in what was considered the minimum peacetime operating level if womanpower was not available to make up for a possible shortfall of male recruits.[72] Although some doubts were expressed as to whether a career in a uniformed military service would prove attractive to women, this time the Air Council gave its consent.[73]

The naval authorities were having second thoughts too. One of the chief objections to a regular WRNS was that it would interfere with the provision of proper periods of home shore service for male ratings. Yet it had become apparent that in certain branches of the Royal Navy, such as those which formed part of its air arm, the likely makeup of the future fleet would result in an 'unduly high' proportion of home shore service. This was considered 'undesirable in itself' and would result in 'invidious comparisons' with service in other naval branches. The institution of a small regular WRNS would help to remedy this imbalance and bring the proportion of home shore service back into line across the service. In addition, it was now recognised that a standing WRNS would allow a reserve organisation to be better prepared for wartime than would otherwise be the case and prevent the repetition of an 'experimental period' as had occurred in 1939 to 1940. Furthermore, there was an acceptance that if, as seemed likely, there was a shortage of manpower for the peacetime Royal Navy, women would provide 'a most useful increment to fill the gap between supply and demand' and that in a number of jobs 'the woman is generally more efficient than the man'. It was conceded, moreover, that at remote naval establishments, in particular, 'the presence of uniformed women had a psychological value and tended to maintain the men's morale'. In any event, it was anticipated that if the army and the RAF maintained regular women's forces there would be 'constant public and political pressure' on the Admiralty to come into line with the other service departments.[74]

When this matter came before the First Lord of the Admiralty, A. V. Alexander, in the spring of 1946 he was not convinced by the change of heart. His inclination was that 'it would be of doubtful wisdom to attempt to maintain active Women's Services in peace-time'. The Royal Navy, he pointed out, would be the smallest of the peacetime services and funding would be limited; the likely work output of the WRNS, along with the extra costs of women's accommodation, would make it cheaper to employ male ratings; and the nature of naval service meant that it would in any case be necessary to train some men in peace to fulfil tasks normally undertaken by the WRNS in war. 'Hence', he cautioned, 'we should not be too ready to follow other services in this matter'.[75] Nevertheless, on the advice of the Admiralty Board, which was under pressure from the other service ministries to finalise its position so that a joint submission could be made to the cabinet, he reluctantly agreed to a regular WRNS.[76]

In early May 1946, an inter-services memorandum on the 'organisation of the women's services in peace' was duly submitted to the cabinet's defence committee. By way of background, it was explained that

> All experience has shown that lack of manpower is one of the strict limitations on this country's capacity to wage a major war. It has accordingly been necessary, both in this and in the last war, to employ women on a very considerable scale in all the Armed Forces. It would appear certain that, in a future war, similar or perhaps even greater requirements will arise for the employment of women in the Royal Navy, the Army and the Royal Air Force.

'One of the main lessons learned from the development of the Women's Services in this war', the document continued, 'has been the impossibility of bringing about a rapid expansion without some peace-time basis of experience, organisation and training'; and, further to this, it would be 'impossible to maintain in peace-time a reserve which would be ready and able to play an immediate part in the opening stage of another war without the backing of a small Regular force which would provide the basis on which to mobilize'. 'It is also important,' the paper added,

> if full co-operation is to be assured between men and women in the Services and the difficulties which arise from prejudice are to be avoided, that the employment of women on full-time duties should come to be regarded as a natural incident of Service life.

The service authorities thus proposed that not only was it essential to maintain post-war women's reserve organisations, but also that regular women's forces needed to be established. These standing institutions would facilitate the deployment of the reserves in an emergency and perform a variety of military tasks for their parent services. What was conceived was a regular WAAF of approximately 8,000 women; a WRNS of between 2,000 and 6,000; and an ATS of some 3,000. The WAAF would be employed across 'a wide range of duties'; the WRNS would focus on 'branches where they have shown themselves to be better at the particular work concerned'; and the ATS likewise on 'jobs at which women have already shown their superiority'. In the case of the ATS, it was envisaged that women would be employed in non-domestic trades such as 'the working of office and statistical machinery, mechanical and technical signal equipment and store keeping, together with certain operational duties in anti-aircraft'.[77]

During the defence committee's discussion of the memorandum, the Home Secretary, James Chuter Ede, raised some concerns about whether the women's services would impact on his department's civil defence organisation in a future war – particularly in view of the threats in the new atomic age – since the latter would again rely heavily on women. Nonetheless, the committee agreed that regular women's forces should be established. In fact, it was suggested that if female recruits were given training in the services as 'typists, book-keepers and domestics' then on discharge they might usefully plug a gap in the civilian labour market by helping to meet the urgent requirements for these categories of workers.[78] At the end of May, the Minister of Labour and National Service, George Isaacs, announced in the House of Commons that a decision had been taken 'to continue the WRNS, the ATS, and the WAAF on a voluntary basis as permanent features of the Forces of the Crown' and a statement to this effect appeared in a government white paper outlining plans for the post-war call-up of men for military service.[79] In regard to her service, Laughton Mathews described the establishment of a regular WRNS as 'the finest monument to the work of Wrens during the war':

> It still seems wonderful that the Royal Navy, the very heart of the British tradition and probably the most conservative institution in the world, should have opened its doors to women. The decision was, of course, very largely due to the manpower situation and the necessity of cutting down the numbers of men in the Services, but all the same, the Navy was with us. The news came at the right moment, when the war was just over and the WRNS stock high and all the Navy were ready to welcome us.[80]

Yet, as she philosophically remarked, the public reaction to the creation of these peacetime forces was distinctly underwhelming:

> The announcement in regard to the 'regular' Women's Services was received in a most remarkable way. Knowing that this revolutionary change was due to be made public, I and others were in a state of excitement, rushing for papers, listening to the radio, and certainly expecting splash headlines ... [But] so

> much interest and controversy were aroused by the terms of
> conscription for men that the paragraph [in the white paper]
> referring to the Women's Services passed unnoticed. There was
> barely a comment. Not a paper gave it a headline or even
> printed it in heavy type ... The complete acceptance of the
> Women's Services could not have been better demonstrated.[81]

Pending the formal establishment of the regular women's forces, opportunities were provided for those still serving in the ATS, WAAF and
WRNS, as well as those who had recently been released, to enter into an
extended service engagement.[82] Meanwhile, preparations were made
for the formation of the new standing institutions. The titles of these
services evoked considerable internal discussion. The Admiralty was
content to retain 'Women's Royal Naval Service' for its force, but the
Air Ministry and the War Office wished to devise new names for their
respective women's organisations. It was believed that the words 'auxiliary' and 'territorial' in the current titles were 'inappropriate' and
'misleading' for regular women's services.[83] The prime minister,
Clement Attlee, was reluctant to see the designations altered for some
'pedantic reason':[84]

> It is always unfortunate to change the name of a Service when
> the name has gathered round it a great amount of goodwill and
> honour. The fact that the present names are not exactly applic-
> able to the future Services does not seem to me necessarily
> conclusive. My own Regiment was called the 'Prince of Wales
> Volunteers' although a regular unit.[85]

Nevertheless, the Air Ministry and the War Office pressed their case and
permission was eventually obtained to adopt new titles. The RAF
authorities, after toying with such names as the 'Royal Air Force
(Women's Section)', the 'Women's Royal Air Service', and the
'Women of the Royal Air Force', opted for the Women's Royal Air
Force (WRAF) – a revival of its original name from the First World
War.[86] The army authorities, following flirtations with the 'Princess
Royal's Women's Regiment', the 'Royal Women's Regiment' and the
'Royal Army Women's Service', settled on the Women's Royal Army
Corps (WRAC).[87] In so doing the War Office rejected a plea from the
ATS old comrades' association – with Helen Gwynne-Vaughan one of
the chief protagonists – that the term 'Women's' be omitted from any

new title. This request was on the grounds that it had been 'one of our sources of pride that the Army could recognise its corps of women without a reiterated reference to their sex' and it had given the service a certain 'superiority over the corresponding bodies of the Navy and Royal Air Force, the names of both of which have always begun with "Women's"'.[88] Gywnne-Vaughan was, however, politely informed that although the new name might disappoint her, the deliberations had been 'long and difficult' and it was 'probably the best that could have been selected'.[89] Some in the service were not quite so certain. One female corporal mused that '"Wrac" sounds a bit like "wreck" to me and someone is sure to get around to "Wreck of the Hesparus"'.[90]

Other aspects of the new regular women's forces also stimulated debate. In the War Office, as Lucy Noakes has demonstrated, there were animated exchanges over the introduction of weapons training for members of the WRAC.[91] The DATS, Mary Tyrwhitt, who had replaced Leslie Whateley in the spring of 1946, believed that even if 'the WRAC do not go forth to meet the enemy', given the use of paratroops and other deep-penetration forces in modern warfare, the enemy was 'more than likely to come to the WRAC'. She therefore proposed that consideration should be given to teaching the WRAC to use small arms as defensive weapons:

> In these days when the enemy may be largely uncivilised, I feel that most women would rather put their trust in their own skill with a rifle than in the finer feelings of an invading army. It might also relieve a Commander's mind (and his available man-power) if the women on his establishment were capable of defending themselves instead of being dependent upon his few men for their protection. There are many precedents for this in history.[92]

However, not only were there concerns about public opposition to such a measure – 'the arming of women in any circumstances', it was opined, 'is distasteful to the British people'[93] – but also the prospect of gun-toting WRACs was clearly anathema to some senior male officers. The Director of Staff Duties, Major-General Richard Hull, was particularly forthright on the issue:

> With the possible exception of those manning AA gun sites ... I consider that it would be psychologically unsound and an

expensive waste of equipment, ammunition and training time to train women in the use of personal arms. The fact that 'little Olga' is trained to kill and prides herself on the number of notches cut on her revolver butt [presumably a reference to the Soviet Union's use of female snipers during the war] is no reason why we, too, should cry 'Annie get your gun'. It is still the soldier's duty to protect his womenfolk whatever they are wearing. Even in these days when war means total war let us at least retain that degree of chivalry.[94]

It was not until 1980 that the government announced that service-women would be trained in the use of arms.[95]

At times, negotiations over the details of the permanent women's services could be a fraught experience for those concerned. During a meeting in the Air Ministry to discuss the issue of illegitimate pregnancies in the WRAF, Felicity Peake, who (as Felicity Hanbury) had taken over as DWAAF from Mary Welsh in late 1946, became so irate with her male colleagues that she left in disgust:

> I listened, spellbound, to these men discussing, apparently in all sincerity, what punishment they should mete out to any air-woman or WRAF officer who became illegitimately pregnant. I was fascinated; I could hardly believe my ears. No one referred to me for my opinion. Eventually I could stand it no longer and burst out, 'And what do you propose to do to the men involved?' – there had been no mention of men – 'Promote them to Air Marshals, I suppose?' Then I stormed out of the meeting. I knew I had behaved very badly, but I was so incensed that I didn't care what happened.[96]

On other occasions, more subtle tactics were employed. Peake found out that the Chancellor of the Exchequer, Sir Stafford Cripps, favoured a separate pay scale for servicewomen, unrelated to the men's scale – a decision, she feared, that would result in protracted arguments over women's pay rates every time the men's rates were increased and make the prospect of eventual parity in pay more remote. So she arranged for Caroline Haslett, an old friend of the Cripps family, who she had met when the engineer gave a lecture at the WAAF officers' school, to 'beard the Chancellor in his den':

When the news came through that she had persuaded Sir Stafford to change his views in our favour I was overcome with joy. I remember literally dancing round my office. Any outsider coming in at that time would undoubtedly have thought that we had all gone mad; for as the news spread, everyone seemed to come bursting into the office to join in the dancing![97]

Inauguration

Despite such behind-the-scenes wrangling, in 1948 an Army and Air Force (Women's Service) Act was passed, which gave effect to the government's decision to form regular women's services, and on 1 February 1949 the WRAF and WRAC were inaugurated, with the permanent WRNS instituted on the same date.[98] To augment these full-time forces, part-time women's reserve units were also established.[99] The WRAF was to be assimilated as closely as possible with the RAF; the WRAC – notwithstanding some discussion over the practicability of incorporating women into the existing male military corps – was to form a distinct corps within the army; and the WRNS was to continue as a separate organisation within the naval service.[100] The WRAF was to offer eighteen categories of work (including such roles as cook, waitress, shorthand typist, engine mechanic, airframe fitter and fighter plotter), the WRNS twenty-four (including steward, hairdresser, sick berth attendant, air mechanic, bomb range assessor and meteorologist) and the WRAC thirty-four (including mess orderly, tailoress, switchboard operator, storewoman, armament artificer and anti-aircraft fire control operator).[101] Female recruits (who could be single or married) were to be entitled to a pension after twenty-two years of regular service.[102] The creation of these new enterprises, which afforded women the opportunity to forge a career with the British armed forces in a way that had not existed before, marked a significant advancement for women in the public sphere. Peake sensed the historical import. 'Women after this war should not "slip-back" as they did after the 1914–18 War', she wrote to her mother about plans for a regular women's air force. 'This may well be the beginning of great things and great changes, particularly as regards equality of opportunity.'[103] By 1952 the WRNS was some 5,000 strong, the WRAC 6,000 and the WRAF 10,000.[104]

Yet although these undertakings might have opened up new career opportunities for women, in a number of respects they remained on a different footing to their male equivalents. The women's services were, for example, to be solely composed of volunteers and exempt from peacetime military conscription.[105] The latter, it was argued, was unnecessary since there would be 'no difficulty' in securing the numbers required through voluntary recruitment.[106] Additionally, in all matters 'distinctively concerning their well-being as women', female personnel were to be administered by those of their own gender and they were entitled to a discharge on marriage if they so desired.[107] Furthermore, these forces were to continue to be non-combatant in nature.[108] Indeed, the mixed anti-aircraft batteries, whose female 'gunners' had perhaps come closest to challenging the combat taboo during the war, disappeared altogether from the army's order of battle when the anti-aircraft command structure in the UK was abolished in 1955.[109] Moreover, servicewomen were to be paid three-quarters of their male equivalents, an agreement reached after a dispute between the service departments and the Treasury over the level of pay – the service ministers holding out for four-fifths of the corresponding male rates, but the chancellor insisting on a lower figure on the grounds, among others, that women were exempted from combat.[110] On top of this, while the WRAC and WRAF were to be subject to the disciplinary codes of the Army and Air Force Acts (including military detention), 'field punishment' (which involved heavy labour and physical restraint) was to be prohibited for female personnel as it was deemed 'not appropriate to women members of the Forces'.[111] As for the WRNS, it was again to be excluded altogether from the Naval Discipline Act. Although this was still a bone of contention for some Wrens – a grievance said to be compounded by constant references to them in the press and elsewhere as 'mere civilians' because they were not subject to naval law[112] – the naval authorities would not budge. The view was held that the peacetime WRNS would not be as closely assimilated with the Royal Navy as the other women's forces with their male 'parent' service and that the Naval Discipline Act was chiefly designed for service afloat and would be inappropriate for women working predominantly in shore-based roles. It was also the case that civilian status was not deemed to be inconsistent with the position in other parts of the naval system where civilians ran ancillary services, such as the supply service. The comparatively small regular force, it was contended, was likely to be highly selective in its recruitment and the present arrangements had 'operated in practice very satisfactorily'.[113] It was to be 1977 before the WRNS was eventually brought under the Naval Discipline Act.[114]

What was also deemed important was that peacetime service-women retained their femininity. This was exemplified in the design of their uniforms in the immediate post-war era. For the WRAC's 'No. 1 dress', a War Office committee chaired by Mary Tyrwhitt solicited designs from leading couturiers, such as Norman Hartnell, Charles Creed, Edward Molyneux and Aage Thaarup and plumped for a pattern submitted by Hartnell, the royal dressmaker, which incorporated a fashionable bottle-green jacket, cut away at the front in the style of the Highland regiments, with a four-gored skirt. It was considered the most suitable choice since it had 'a feminine line and yet is reminiscent of Military Uniforms of the early nineteenth century'.[115] The new uniform was unveiled in 1949.[116]

The development of the WRAF's 'No. 1 dress' was more rancorous. After the brief, unsuccessful trial of a design based on the uniform worn by the WRAF's Central Band, in 1952 Nancy Salmon, who had taken over from Peake as DWRAF in the summer of 1950, approached Victor Stiebel, another prominent couturier who was based at the Jacqmar fashion house in Mayfair, with a view to creating a uniform 'specifically for the feminine figure'.[117] But his design, which featured a stylish, shorter air force blue jacket with less square shoulders and a more accentuated waist, together with a flared skirt, met with opposition from a number of senior WRAF officers. The inspector of the WRAF, Group Officer Anne Stephens, took particular offence. In a strongly-worded letter to Salmon, in which she complained that she was 'dismayed and greatly perturbed' to find plans for a new uniform so greatly advanced without having been formally consulted, Stephens protested that she was 'completely opposed for reason of both morale and practical value to a departure from the tradition of wearing the same uniform as the Royal Air Force'. She laid out her objections under a series of headings:

Need for femininity

I understand that your desire to encourage the women of the service to both look and be feminine is your biggest reason for instigating a new design of uniform. I could not be more in agreement with you regarding the need for femininity in the service particularly in view of the masculine life and work in which we are engaged; but are you really dissatisfied with the degree of femininity which prevails to-day? Surely our ideal for a member of the WRAF is a woman who always maintains her ladylike qualities coupled with a sense of discipline which prevents her displaying the temperamentalness sometimes associated with our sex. I would claim that apart from the small and hard core of 'tough' women which no change of uniform will alter we are in the happy position of having a vast majority of officers and airwomen who are both disciplined and ladylike, and that there is no need for a special crusade to feminise the service and therefore no need for a specially feminine cut of uniform.

Pride of service
In my experience members of the WRAF are tremendously proud of belonging to the Royal Air Force. This is certainly the biggest morale factor in their service lives; the loyalty which members of the WRAF give to the WRAF is but secondary, and only called forth when vis-a-vis the other women's services. The basic loyalty of the WRAF is to the Royal Air Force and great pride is felt in wearing the same uniform as the Royal Air Force. I do not think we shall ever succeed in building up a pride in and loyalty to a WRAF uniform which may appear to some to symbolise a separate WRAF service. You know better than I the need for pride of service and esprit de corps to support the service man or woman in the day of trial and danger and in giving the WRAF a uniform different from the RAF I think we should strike a grave blow at the morale of the service. For these reasons I am strongly opposed to a departure from the traditional RAF design. I am prepared to say that 90% of the officers and airwomen of the service would resent being put into a uniform which differed from the RAF and I would further say that the 10% (or even 20%) who welcomed a new design would be made up of those who cared least for the traditions of the Royal Air Force and had least knowledge of the service.

Integration
The policy of integration has been and is being successfully pursued, but as you are well aware there is still a degree of prejudice to the full employment of WRAF personnel in male

posts. This prejudice is more marked amongst the lower ranking RAF officers at station level and it is here that the WRAF uniform is seen daily. I feel that to put members of the WRAF into a uniform of their own will encourage those RAF officers who are opposed to integration in their belief that the woman is not a proper substitute for the man. It will, as it were, give visual expression to their feeling that 'the WRAF are different'.

Dating

I have already expressed verbally my fears regarding the effect of changes in women's fashions on a specifically WRAF uniform design. The model which I saw last week with its short jacket and slightly flared skirt is essentially a 1952 fashion; I wonder if women may not be wearing Edwardian cut coats and mutton chop sleeves in 1962, which will make our 1952 model look very démodé.

I feel that adherence to the RAF pattern would by the fact that it is a well known and universally accepted uniform exempt us from comparison with feminine fashions current at any time.

Publicity

I believe that you are hoping that a new pattern uniform would have good publicity value and enhance recruiting. I think that this would in fact be true for the first few weeks or months after its introduction but fear that the initial impetus would soon be lost. Should the pattern date it would, of course, become a deterrent to recruiting.

At present in the eyes of the public every officer and airwoman is patently a member of the Royal Air Force; it is possible that, dressed in a uniform which differed from the Royal Air Force, members of the WRAF might be mistaken for Air Hostesses or Air Rangers [a branch of the Girl Guides Association] or members of the WJAC [Women's Junior Air Corps]. Should such mistakes be made the publicity value of the new design would be lost and the sense of insult a grievance amongst members of the WRAF would be very bitter.[118]

The Air Council was asked to adjudicate on the matter and, despite Stephens's lengthy objections, gave its consent to Stiebel's design. Not only was its potential recruitment value alluded to – Hartnell's creation was said to have acted as an excellent recruiting agent for the WRAC – but also a survey of members of the WRAF who had seen it modelled at RAF Hawkinge (a WRAF training centre) had revealed a clear margin in its favour over the present design. While opinion had been evenly divided among officers, it had 'been acclaimed by the majority of the airwomen'.[119] The new uniform was launched in 1954.[120]

Figure 10.3 WRNS officers' mess dress designed by Victor Stiebel, 1951 (© Mary Evans Picture Library)

As for the WRNS, an evening mess dress for its officers was adopted. On hearing of proposals for this new item of uniform, a group of WRNS officers in Portsmouth Command took the liberty of producing their own design which was forwarded to the Admiralty for scrutiny. It was described as 'essentially feminine, whilst remaining unmistakably uniform', 'becoming to all figures' and successful in avoiding 'the pitfall, so dear to the caricaturist, of arraying young ladies in quasi-military attire'.[121] But various shortcomings were identified in this pattern by the new DWRNS, Mary Lloyd, and in 1950 Stiebel was called upon to design the mess dress.[122] He was, however, to be left in little doubt as to the brief. Instructions were given that the views of Vice-Admiral Lord Mountbatten, at this time the Fourth Sea Lord (who was responsible for supplying the Royal Navy), should be brought to the couturier's attention: 'I shall not approve of any masculinity in the evening', insisted Mountbatten, 'and am glad to find the Queen [Commandant-in-Chief of the WRNS] shares my views.'[123] The resulting creation, an elegant combination of long, flowing skirt and bolero jacket of black ottoman rayon, complemented by a white marcella blouse with revered collar, was revealed in 1951.[124] It exuded naval femininity.[125]

CONCLUSION

The wartime women's auxiliary services were born out of necessity rather than desire. In this regard, the manpower requirements of the armed forces were clearly of central importance in accounting for their revival in the late 1930s. After the experience of the First World War, it never seemed in doubt that in another major conflict the service departments would need to employ women in auxiliary roles in order to free up their male personnel for combatant duties. As the threat of war loomed, especially in the wake of the Munich crisis, the armed forces were compelled to make contingency plans in peacetime to ensure that they would have a trained pool of womanpower available to them on the outbreak of hostilities. The War Office and the Air Ministry were in the vanguard over this, but even the Admiralty, which was less enthusiastic, came to recognise the requirement for such measures.

But what was also important, and what can be contrasted with the focus on the anti-militarist activities of women in the inter-war years,[1] was the part women themselves played in pressurising the armed forces to readmit them into their sphere. In this respect the 'enthusiastic ladies' of the women's bodies, as the Air Member for Personnel termed them, played a key role both in persuading the service authorities of the military utility of women auxiliaries and in keeping the issue on the 'rearmament' agenda.[2] Indeed, Constance Woodhead, who authored the Air Ministry's internal history of the WAAF, argued that 'it was the enthusiasm of the various women's organisations which before 1939 overcame governmental and departmental resistance and finally brought the women's services into existence'.[3] At the forefront of this effort were Lady Londonderry and Helen Gwynne-Vaughan (with Katharine Furse playing a similar role in relation to the Royal Navy). Before the First World War, both these figures had been active suffragists who had campaigned for the political rights of women.[4] Now, as a new war approached, they used their formidable lobbying skills to press for women's military rights. Yet this was to be a battle fought from the sofa rather than the soap box. As Mollie Izzard noted: 'they attacked on a broad front at the luncheon and dinner table, and harassed by means of the telephone'.[5] What sealed the matter were the hordes of patriotic women who clamoured to undertake national service at the time of Munich and thereafter, forcing the service authorities to act. Felicity Peake of the WAAF typified their attitude: 'Like so many others', she stated, 'I merely wanted to serve my country.' It would not be long before she was doing her duty on the 'frontline' at Biggin Hill during the Battle of Britain.[6]

In many respects the wartime women's auxiliary services represented a considerable gender advance for women. From a position shortly before the war in which there were no such official women's forces, by the end of the conflict over 400,000 women were serving with the ATS, WAAF and WRNS at home and overseas. Servicewomen now undertook a range of military duties, including manning the fire-control instruments on anti-aircraft guns, that few could have anticipated five years earlier. Furthermore, rather than being 'camp followers', these women (with the exception of the WRNS) were endowed with a military status that designated them members of the armed forces of the crown and entitled their officers to hold the king's commission. In certain circumstances, female officers were permitted to issue orders to servicemen. Although this journey was fraught with difficulties as gender identities were renegotiated, servicewomen came to play such an integral role in the wartime armed forces that the military authorities found it necessary to establish permanent regular post-war women's services and, in so doing, opened up a military career for women for the first time. Some justly regard these women as feminist pioneers. 'The woman who, today, goes to sea in a warship or flies a jet aircraft', writes Colin Dobinson, 'is heir to the tradition begun by Pile's "gunner girls".'[7]

The women's forces performed an important military function for their wartime 'parent' services. At their peak numbers, the ATS made up 7% of the total combined strength of the ATS and the army, the WRNS 9% of the combined strength of the WRNS and the Royal

Navy and the WAAF 16% of the combined strength of the WAAF and the RAF.[8] In the United Kingdom, the WAAF made up 22% of the combined strength.[9] Overall, this represented a significant female labour force for the armed services. It was calculated, for example, that without the WAAF the RAF would have required an additional 150,000 men who could only have been provided at the expense of the other services or war production.[10] Likewise, the ATS 'gunners' in the mixed batteries in AA Command were alone estimated to have saved the army 28,000 men.[11] This was the equivalent of roughly thirty-five infantry battalions – or the rifle strength of four frontline infantry divisions.[12] By the same token, some of the non-combatant branches of the armed forces became very reliant on female personnel. It was reported in 1945, for instance, that in the British army at home service-women made up 50% of those undertaking pay, records and signals duties; in the RAF, they accounted for 50% of those employed as clerks and 86% as teleprinter operators; and in the Royal Navy, they constituted 88% of the clerical and 97% of the telephone branches.[13] In fact, during Operation Overlord much of the Royal Navy's vital shore-based communications was in the hands of Wrens.[14] At the commander-in-chief's signals distribution office in Portsmouth, such was the burden of responsibility that some of the women had 'tears of fatigue running down their faces'.[15] It was a powerful indication of the importance of the women's services to the functioning of the armed forces that when in the summer of 1945 Churchill called for servicewomen to be demobilised as and when they wished, regardless of their release category – 'the sooner they are back at their homes the better'[16] – this was firmly opposed by the manpower authorities. Their view was that if women were allowed to leave on such a basis this would 'seriously impair the efficiency of the Services, and in some branches even lead to a complete breakdown'.[17]

As for the servicewomen themselves, although distinctions of social class, age, race and ethnicity, sexuality, rank, military occupation, type of auxiliary service and status as conscript or volunteer, intersected with those of gender,[18] most seem to have regarded their experiences in the forces with a good deal of satisfaction. Admittedly, as Dorothy Sheridan reminds us, some reflected on their period in uniform as merely a temporary interruption to their peacetime lives: 'we wanted to get back home and pick up the threads of normal life once again', recalled a former member of the ATS.[19] Others, by their own admission, were just not cut out for service life and never fitted in. 'I look back on those years', confessed one ex-Wren, 'as the most miserable I have ever spent.'[20] Yet the majority who have placed their experiences on record appear to have enjoyed and benefitted from their time in the forces. There were strong bonds of friendship forged. Waaf Mary Hickes recounted that 'The camaraderie was excellent – we were all in the same boat and helped one another; many missed that part of service life more than anything else on demobilisation.'[21] There was a broadening of outlook. 'I think the whole thing was very very salu-tary,' ruminated Wren Ann Tomlinson. 'I think I learned how to like and respect other people who were not of backgrounds like mine, who had very different experiences.'[22] There was a sense of empowerment. Waaf Jean Wright reminisced that 'for us it was the chance of a lifetime, expressing ourselves, doing jobs and experiencing a way of life we had never had a chance to experience before, and all within the protective framework of the services'.[23] There were feelings of pride. 'Pride – yes,' stressed Vee Robinson of the ATS, 'for with thousands of other girls I had helped defend this land of ours against an enemy who threatened us with slavery. That may sound melodramatic; nevertheless it was true.'[24] And there was mischief and laughter to be had. 'There was so much natural fun . . .', remembered Waaf Rebecca Barnett. 'In a way we behaved at times like a slightly older version of the St Trinians' girls.'[25] Female veterans were, moreover, linked together by an invisible chain. Winifred Lane of the ATS commented that 'For some years after the war, whenever I met women for the first time, I knew if they had been in any of the women's Forces. Common experience bred a kindness, a greater understanding and sympathy between women, unknown before or since.'[26] Penny Summerfield has written of former service-women looking back on their wartime lives and reconstructing their time in the forces around such transformative concepts as becoming 'better and more complete people', understanding their 'spiritual and corporeal humanity with others', gaining 'a sense of identification with the nation' and acquiring 'a new gender identity'.[27]

Yet the more affirmative aspects of service life could be tem-pered by moments of great pathos. In one of the German 'tip and run' raids on British coastal towns in May 1943, twenty-six members of the ATS serving in 103 AA Brigade were killed. Twelve Focke-Wulf fighter-bombers attacking Great Yarmouth destroyed their hostel at Sefton House, close to the seafront, just after they had returned from early morning PT. Six of the ATS dead were laid to rest in nearby Caister Old Cemetery, including nineteen-year-old Private Lilian Grimmer, a local recruit who had reputedly swopped her leave with a friend who was eager to celebrate her twenty-first birthday.[28] A marble memorial tablet now commemorates the fallen at the site of the former hostel.[29] There were also tragic accidents. In November 1943 two WAAF officers, Section Officers Ruth Watson and Monica Daventry, were fatally injured when, being driven back to their quarters late one night after duty with the RAF delegation in Washington DC, their vehicle collided with another at the junction of Albermarle Street and Nebraska Avenue Northwest. The two Waafs were buried in Arlington National Cemetery with military honours, their coffins borne on horse-drawn caissons and draped in Union Jacks with a detail of American soldiers acting as pallbearers. They were the first foreign servicewomen to be interred at the US national shrine.[30]

The deaths of servicewomen could leave an indelible mark on those who witnessed such events. WAAF officer, Muriel Gane Pushman, was deeply traumatised when several of her barrage balloon operators were killed during a bombing raid on Cardiff in 1943:

> In the early hours of the next morning, we were awakened by the heart-stopping wail of the air raid sirens. Immediately we scrambled out of bed, grabbed our clothes, ran to our bicycles, and raced down the long Castle drive to spread out like a fan, each of us going to a different balloon site . . . .
>
> As I pedalled frantically, I had to admit to myself that I was terrified. The noise of the guns blazing away in the dark was deafening, and I felt, rather irrationally, that I was alone in a city on the brink of destruction. With the exception of the odd policeman or air raid warden, I saw no one about, until my bicycle was joined on the main road by fire engines and ambulances, coming and going in all directions. Dear God, I prayed, please don't let me be killed tonight. A line from some half-forgotten poem filtered into my mind – 'nor let me die before I have begun to live.' I think I was crying, but being so alone, consoled myself with the knowledge that no one else would ever know.
>
> I arrived at the balloon site. All was calm. While the world exploded around them, these incredible girls were quietly

tending their balloons. I sent a silent thank-you towards the heavens for our safety to this point, followed by another flurry of prayers to keep it that way . . . .

The violence of the raid increased, and finally we had to dash into the little aid raid shelter on the site and sit it out in the dark. The only comfort was the proximity of others. We were packed in and felt the closeness, emotionally as well as physically. None of us spoke, listening instead to the terrible, persistent bombing in the world outside our temporary cocoon of safety.

It was not until daybreak that the full horror became known. One of our balloon sites up on a hill on the far side of the city had received a direct hit, blowing the Nissen hut to smithereens and instantly killing several of the girls. The pretty little corporal in charge had her arm and shoulder blown off and suffered dreadful damage to one side of her face. In this appalling condition, she had managed to crawl to the Pioneer Corps position – nearly a quarter of a mile away – to raise the alarm. She had only been married the previous week, and her husband, an able seaman in the Navy, had just left for sea duty, destination unknown.

The ruin of these young lives, and the feeling of sick helplessness at the carnage of that night, marked a watershed in my life. Painful as my wartime losses had been, I had not been there at the ending of lives dear to me. I had been able to protect myself by giving dignity and purpose to their deaths, mentally burying the realities in flag-draped coffins. Now, as I stood with the other officers while parts of bodies were collected, I found myself shivering despite the warm sunshine. No one spoke and no one cried. The hurt was too deep, and our eyes too dry for tears. How could all this youth and freshness, this joy and promise, have ended in these torn, sad remnants? . . .

The next week was a blur. Nothing seemed quite real. We were called upon to accompany the bodies to their respective home towns and attend the funerals alongside the families. I was emotionally keyed up with pity, concern, and nerves, but what does remain in my mind after all these years was the pride and unaffected dignity with which these ordinary and unheroic people buried their children . . . . There were no parents to whom I spoke during that agonizing week who did not truly believe that the daughters they loved had died with honour in a just cause.[31]

Whilst the wartime women's auxiliary services might have represented a considerable gender advance for women, they did not, however, achieve equality with their 'parent' services. The ATS, WAAF and WRNS remained essentially auxiliary forces and across a wide spectrum of military life servicewomen were treated differently to their male counterparts. Despite nuances between the services, they continued, for example, to be predominantly utilised in 'feminine' jobs; they retained their own corps of 'administrative' officers who looked after the women's 'well being'; they did not receive equal pay; they were not subject to the same disciplinary sanctions (and in the case of the WRNS were not subject to the Naval Discipline Act at all); they faced restrictions on their overseas service; they received priority for release at the end of the war if they were married; and they were generally held to higher standards of off-duty behaviour. Above all, and in spite of some ambiguities, they were not to be used in direct combat roles. The voracious demands of 'total war' were thus undercut by the need to maintain gender conventions. Furthermore, the service departments' assessments of female performance were highly gendered. Whilst they were regarded as being more proficient than their male counterparts at routine sedentary jobs that required 'manual dexterity, neatness or accuracy' – skills, it might be added, that the RAF's Director of Technical Training was reported to have attributed to 'generations of patient delicate-fingered females who had devoted long hours to cross-stitch, petit-point or invisible mending'[32] – they were considered less accomplished in tasks that called for 'initiative, responsibility and drive', inclined 'to get flustered in emergency and more easily discouraged when up against difficulties'. In fact, their presence on occasion was justified on the grounds of maintaining male morale. Margaret and Patrice Higonnet have used the metaphor of a double helix to delineate a model of wartime gender relations in which women might have challenged conventional gender boundaries, but the underlying structures of female subordination remained the same. 'In this social dance,' they contend, 'the woman appears to have taken a step forward as the partners change places – but in fact he is still leading her'.[33]

    In explaining why the women's forces did not achieve greater wartime equality, the intractability of the male service establishment undoubtedly played a role. As the ATS hierarchy delicately put it, 'many cherished traditions and ideals, both of women as such and their place in a hitherto purely masculine organisation, had to be overcome'.[34] There was also public resistance to the creation of a female warrior corps. 'Boadicea was, in some ways, a noble character', remarked one male MP, 'but she has never been held up as the ideal of British womanhood. We do not want to see the ideal of British womanhood brought down to the pagan level of the Amazons or even to the level of Boadicea.'[35] But it was further due in part to the attitude of senior servicewomen and their perception of gender differences within the armed forces.[36] In the WRNS, Vera Laughton Mathews strongly believed that 'a woman's Service must be largely run by women' and its distinctive way of administering things 'was better for women than if it had been exactly on naval lines'.[37] In the ATS, Leslie Whateley contended that as a result of 'the peculiar psychology of women' it was 'utterly impossible ... to try to run a women's service on identical lines with those of a male organization'.[38] As for the WAAF, which was more closely assimilated in organisational terms with its 'parent' service than the other women's services, similar views were aired within Jane Trefusis-Forbes's directorate:

> It has been generally agreed that a service of women cannot in every way be run on similar lines as a force of men. The average woman, apart from her physique, it not likely naturally to adapt herself to Service conditions, unless handled sensitively and carefully.[39]

In a revealing interview with the American journalist and author Margaret Goldsmith, Jean Knox, head of the ATS from 1941 to 1943, almost seemed to decry the wartime gender advances of servicewomen:

> 'To build up an effective women's service like the ATS,' she said, 'one must always bear in mind that there are great psychological differences between men and women, and to get the best contribution for the country out of the women, this fact must be born in mind so that their special feminine talents and abilities can be used most effectively. The valuable contribution of women should be kept separate from that of men. They should not really walk side by side, for then women would inevitably get ahead, and this would have a disruptive effect on society. In an ideal world,' Mrs Knox added, 'women should be able to look up to men.'[40]

ATS staff officer Mary Thomson recalled that establishing a close working relationship with her male counterparts in AA Command was frowned upon by some in her service as somehow suspicious and as exploiting her feminine wiles: 'You weren't supposed to be helped by the men. If you said the men were helpful then immediately they thought, ah, ah, what's going on'. She felt she was walking 'a tightrope' and that 'she *gets on* with the men' was sometimes used as 'a derogatory remark'.[41]

Meanwhile, women in the forces appeared determined to retain their femininity whilst in uniform. It was reported that when ATS 'gunners' assumed operational duties in anti-aircraft batteries there was an increased interest in 'feminine matters of dress and appearance'.[42] In similar terms, PT sessions in the WAAF were said to have only been made tolerable to airwomen at RAF stations when presented, against the regulations, as 'health and beauty' classes.[43] Alongside this, reassuring messages were conveyed to the public to counter fears about the defeminising effects of military life. In a War Office-approved lecture to a conference on maternity and child welfare in 1942, the recently retired chief woman medical adviser to the ATS, Dr Letitia Fairfield, sought to allay such anxieties:

> It is sometime suggested that by working in close association with men on jobs usually reserved for men, and in men's clothes, women may be 'psychologically damaged' and find themselves turning into men. In my experience, for what it is worth, there is no cause for worry. Service women do not even get these ideas unless someone else puts them into their heads. They value their own homes all the more because they have had to leave them, and the more they work on men's jobs the more charmingly feminine do they become.[44]

Princess Elizabeth reinforced this message. At an ATS reunion in 1949 at the Royal Albert Hall, she observed that 'the rough, no less than the smooth, gave us a chance to develop qualities which should make us better wives, mothers, and citizens'.[45]

What was more, in the view of Wren Angela Mack, the majority of servicewomen did not see their military service as primarily a chance to break down doors marked 'men only'. 'There were certainly a few, but only a few, who enjoyed the idea of being male impersonators', she remarked. 'These pseudo macho characters sported Eton-cropped hair and enjoyed giving out crisp orders and relished prancing about on the parade ground.' Nonetheless, she argued that

> Looking back, I'm sure that most of us newcomers hoping to become members of the Women's Royal Naval Service were clear about one thing and that was that we were feminine creatures putting our normal lives on one side to help with the war effort. I don't remember that we thought much about 'freedom of opportunity' or the chance at last to show men what stuff we were made of.[46]

But the strongly masculine workplace culture within the armed forces could be inimical to servicewomen. The high proportion of men to women serving in these forces, combined with a working environment in which they worked and lived closely together in challenging and confined circumstances and a rank structure that could lead to abuses of power, were fertile grounds for sexual harassment by servicemen – a number of whom regarded their female counterparts as little more than 'slap-and-tickle girls' or 'comforts for the troops'.[47] Some women never seem to have encountered such behaviour. 'I think it is forgotten today', insisted WAAF clerk Dorothea Gray, 'how respectful men were with women during the war. There was never, although I worked in an office with seven or eight men, any of the sly nudging, the innuendos, the blue jokes or even the swearing one might have expected.'[48] Similarly, ATS driver Joan Stewart reminisced of her posting to a REME unit, in which five auxiliaries worked alongside a platoon of soldiers, that 'The men were lovely! They treated us like sisters. It was like belonging to a big family.'[49] Others, however, as we have seen, did experience sexual harassment and Alice Kessler-Harris has argued that such coercive behaviour in the workplace has 'long sustained male prerogative and unequal power relationships' and been 'a prime driver of persistent gender inequalities'.[50]

Some servicewomen looked back on their wartime lives and regarded the sexual harassment they encountered as little more than harmless fun. 'We took it all in good part', recollected Morfydd Brooks of the sexual 'banter' directed at her from RAF aircrew, 'because we knew the great strains they were under and the dangers they would soon face.'[51] But this was not the case for others. ATS cook, Constance Poolman, admitted that she was so distressed by the soldiers' wolf whistles and cat calls that she often had to hide away after doling out their tea in order to compose herself: 'I was so nervous I was trembling.'[52] On occasion, they suffered sickening physical injuries. One Waaf revealed that she and her fellow airwomen could not visit their latrines after dark for fear of being raped by soldiers from a nearby transit camp and that 'several girls had scars and black eyes' after violent assaults. Thereafter armed airmen were assigned to guard them with orders to shoot any intruder found on their site at night.[53]

At the end of the war, many of the gender complexities and ambiguities that characterised the wartime women's auxiliary services were still at play in the decision to create the permanent regular post-war women's forces. Again, the Admiralty was less eager to follow this path but eventually came into line with the War Office and the Air Ministry. On the face of it, this historic development could be interpreted as a feminist victory for servicewomen that rewarded them for their contribution to the British military war effort by opening up a new career for female personnel in the armed forces. But whilst the role of women was acknowledged by the service departments, and there was some recognition that they might well now expect to take their place alongside the peacetime regulars and be disappointed if excluded, the creation of these standing women's services was not the result of a great surge of feminism through the corridors of Whitehall. It was more the consequence of hard-headed calculations about the manpower requirements of the post-war armed forces and the need to create small regular women's cadres that were capable of expansion in times of future war – partly, it should be noted, in order to try and prevent a repetition of the male prejudices that had characterised male-female service relations in the early years of the 1939–45 conflict. Lucy Noakes has observed that the motto of the WRAC, '*suaviter in modo, fortiter in re*' ('gentle in manner, resolute in deed'), which fused the military attributes of strength and tenacity with the womanly virtues of tenderness and compassion, symbolised the gender tensions within the post-war services. 'Although the work of women in the military had finally been recognised and rewarded by the creation of a permanent space for them within the British armed forces,' she argues, 'this space was one which was entirely defined by their gender.'[54]

Perceptions of bravery could also be gendered. On 30 June 1942 Audrey Roche (then Audrey Coningham), a twenty-three-year-old WRNS officer from Sussex, was aboard the submarine depot ship HMS *Medway II*, having been evacuated from Alexandria as the

Figure C.1 WRNS officer Audrey Roche (then Audrey Coningham) who saved the life of Leading Seaman Leslie Crossman in 1942 (© Imperial War Museum)

Germans advanced into Egypt. Her ship, however, was sunk en route to Haifa by a German U-boat in the Mediterranean, with the loss of thirty of those on board and Roche was forced into the sea. Whilst swimming to safety, she came across Leading Seaman Leslie Crossman clinging to another sailor. Crossman was injured, could not swim and with no lifebelt was in imminent danger of drowning as his head kept disappearing beneath the waves. Even though she did not know how long she would be in the water, she unthinkingly gave the man her lifebelt and told him 'Lie still. You'll be all right. Trust me'. Her selfless act enabled Crossman to stay afloat until rescued by a boat while she eventually managed to reach another ship and was hauled aboard. The captain of the *Medway* reported that she had 'undoubtedly saved this man's life'. For her gallantry, Roche was recommended for the immediate award of the Albert Medal (which has since been superseded by the George Cross) and this nomination received the backing of the Commander-in-Chief of the Mediterranean fleet, Admiral Sir Henry Harwood, who had won fame at the Battle of the River Plate. However, the honours and awards committee in London decided that since a nearby male officer in the water had helped Roche to put the lifebelt on Crossman, and she was a strong swimmer, she had not put herself in undue danger and thus should be merely mentioned in despatches. It was suggested that some publicity should be given to her action 'which will bring credit to the WRNS', but that this 'would not redound nearly so favourably if there were any suggestion that Miss Coningham was granted a decoration which might be regarded as easily won'. Despite the parsimony of the authorities, Roche wore her Oak Leaf decoration with pride and is thought to be the only women to have been decorated for bravery at sea during the war. Yet it was an indication of some of the challenges that Roche and others like her posed to the male warrior culture that the reaction of one naval officer to seeing her display the decoration was said to have been 'outrage' since he simply 'could not believe that she was entitled to it'. On a happier note, it might be recorded that, unlike Daphne Pearson, Roche *was* able to meet again the man she saved. At a reunion in 1987 a grinning Crossman, who had gone on to be decorated himself for gallantry, was reintroduced to his wartime saviour. Roche, however, did not immediately recognise him. 'I can't pretend I would have picked you out', she quipped to Crossman. 'You weren't smiling when we last met.'[55]

NOTES

Prologue

1. *Instructions for American servicemen in Britain 1942* (Washington DC: War Department, 1942; Oxford: Bodleian Library, 2004), p. 25.
2. Imperial War Museum, Southwark, London (IWM), papers of J. D. M. Pearson, Documents.2442, letter from Daphne Pearson to her mother, May 1940; IWM, Pearson, Documents.2442, R. Brooks, 'A Waaf at Detling 40 years ago', *Bygone Kent*, undated; The National Archives of the UK, Kew, London (TNA), Air Ministry papers (AIR), AIR 2/8883, letter from R. Knox to Sir Arthur Street, 8 July 1940; 'Corporal (now Assistant Section Officer) Joan Daphne Mary Pearson, Women's Auxiliary Air Force', *London Gazette*, 19 July 1940, p. 4434; D. Pearson, *In war and peace: the life and times of Daphne Pearson GC: the first woman to receive the George Cross* (London: Thorogood, 2001), pp. 84–6; 'Daphne Pearson GC', obituary, *Daily Telegraph*, 26 July 2000, p. 29; 'Daphne Pearson GC', obituary, *Times*, 26 July 2000, p. 19; A. B. Sainsbury, 'Daphne Pearson', obituary, *Independent*, 31 July 2000, p. 6; D. Condell, 'Daphne Pearson: first woman to receive a gallantry award in the Second World War', *Guardian*, 31 July 2000, p. 18.
3. M. Goldsmith, *Women at war* (London: Lindsay Drummond, 1943), p. 76.
4. Central Statistical Office, *Fighting with figures* (London: HMSO, 1995), p. 39. The ATS strength peaked in September 1943, that of the WAAF in June 1943 and that of the WRNS in September 1944.
5. TNA, War Office papers (WO), WO 73/159, 'Analysis of strength by nationality' in 'General return of the strength of the British army on the 31 Dec. 1943', table vii, pp. 287–8.
6. Central Statistical Office, *Fighting with figures*, p. 40. It was reported that between 1942 and 1944, 92% of ATS recruits had had an elementary and post-primary education without taking a school certificate; 5.3% had taken a school certificate; and 0.7% a higher school certificate. Before joining up, 31% were said to have worked in clerical jobs; 15% in shops; 16% in domestic service; and 23% in unskilled manual work. See T. H. Hawkins and L. J. F. Brimble, *Adult education: the record of the British army* (London: Macmillan & Co, 1947), p. 148.
7. This figure is calculated from the lists of members of the three women's services who died between September 1939 and September 1945, as recorded by the Commonwealth

War Graves Commission: www.cwgc.org (accessed 16 September 2019). Also see TNA, WO 277/6, 'The Auxiliary Territorial Service', compiled by Controller J. M. Cowper ATS, War Office, 1949, app. vi, p. 279; B. E. Escott, *Women in air force blue: the story of women in the Royal Air Force from 1918 to the present day* (Wellingborough: Patrick Stephens, 1989), app. 'm', p. 303; *Strength and casualties of the armed forces and auxiliary services of the United Kingdom 1939 to 1945*, Cmd. 6832 (London: HMSO, 1946), p. 9.

8. P. Scott, *They made invasion possible* (London: Hutchinson, 1944), p. 31.

9. B. Pimlott, *The Queen: a biography of Elizabeth II* (London: Harper Collins, 1996), pp. 74–5; L. Whateley, *As thoughts survive* (London: Hutchinson, 1949), pp. 152, 158–9; B. Castle, *The Castle diaries 1964–1976* (London: Papermac, 1990), p. 213.

10. 'Court Circular', *Times*, 21 Nov. 1947, p. 8.

11. See, for example, J. Terraine, *The right of the line: the Royal Air Force in the European war 1939–1945* (Sevenoaks: Sceptre, 1988); P. Bishop, *Air force blue: the RAF in World War Two: spearhead of victory* (London: William Collins, 2017); C. Barnett, *Engage the enemy more closely: the Royal Navy in the Second World War* (London: Penguin Books, 2000); D. Redford, *A history of the Royal Navy: World War II* (London: I. B. Tauris, 2014); G. Prysor, *Citizen sailors: the Royal Navy in the Second World War* (London: Penguin Books, 2012); D. Fraser, *And we shall shock them: the British army in the Second World War* (Sevenoaks: Sceptre, 1988); D. French, *Raising Churchill's army: the British army and the war against Germany 1919–1945* (Oxford: Oxford University Press, 2000); A. Allport, *Browned off and bloody-minded: the British soldier goes to war, 1939–1945* (London: Yale University Press, 2015); J. Fennell, *Fighting the people's war: the British and Commonwealth armies and the Second World War* (Cambridge: Cambridge University Press, 2019). The present author is also guilty of this in a previous work: J. A. Crang, *The British army and the people's war 1939–1945* (Manchester: Manchester University Press, 2000).

12. See, for example, K. Bentley Beauman, *Partners in blue: the story of women's service with the Royal Air Force* (London: Hutchinson, 1971); Escott, *Women in air force blue*; T. Stone, 'Creating a (gendered?) military identity: the Women's Auxiliary Air Force in Great Britain during the Second World War', *Women's History Review*, vol. 8, no. 4 (1999); M. H. Fletcher, *The WRNS: a history of the Women's Royal Naval Service* (London: Batsford, 1989); U. Stuart Mason, *Britannia's daughters: the story of the WRNS* (London: Leo Cooper, 1992); J. Stanley, *Women and the Royal Navy* (London: I. B. Tauris, 2018); H. Roberts, *The WRNS in wartime: the Women's Royal Naval Service 1917–45* (London: I. B. Tauris, 2018); S. Bidwell, *The Women's Royal Army Corps* (London: Leo Cooper, 1977); R. Terry, *Women in khaki: the story of the British woman soldier* (London: Columbus Books, 1988); L. Noakes, *Women in the British army: war and the gentle sex 1907–1948* (London: Routledge, 2006).

13. See, for example, G. J. DeGroot, '"I love the scent of cordite in your hair": gender dynamics in mixed anti-aircraft batteries during the Second World War', *History*, vol. 82, no. 265 (1997); G. J. DeGroot, 'Whose finger on the trigger? Mixed anti-aircraft batteries and the female combat taboo', *War in History*, vol. 4, no. 4 (1997); J. Schwarzkopf, 'Combatant or non-combatant? The ambiguous status of women in British anti-aircraft batteries during the Second World War', *War & Society*, vol. 28, no. 2 (2009); G. Natzio, 'Homeland defence: British gunners, women and ethics during the Second World War' in C. Lee and P. E. Strong (eds), *Women in war* (Barnsley: Pen & Sword, 2012).

14. Pearson, *In war and peace*, pp. 172–213; 'Her act of courage means everything to the Bond family: she ignored flames and bombs to rescue man who would become helicopter king', *Daily Mail*, 15 May 1995, p. 23.
15. Quoted in Pearson, *In war and peace*, p. i.
16. Quoted in 'Her act of courage'.
17. It is said that Knight agreed to paint the portrait for a fee of thirty-five guineas. See J. Dunbar, *Laura Knight* (London: Collins, 1975), p. 157.
18. IWM, Pearson, Documents.2442, letter from Daphne Pearson to her mother, 31 Aug. 1940.
19. Pearson, *In war and peace*, p. 97; R. Aspden, 'War through women's eyes', *New Statesman*, 16 Mar. 2009, p. 46; K. Palmer, *Women war artists* (London: Tate Publishing, 2011), pp. 31, 33; B. C. Morden, *Laura Knight: a life* (Pembroke Dock, Pembrokeshire: McNidder & Grace, 2014), p. 209.
   A note on surnames: it should be recorded that, for the convenience of readers, the surnames of former members of the women's services whose experiences are cited in this book generally appear as the surnames under which the women's memoirs have been published, or the surnames under which their papers have been catalogued in the archives. In a number of cases these might be the later married names of the women concerned, rather than their wartime maiden names.

Revival

1. H. Popham, *The FANY in peace & war: the story of the First Aid Nursing Yeomanry 1907–2003* (London: Leo Cooper, 2003), pp. 15–46; Marchioness of Londonderry, *Retrospect* (London: Frederick Muller, 1938), pp. 111–24; H. Gwynne-Vaughan, *Service with the army* (London: Hutchinson, 1942), pp. 9–71; Bidwell, *The Women's Royal Army Corps*, pp. 1–29; Terry, *Women in khaki*, pp. 32–84; C. Messenger, *Call to arms: the British army 1914–18* (London: Weidenfeld and Nicholson, 2005), pp. 243–64; Noakes, *Women in the British army*, pp. 53–81; S. Philo-Gill, *The Women's Army Auxiliary Corps in France, 1917–1921* (Barnsley: Pen & Sword, 2017), passim; Beauman, *Partners in blue*, pp. 1–53; Escott, *Women in air force blue*, pp. 9–73; K. Furse, *Hearts and pomegranates: the story of forty-five years, 1875–1920* (London: Peter Davies, 1940), pp. 360–90; Fletcher, *The WRNS*, pp. 11–24; Stuart Mason, *Britannia's daughters*, pp. 1–31; Roberts, *The WRNS in wartime*, pp. 16–61; National Army Museum, Chelsea, London (NAM), papers of F. Coulshed, 9401-243-158, N. L. Goldman, 'The utilization of women in combat: the armed forces of Great Britain, World War I and World War II', 13 Oct. 1978, pp. 40–6. For the sake of brevity, the term 'military authorities' will encompass the army, RAF and Royal Navy. An earlier version of this chapter appeared in *Historical Research*, vol. 83, issue 220 (2010), 'The revival of the British women's auxiliary services in the late nineteen-thirties,' pp. 343–57. I am grateful to the executive editor for permission to reproduce it here.
2. J. M. Gould, 'The women's corps: the establishment of women's military services in Britain' (PhD thesis, University of London, 1988), pp. 341–54; L. Noakes, 'Demobilising the military women: constructions of class and gender in Britain after the First World War', *Gender & History*, vol. 19, no. 1 (2007), pp. 147–8; M. Pugh, *Women and the women's movement in Britain 1914–1959* (London: Macmillan, 1992), p. 72; Noakes, *Women in the British army*, pp. 84–5; Bidwell, *The Women's Royal Army Corps*, pp. 28, 31; Escott, *Women in air force blue*, pp. 70–3, 84; Stuart Mason, *Britannia's daughters*, pp. 28–31. One naval commander commented retrospectively in 1941 that 'In the last war some of the Women's

Services were controlled by women who were strong Feminists and there is a widely held opinion that the Services did not in the final outcome profit by the intrusion of strong Feminist ideas'. See TNA, ADM 116/5102, letter from Commander-in-Chief, Portsmouth, to Secretary of the Admiralty, 10 Apr. 1941.

3. TNA, WO 32/10652, 'Report of the women's reserve committee', 3 Dec. 1920; TNA, WO 163/26, minutes of the 281st meeting of the Army Council, 2 June 1921; Gould, 'The women's corps', pp. 354–8; Noakes, 'Demobilising the military women', pp. 151–2.

4. Bidwell, *The Women's Royal Army Corps*, pp. 32–3; J. M. Cowper, 'Women in the fighting services', in H. G. Thursfield (ed.), *Brassey's annual: the armed forces yearbook 1957* (London: William Clowes & Sons, 1957), pp. 291–2.

5. D. Urquhart, 'Stewart, Edith Helen Vane-Tempest-, marchioness of Londonderry (1878–1959)', *Oxford Dictionary of National Biography (ODNB)*, online edition (2008): www.oxforddnb.com/view/10.1093/ref:odnb/9780198614128.001.0001/odnb-9780198614128-e-45461 (accessed 26 July 2019); A. Jackson, 'Stewart, Charles Stewart Henry Vane-Tempest-, 7th marquess of Londonderry (1878–1949)', *ODNB*, online edition (2008): www.oxforddnb.com/view/10.1093/ref:odnb/9780198614128.001.0001/odnb-9780198614128-e-36627 (accessed 26 July 2019); R. M. Douglas, *Feminist freikorps: the British Voluntary Women Police 1914–1940* (Westport, Conn: Praeger, 1999), pp. 115–24; M. S. Allen, *Lady in blue* (London: Stanley & Co., 1936), pp. 272–3; E. Londonderry, 'National efficiency: a plea for the organisation of women', *The Nineteenth Century and After*, vol. 115 (1934), pp. 85–90; TNA, WO 32/10650, E. Londonderry, letter to the editor, *Times*, 9 Nov. 1933; TNA, WO 32/10650, M. S. Allen, letter to the editor, *Times*, 15 Dec. 1933; TNA, WO 32/10650, draft letter from Lady Londonderry, 16 Dec. 1933; National Maritime Museum, Greenwich, London (NMM), papers of HMS *Dauntless* (DAU) 180/2, 'The Women's Legion', undated.

6. TNA, WO 32/10650, letter from P. Synnott to Private Secretary, 24 Jan. 1934; TNA, WO 32/10650, letter from H. Creedy to Lady Londonderry, 26 Jan. 1934; TNA, WO 32/10650, 'Women's legion', draft memorandum for the cabinet, 29 May 1935; TNA, AIR 2/3036, 'Notes in connection with Marchioness of Londonderry's letter of 29 March 1938'.

7. TNA, Admiralty papers (ADM), ADM 116/3701, minute by DP, 14 Aug. 1934; TNA, AIR 2/1601, notes of a meeting, 27 Feb. 1935; TNA, ADM 116/3701, 'Women's reserve', War Office, Apr. 1937.

8. M. R. S. Creese, 'Vaughan, Dame Helen Charlotte Isabella Gwynne- (1879–1967)', *ODNB*, online edition (2004): www.oxforddnb.com/view/10.1093/ref:odnb/9780198614128.001.0001/odnb-9780198614128-e-33623 (accessed 26 July 2019); Gwynne-Vaughan, *Service with the army*, pp. 12–14, 66–7, 76–8; M. Izzard, *A heroine in her time: a life of Dame Helen Gwynne-Vaughan, 1879–1967* (London: Macmillan, 1969), pp. 184–5, 261–2.

9. Gwynne-Vaughan, *Service with the army*, p. 78; Izzard, *A heroine in her time*, p. 263.

10. TNA, Cabinet papers (CAB), CAB 57/18, letter from H. Gwynne-Vaughan to War Office and Air Ministry, 5 Feb. 1936.

11. NAM, papers of H. Gwynne-Vaughan, 9401-253-104, letter from H. Gwynne-Vaughan to Lt.-Gen. Sir Harry Knox, 5 Feb. 1936.

12. NAM, Gwynne-Vaughan, 9401-253-105, letter from Lt.-Gen. Sir Harry Knox to H. Gwynne-Vaughan, 6 Feb. 1936.

13. TNA, CAB 57/18, Committee of Imperial Defence, sub-committee on man-power, women's reserve sub-committee, minutes of meeting, 10 Oct. 1935; TNA, WO 32/

10652, Committee of Imperial Defence, sub-committee on man-power, women's reserve sub-committee, report, 12 May 1936.

14. TNA, AIR 10/5546, 'The Women's Auxiliary Air Force', Air Ministry (AHB), 1953, p. 2; Noakes, *Women in the British army*, pp. 96–7.

15. TNA, AIR 2/3036, memorandum by Lady Londonderry, 29 Mar. 1938; NAM, Gwynne-Vaughan, 9401-253-118, letter from H. Gwynne-Vaughan to the Secretary, War Office, 5 Oct. 1936.

16. TNA, WO 32/10652, women's reserve sub-committee, report.

17. Gwynne-Vaughan, *Service with the army*, p. 79; Izzard, *A heroine in her time*, pp. 267–8.

18. Gwynne-Vaughan, *Service with the army*, p. 81; Izzard, *A heroine in her time*, pp. 265, 268; NAM, Gwynne-Vaughan, 9401-253-280, letter from H. Gwynne-Vaughan to Lord Wakefield, 12 Feb. 1938.

19. NAM, Gwynne-Vaughan, 9401-253-242, letter from Kitty Trenchard to H. Gwynne-Vaughan, 31 Oct. 1937; NAM, Gwynne-Vaughan, 9401-253-243, letter from Gwynne-Vaughan to Trenchard, 1 Nov. 1937; NAM, Gwynne-Vaughan, 9401-253-244, letter from Trenchard to Gwynne-Vaughan, 3 Nov. 1937; NAM, Gwynne-Vaughan, 9401-253-246, draft letter to Unity Mitford, undated; Izzard, *A heroine in her time*, p. 265; D. Pryce-Jones, *Unity Mitford: a quest* (London: Phoenix Giants, 1995), pp. 178–9.

20. Gwynne-Vaughan, *Service with the army*, pp. 79–81; TNA, AIR 2/2694, 'A women's OTC', *Times*, 16 Oct. 1937.

21. Quoted in Gwynne-Vaughan *Service with the army*, p. 81.

22. Ibid., p. 80.

23. TNA, AIR 2/1601, '"Commandant" Mary Allen and the Women's Reserve', Home Office, Sept. 1936.

24. Douglas, *Feminist freikorps*, p. 126. Also see L. A. Jackson, *Women police: gender, welfare and surveillance in the twentieth century* (Manchester: Manchester University Press, 2006), p. 22.

25. TNA, AIR 2/1601, letter from H. L. Ismay to Miss Allen, 13 Oct. 1936.

26. TNA, AIR 2/3036, memorandum by Lady Londonderry, 29 March 1938.

27. TNA, ADM 116/3701, 'Women's reserve', War Office, Apr. 1937; TNA, ADM 116/3701, letter from A. Duff Cooper to Ernest Brown, 27 Apr. 1937; TNA, ADM 116/3701, letter from Brown to Duff Cooper, 28 May 1937.

28. TNA, AIR 2/2694, letter from H. Knox to Lady Loch and Dame Helen Gywnne-Vaughan, 4 Aug. 1937.

29. TNA, WO 163/47, Informal Army Council, précis No. 5, 'Supply of women for supervisory posts in war', by H. J. Creedy, 6 Nov. 1937; Gould, 'The women's corps', pp. 366-7.

30. Gould, 'The women's corps', p. 367.

31. Churchill Archives Centre, Churchill College, Cambridge (CAC), papers of I. L. Hore-Belisha, HOBE 1/5, diary entry, 14 Jan. 1938; TNA, WO 277/6, 'The Auxiliary Territorial Service', p. 2.

32. CAC, Hore-Belisha, HOBE 5/17, 'The organisation of the army for its role in war', cabinet paper by L. H.-B., 10 Feb. 1938, pp. 4–5. Also see TNA, CAB 92/112, 'Women's auxiliary services', note prepared by the Air Ministry, 6 Apr. 1943.

33. Bidwell, *The Women's Royal Army Corps*, pp. 36–7; TNA, WO 32/10652, AG to PUS, 14 Jan. 1938.

34. Izzard, *A heroine in her time*, p. 271.

35. NAM, Gwynne-Vaughan, 9401-253-274, letter from Dorothy Jackson to H. Gywnne-Vaughan, 31 Dec. 1937.

36. NAM, Gwynne-Vaughan, 9401-253-133, letter from Jackson to Gwynne-Vaughan, 6 Dec. 1937.

37. TNA, WO 163/47, proceedings of the 11th meeting of the Informal Army Council, 22 Nov. 1937; TNA, WO 32/10652, 'Formation of a women's reserve in peace to embrace all branches of the army', by J. Patrick, 22 Dec. 1937.

38. CAC, Hore-Belisha, HOBE 1/5, diary entry, 12 Jan. 1938.

39. TNA, WO 32/10652, minutes of a meeting of the co-ordinating committee of the Army Council, 1 Apr. 1938.

40. Gwynne-Vaughan, *Service with the army*, pp. 82–3; TNA, WO 32/10652, letter from H. J. Creedy to the Secretary, Committee of Imperial Defence, 6 Apr. 1938.

41. TNA, CAB 57/27, Committee of Imperial Defence, man-power sub-committee, sub-committee on the control of man-power, minutes of the 4th meeting, 12 May 1938.

42. TNA, WO 32/10652, record of a meeting to consider the formation of a women's auxiliary corps, 6 May 1938; TNA, WO 32/10652, record of a meeting, 23 June 1938; TNA, WO 277/6, 'The Auxiliary Territorial Service', p. 2; Izzard, *A heroine in her time*, pp. 268, 328; L. Beardwood, 'Ellis, Mary Baxter (1892–1968)', *ODNB*, online edition (2004): www.oxforddnb.com/view/10.1093/ref:odnb/9780198614128.001.0001/odnb-9780198614128-e-70523 (accessed 27 July 2019).

43. TNA, WO 32/10652, 'Women's auxiliary corps', record of a meeting, 5 May 1938; TNA, AIR 2/3036, W. G. Clements to AMP, 6 July 1938; TNA, ADM 234/219, 'Histories of special subjects 1939–1945', BR 1076, 'The Women's Royal Naval Service', Admiralty, 1956, pp. 2–3.

44. TNA, WO 32/10652, 'Auxiliary Territorial Service', draft scheme, June 1938; TNA, WO 32/10652, DDTA to US of S, 24 June 1938; TNA, WO 277/6, 'The Auxiliary Territorial Service', pp. 2–4; Gwynne-Vaughan, *Service with the army*, p. 87.

45. TNA, WO 277/6, 'The Auxiliary Territorial Service', pp. 2–3.

46. Izzard, *A heroine in her time*, pp. 280–1. See also R. J. Minney, *The Private Papers of Hore-Belisha* (London: Collins, 1960), pp. 67–8, 78; and A. Boyle, *Trenchard: man of vision* (London: Collins, 1962), p. 710.

47. Terry, *Women in khaki*, pp. 95–6.

48. Izzard, *A heroine in her time*, p. 281.

49. Gwynne-Vaughan, *Service with the army*, pp. 94–5.

50. NAM, Gywnne-Vaughan, 9401-253-471, letter from Molly Grundy to H. Gwynne-Vaughan, 24 Oct. 1938.

51. TNA, WO 277/6, 'The Auxiliary Territorial Service', pp. 8–9, 277.

52. Whateley, *As thoughts survive*, p. 15.

53. TNA, WO 32/13160, 'Army post-war problems: future of the women's services', report of the standing committee on army post-war problems, 15 May 1945.

54. TNA, WO 277/6, 'The Auxiliary Territorial Service', p. 5; Gwynne-Vaughan, *Service with the army*, pp. 89, 100; J. Rosenzweig, 'The construction of policy for women in the British armed forces 1938–45' (M.Litt thesis, University of Oxford, 1993), pp. 83–4.

55. Izzard, *A heroine in her time*, pp. 284–5.

56. Ibid., pp. 277, 285.

57. NAM, Gwynne-Vaughan, 9401-253-861, letter from H. Gwynne-Vaughan to Mrs. Ross, 28 Apr. 1939.

58. NAM, Gwynne-Vaughan, 9401-253-890, letter from Justina Collins to H. Gwynne-Vaughan, 2 May 1939.

59. NAM, Gwynne-Vaughan, 9401-253-891, letter from Gwynne-Vaughan to Collins, 3 May 1939.

60. Terry, *Women in khaki*, p. 102; Izzard, *A heroine in her time*, p. 295.

61. Terry, *Women in khaki*, pp. 99–103; A. De Courcy, *Debs at war 1939–45: how wartime changed their lives* (London: Weidenfeld and Nicolson, 2005), pp. 53, 73–5; Izzard, *A heroine in her time*, pp. 321–4; Popham, *The FANY in peace & war*, pp. 61–9; I. Ward, *FANY invicta* (London: Hutchinson, 1955), pp. 109–38. The FANY claimed that the War Office reneged on a promise that it would be allowed to retain its 'entity' if incorporated into the ATS.

62. TNA, AIR 10/5546, 'The Women's Auxiliary Air Force', pp. 3–4; TNA, AIR 2/3036, D of O to AMSO, Dec. 1938; TNA, AIR 2/3036, letter from Air Ministry to the Secretaries, Territorial Army and Air Force Associations, 27 Jan. 1939.

63. TNA, AIR 10/5546, 'The Women's Auxiliary Air Force', pp. 4–5; TNA, AIR 2/3115, 'Auxiliary Territorial Service: Royal Air Force companies', minutes of a meeting, 20 Apr. 1939; TNA, AIR 2/3115, AMP to S of S, 25 Apr. 1939; TNA, AIR 2/3115, CAS to S of S, 27 Apr. 1939; TNA, AIR 2/3115, AWS to US of S and S of S, 6 May 1939.

64. TNA, AIR 10/5546, 'The Women's Auxiliary Air Force', pp. 5–7; TNA, AIR 41/65, 'Manning: plans and policy', RAF monograph, air historical branch, Air Ministry, 1958, pp. 199–200; TNA, AIR 2/3115, letter from E. A. Shearing to Air Officers Commanding-in-Chief, Bomber Command, Fighter Command, Coastal Command, Balloon Command, 18 July 1939; Beauman, *Partners in blue*, pp. 68–9; 'Women's Auxiliary Air Force', *Times*, 3 July 1939, p. 8; Royal Air Force Museum, Hendon, London (RAFM), papers of K. J. Trefusis Forbes, AC 72/17/1, box 1, 'Discipline', undated; T. Stone, 'Forbes, Dame (Katherine) Jane Trefusis (1899–1971)', *ODNB*, online edition (2008): www.oxforddnb.com/view/10.1093/ref:odnb/9780198614128.001.0001/odnb-9780198614128-e-51971 (accessed 27 July 2019).

65. P. Joubert de la Ferté, *The forgotten ones: the story of the ground crews* (London: Hutchinson & Co., 1961), p. 150.

66. F. Peake, *Pure chance* (Shrewsbury: Airlife, 1993), p. 23.

67. TNA, AIR 10/5546, 'The Women's Auxiliary Air Force', pp. 7, 131; Beauman, *Partners in blue* p. 68; T. Stone, 'The integration of women into a military service: the Women's Auxiliary Air Force in the Second World War' (PhD thesis, University of Cambridge, 1998), pp. 48–9.

68. TNA, ADM 234/219, 'The Women's Royal Naval Service', pp. 1–2; V. L. Mathews, 'Furse, Dame Katharine (1875–1952)', rev. A. McConnell, *ODNB*, online edition (2004): www.oxforddnb.com/view/10.1093/ref:odnb/9780198614128.001.0001/odnb-9780198614128-e-33300/version/0 (accessed 27 July 2019); TNA, ADM 116/3701, letter from K. Furse to the Secretary, the Admiralty, 8 Sept. 1937; TNA, ADM 116/3701, letter from H. Eastwood to Furse, 12 Oct. 1937; TNA, ADM 116/3701, letter from Furse to Eastwood, 27 Oct. 1937; TNA, ADM 116/3701, letter from Eastwood to Furse, 12 Nov. 1937; TNA, ADM 116/3701, letter from Furse to Eastwood, 28 Mar. 1938; TNA, ADM 116/3701, letter from Eastwood to Furse, 30 Mar. 1938; TNA, ADM 116/3701, 'Correspondence between Dame Katharine Furse and the Prime Minister's private secretary on the subject of women's activities in war or emergency', 26 May 1938.

69. TNA, ADM 116/3701, 'Women's auxiliary corps', 31 May 1938; TNA, ADM 116/3701, A. S. Le Maitre to Deputy Secretary, undated; TNA, ADM 116/3701, Admiralty Board minutes, 25 July 1938; TNA, ADM 116/3701, letter from S. H. Phillips to Commanders-in-Chief, Portsmouth, Plymouth, The Nore, Rear Admiral and Commanding Officer, Coast of Scotland, Admiral Commanding Reserves, Adjutant-General Royal Marines, 19 Aug. 1938; TNA, ADM 234/219, 'The Women's Royal Naval Service', pp. 2–11.

70. TNA, ADM 234/219, 'The Women's Royal Naval Service', pp. 5–6; Ministry of Labour, *National service: a guide to the ways in which the people of this country may give service* (London: HMSO, 1939), p. 32; V. L. Mathews, *Blue tapestry* (London: Hollis & Carter, 1948), p. 51.

71. Mathews, *Blue tapestry*, pp. 50–3; L. Thomas, 'Mathews, Dame Elvira Sibyl Maria Laughton (1888–1959)', *ODNB*, online edition (2004): www.oxforddnb.com /view/10.1093/ref:odnb/9780198614128.001.0001/odnb-9780198614128-e-34937 (accessed 27 July 2019). Laughton Mathews's father was the eminent naval historian, Professor Sir John Laughton.

72. Mathews, *Blue tapestry*, p. 61; Stuart Mason, *Britannia's daughters*, p. 37. The announcement appeared in newspapers on 14 Apr.

73. TNA, ADM 234/219, 'The Women's Royal Naval Service', pp. 21–4, 28; NMM, DAU 168, 'Women's Royal Naval Service', lecture to SOTC, 9 Jan. 1953.

74. Mathews, *Blue tapestry*, p. 79.

75. Ibid., p. 68.

76. TNA, ADM 234/219, 'The Women's Royal Naval Service', p. 45; NMM, DAU 168, 'Women's Royal Naval Service', lecture to SOTC.

Organisation and Recruitment

1. TNA, AIR 10/5546, 'The Women's Auxiliary Air Force', pp. 9–17; TNA, AIR 2/9408, 'Duties and status of the Director of the Women's Auxiliary Air Force', Air Ministry Order A567, 8 Aug. 1940; TNA, AIR 2/9408, 'The Women's Auxiliary Air Force', Air Ministry order A578, 8 Aug. 1940; TNA, AIR 72/26, 'The Women's Auxiliary Air Force', Air Ministry Order A83, 29 Jan. 1942; *Report of the committee on amenities and welfare conditions in the three women's services*, cmd. 6384 (London: HMSO, 1942), pp. 13–14; Escott, *Women in air force blue*, p. 113; Stone, 'The integration of women into a military service', pp. 57–62, 68–84. Stone provides an excellent overview of the development of WAAF organisation and administration. It should be noted that material from this chapter appeared in *Defence Studies*, vol. 8, no. 3 (2008): '"Come into the Army, Maud": Women, military conscription and the Markham Inquiry', pp. 381–95. I am grateful to Taylor and Francis for permission to reproduce it here.

2. TNA, ADM 1/11837, 'Disciplinary regulations for the Women's Royal Naval Service', Admiralty, 1940; TNA, ADM 182/113, 'WRNS administration', Admiralty Fleet Order 261, 21 Jan. 1943; NMM, DAU 169, 'The organisation and activities of the WRNS during the war', undated; *Report of the committee on amenities and welfare conditions in the three women's services*, p. 12; Mathews, *Blue tapestry*, pp. 128–9; Stuart Mason, *Britannia's daughters*, p. 50.

3. TNA, WO 277/6, 'The Auxiliary Territorial Service', pp. 10–14, 23–7, 43–4, 53–9, 90; War Office, *Regulations for the Auxiliary Territorial Service* (London: HMSO, 1941); *Report of the committee on amenities and welfare conditions in the three women's services*, pp. 13–15; Liddell Hart Centre for Military Archives, King's College, London (LHCMA), papers of R. F. Adam, 3/13, 'Various administrative aspects of the Second World War', 1960, ch. viii, p. 3; Whateley, *As thoughts survive*, p. 86.

4. Stone, 'The integration of women into a military service', p. 161.

5. TNA, AIR 2/8362, 'Organisation of the Women's Auxiliary Air Force', note by AMSO and AMP, 5 Dec. 1941.

6. M. Francis, *The flyer: British culture and the Royal Air Force, 1939–1945* (Oxford: Oxford University Press, 2008), pp. 14–16, 32–5.

7. Joubert de la Ferté, *The forgotten* ones, p. 150
8. RAFM, Trefusis Forbes, AC 72/17/1, box 7, 'Talk by the DWAAF to officers at Air Ministry', 26 Jan. 1940, p. 5.
9. RAFM, Trefusis Forbes, AC 72/17/1, box 3, notes of a meeting with Mr Shearing, 3 Nov. 1942. It was claimed that the WAAF was mocked by the ATS and WRNS for being 'run by the RAF'. See RAFM, papers of C. Woodhead, X002-5638, box 1, '"As we knew them": a brief account of the WAAF from 1939 to 1945', by C. Woodhead (with the final chapter written by Vera Atkins), undated, ch. vii, 'The WAAF is taken for granted', p. 14.
10. TNA, AIR 2/9408, 'Notes of discussion on WAAF administration', 4 May 1940.
11. *Report of the committee on amenities and welfare conditions in the three women's services*, p. 14.
12. TNA, Treasury papers (T), T 189/10, 'Question 7', app. 'g' to 'Work and remuneration of women in the Auxiliary Territorial Service', War Office, 1945; TNA, T 189/10, 'Question 7', enclosure with Air Ministry letter to Royal Commission on Equal Pay, Air Ministry, 5 June 1945; TNA, T 189/12, 'Statement for the Royal Commission on Equal Pay', Admiralty, 1945.
13. RAFM, Woodhead, X002-5638, box 2, AHB monograph, no author [but C. Woodhead], undated, ch. v, 'System of administration', p. 15; G. J. DeGroot, '"I love the scent of cordite in your hair"', p. 87.
14. TNA, WO 32/10031, 'It is an honour to serve your country with the Auxiliary Territorial Service', War Office, Apr. 1941; TNA, WO 277/6, 'The Auxiliary Territorial Service', pp. 15–17, 28–31, 67–71, 216–17; *Regulations for the Auxiliary Territorial Service 1941*, pp. 27–30; TNA, WO 32/10663, JAG to AUS, 30 Dec. 1944; TNA, AIR 2/6373, 'Women's Auxiliary Air Force: notes for the information of candidates', Air Ministry, July 1941; TNA, AIR 10/5546, 'The Women's Auxiliary Air Force', pp. 7–8, 38, 59–62; R. Vogeleisen, *In their own words: women who served in World War II* (Cirencester: Mereo Books, 2015), p. 28; TNA, AIR 2/9278, JAG to DPS, 30 Dec. 1944; TNA, WO 32/10663, 'Compulsory posting overseas of members of Auxiliary Territorial Service and Women's Auxiliary Air Force: case for the opinion of the law officers', by Treasury Solicitor, 11 Jan. 1945; TNA, WO 32/10663, 'Compulsory posting overseas of members of Auxiliary Territorial Service and Women's Auxiliary Air Force: opinion: the law officers of the crown', by D. B. Somervell and D. P. Maxwell Fyfe, 12 Jan. 1945; National Museum of the Royal Navy (NMRN), WRNS collection, RNM 1990/230/10, 'Women's Royal Naval Service: join the Wrens and free a man for the fleet', Admiralty, undated; TNA, ADM 234/219, 'The Women's Royal Naval Service', pp. 45–51, 54–6, 81; TNA, ADM 116/5725, 'Notes on the maintenance of WRNS organisation in peace for embodiment in draft cabinet paper', by J. G. Lang, 30 Mar. 1946. The upper age limit for the WRNS was forty-five (rather than forty-three for the ATS and WAAF) but all the women's services were prepared to accept women up to and including the age of forty-nine if they had exceptional qualifications or experience. For a period in 1941 some volunteers for the ATS were able to enrol for UK service only. From the autumn of 1943, the WRNS 'immobile' branch was no longer open to new volunteers.
15. TNA, WO 277/6, 'The Auxiliary Territorial Service', pp. 31, 69. The WAAF also admitted enemy aliens, but the WRNS did not. See N. Bentwich, *I understand the risks: the story of refugees from Nazi oppression who fought in the British forces in the World War* (London: Victor Gollancz, 1950), pp. 154–9.
16. TNA, Records of the Government Social Survey Department (RG), RG 23/5, 'An investigation of the attitudes of women, the general public and ATS personnel to

the Auxiliary Territorial Service', the Social Survey, Oct. 1941, pp. 30–1; The Mass Observation Archive, University of Sussex, The Keep, Brighton (MOA), 'General picture of WAAF life', file report 757, 25 June 1941, p. 1; J. Nicholson, *Kiss the girls goodbye!* (London: Hutchinson & Co., 1944), p. 42; J. Waller and M. Vaughan-Rees, *Women in uniform 1939–45* (London: Papermac, 1989), pp. 11–12; E. Taylor, *Women who went to war 1938–1946* (London: Grafton Books, 1989), pp. 27–9; G. Braybon and P. Summerfield, *Out of the cage: women's experience in two world wars* (London: Pandora, 1987), p. 165; J. Rice, *Sand in my shoes: coming of age in the Second World War: a WAAF's diary* (London: Harper Perennial, 2007), p. 4.

17. TNA, RG 23/5, 'An investigation of the attitudes of women, the general public and ATS personnel to the Auxiliary Territorial Service', p. 31; MOA, 'General picture of WAAF life', p. 1; IWM, 'Material contributed for the book women in uniform 1939–45', Documents.1553, ATS file, E. M. Hazell, 14 Nov. 1987, p. 1; P. Summerfield, *Reconstructing women's wartime lives: discourse and subjectivity in oral histories of the Second World War* (Manchester: Manchester University Press, 1998), p. 83.

18. Quoted in Waller and Vaughan-Rees, *Women in uniform*, p. 11.

19. TNA, RG 23/5, 'An investigation of the attitudes of women, the general public and ATS personnel to the Auxiliary Territorial Service', pp. 30–1.

20. IWM, papers of J. Myler, Documents.7972, 'The war under the city', undated, p. 2; IWM, papers of D. Coyne, Documents.2349, untitled manuscript, undated, p. 126.

21. IWM, papers of J. F. Wheatley, Documents.1530, 'WRNS 1943–1946', May 1991, p. 1; IWM, Documents.1553, WRNS file, P. Burningham, undated, p. 3; Waller and Vaughan-Rees, *Women in uniform*, p. 6; Summerfield, *Reconstructing women's wartime lives*, p. 50; Roberts, *The WRNS in wartime*, p. 113.

22. Stone, 'The integration of women into a military service', p. 193; De Courcy, *Debs at war*, p. 205.

23. Quoted in G. Page (ed.), *We kept the secret: now it can be told: some memories of Pembroke V Wrens* (Wymondham, Norfolk: Geo. R. Reese, 2002), p. 5.

24. IWM, papers of C. I. Lambert, Documents.504, untitled manuscript, undated, p. 1.

25. TNA, RG 23/5, 'An investigation of the attitudes of women, the general public and ATS personnel to the Auxiliary Territorial Service', p. 47.

26. Ibid., pp. iii, 7.

27. Waller and Vaughan-Rees, *Women in uniform*, pp. 5–6.

28. Summerfield, *Reconstructing women's wartime lives*, p. 44.

29. IWM, Myler, Documents.7972, p. 1; IWM, Coyne, Documents.2349, pp. 127–8.

30. IWM, Documents.1553, WAAF file, H. L. Williams, 8 May 1988, p. 3.

31. TNA, AIR 10/5546, 'The Women's Auxiliary Air Force', p. 63; TNA, WO 277/12, 'Manpower problems', compiled by Maj-Gen. A. J. K. Pigott, War Office, 1949, app. 'c', p. 80; TNA, ADM 234/219, 'The Women's Royal Naval Service', pp. 63–4; TNA, Ministry of Labour papers (LAB), LAB 76/13, 'Women's auxiliary services', by J. L. Brooke-Wavell, Ministry of Labour and National Service, undated [c. 1949], pp. 17, 106; H. M. D. Parker, *Manpower: a study of war-time policy and administration* (London: HMSO, 1957), table iv, p. 486. These figures exclude women locally enlisted abroad. Precise volunteering figures for September 1939 to December 1940 do not seem to be available for the WRNS and those for the ATS and WAAF seem variable in their accuracy, so the totals should be regarded as approximations.

32. Parker, *Manpower*, table iv, p. 485. Between 1939 and 1945, approximately 1.4 million male volunteers joined the armed forces out of a total of 4.6 million men who were enlisted for service (this figure does not include some 120,000 direct officer intakes). Volunteers made up 20% of the army's total intake, 40% of the Royal Navy's total intake, and 50% of the RAF's total intake.

33. 'Oldest ATS' age is a secret', *Daily Mirror*, 12 Mar. 1945, p. 5; NAM, press cutting from the *Daily Mirror*, 9802-158-1, letter from Irene Walker, 7 July 1984.

34. TNA, LAB 76/13, 'Women's auxiliary services', pp. 14–23; Parker, *Manpower*, p. 283.

35. MOA, 'Summary of report on ATS campaign', file report 1083, 2 Feb. 1942, p. 7; IWM, papers of M. V. Hazell, Documents.7535, 'Just like the men', undated, pp. 1–4.

36. Nicholson, *Kiss the girls goodbye!*, p. 9.

37. IWM, Hazell, Documents.7535, p. 4.

38. Nicholson, *Kiss the girls goodbye!*, pp. 7–8.

39. TNA, RG 23/5, 'An investigation of the attitudes of women, the general public and ATS personnel to the Auxiliary Territorial Service', p. 45; MOA, 'Summary of report on ATS campaign', p. 10.

40. *Twelfth report from the select committee on national expenditure* (London: HMSO, 1940), p. 8; *Report of the committee on amenities and welfare conditions in the three women's services*, pp. 5, 9; TNA, LAB 76/13, 'Women's auxiliary services', pp. 139–40; MOA, 'Summary of report on ATS campaign', p. 10; Noakes, *Women in the British army*, p. 107.

41. Quoted in Izzard, *A heroine in her time*, p. 301.

42. TNA, RG 23/5, 'An investigation of the attitudes of women, the general public and ATS personnel to the Auxiliary Territorial Service', pp. 45, 47–8; MOA, 'Summary of report on ATS campaign', p. 9; MOA, 'ATS', file report 955, Nov. 1941, pp. 3–5; DeGroot, 'I love the scent of cordite in your hair', p. 79.

43. TNA, RG 23/5, 'An investigation of the attitudes of women, the general public and ATS personnel to the Auxiliary Territorial Service', p. 47.

44. Quoted in P. Summerfield and N. Crockett, '"You weren't taught that with the welding": lessons in sexuality in the Second World War', *Women's History Review*, vol. 1, no. 3 (1992), p. 442.

45. Quoted in V. Nicholson, *Millions like us: women's lives in war and peace 1939–1949* (London: Viking, 2011), p. 146. Contemporary observers such as Edith Summerskill contended that such attitudes were part of a longer-term suspicion of women in public roles that 'struck a mid-Victorian note': 'There is a certain type of individual who is always ready to suspect the morals of women who indulge in activities outside the home and who is obsessed with the idea that a girl in uniform attracts certain undesirable characters'. See E. Summerskill, 'Conscription and women', *The Fortnightly*, vol. 151 (March 1942), p. 209. Also see P. Summerfield, 'Women and war in the twentieth century' in J. Purvis (ed.), *Women's history: Britain 1850–1945: an introduction* (London: Routledge, 2000), p. 329. This opprobrium was not aimed exclusively at the ATS. Jean Wallace of the WAAF wrote of 'self-righteous middle class ladies' who 'thought of us girls in uniforms and away from home as promiscuous sluts' and who 'made damned sure that their daughters were in reserved occupations and who could thus stay at home'. See IWM, papers of J. Wallace, Documents.1161, 'Recollections of a servicewoman in the Women's Auxiliary Air Force during the Second World War', undated, pp. 15–16. When, early in the war, the *Daily Mail* invited its readers

to rank their wartime grouches, 'women in uniform' was reported to have come top of the list. See 'I see life ... by Charles Graves', *Daily Mail*, 16 Jan. 1940, p. 6.

46. Izzard, *A heroine in her time*, pp. 330–342; Terry, *Women in khaki*, pp. 123–30; LHCMA, Adam, 3/13, 'Various administrative aspects of the Second World War', ch. viii, p. 3; TNA, WO 277/6, 'The Auxiliary Territorial Service', pp. 184–5, 203–4; Noakes, *Women in the British army*, p. 110.

47. NAM, Cowper, 9401-247-572, draft memoir, undated, pp. 112–13.

48. Whateley, *As thoughts survive*, p. 30.

49. TNA, LAB 76/13, 'Women's auxiliary services', pp. 95–6; Terry, *Women in khaki*, p. 130; Noakes, *Women in the British army*, pp. 113–14.

50. TNA, LAB 76/13, 'Women's auxiliary services', pp. 18–20, 89–96; TNA, WO 32/10031, extract from conclusions of a meeting of the War Cabinet, 10 Nov. 1941; *Ministry of Labour and National Service: report for the years 1939–1946*, Cmd. 7225 (London: HMSO, 1947), pp. 42–3; Parker, *Manpower*, pp. 143–5, 223–4, 284–5.

51. TNA, LAB 76/13, 'Women's auxiliary services', pp. 26, 97; *Parliamentary debates*, House of Commons, 5th series, vol. 376, 2 Dec. 1941, cols. 1035–6.

52. TNA, LAB 76/13, 'Women's auxiliary services', p. 25.

53. Ibid., pp. 26–8.

54. Ibid., p. 29; TNA, WO 32/10031, extract from conclusions of a meeting of the War Cabinet, 10 Nov. 1941.

55. Quoted in TNA, LAB 76/13, 'Women's auxiliary services', p. 29.

56. TNA, WO 32/10031, extract from conclusions of a meeting of the War Cabinet, 10 Nov. 1941.

57. TNA, LAB 76/13, 'Women's auxiliary services', p. 32; TNA, CAB 65/20, conclusions of a meeting of the War Cabinet, 28 Nov. 1941; A. Bullock, *The life and times of Ernest Bevin*, vol. 2, *Minister of Labour 1940–1945* (London: Heinemann, 1967), pp. 137–9.

58. *Parliamentary debates*, vol. 376, 2 Dec. 1941. col. 1079.

59. *Parliamentary debates*, vol. 376, 4 Dec. 1941, col. 1310.

60. Noakes, *Women in the British army*, pp. 53, 117.

61. *Parliamentary debates*, vol. 376, 2 Dec. 1941, col. 1087.

62. *Parliamentary debates*, vol. 376, 2 Dec. 1941, col. 1082.

63. *Parliamentary debates*, vol. 376, 3 Dec. 1941, col. 1158.

64. TNA, LAB 76/13, 'Women's auxiliary services', p. 37; V. Douie, *The lesser half* (London: Women's Publicity Planning Association, 1943), p. 32; *Ministry of Labour and National Service: report for the years 1939–1946*, p. 10.

65. Goldsmith, *Women at war*, p. 36.

66. TNA, LAB 76/13, 'Women's auxiliary services', pp. 31–7, 107–10; *Ministry of Labour and National Service: report for the years 1939–1946*, pp. 30–1; Parker, *Manpower*, pp. 286–7; Bullock, *The life and times of Ernest Bevin*, p. 139. It should be noted that women between the ages of eighteen and fifty could theoretically be called-up under the act, but it was indicated in the parliamentary debate that only those between twenty and thirty would be summoned (although it was subsequently announced in 1943 that the call-up age for women would be reduced to nineteen). The liability to serve did not extend to women in Northern Ireland (see J. W. Blake, *Northern Ireland in the Second World War* (Belfast: Blackstaff Press, 2000), pp. 197–9). Some 900 women were successful in obtaining official status as conscientious objectors (see H. Nicholson, 'A disputed identity: women conscientious objectors in Second World War Britain', *Twentieth Century British History*, vol. 18, no. 4 (2007), p. 416).

67. TNA, LAB 76/13, 'Women's auxiliary services', pp. 33–4, 112, 128–9; 'How the "call-up" affects the women of Britain: an official explanation of registration and compulsory call-up', *Times*, 24 Feb. 1942, p. 8. The civil defence option was withdrawn after a few months because of the restricted number of vacancies, but the choice between the women's services and industry remained.

68. TNA, LAB 76/13, 'Women's auxiliary services', pp. 128–9; TNA, ADM 234/219, 'The Women's Royal Naval Service', pp. 47–8.

69. TNA, LAB 76/13, 'Women's auxiliary services', pp. 39, 113–19, 130–4; TNA, WO 32/10663, JAG to AUS, 30 Dec. 1944; TNA, WO 32/10663, 'Compulsory posting overseas of members of Auxiliary Territorial Service and Women's Auxiliary Air Force: case for the opinion of the law officers', by Treasury Solicitor, 11 Jan. 1945; TNA, WO 32/10663, 'Compulsory posting overseas of members of Auxiliary Territorial Service and Women's Auxiliary Air Force: opinion: the law officers of the crown', by D. B. Somervell and D. P. Maxwell Fyfe, 12 Jan. 1945; TNA, ADM 234/219, 'The Women's Royal Naval Service', p. 81; NMM, DAU 171/2, 'National Service Acts 1939 to 1941: position of women: explanatory note', 1942; *Ministry of Labour and National Service: report for the years 1939–1946*, pp. 9–10, 30; E. Summerskill, *A woman's world* (London: Heinemann, 1967), pp. 76–7. It was reported that 'a handful of the most respectable ladies' entered 'prostitute' as their profession on their calling-up papers in order to avoid conscription. See G. B. Stern, *Trumpet voluntary* (London: Cassell and Co., 1944), p. 121.

70. TNA, LAB 76/13, 'Women's auxiliary services', pp. 75–7, 138.

71. Ibid., p. 111; Parker, *Manpower*, table iv, p. 486.

72. TNA, LAB 76/13, 'Women's auxiliary services', p. 110.

73. Parker, *Manpower*, table iv, p. 485. Between 1939 and 1945, approximately 3.2 million male conscripts joined the armed forces out of the total of 4.6 million men who were enlisted for service. Conscripts made up 80% of the army's total intake, 60% of the Royal Navy's total intake, and 50% of the RAF's total intake.

74. IWM, papers of J. R. Macbeth, Documents.1214, 'Lecture to the Reay women's guild', Feb. 1943, p. 2.

75. Quoted in A. Hall (ed.), *We, also, were there: a collection of recollections of wartime women in Bomber Command* (Braunton, Devon: Merlin Books, 1985), p. 103.

76. I. R. Bet-El, *Conscripts: forgotten men of the Great War* (Stroud: Sutton, 1999), p. 16.

77. R. Howard, *In search of my father: a portrait of Leslie Howard* (New York: St Martin's Press, 1981), pp. 124–6; A. Lant, *Blackout: reinventing women for wartime British cinema* (Princeton: Princeton University Press, 1991), pp. 89–98; E. Eforgan, *Leslie Howard: the lost actor* (London: Vallentine Mitchell, 2010), pp. 196–200; Noakes, *Women in the British army*, pp. 123–4.

78. Quoted in Howard, *In search of my father*, p. 125.

79. Whateley, *As thoughts survive*, p. 74.

80. Quoted in Eforgan, *Leslie Howard*, p. 200; Lant, *Blackout*, p. 93.

81. Nicholson, *Kiss the girls goodbye!*, pp. 75–6.

82. Noakes, *Women in the British army*, p. 124.

83. *The Gentle Sex*, Two Cities/Concanen (1943).

84. *Parliamentary debates*, vol. 376, 2 Dec. 1941, cols. 1066, 1087–8; ibid., 4 Dec. 1941, col. 1341; ibid., 9 Dec. 1941, cols. 1453–4; ibid., 10 Dec. 1941, col. 1568.

85. TNA, AIR 2/6374, letter from Ernest Bevin to Sir Archibald Sinclair, 24 Dec. 1941.

86. TNA, AIR 2/6374, letter from David Margesson to Ernest Bevin, 30 Dec. 1941; TNA, AIR 2/6374, letter from Archibald Sinclair to Ernest Bevin, 1 Jan. 1942.

87. TNA, AIR 2/6374, letter from Sinclair to Bevin, 1 Jan. 1942.

88. TNA, AIR 2/6374, 'Discussion between the ministers concerned about the establishment of uniform standards for the welfare of women in the services', 1 Jan. 1942; TNA, AIR 2/6374, minutes of the 1st meeting of the committee of parliamentary under-secretaries of the three service departments and the Ministry of Labour, 19 Jan. 1942.

89. TNA, Prime Minister's papers (PREM), PREM 4/14/11, letter from Gwendolen Peel to Winston S. Churchill, 23 Dec. 1941; TNA, PREM 4/14/11, letter from Irene Ward to Sir John Anderson, 11 Jan. 1942; H. L. Smith, 'The womanpower problem in Britain during the Second World War', *The Historical Journal*, vol. 27, no. 4 (1984), pp. 928–32.

90. TNA, PREM 4/14/11, letter from Ward to Anderson, 11 Jan. 1942.

91. TNA, PREM 4/14/11, extract from parliamentary debates, vol. 377, 3 Feb. 1942, cols. 1040–2; T. Cazalet-Keir, *From the wings* (London: The Bodley Head, 1967), p. 131; J. Grigg, 'Keir, Thelma Cazalet- (1899–1989)', rev. H. C. G. Matthew, *ODNB*, online edition (2004): www.oxforddnb.com/view/10.1093/ref:odnb/9780198614128 .001.0001/odnb-9780198614128-e-39850/version/o (accessed 27 July 2019); Smith, 'The womanpower problem', p. 936.

92. Rosenzweig, 'The construction of policy for women in the British armed forces 1938–1945', pp. 107–8.

93. TNA, PREM 4/14/11, TLR [Thomas Leslie Rowan] to Prime Minister, 23 Jan. 1942; TNA, PREM 4/14/11, WSC to TLR, 3 Feb. 1942.

94. TNA, PREM 4/14/11, TLR to Prime Minister, 4 Feb. 1942; TNA, PREM 4/14/11, note by TLR, 5 Feb. 1942.

95. TNA, PREM 4/14/11, 'Conditions in the women's services', by CRA, undated.

96. Ibid.

97. TNA, PREM 4/14/11, WSC to Lord Privy Seal and Sir Edward Bridges, 14 Feb. 1942.

98. V. R. Markham, *Return passage: the autobiography of Violet. R. Markham* (London: Oxford University Press, 1953), pp. 155, 225–6; H. Jones, 'Markham, Violet Rosa (1872–1959)', *ODNB*, online edition (2004): www.oxforddnb.com /view/10.1093/ref:odnb/9780198614128.001.0001/odnb-9780198614128- e-34881 (accessed 27 July 2019); Ministry of Labour, *Report of the commission of enquiry appointed by the Minister of Labour to enquire into the Women's Army Auxiliary Corps in France* (London: HMSO, 1918); Cazalet-Keir, *From the wings*, p. 131; Summerskill, *A woman's world*, pp. 75–6; J. Stewart, 'Summerskill, Edith Clara, Baroness Summerskill (1901–1980)', *ODNB*, online version (2011): www .oxforddnb.com/view/10.1093/ref:odnb/9780198614128.001.0001/odnb- 9780198614128-e-31734 (accessed 27 July 2019); M. Stocks, *My commonplace book* (London: Peter Davies, 1970), p. 170; D. Sutherland, 'Stocks, Mary Danvers, Baroness Stocks (1891–1975)', *ODNB*, online version (2004): www .oxforddnb.com/view/10.1093/ref:odnb/9780198614128.001.0001/odnb- 9780198614128-e-31721 (accessed 27 July 2109); M. Linklater, 'Elliot, Katharine, Baroness Elliot of Harwood (1903–1994)', *ODNB*, online version (2004): www.oxforddnb.com/view/10.1093/ref:odnb/9780198614128.001.0001 /odnb-9780198614128-e-54942 (accessed 27 July 2019).

99. *Report of the committee on amenities and welfare conditions in the three women's services*, pp. 6–7; Rosenzweig, 'The construction of policy for women in the British armed forces 1938–1945', pp. 111–12.

100. *Report of the committee on amenities and welfare conditions in the three women's services*, pp. 8–9, 24–5.
101. Ibid., p. 9.
102. Ibid., p. 8.
103. Rosenzweig, 'The construction of policy for women in the British armed forces 1938–1945', pp. 116–17.
104. Douie, *The lesser half*, p. 35; Nicholson, *Kiss the girls goodbye!*, p. 26.
105. Summerskill, *A woman's world*, p. 75.
106. *Report of the committee on amenities and welfare conditions in the three women's services*, pp. 49–52. It was noted that while the pregnancy rate among unmarried members of the ATS was running at 15.4 cases per 1,000 of the unmarried strength per annum, the illegitimate birth rate among similar civilian age groups was 21.8 per 1,000.
107. Ibid., p. 51.
108. TNA, AIR 2/8370, 'The Markham committee report', joint handout by Press Division, Admiralty, DPR, War Office, and DPR, Air Ministry, 18 Aug. 1942; TNA, AIR 2/8370, 'The Markham report', joint handout by Press Division, Admiralty, DPR, War Office, and DPR, Air Ministry, 21 Aug. 1942.
109. Whateley, *As thoughts survive*, p. 71; LHCMA, Adam, 3/13, 'Various administrative aspects of the Second World War', ch. viii, p. 4; TNA, LAB 76/13, 'Women's auxiliary services', pp. 150–1.
110. Whateley, *As thoughts survive*, p. 152.

Training and Selection

1. D. Collette Wadge, *Women in uniform* (London: Sampson Low, Marston, 1946), pp. 63, 116, 174. It should be noted that during certain periods, Waafs were sent in the first instance to a 'reception' camp for a few days, before being transferred to a basic training centre.
2. TNA, ADM 234/219, 'The Women's Royal Naval Service', p. 55. From 1943, this privilege was not extended to WRNS conscripts. See 'New conditions for WRNS', *Times*, 26 Jan. 1943, p. 2.
3. RAFM, Woodhead, X002-5638, box 1, 'As we knew them', ch. vii 'The WAAF is taken for granted', pp. 3–4.
4. R. Houston, *Changing course: the wartime experiences of a member of the Women's Royal Naval Service, 1939–1945* (London: Grub Street, 2005), p. 36.
5. IWM, papers of M. Brookes, Documents.358, 'My service with the ATS 15/1/43–24/5/46', undated, pp. 3–5; IWM, papers of I. Bryce, Documents.3680, 'Greenwich to Woolwich', undated, p. 1; WO 277/6, 'The Auxiliary Territorial Service', p. 185 and app. v, pp. 259–60. The ATS 'Home Scale' for 'clothing', 'personal equipment', 'cleaning and toilet articles', and 'necessaries', numbered approximately 100 items. Pyjamas were introduced in 1942.
6. IWM, papers of W. Lane, Documents.137, '"It was rather like this, Miranda"', undated, p. 29.
7. IWM, Bryce, Documents.3680, p. 5.
8. Quoted in Waller and Vaughan-Rees, *Women in uniform*, p. 15
9. Ibid., pp. 14–15.
10. E. Smith, *Why did we join? A former Waaf remembers service life in World War II* (Bognor Regis: Woodfield, 2003), pp. 25–6.
11. IWM, Documents.5539, ATS job analyses, War Office, 1946, p. xii; TNA, AIR 10/5546, 'The Women's Auxiliary Air Force', p. 66; NMRN, WRNS collection, RNM

1988/350/96/47–8, 'KMP', 'Wrens in the making', *Yachting Monthly & RNVR Journal* (April 1944); NAM, Cowper, 9401-247-575, WRAC history, undated, pp. 216–17. Roxane Houston, however, appears to have been taught to fire a .303 rifle and a .45 Webley Scott revolver during her initial training at the Royal Naval air station at St Merryn, Padstow, in August 1940. See Houston, *Changing course*, pp. 46–7.

12. IWM, Documents.1553, WAAF file, J. Thrush, undated, p. 1; IWM, Documents.1553, WRNS file, E. Sealey, undated, p. 2; NAM, papers of J. Button, 9802-46-2-1, 'My memories of the ATS by Joan Button', 25 Feb. 1992, p. 1.

13. IWM, papers of E. M. C. McMurdo, Documents.3575, 'One girl's war', 1983, pp. 6–7.

14. Quoted in Waller and Vaughan-Rees, *Women in uniform*, p. 20.

15. IWM, Documents.1553, ATS file, H. Mason, 4 Mar. 1988, p. 1.

16. M. G. Pushman, *We all wore blue* (London: Robson Books, 1994), p. 25.

17. Houston, *Changing course*, p. 40.

18. M. L. Settle, *All the brave promises: the memories of Aircraftwoman 2nd Class 2146391* (London, Heinemann, 1966), p. 42.

19. IWM, Bryce, Documents.3680, pp. 2–3.

20. IWM, Documents.1553, WAAF file, G. Reilly, undated, p. 2.

21. V. Robinson, *Sisters in arms* (London: Harper Collins, 1996), p. 29.

22. Quoted in S. Saywell, *Women in war* (Tunbridge Wells: D. J. Costello, 1987), p. 15.

23. IWM, Bryce, Documents.3680, pp. 3–4.

24. RAFM, Trefusis Forbes, AC 72/17/1, box 4, untitled memorandum by Trefusis Forbes, 4 July 1941.

25. Pushman, *We all wore blue*, p. 32.

26. IWM, Bryce, Documents.3680, p. 3.

27. IWM, McMurdo, Documents.3575, p. 9.

28. A. Mack, *Dancing on the waves* (Little Hatherden, near Andover: Benchmark Press, 2000), p. 16.

29. J. Wyndham, *Love lessons and love is blue* (London: Mandarin, 1995), p. 194.

30. R. Barnett, *Lambs in blue: the experiences of three lasses from Tyneside in the wartime WAAF* (Bognor Regis: Woodfield Publishing, 1999), p. 20.

31. Settle, *All the brave promises*, p. 40.

32. TNA, WO 277/6, 'The Auxiliary Territorial Service', app. iv, p. 253; IWM, Documents.1553, WAAF file, P. Machray, undated, p. 1.

33. Beauman, *Partners in blue*, p. 167; TNA, AIR 41/65, 'Manning: plans and policy', p. 209; TNA, AIR 10/5546, 'The Women's Auxiliary Air Force', pp. 67–8; TNA, WO 277/6, 'The Auxiliary Territorial Service', p. 152.

34. Beauman, *Partners in blue*, p. 167.

35. TNA, AIR 41/65, 'Manning: plans and policy', p. 209.

36. D. Calvert, *Bull, battle-dress, lanyard & lipstick* (Bognor Regis: New Horizon, 1978), pp. 17–18.

37. TNA, WO 277/6, 'The Auxiliary Territorial Service', pp. 142, 252; TNA, AIR 10/5546, 'The Women's Auxiliary Air Force', pp. 73–5; TNA, ADM 234/219, 'The Women's Royal Naval Service', p. 104.

38. TNA, AIR 10/5546, 'The Women's Auxiliary Air Force', p. 74; Wadge, *Women in uniform*, pp. 117–18; Mack, *Dancing on the waves*, pp. 49–56.

39. Nicholson, *Kiss the girls goodbye!*, pp. 51–3, 55–6.

40. Quoted in Summerfield, *Reconstructing women's wartime lives*, p. 186.

41. IWM, papers of B. B. Littlejohn, Documents.2879, 'Eavesdropping on the enemy: my time in the 'Y' Service 1941–1946', Jun. 1994, pp. 25–6.

42. IWM, papers of J. E. Peyman, Documents.9600, 'In the ATS', undated, p. 82.

43. IWM, Coyne, Documents.2349, p. 156.

44. Wyndham, *Love lessons and love is blue*, p. 228.
45. TNA, WO 277/6, 'The Auxiliary Territorial Service', pp. 142–4; TNA, AIR 10/ 5546, 'The Women's Auxiliary Air Force', pp. 76–81.
46. Whateley, *As thoughts survive*, p. 49; Bidwell, *The Women's Royal Army Corps*, p. 65; TNA, WO 277/6, 'The Auxiliary Territorial Service', pp. 143, 252.
47. Whateley, *As thoughts survive*, p. 49.
48. TNA, WO 277/6, 'The Auxiliary Territorial Service', pp. 28–32; E. O. Mercer, 'Psychological methods of personnel selection in a women's service', *Occupational Psychology*, vol. 19, no. 4 (1945), p. 190; P. E. Vernon and J. B. Parry, *Personnel selection in the British forces* (London: University of London Press, 1949), p. 47; IWM, papers of F. Hill, Documents.4782, 'The sure possession', undated, p. 28; IWM, papers of B. J. Wright, Documents. 4298, 'The adventures of a nobody in the WAAF 1941–1946', 1981, p. 6; IWM, Coyne, Documents.2349, pp. 127–9; IWM, papers of E. Hodges, Documents.8249, 'My time in the Wrens during World War II', undated, p. 28.
49. Mercer, 'Psychological methods of personnel selection', pp. 180–1. Also see E. Mercer, 'A woman psychologist at war', *The Psychologist*, vol. 4, no. 9 (1991).
50. Mercer, 'Psychological methods of personnel selection', p. 181.
51. Vernon and Parry, *Personnel Selection*, pp. 46–8; TNA, WO 277/6, 'The Auxiliary Territorial Service', pp. 59–61.
52. TNA, AIR 10/5546, 'The Women's Auxiliary Air Force', p. 61; TNA, ADM 234/ 219, 'The Women's Royal Naval Service', pp. 105–6; H. R. Rollin, 'Trade training failures in the WAAF: factors in predisposition and precipitation', *British Journal of Medical Psychology*, vol. 20, issue 1 (1944), p. 65.
53. TNA, CAB 98/28, 'Psychological work in the ATS', by E. O. Mercer, app. to War Cabinet, expert committee on the work of psychologists and psychiatrists in the services, services sub-committee, minutes of the 21st meeting, 20 Oct. 1943. For an overview of the other rank selection system adopted by the army, see Crang, *The British army and the people's war 1939–1945*, ch. 1.
54. Mercer, 'Psychological methods of personnel selection', p. 189; J. Lingwood, 'Test performances of ATS recruits from certain civilian occupations', *Occupational Psychology*, vol. 26, no. 1 (1952), p. 36.
55. Mercer, 'Psychological methods of personnel selection', pp. 183–4, 190; Lingwood, 'Test performances of ATS recruits', p. 36.
56. Vernon and Parry, *Personnel Selection*, pp. 47–8. An agility test was taken by the men.
57. P. E. Vernon, 'Psychological tests in the Royal Navy, army and ATS', *Occupational Psychology*, vol. 21, no. 2 (1947), pp. 61–2.
58. Ibid., p. 66.
59. Mercer, 'Psychological methods of personnel selection', pp. 182–3, 185–91; TNA, WO 277/6, 'The Auxiliary Territorial Service', pp. 60–1.
60. IWM, McMurdo, Documents.3575, p. 7.
61. IWM, Documents.5539, 'The post basic training follow-up ATS', by Senior Commander M. Wickham, undated, pp. 1, 3–4, 14; M. Wickham, 'Follow-up of personnel selection in the ATS', *Occupational Psychology*, vol. 23, no. 3 (1949), pp. 153, 156–7; Mercer, 'Psychological methods of personnel selection', pp. 194–6.
62. Wickham, 'Follow-up of personnel selection in the ATS', p. 169.
63. TNA, WO 277/6, 'The Auxiliary Territorial Service', pp. 14, 28; TNA, WO 163/50, 'Selection of officers for the Auxiliary Territorial Service', by P. J. G., AC/P(41)49, 25 July 1941; TNA, AIR 10/5546, 'The Women's Auxiliary Air Force', pp. 22–4;

Wadge, *Women in uniform*, p. 61; N. Spain, *Thank you – Nelson* (London: Hutchinson/Arrow Books, c. 1950), pp. 172–6.

64. De Courcy, *Debs at war*, pp. 63–4.
65. Quoted in ibid., pp. 90–1.
66. Bidwell, *The Women's Royal Army Corps*, pp. 65–6; Whateley, *As thoughts survive*, p. 67.
67. Wyndham, *Love lessons and love is blue*, p. 226. Also see TNA, WO 32/10040, EG to S of S, 20 July 1940; RAFM, Trefusis Forbes, AC 72/17/1, box 5, P. Babington to Air Vice-Marshal K. R. Park, 23 Apr. 1941; Stone, 'The integration of women into a military service', p. 88.
68. TNA, WO 277/6, 'The Auxiliary Territorial Service', pp. 62–3; LHCMA, Adam, 3/13, 'Various administrative aspects of the Second World War', ch. viii, p. 6.
69. Bidwell, *The Women's Royal Army Corps*, p. 66; Wadge, *Women in uniform*, p. 117; H. Harris, *The group approach to leadership testing* (London: Routledge & Kegan Paul, 1949), p. 255; TNA, CAB 21/918, expert committee on the work of psychologists and psychiatrists in the services, draft note by the Joint Secretaries, 2 June 1943; IWM, papers of E. O. Scovell, Documents.6785, 'Live a little: die a little', 1978, pp. 191–6; W. Raphael, 'An autobiography', *Occupational Psychology*, vol 38. no. 1 (1964), p. 65; R. Hubback, *Winifred Raphael (1898–1978)* (London: CFT, 1983), p. 31; Whateley, *As thoughts survive*, pp. 67–8; 'Candidates for ATS commissions', *Times*, 3 Aug. 1943, p. 2. For a description of the officer selection system adopted by the army, see Crang, *The British army and the people's war*, ch. 2.
70. London School of Economics, Women's Library, Holborn, London (LSE), papers of Violet Markham, Markham 24/29, 'Job analysis of ATS officers', 2nd report by the National Institute of Industrial Psychology, investigator W. Raphael, 22 Mar. 1943, pp. 39, 46–8. Henry Harris, a psychologist closely involved in wartime officer selection techniques, surmised that one of the 'temptations' that the 'all-women' WOSBs might succumb to, was 'a difficulty – that should be obvious enough – in being objective about candidates who happen to be attractive to men'. Presumably, 'attractiveness' to men might have been regarded as a negative attribute by a WOSB, but this statement can be read both ways. See Harris, *The group approach to leadership testing*, p. 255.
71. TNA, WO 165/101, war diary of the Directorate of Selection of Personnel, entries for Dec. 1943 and Dec. 1943–Jan. 1944.
72. IWM, Scovell, Documents.6785, p. 192.
73. Ibid., pp. 192–4.
74. IWM, Scovell, Documents.6785, p. 196.

Work

1. TNA, AIR 10/5546, 'The Women's Auxiliary Air force', p. 84.
2. IWM, Documents.5539, 'ATS job analyses', preface; Gwynne-Vaughan, *Service with the army*, p. 129.
3. NMM, DAU 168, 'Women's Royal Naval Service', lecture to SOTC.
4. Mathews, *Blue tapestry*, p. 136.
5. TNA, WO 277/6, 'The Auxiliary Territorial Service', p. 22; TNA, AIR 41/65, 'Manning: plans and policy', p. 204; TNA, ADM 234/219, 'The Women's Royal Naval Service', p. 61.
6. TNA, WO 277/6, 'The Auxiliary Territorial Service', pp. 21–2; Mathews, *Blue tapestry*, p. 136.

7. TNA, WO 277/6, 'The Auxiliary Territorial Service', pp. 31–5, 47–53, 85–90; TNA, ADM 234/219, 'The Women's Royal Naval Service', pp. 57–103; Rosenzweig, 'The construction of policy for women in the British armed forces 1938–1945', pp. 129–30.
8. TNA, AIR 2/8207, standing committee to consider substitution of WAAF for RAF personnel: interim report, Apr. 1941; TNA, AIR 41/65, 'Manning: plans and policy', p. 205; TNA, AIR 10/5546, 'The Women's Auxiliary Air Force', p. 84.
9. RAFM, Trefusis Forbes, AC 72/17/1, box 4, 'The Women's Auxiliary Air Force' (1): history of women in the RAF', by Dame K. Forbes, Oct. 1945, pp. 3–4.
10. TNA, AIR 2/8207, standing committee to consider substitution of WAAF for RAF personnel: interim report; TNA, AIR 10/5546, 'The Women's Auxiliary Air Force', p. 86.
11. TNA, AIR 2/8207, standing committee to consider substitution of WAAF for RAF personnel: 2nd interim report, Nov. 1941; TNA, AIR 2/8207, standing committee to consider substitution of WAAF for RAF personnel: 3rd interim report, Nov. 1942; TNA, AIR 2/8207, standing committee to consider the substitution of WAAF for RAF personnel: 4th interim report, Oct. 1943; TNA, AIR 2/6097, standing committee to consider the substitution of WAAF for RAF personnel: 5th and final report, Aug. 1945; TNA, AIR 10/5546, 'The Women's Auxiliary Air Force', pp. 86–8; TNA, AIR 41/65, 'Manning: plans and policy', p. 207; Stone, 'The integration of women into a military service', pp. 108–9.
12. RAFM, Woodhead, X002-5638, box 2, AHB monograph, ch. xii, 'Substitution', p. 2.
13. L. Whateley, 'The work of the Auxiliary Territorial Service in the war', *Royal United Service Institution Journal*, vol. 91 (1946), p. 242.
14. TNA, AIR 2/6097, standing committee to consider the substitution of WAAF for RAF personnel: 5th and final report; RAFM, Woodhead, X002-5638, box 2, AHB monograph, ch. i, 'Prologue', p. 1; Stuart Mason, *Britannia's daughters*, p. 92; NMM, DAU 168, 'Women's Royal Naval Service', lecture to SOTC; TNA, ADM 234/219, 'The Women's Royal Naval Service', pp. 61, 68–9, 74; Fletcher, *The WRNS*, p. 45; IWM, Documents.5539, 'ATS job analyses', preface; Wadge, *Women in uniform*, pp. 72–4, 118–19, 177–81. It is likely that the services classified their categories of work differently, so these figures might not be strictly comparable. The number of categories also varies between sources, so it is difficult to establish agreed totals. See, for example, K. L. Sherit, 'The integration of women into the Royal Navy and the Royal Air Force, post-World War II to the mid 1990s' (PhD thesis, King's College, London, 2013), pp. 30–1; and K. Sherit, *Women on the front line: British servicewomen's path to combat* (Stroud: Amberley, 2020), pp. 31, 33.
15. V. Douie, *Daughters of Britain: an account of the work of British women during the Second World War* (Oxford: George Ronald, 1950), p. 21.
16. J. J. Halley, 'Operation Outward: the Royal Navy's strategic air command', *Aviation News Magazine*, vol. 15, no. 1 (1986), pp. 590–1; Mathews, *Blue tapestry*, p. 226; NMRN, WRNS collection, RNM 1991/24/79, letter from Antoinette Porter to Commandant Fletcher, 1987; NMRN, WRNS collection, RNM 1991/24/68, letter from Mary Beck, 1987; NMRN, WRNS collection, RNM 1991/24/48, letter from Madeleine Cowans, 1987; IWM, papers of S. M. Bywater, Documents.13103, 'Small part, big war', undated, pp. 1–2; A. Porter, 'Tuppence a day danger money',WW2 people's war,www.bbc.co.uk/history/ww2peopleswar/stories/19/a3112219.shtml (accessed 27 Apr. 2019).

17. TNA, AIR 2/5868, letter from F. H. Sandford to W. G. Maclagan, 5 Mar. 1946; IWM, papers of I. Forsdyke, Documents.2745, 'Barrage balloon operator 1941–1943', 1985, p. 1.
18. Wadge, *Women in uniform*, pp. 119–20; IWM, Documents.5539, 'ATS job analyses', pp. 167–89.
19. TNA, T 189/12, Royal Commission on Equal Pay, 'Discussion with the Adjutant-General to the Forces, General Sir Ronald F. Adam', by WGM, 13 July 1945. Also see Schwarzkopf, 'Combatant or non-combatant?', p. 122.
20. D. Sheridan, 'ATS women: challenge and containment in women's lives in the military during the Second World War' (MA thesis, University of Sussex, 1988), pp. 34, 37; IWM, papers of E. Hunter, Documents.2506, 'Service in the ATS', Jan. 1993, p. 4; J. Costello, *Love, sex and war: changing values 1939–45* (London: Pan, 1986), p. 45.
21. Stone, 'The integration of women into a military service', pp. 127–31; Stone, 'Creating a (gendered?) military identity', pp. 612–15; Braybon and Summerfield, *Out of the cage*, p. 198.
22. IWM, Documents.1553, WAAF file, Williams, p. 3.
23. Barnett, *Lambs in blue*, p. 36.
24. 'Muriel Petch: WAAF sergeant and "ops room" plotter at RAF Hornchurch who helped win the Battle of Britain', obituary, *Independent*, 21 Apr. 2014, p. 50.
25. IWM, papers of R. Britten, Documents.2903, 'F/O Rosemary Britten, 38 Group, RAF, Operation Varsity 24 March 1945', undated, pp. 1–8; A Cooper, *Wot! No engines? Royal Air Force glider pilots in Operation Varsity* (Bognor Regis: Woodfield Publishing, 2012), pp. 157–9. Also see Stone, 'The integration of women into a military service', p. 209, ftn. 3; B. Cumming 'The only WAAF to go on a wartime bombing raid', *Flightlines* (March/April 2018), pp. 8–10; and K. Mackesy, *The searchers: radio intercept in two world wars* (London: Cassell, 2004), p. 199.
26. NMRN, WRNS collection, RNM 1988/350/72/1, 'Notes for naval estimates for the year ending 31 January 1944', by DWRNS, undated, p. 2; Escott, *Women in air force blue*, app. 'h', p. 301; IWM, Documents.5539, 'ATS job analyses', p. xvii. It is difficult to be precise here because the three services used different work categorisations or trade groups and numbers fluctuated over time. However, in January 1944 the WRNS 'domestic, clerical, and communications' categories accounted for 68% of its total service personnel; in September 1944 the WAAF 'admin, domestic, and ground signals' categories accounted for 70% of its total service personnel; and in January 1945 the ATS 'catering, communications, domestic, and clerical' categories accounted for 70% of its total service personnel.
27. IWM, Documents.5539, 'ATS job analyses', p. xvii.
28. IWM, papers of N. E. Lodge, Documents.7523, 'The employment of women in the Second World War as radio location mechanics – an experience', undated, p. 4. They were working at a RAOC camp at Charminster in Dorset.
29. J. Bulpitt, WW2 people's war, www.bbc.co.uk/history/ww2peopleswar/stories/41/a4508741.shtml (accessed 27 Dec. 2018). The NAAFI (Navy, Army and Air Force Institutes) ran canteens for the armed forces.
30. TNA, T 189/10, 'Question 1', app. 'a' and annex 'I', 'Work and remuneration of women in the Auxiliary Territorial Service'.
31. TNA, T 189/10, app. 'a', enclosure with Air Ministry letter to Royal Commission on Equal Pay.

32. S. C. Rexford-Welch (ed.), *The Royal Air Force Medical Services*, vol. 1, *adminis-tration*, (London: HMSO, 1954), p. 444; TNA, AIR 10/5546, 'The Women's Auxiliary Air Force', pp. 35–6. Also see D. Ellin, 'The many behind the few: the lives and emotions of Erks and WAAFs of RAF Bomber Command 1939–1945' (PhD thesis, University of Warwick, 2015), p. 182.

33. C. Lamb, *I only joined for the hat: redoubtable Wrens at war: their trials, tribula-tions and triumphs* (London: Bene Factum Publishing, 2007), pp. 58–63.

34. Quoted in Stone, 'The integration of women into a military service', p. 111; TNA, AIR 2/8207, standing committee to consider substitution of WAAF for RAF personnel: 3rd interim report, p. 3. The flight simulator was known as a Link Trainer.

35. P. Elliot, 'The RAF's first women pilots', *Air Clues*, vol. 44, no. 5 (1990), pp. 170–1. I am grateful to Mr Elliot for drawing this article to my attention.

36. TNA, AIR 8/793, letter from T. Leigh Mallory to the Under-Secretary of State, Air Ministry, 3 Jan. 1944.

37. NAM, Coulshed, 9401-243-158, Goldman, 'The utilization of women in combat', pp. 2–3; Stone, 'The integration of women into a military service', pp. 208–9. It is possible that one woman, Helen Wynne-Eyton, might have been temporarily attached to the RAF in the Middle East as a sergeant pilot, but the evidence is inconclusive. See Elliot, 'The RAF's first women pilots', p. 174.

38. D. Parkin, 'Women in the armed services, 1940–5' in R. Samuel (ed.), *Patriotism: the making and unmaking of British national identity*, vol. 2, *Minorities and out-siders* (London: Routledge, 1989), p. 159.

39. C. Peniston-Bird, 'Of hockey sticks and Sten guns: British auxiliaries and their weapons in the Second World War', *Women's History Magazine*, issue 76 (Autumn, 2014), pp, 13–20; Wadge, *Women in uniform*, pp. 118, 178; IWM, papers of L. Orde, Documents.6468, 'Better late than never', undated, p. 118; IWM, papers of D. Gray, Documents.5561, untitled manuscript, undated, p. 12; IWM, papers of M. W. Ackroyd, Documents.660, 'Women's Royal Naval Service: service as a special duties (languages) Wren 5 August 1940 to 28 December 1943', by E. Marshall, 2 Nov. 1989, p. 25.

40. TNA, AIR 2/5868, 'Royal Commission on Equal Pay: part 'c' of first Treasury memorandum: the armed forces', undated; *Royal Commission on Equal Pay 1944–46: report*, cmd. 6937 (London: HMSO, 1946), p. 17; Peniston-Bird, 'Of hockey sticks and Sten guns', pp. 13–14.

41. TNA, WO 32/13173, 'The defensive role in war of the Women's Royal Army Corps', by DPA, July 1948.

42. TNA, WO 32/13173, DATS to AG, 22 Apr. 1948.

43. *Parliamentary Debates*, vol. 365, 19 Nov. 1940, col. 1932. Also see P. Summerfield and C. Peniston-Bird, *Contesting home defence: men, women and the Home Guard in the Second World War* (Manchester: Manchester University Press, 2007), p. 67.

44. P. Summerfield, '"She wants a gun not a dishcloth!": gender, service and citizenship in Britain in the Second World War' in G. J. DeGroot and C. Peniston-Bird, (eds.) *A soldier and a woman: sexual integration in the military* (London: Longman, 2000), pp. 133–4.

45. Mathews, *Blue tapestry*, pp. 226–7. Also see TNA, ADM 116/5102, minute by DWRNS, 21 Nov. 1942.

46. 'Women are not killers – ATS Chief', *Courier and Advertiser*, 1 Oct. 1942, p. 2.

47. RAFM, Trefusis Forbes, AC 72/17/1, box 10, 'Women's Auxiliary Air Force: preliminary and personal notes by DWAAF', May 1942, p. 2; TNA, AIR 24/

1645, app. x, 'Minute to AMP from DWAAF re. the use of firearms in the WAAF – dated 24. 11. 41'. Also see Stone, 'The integration of women into a military service', pp. 213-14.

48. TNA, WO 32/13173, DATS to AG, 22 Apr. 1948.

49. F. Pile, *Ack-Ack: Britain's defence against air attack during the Second World War* (London: George Harrap, 1949), p. 186; Citrine, 'Haslett, Dame Caroline Harriet (1895–1957)', rev. E. Putnam Symons, *ODNB*, online edition (2011): www.oxforddnb.com/view/10.1093/ref:odnb/9780198614128.001.0001/odnb-9780198614128-e-33751 (accessed 27 July 2019).

50. Pile, *Ack-Ack*, p. 186; TNA, WO 193/204, DDMO to DMO & P, 21 Nov. 1939.

51. TNA, WO 193/204, DMO & P to DPS, 24 Nov. 1939.

52. TNA, CAB 44/48, 'History of AA Command', by HQ AA Command, Stanmore, undated, p. 84; Pile, *Ack-Ack*, pp. 186-7.

53. TNA, CAB 44/48, 'History of AA Command', p. 84.

54. TNA, WO 163/84, Anti-aircraft reorganisation committee: 1st interim report, 1 Feb. 1941.

55. Pile, *Ack-Ack*, p. 188; TNA, WO 163/50, minutes of the 4th meeting of the Army Council, 12 Mar. 1941.

56. TNA, CAB 66/15, 'Status and future employment of the ATS: memorandum by the Secretary of State for War', 29 Mar. 1941; TNA, ADM 116/5102, extract from conclusions of a meeting of the War Cabinet, 31 Mar. 1941.

57. Pile, *Ack-Ack*, p. 193.

58. TNA, CAB 44/48, 'History of AA Command', p. 104.

59. Bidwell, *The Women's Royal Army Corps*, pp. 119, 126; Pile, *Ack-Ack*, p. 186; G. DeGroot, 'Whose finger on the trigger?', p. 436.

60. Pile, *Ack-Ack*, p. 193.

61. Robinson, *Sisters in arms*, pp. 77-8; Summerfield, *Reconstructing women's wartime lives*, p. 89. This ambivalence over the auxiliaries' combatant status also led to their ineligibility for certain gallantry awards available to soldiers. A woman in a mixed battery could, for example, be awarded the Victoria Cross, but could not receive the Military Cross or the Distinguished Conduct Medal. See *Parliamentary debates*, vol. 398, 28 Mar. 1944, cols. 1226-7.

62. TNA, WO 32/10027, 'Policy of employment of ATS in the ADGB (heavy AA btys)', minutes of a meeting, 6 May 1941; TNA, CAB 44/48, 'History of AA Command', p, 107; NAM, Cowper, 9401-247-575, WRAC history, pp. 235, 237.

63. NAM, Cowper, 9401-247-280, '129 (M) HAA Regiment or reminiscences run riot', by K. Manton, undated, p. 3.

64. MOA, Topic Collection, 'Women in wartime 1939–1945', box 1, 32-1-F, 'Soldiers' feelings about ATS', by R. D. Gray, 19 Oct. 1941. Muriel Barker wrote of a 'po-faced' male troop commander in her mixed battery who 'hated the ATS' and would require the auxiliaries to undertake labouring tasks such as laying down clinker paths around the gun site, while their male colleagues played football on Sunday afternoons. See IWM, papers of M. I. D. Barker, Documents.13791, 'Freddy Pile's Popsies', 1972, p. 91.

65. Quoted in Saywell, *Women in war*, p. 18.

66. NAM, Cowper, 9401-247-280, '129 (M) HAA Regiment or reminiscences run riot', by K. Manton, p. 3.

67. Ibid., pp. 3-6; J. W. N [Lieut-Col. J. W. Naylor], '"Mixed" batteries', *Journal of the Royal Artillery*, vol. 69, no. 3 (1942), p. 205; J. R. Rees, *The shaping of psychiatry by war* (London: Chapman and Hall, 1945), p. 94; Pile, *Ack-Ack*, p. 193.

68. J. W. N, '"Mixed" batteries', pp. 202, 205–6.
69. TNA, WO 277/6, 'The Auxiliary Territorial Service', app. vi, p. 278. This figure includes 'operators fire-control' and 'instrument numbers/NCOs'; F. Pile, 'The anti-aircraft defence of the United Kingdom from 28 July 1939 to 15 April 1945', *Supplement to the London Gazette*, 18 Dec. 1947, p. 5981.
70. Pile, *Ack-Ack*, p. 194.
71. Schwarzkopf, 'Combatant or non-combatant?', p. 125. Also see IWM, Barker, Documents.13791, p. 53.
72. M. Thomson, interview with the author, 31 July 2002.
73. 'ATS killed in action', *Times*, 21 April 1942, p. 2; Bidwell, *The Women's Royal Army Corps*, p. 130; NAM, Cowper, 9401-247-575, WRAC history, p. 259; D'A. Campbell, 'Women in combat: the World War II experience in the United States, Great Britain, Germany, and the Soviet Union', *Journal of Military History*, vol. 57, no. 2 (1997), p. 309. When Clementine Churchill learnt of Caveney's death, she wrote to her daughter, Mary, who was serving in 469 Battery: 'My first agonizing thought was – it might have been Mary – my second thought was satisfaction & pride that the other girls on duty continued their work smoothly without a hitch "like seasoned soldiers".' Quoted in M. Soames, *A daughter's tale: the memoir of Winston and Clementine Churchill's youngest child* (London: Doubleday, 2011), pp. 232–3.
74. M. R. D. Foot, 'Szabo, Violette Reine Elizabeth (1921–1945)', rev. R. Brown, *ODNB*, online edition (2008): www.oxforddnb.com/view/10.1093/ref:odnb/9780198614128.001.0001/odnb-9780198614128-e-38046/version/3 (accessed 27 July 2019); R. J. Minney, *Carve her name with pride: the story of Violette Szabo* (London: George Newnes, 1956; Barnsley: Pen & Sword, 2011), pp. 44–52. Szabo's wartime exploits were to be immortalised in the film *Carve her name with pride* (1958) based on Minney's book.
75. Minney, *Carve her name with pride*, p. 49.
76. IWM, papers of B. M. Holbrook, Documents.3311, 'No medals for us', 1993, p. 9.
77. IWM, Hunter, Documents.2506, p. 4.
78. NAM, Cowper, 9401-247-280, '129 (M) HAA Regiment or reminiscences run riot', by K. Manton, p. 4.
79. Calvert, *Bull, battle-dress, lanyard & lipstick*, pp. 93, 101, 120.
80. Ibid., pp. 74–5.
81. Ibid., p. 40.
82. Pile, *Ack-Ack*, pp. 188–9; TNA, WO 163/50, 'Status and employment of the Auxiliary Territorial Service', by Under-Secretary of State (Civil Member), 4 Apr. 1941.
83. Pile, *Ack-Ack*, p. 187.
84. NAM, Cowper, 9401-247-279, letter from Kina Manton to Julia Cowper, 25 Apr. 1956.
85. NAM, Cowper, 9401-247-280, '129 (M) HAA Regiment or reminiscences run riot', p. 3.
86. LHCMA, Adam, 3/13, 'Various administrative aspects of the Second World War', ch. viii, p. 7; Rosenzweig, 'The construction of policy for women in the British armed forces 1938–1945', pp. 131–3.
87. Pile, *Ack-Ack*, p. 189.
88. Bidwell, *The Women's Royal Army Corps*, p. 126.
89. Ibid.
90. 'Chief controller Knox resigns', *Times*, 21 Oct. 1943, p. 4; A. Danchev and D. Todman (eds.), *War diaries 1939–1945: Field Marshal Lord Alanbrooke* (London, Weidenfeld and Nicolson, 2001), p. 389; Whateley, *As thoughts survive*,

p. 79; CAC, papers of W. L. S. Churchill, CHAR 20/104/4, WSC to Secretary of State for War, 14 Oct. 1943; CAC, papers of C. O. Spencer-Churchill, CSCT 1/27, letter from Clementine Churchill to Winston, Oct. 1943; Terry, *Women in khaki*, pp. 132–3.

91. TNA, WO 32/9752, 'Employment of ATS in searchlights', by DAA & CD, 8 Jan. 1942.

92. Bidwell, *The Women's Royal Army Corps*, p. 128; TNA, WO 277/6, 'The Auxiliary Territorial Service', pp. 48, 88. It might be noted that the 93rd did have a male Royal Artillery commanding officer and male Royal Artillery battery commanders. See I. Corrigan, '"Put that light out!" The 93rd Searchlight Regiment Royal Artillery' in Lee and Strong, *Women in war*, p. 82.

93. Pile, *Ack-Ack*, p. 227.

94. NAM, Cowper, 9401-247-283, letter from Kina Manton to Julia Cowper, 1 Aug. 1956. Also see Pile, *Ack-Ack*, p. 193; and TNA, WO 277/6, 'The Auxiliary Territorial Service', p. 49.

95. Pile, *Ack-Ack*, pp. 227–8.

96. Quoted in K. Adie, *Corsets to camouflage: women and war* (London: Coronet, 2004), p. 155.

97. IWM, Documents.1553, WAAF file, D. Hobson, 14 July 1988, p. 6.

98. IWM, Documents.1553, WRNS file, Burningham, p. 7.

99. TNA, AIR 10/5546, 'The Women's Auxiliary Air Force', p. vi.

100. Quoted in C. Harris, *Women at war in uniform 1939–1945* (Stroud: Sutton Publishing, 2003), p. 90.

101. IWM, Documents.1553, WRNS file, J. Rawson, undated, p. 1.

102. IWM, Documents.1553, WAAF file, P. Wells, undated, p. 2.

103. IWM, papers of K. P. Mannock, Documents.7538, 'Mentioned in despatches', undated, p. 51. One army officer disclosed that 'On the whole, ATS are looked on as rather a joke. There is no scorn or malice, but the male is taken for granted as the superior. Hence the name of Queen AT for commissioned ATS.' See MOA, 'Women in wartime 1939–1945', 'Soldiers' feelings about ATS'.

104. IWM, Documents.1553, WRNS file, Burningham, p. 6.

105. IWM, papers of P. Brisley-Wilson, Documents.4009, 'Backward Glance', 14 Nov. 1995, p. 86.

106. RAFM, papers of M. Brooks, B3940, 'A Waaf's tale', 2 July 1993, pp. 4–5.

107. IWM, papers of L. Goossens, Documents.2139, 'Lois – her wartime exploits', Sept. 1992, p. 7.

108. IWM, papers of P. T. Martin, Documents.11884, 'Penny's story', 1994, p. 16.

109. Summerfield, *Reconstructing women's wartime lives*, p. 159.

110. M. Thomson, interview with the author, 17 July 2003. I am grateful to Mary Thomson's son, Professor Richard Thomson, for further information on this episode. The military authorities do seem to have taken action in certain cases. It was reported, for example, that a RAF warrant officer was reduced to the ranks for 'kissing' and 'cuddling' airwomen under his command. See 'Waaf-cuddling WO is sentenced – reduced to ranks', *Daily Mirror*, 3 Oct. 1944, p. 1.

111. Mathews, *Blue tapestry*, p. 213; TNA, ADM 178/291, letter from N. C. Deans to the Commanding Officer HMS *Proserpine*, 3 Nov. 1943.

112. TNA, ADM 178/291, letter from E. Macpherson to Admiral Commanding Orkney and Shetland, 18 Nov. 1943.

113. Mathews, *Blue tapestry*, p. 215; TNA, ADM 178/291, letter from N. C. Deans to the Commanding Officer HMS *Proserpine*, 3 Nov. 1943.

114. TNA, ADM 178/291, letter from E. Macpherson to Admiral Commanding Orkney and Shetland, 18 Nov. 1943; TNA, ADM 178/291, letter from M. Fogg-Elliot to Admiral Commanding Orkney and Shetland, 3 Nov. 1943.

115. Mathews, *Blue tapestry*, pp. 215-6; TNA, ADM 178/291, Vera Laughton Mathews to C. W. Branch, 25 Nov. 1943; TNA, ADM 178/291, minute from Vera Laughton Mathews, 4 Dec. 1943.

116. D. Lindsay, *Forgotten general: a life of Andrew Thorne* (Salisbury: Michael Russell, 1987), pp. 152-3; 'Women who are helping in Britain's war effort', *The Sphere*, 18 Oct. 1941, p. 90.

117. IWM, Documents.1553, WAAF file, Hobson, pp. 6-7.

118. IWM, Documents.1553, WRNS file, Burningham, p. 7.

119. IWM, papers of C. E. De Wolff, Documents.742, 'Odd notes', 1975, p. 99.

120. NMRN, WRNS collection, RNM 1988/350/113/4, 'History of Blockhouse Wrens', lecture notes by Rear Admiral R. B. Darke, undated.

121. RAFM, Trefusis Forbes, AC 72/17/1, box 6, 'Women's Auxiliary Air Force', by a group captain, 27 June 1941.

122. RAFM, Woodhead, X002-5638, box 2, AHB monograph, ch. ii, 'Inherent difficulties', p. 3.

123. P. Beck, *A WAAF in Bomber Command* (London: Goodall Publications, 1989), p. 19.

124. Quoted in P. Schweitzer, L. Hilton and J. Moss (eds.), *What did you do in the war, mum?* (London: Age Exchange Theatre Company, 1993), p. 19; Braybon and Summerfield, *Out of the cage*, p. 188.

125. RAFM, Brooks, B3940, 'A Waaf's tale', pp. 6-7.

126. Francis, *The flyer*, p. 83.

127. Quoted in Hall, *We, also, were there*, p. 53.

128. Ibid., p. 41.

129. IWM, papers of E. M. Kup, Documents.507, 'Memoirs of a wartime Waaf', undated, p. 62. Also see Francis, *The flyer*, p. 82.

130. Nicholson, *Kiss the girls goodbye!*, p. 78.

131. A. Clayton, *The enemy is listening: the story of the Y Service* (Manchester: Crécy Books, 1993), p. 48.

132. Ibid., p. 39.

133. Summerfield, *Reconstructing women's wartime lives*, pp. 185-6; Roberts, *The WRNS in wartime*, p. 212.

134. Quoted in Waller and Vaughan Rees-Rees, *Women in uniform*, p. 68.

135. Quoted in Summerfield, *Reconstructing women's wartime lives*, p. 186.

136. RAFM, Woodhead, X002-5638, box 2, AHB monograph, ch. xiii, 'Officers', pp. 3-4.

137. Settle, *All the brave promises*, p. 66. Also see G. G. Field, *Blood, sweat, and toil: remaking the British working class, 1939-1945* (Oxford: Oxford University Press, 2011), pp. 165, 172.

138. IWM, papers of M. O. Stewart, Documents.7974, untitled manuscript, undated, p. 11.

139. RAFM, Woodhead, X002-5638, box 2, AHB monograph, ch. xiii, 'Officers', p. 4; RAFM, Woodhead, X002-5638, box 2, AHB monograph, ch. xxxvi, 'Conclusions', p. 3. Also see Stone, 'The integration of women into a military service', pp. 91-2. The WRNS and the ATS also embodied 'substitution' officers. See *Report of the committee on amenities and welfare conditions in the three women's services*, p. 14.

140. Pushman, *We all wore blue*, pp. 75-6.

141. D. Morgan and M. Evans, *The battle for Britain: citizenship and ideology in the Second World War* (London: Routledge, 1993), p. 80.
142. Wadge, *Women in uniform*, p. 188; 'Elspeth Green', obituary, *Daily Telegraph*, 30 Aug. 2006, p. 21.
143. Wadge, *Women in uniform*, p. 78; NMRN, WRNS collection, RNM 1988/350/123/1, J. Clew, 'Wrens on wheels', *The Classic Motor Cycle* (Feb. 1987), p. 20; Taylor, *Women who went to war*, p. 50.
144. Wadge, *Women in uniform*, p. 123; NAM, Cowper, 9401-247-575, WRAC history, p. 340.
145. C. Babington Smith, *Evidence in camera: the story of photographic intelligence in the Second World War* (Stroud: Sutton Publishing, 2004), pp. 176-201; 'Constance Babington Smith', obituary, *Daily Telegraph*, 9 Aug. 2000, p. 23. Also see C. Halsall, *Women of intelligence: winning the Second World War with air photos* (Stroud: Spellmount, 2012). Babington Smith was played by Sylvia Syms in Carlo Ponti's 1965 film *Operation Crossbow*.
146. Citation for Legion of Merit quoted in A. Williams, *Operation Crossbow: the untold story of photographic intelligence and the search for Hitler's V Weapons* (London: Preface, 2013), p. 361. I am grateful to Dr Allan Williams for his insights on Babington Smith.
147. S. Parkin, *A game of birds and wolves: the secret game that won the war* (London: Sceptre, 2019), pp. 144-92, 272-8.
148. Quoted in ibid., p. 184. Also see D. Macintyre, *U-boat killer: fighting the U-boats in the Battle of the Atlantic* (London: Cassell, 2002), p. 118.
149. K. Johnson and J. Gallehawk, *Figuring it out at Bletchley Park 1939-1945* (Redditch: Book Tower Publishing, 2007), tables 8-10, pp. 40-51.
150. D. Payne, 'The bombes' in F. H. Hinsley and A. Stripp (eds.), *Codebreakers: the inside story of Bletchley Park* (Oxford: Oxford University Press, 1993), p. 135.
151. Ibid.
152. Ibid., p. 136.
153. Ibid., p. 135.
154. F. W. Winterbotham, *The Ultra Secret* (London: Weidenfeld and Nicolson, 1974).
155. C. Smith, *The hidden history of Bletchley Park: a social and organisational history, 1939-1945* (Basingstoke: Palgrave Macmillan, 2015), pp. 50-3, 57.
156. T. Dunlop, *The Bletchley girls: war, secrecy, love and loss: the women of Bletchley Park tell their story* (London: Hodder, 2015), p. 8.
157. Quoted in Goldsmith, *Women at war*, p. 98. Also see Whateley, *As thoughts survive*, p. 101 and Taylor, *Women who went to war*, p. 129. In another example of highly secret work, members of the ATS were employed as laboratory assistants, and in the associated rat houses, producing scrub typhus vaccine for troops in south-east Asia. See Whateley, 'The work of the Auxiliary Territorial Service in the war', pp. 245-6.
158. TNA, T 189/12, 'Statement for the Royal Commission on Equal Pay'. Also see the discussion of individual categories of work in ADM, 1/18884: 'Comparative quality of the work of RN and WRNS personnel', minutes of a meeting, 19 Apr. 1945; and 'Comparative quality of the work of RN and WRNS personnel', by Head of Naval Branch, 14 May 1945. Kathleen Sherit has pointed out that the evidence to the commission might have been partly intended to highlight gender differences in order to undermine the case for equal pay. See Sherit, 'The integration of women into the Royal Navy and the Royal Air Force', p. 37; and Sherit, *Women on the front line*, p. 39.

159. TNA, T 189/10, 'Question 5', app. 'e' to 'Work and remuneration of women in the Auxiliary Territorial Service'.
160. TNA, T 189/10, 'Question 5', enclosure with Air Ministry letter to Royal Commission on Equal Pay.
161. TNA, T 189/10, app. 'a (airwomen)' to Air Ministry letter to Royal Commission on Equal Pay. Also see the reports of the various RAF commands on these matters in AIR 2/5868.
162. B. E. Escott, 'Welsh, Dame (Ruth) Mary Eldridge (1896–1986)', *ODNB*, online edition (2009): www.oxforddnb.com/view/10.1093/ref:odnb/9780198614128 .001.0001/odnb-9780198614128-e-68169 (accessed 27 July 2019).
163. TNA, AIR 2/5868, DDWAAF(O) to Head of S11, 6 Apr. 1945; TNA, T 189/10, 'Question 3', enclosure with Air Ministry letter to Royal Commission on Equal Pay; Stone, 'The integration of women into a military service', p. 142.
164. TNA, AIR 2/5868, PUS to AUS(P), 15 May 1945.
165. TNA, AIR 2/5868, DWAAF to DGP1, 21 Aug. 1945; TNA, AIR 2/5868, DWAAF to DGP(1), 5 Nov. 1945. Some of DWAAF's views were alluded to in a brief covering letter with the submission.

Status and Discipline

1. TNA, ADM 116/5102, War Cabinet, Home Policy committee, 'Discipline in the Women's Royal Naval Service, Auxiliary Territorial Service, and the Women's Auxiliary Air Force', 'Memorandum by the First Lord of the Admiralty and the Secretaries of State for War and Air', 3 Aug. 1940.
2. TNA, ADM 116/5102, letter from G. D. Roseway to E. A. Seal, 24 Feb. 1939.
3. *Report of the committee on amenities and welfare conditions in the three women's services*, p. 4. 'Camp followers' was a term used to denote civilians, often women, who in previous eras accompanied armies in the field and provided a range of services for the troops such as cooking, cleaning and nursing. See Noakes, *Women in the British army*, pp. 2, 4, 20.
4. TNA, ADM 116/5102, report of a meeting held at the office of the Judge Advocate General, 23 May 1940; NAM, Cowper, 9401-247-575, WRAC history, p. 212; TNA, WO 32/10031, 'Auxiliary Territorial Service', app. 'b' to 'Recruiting in the ATS', memorandum by CM, 10 Dec. 1940.
5. TNA, ADM 116/5102, report of a meeting held at the office of the Judge Advocate General, 23 May 1940; TNA, ADM 116/5102, 'Discipline in the Women's Royal Naval Service, Auxiliary Territorial Service, and the Women's Auxiliary Air Force', 3 Aug. 1940.
6. TNA, AIR 2/4090, 'Discipline-WAAF', letter from Barbara Whittingham-Jones to headquarters No. 12 group, 10 May 1940; RAFM, Trefusis Forbes, AC 72/17/1, box 1, 'Discipline', undated.
7. Peake, *Pure chance*, p. 36.
8. TNA, ADM 116/5102, 'Discipline in the Women's Royal Naval Service, Auxiliary Territorial Service, and the Women's Auxiliary Air Force', 3 Aug. 1940.
9. TNA, ADM 116/5102, War Cabinet, Home Policy committee, discipline in the women's forces, draft minutes of a meeting, 3 Sept. 1940; TNA, ADM 116/5102, Civil Lord to Secretary, 3 Sept. 1940; TNA, AIR 2/4646, AMP to PUS, 3 Sept. 1940; TNA, AIR 10/5546, 'The Women's Auxiliary Air Force', pp. 18–19. It might be noted that the WRNS included the punishment of 'deductions from pay for improper absence' in its disciplinary regulations issued in the summer of 1940. See TNA, ADM

1/11837, 'Disciplinary regulations for the Women's Royal Naval Service', Admiralty, 1940.

10. TNA, AIR 2/4646, Women's corps status committee, notes of a meeting, 18 Feb. 1941; TNA, ADM 116/5102, 'Women's services: memorandum on the question of military status', War Office, undated; TNA, CAB 66/15, 'Status and future employment of the ATS: memorandum by the Secretary of State for War', 29 Mar. 1941.

11. TNA, CAB 66/15, 'Status and future employment of the ATS: memorandum by the Secretary of State for War', 29 Mar. 1941; TNA, ADM 116/5102, extract from conclusions of a meeting of the War Cabinet, 31 Mar. 1941.

12. TNA, WO 277/6, 'The Auxiliary Territorial Service', app. 1, p. 243; TNA, AIR 10/5546, 'The Women's Auxiliary Air Force', app. 1, pp. 129–30.

13. NAM, Gwynne-Vaughan papers, 9401-253-1343-1, letter from H. Gwynne-Vaughan to Sir John Brown, 14 Sept. 1938; Gwynne-Vaughan, *Service with the army*, pp. 113–14, 135–7.

14. TNA, WO 277/6, 'The Auxiliary Territorial Service', pp. 43–6; Escott, *Women in air force blue*, app. 'a', p. 291; K. J. Trefusis Forbes, 'Women's Auxiliary Air Force', *Flying and Popular Aviation* (Sept. 1942), p. 127. In regard to badges of rank, the ATS came into line here with the practice of the WAAF, which already used RAF badges. See TNA, WO 163/50, 'Status and employment of the Auxiliary Territorial Service', memorandum by Under-Secretary of State for War (Civil Member), 4 Apr. 1941.

15. *Regulations for the Auxiliary Territorial Service 1941*, pp. 42–3.

16. TNA, AIR 2/6239, Air Ministry Order A.466/1941, June 1941, p. 2. It was said that servicewomen had already issued orders to male subordinates on occasions. See, for example, RAFM, Trefusis Forbes, AC 72/17/1, box 4, 'The Women's Auxiliary Air Force', by Dame K. Trefusis Forbes, Oct. 1945, p. 5; and Gwynne-Vaughan, *Service with the army*, p. 127.

17. Nicholson, *Kiss the girls goodbye!*, p. 78.

18. TNA, AIR 2/6239, Air Ministry Order A.466/1941; TNA, AIR 10/5546, 'The Women's Auxiliary Air Force', pp. 19–21; *Regulations for the Auxiliary Territorial Service 1941*, pp. 45–68; TNA, WO 277/6, 'The Auxiliary Territorial Service', pp. 44–5; 'An Act to consolidate the Army Discipline and Regulation Act, 1879, and the subsequent acts amending the same' in *The statutes: third revised edition*, vol. 10, *from the forty-first and forty-second to the forty-sixth and forty-seventh years of Queen Victoria AD 1878–1883* (London: HMSO, 1950), pp. 457–505; 'Air Force Act' in Air Ministry, *Manual of Air Force law* (London: HMSO, 1939), pp. 219–96. It should be noted that, in contrast to the position in the WAAF, army commanding officers did not have powers of summary punishment over ATS personnel in their mixed sex units. Only army area or divisional commanders, or those above, could exercise these powers.

19. TNA, WO 32/10072, 'The application of the Army Act to personnel of the women's forces serving abroad', memorandum by PUS, 28 July 1941; TNA, WO 32/10072, 'Women's forces: administration of discipline', memorandum by AG, 28 June 1943; TNA, AIR 2/6486, 'WAAF disciplinary code', note by AMP, 10 Sept. 1943; TNA, WO 277/6, 'The Auxiliary Territorial Service', p. 77; TNA, AIR 10/5546, 'The Women's Auxiliary Air Force', p. 19.

20. TNA, ADM 116/5102, minute by Head of CEI, 13 June 1940.

21. TNA, ADM 116/5102, 'Status of WRNS', by Admiral Sir Charles Little, 9 June 1941.

22. TNA, ADM 116/5102, 'Disciplinary status of the Women's Royal Naval Service', by DWRNS, 8 Apr. 1941.

23. TNA, ADM 116/5102, letter from Richmond Walton to Commanders-in-Chief, Portsmouth, Plymouth, The Nore, Western Approaches, Rosyth, and Flag Officer Commanding, Orkneys and Shetland, 2 Apr. 1941; TNA, ADM 116/5102, letter from Commander-in-Chief, Portsmouth, to Secretary of the Admiralty, 10 Apr. 1941.

24. TNA, ADM 116/5102, 'Status of WRNS', by Admiral Sir Charles Little.

25. Mathews, *Blue tapestry*, p. 116.

26. Ibid., pp. 132-3; Roberts, *The WRNS in wartime*, p. 207; TNA ADM 116/5102, extract from board minutes, 12 June 1941; TNA, ADM 234/219, 'The Women's Royal Naval Service', pp. 37-40; Sherit, 'The integration of women into the Royal Navy and the Royal Air Force', pp. 41-3; Sherit, *Women on the front line*, pp. 46-7. Under an Admiralty Fleet Order issued in early 1943, it was laid down that disciplinary offences were to be dealt with by Royal Navy commanding officers, but a WRNS officer was to be present at all investigations. See TNA, ADM 182/113, Admiralty Fleet Order 261, 21 Jan. 1943. Wrens wore similar rank insignia as their male equivalents, but in blue instead of gold. The 'curls' atop officers' rank stripes were diamond-shaped rather than circular.

27. TNA, AIR 2/4090, S7(g) to AMP, 17 Jan. 1942; TNA, AIR 2/4090, letter from Air Marshal, Air Officer Commanding-in-Chief, Technical Training Command, to Under-Secretary of State, Air Ministry, 12 Dec. 1941; TNA, AIR 2/4090, letter from Air Vice Marshal, Air Officer Commanding, No. 24 group, to Under-Secretary of State, Air Ministry, 2 Jan. 1942; TNA, AIR 2/4090, letter from Air Marshal, Air Officer Commanding-in-Chief, Flying Training Command, to Under-Secretary of State, 28 Jan. 1942; TNA, AIR 2/4090, letter from Air Chief Marshal, Air Officer Commanding-in-Chief, Coastal Command, to Under-Secretary of State, Air Ministry, 25 Mar. 1942.

28. TNA, AIR 2/4090, Air Vice Marshal, Air Officer Commanding, No. 24 Group, to Under-Secretary of State, Air Ministry, 2 Jan. 1942.

29. RAFM, Trefusis Forbes, AC 72/17/1, box 6, extracts from discharge case of 2006569 ACW2 Silvie, undated.

30. Joubert de la Ferté, *The forgotten ones*, p. 151.

31. RAFM, Trefusis Forbes, AC 72/17/1, box 9, JAG to PAS(P), Air Ministry, 13 June 1940; TNA, AIR 24/1645, app. 8, 'Minute to AMP from S.11 re. position of WAAF in relation to relief from death duties – dated 8. 5. 42'; Stone, 'The integration of women into a military service', pp. 162-3.

32. Joubert de la Ferté, *The forgotten ones*, p. 151.

33. TNA, WO 277/6, 'The Auxiliary Territorial Service', p. 76.

34. TNA, AIR 2/4090, S7(g) to AMP, 17 Jan. 1942.

35. TNA, AIR 2/4090, 'WAAF discipline', letter from R. C. Richards to AO C-in-C, Bomber, Maintenance, Army Co-operation, Flying Training, Technical Training, Northern Ireland and Balloon Commands, 19 June 1942; TNA, AIR 2/4090, minute by DPS, 13 Feb. 1942; TNA, AIR 2/4090, AMP to DPS and PAS(P), 14 Feb. 1942.

36. *Report of the committee on amenities and welfare conditions in the three women's services*, pp. 20, 55.

37. TNA, AIR 2/4090, Markham report, extract from conclusions of the 2nd meeting of the Air Council committee, 28 Sept. 1942; TNA, AIR 2/6486, 'WAAF disciplinary code', note by AMP, 10 Sept. 1943; TNA, AIR 2/6486, minute by DWAAF, 5 July 1943.

38. TNA, WO 32/10072, 'Women's forces: administration of discipline', memorandum by AG, 28 June 1943; TNA, WO 32/10072, extract from the minutes of the 117th meeting of the executive committee of the Army Council, 2 July 1943.

39. TNA, WO 32/10072, PJG to PUS, 15 July 1943; TNA, WO 32/10072, extract from the minutes of the 34th meeting of the Army Council, 16 July 1943; TNA, AIR 2/6486, letter from P. J. Grigg to Sir Archibald Sinclair, 20 Sept. 1943; TNA, AIR 2/6486, extracts from Air Ministry draft conclusions of meeting, 28 Sept. 1943.

40. TNA, AIR 2/6486, Grigg to Sinclair, 20 Sept. 1943.

41. TNA, AIR 2/6486, letter from A. W. Street to Sir Frederick Bovenschen, 22 July 1943.

42. TNA, AIR 2/6486, 'WAAF disciplinary code', note by AMP, 10 Sept. 1943; TNA, AIR 2/6486, draft conclusions of a meeting of the Air Council, 14 Sept. 1943.

43. TNA, AIR 2/6486, S11 to DGPS, 9 Dec. 1943; TNA, AIR 2/6486, minute by DWAAF, 17 Nov. 1943; TNA, AIR 2/6486, letter from E. A. Shearing to Violet Markham, 25 Nov. 1943.

44. TNA, AIR 2/6486, 'WAAF disciplinary code', note of a meeting, 14 Dec. 1943. According to the minutes of this meeting, as well as the recollections of Mary Lee Settle, who had witnessed airwomen incarcerated in a barbed-wire enclosure during her initial training, some measure of detention already seems to have been in operation at one WAAF depot, even if unofficially or as a trial. See Settle, *All the brave promises*, pp. 28–9.

45. TNA, AIR 2/6486, 'WAAF disciplinary code', note by AMP, 18 Feb. 1944; TNA, AIR 2/6486, extract from draft conclusions of a meeting of the Air Council, 7 Mar. 1944; TNA, AIR 10/5546, 'The Women's Auxiliary Air Force', pp. 20–1.

46. TNA, AIR 2/6486, 'Report on a visit to Fort Darland military detention barracks, Chatham', undated; TNA, AIR 2/6486, letter from E. A. Shearing to M. Mellanby, 28 Apr. 1944; TNA, AIR 2/6486, 'WAAF disciplinary code', minute from S11 to DGPS, 29 Apr. 1944.

47. TNA, AIR 2/6486, note of a meeting held by DPS to discuss points arising from the proposal to introduce detention as a punishment for the WAAF, 6 May 1944; TNA, AIR 2/6486, 'Detention for the WAAF', draft of proposed regulations, undated.

48. TNA, AIR 2/6486, note of a meeting held by DPS to discuss points arising from the proposal to introduce detention as a punishment for the WAAF; TNA, AIR 2/6486, 'WAAF disciplinary code', draft note by AMP; undated; TNA, AIR 2/8793, WAAF Advisory Council, minutes of the 12th meeting, 4 Oct. 1944.

49. TNA, AIR 2/6486, DGPS to AMP, 20 May 1944.

50. TNA, AIR 2/6486, 'WAAF disciplinary code', note by AMP, 20 July 1944; TNA, AIR 2/6486, 'WAAF disciplinary code', note by AMP, 25 Aug. 1944.

51. TNA AIR 6/75, draft conclusions of a meeting of the Air Council, 28 July 1944.

52. TNA AIR 6/75, draft conclusions of a meeting of the Air Council, 29 Aug. 1944; TNA, AIR 2/8793, 'WAAF disciplinary code', note by DWAAF, Sept. 1944; TNA, AIR 2/8793, WAAF Advisory Council, minutes of the 12th meeting, 4 Oct. 1944.

53. RAFM, Woodhead, X002-5638, box 2, AHB monograph, ch. xiii, 'WAAF discipline', pp. 8–10; TNA, AIR 10/5546, 'The Women's Auxiliary Air Force', p. 21.

54. TNA, AIR 2/5868, letter from Air Marshal, Air Officer Commanding-in-Chief, Fighter Command, to the Under-Secretary of State, Air Ministry, 17 Mar. 1945. The number of absentees in Fighter Command was put at 2.28% of airwomen and 1.35% of airmen. Across the service it was reported that cases of absence without leave were running at a ratio of approximately four airwomen to three airmen. See TNA, T 189/10, 'Question 4', enclosure with Air Ministry letter to Royal Commission on Equal Pay.

55. RAFM, Woodhead, X002-5638, box 2, AHB monograph, ch. xxxi, 'Conclusions', pp. 4–5.
56. F. Ashbee, *For the duration: a light-hearted WAAF memoir* (Syracuse, New York: Syracuse University Press, 2012), pp. 140–2. Minor amendments to the vernacular dialogue in this quotation have been made for the sake of clarity but without changing the meaning.
57. *Report of the committee on amenities and welfare conditions in the three women's services*, p. 55.
58. TNA, ADM 116/5102, minute by DWRNS, 21 Nov. 1942; TNA, ADM 116/5102, minute by Head of NL, July 1942.
59. TNA, ADM 116/5102, minute by DPS, 24 Nov. 1942.
60. TNA, ADM 116/5102, minute by Head of NL, 27 Nov. 1942; TNA, ADM 116/5102, minute by HMV, 8 Dec. 1942; TNA, ADM 116/5102, percentage of deserters to total personnel for the years 1941 to 1943, undated.
61. TNA, ADM 116/5102, extract from board minutes, 12 Feb. 1943.
62. TNA, ADM 116/5102, summary of views of commanders-in-chief etc., undated; NMRN, WRNS collection, RNM 1988/350/72/1, 'Notes for naval estimates for the year ending 31 January 1943', by DWRNS, undated, p. 1.
63. TNA, ADM 116/5102, letter from Commander-in-Chief, Plymouth, to Secretary of the Admiralty, 18 Mar. 1943.
64. TNA, ADM 116/5102, extract from board minutes, 16 July 1943; TNA, ADM 234/219, 'The Women's Royal Naval Service', pp. 40–4.
65. TNA, ADM 116/5102, minute by DWRNS, 27 Jan. 1944; TNA, ADM 116/5102, percentage of deserters to total personnel for the years 1941 to 1943; TNA, ADM 116/5102, letter from A. V. Alexander to Sir John Anderson, 22 Oct. 1943; TNA, ADM 116/5102, letter from John Anderson to A. V. Alexander, 13 Dec. 1943.
66. TNA, ADM 116/5102, 'Immobiles' by DWRNS, 31 Jan. 1944.
67. TNA, ADM 116/5102, letter from Commander-in-Chief, the Nore, to Secretary of the Admiralty, 13 Mar. 1944.
68. TNA, ADM 116/5102, letter from Commander-in-Chief, Rosyth, to Secretary of the Admiralty, 28 Mar. 1944.
69. TNA, ADM 116/5102, minute by Head of NL, 29 Feb. 1944; TNA, ADM 116/5102, minute by Head of NL, 21 Apr. 1944; TNA, ADM 116/5102, minute by PAS (NP), 8 May 1944; TNA, ADM 116/5102, minute by HVM [Sir Henry Markham], 28 May 1944; TNA, ADM 116/5102, minute by AUW [Sir Algernon Willis], 6 June 1944; TNA, ADM 116/5102, minute by B, 16 June 1944; TNA, ADM 116/5102, letter from J. G. Lang to Commanders-in-Chief, the Nore, Portsmouth, Plymouth, Rosyth, Western Approaches, Admiral Commanding Orkneys and Shetland, Flag Officer Naval Air Stations, Flag Officer Commanding Dover, 10 Aug. 1944; Sherit, 'The integration of women into the Royal Navy and the Royal Air Force', p. 43; ADM 182/138, 'Members of the WRNS – incitement to desert', Confidential Admiralty Fleet Order 1748, 10 Aug. 1944.
70. NMM, DAU 163, 'WRNS and the Naval Discipline Act', memorandum by Superintendent, the Nore, 25 Mar. 1943.
71. Mathews, *Blue tapestry*, p. 117.

Necessities of Life

1. TNA, WO 277/6, 'The Auxiliary Territorial Service', p. 181; TNA, AIR 10/5546, 'The Women's Auxiliary Air Force', p. 33; D. Jarrett, *British naval dress* (London: J. M. Dent, 1960), p. 135.

2. Wadge, *Women in uniform*, pp. 69–71, 137–8, 183–4; Harris, *Women at war*, pp. 30–1, 76–81, 91–5; A. Cormack, *The Royal Air Force 1939–45* (Oxford: Osprey, 1990), pp. 12–13; I. Sumner, *The Royal Navy 1939–45* (Oxford: Osprey, 2001), p. 59; TNA, WO 277/6, 'The Auxiliary Territorial Service', pp. 183, 259–60, 274–6; IWM, Bryce, Documents.3680, p. 1; IWM, papers of K. M. Ball, Documents.571, 'A short account of life in the Women's Auxiliary Air Force', undated, p. 3. The WRNS jacket buttoned to the left side.

3. IWM, Hazell, Documents.7535, p. 221.

4. Harris, *Women at war*, pp. 31–2; Wadge, *Women in uniform*, pp. 212–15; Sumner, *The Royal Navy*, p. 58.

5. TNA, AIR 2/4085, DWAAF to DPS and AMP, 21 Oct. 1939.

6. TNA, AIR 2/4085, S7(g) to DPS, 28 Oct. 1939; TNA, AIR 2/4085, D of E to E13, 31 Oct. 1939; TNA, AIR 2/4085, D of E to DPS, 31 Oct. 1939.

7. TNA, AIR 2/4085, DWAAF to D of E, 31 Oct. 1939; TNA, AIR 2/4085, slacks for WAAF, minutes of a conference, 2 Nov. 1939.

8. TNA, AIR 2/4085, letter from E. A. Shearing to Air Officers Commanding-in-Chief, Bomber Command, Fighter Command, Training Command, and Air Officers Commanding Maintenance Command, Reserve Command, Balloon Command, 6 Nov. 1939; TNA, AIR 2/4085, letter from C. L. Boxshell to Under-Secretary of State for Air, Air Ministry, 9 Mar. 1940.

9. TNA, AIR 2/4085, letter from Boxshell to Under-Secretary of State, Air Ministry, 27 June 1940; TNA, AIR 2/4085 letter from Group Captain, Senior Medical Officer, headquarters No. 23 Group, to Principal Medical Officer, headquarters Flying Training Command, 28 June 1940.

10. TNA, AIR 2/4085, DWAAF to DPS, 3 July 1940.

11. TNA, AIR 2/4085, F7 to DDE(6) and DWAAF, 14 Aug. 1940.

12. TNA, AIR 2/4085, minute by DWAAF, 20 Aug. 1940.

13. TNA, AIR 2/4085, letter from L. G. S. Reynolds to the Secretary, the Treasury, 7 Sept. 1940; TNA, AIR 2/4085, letter from W. S. Douglas to Under-Secretary of State, Air Ministry, 12 Oct. 1940.

14. TNA, AIR 2/4085, letter from L. G. S. Reynolds to the Secretary, the Treasury, 20 Dec. 1940.

15. TNA, AIR 2/4085, letter from H. Parker to Under-Secretary of State, Air Ministry, 15 Jan. 1941; TNA, AIR 2/4085, 'Issue of blue slacks to WAAF personnel', Air Ministry Order N1365, 13 Nov. 1941.

16. TNA, AIR 2/4085, 'Issue of blue slacks to WAAF personnel', Air Ministry Order A417, 23 Apr. 1942.

17. Stone, 'Creating a (gendered?) military identity', pp. 617–19.

18. RAFM, Woodhead, X002-5638, box 1, 'As we knew them', ch. xix, 'Releases and conclusion', p. 2. Also see IWM, Hill, Documents.4782, p. 30.

19. P. Kirkham, 'Beauty and duty: keeping up the (home) front', in P. Kirkham and D. Thoms (eds.), *War culture: social change and changing experience in World War Two* (London: Lawrence and Wishart, 1995), pp. 24–5; P. Kirkham, 'Keeping up home front morale: "beauty and duty" in wartime Britain', in J. M. Atkins (ed.), *Wearing propaganda: textiles on the home front in Japan, Britain, and the United States, 1931–1945* (New Haven, CT: Yale University Press, 2005), p. 216.

20. Mary Thomson, interview with the author, 17 July 2003; Babington Smith, *Evidence in camera*, p. 215.

21. Pushman, *We all wore blue*, p. 143.

22. TNA, ADM 1/16887, report of a board of enquiry, HMS *Hopetoun*, South Queensferry, 9 Feb. 1944; Taylor, *Women who went to war*, pp. 34–5.

23. TNA, ADM 1/16887, minute by DWRNS, 21 Mar. 1944; TNA, ADM 1/16887, minute by Head of L, 14 Apr. 1944; TNA, ADM 182/118, 'WRNS – ratings working on or in the vicinity of moving machinery', Admiralty Fleet Order 2929, 1 June 1944.

24. IWM, papers of J. Stallard, Documents.485, 'WAAF service during World War II', 1989, p. 3; J. Summers, *Fashion on the ration: style in the Second World War* (London: Profile Books, 2016), p. 44. It was said that after the war the British airline, BAOC, purchased surplus WRNS uniforms for their stewardesses. See Harris, *Women at war*, p. 91.

25. De Courcy, *Debs at war*, p. 205.

26. *Report of the committee on amenities and welfare conditions in the three women's services*, pp. 23–6; Waller and Vaughan-Rees, *Women in uniform*, pp. 14, 61–3; Escott, *Women in air force blue*, pp. 137–40; TNA, AIR 10/5546, 'The Women's Auxiliary Air Force', pp. 30–1.

27. Quoted in Waller and Vaughan-Rees, *Women in uniform*, p. 63.

28. TNA, T 189/10, 'Question 7', app. 'g' to 'Work and remuneration of women in the Auxiliary Territorial Service'; TNA, T 189/10, 'Question 7', enclosure with Air Ministry letter to Royal Commission on Equal Pay; TNA, T 189/12, annex 1 to 'Statement for the Royal Commission on Equal Pay'; TNA, AIR 10/5546, 'The Women's Auxiliary Air Force', pp. 29–30; TNA, WO 277/6, 'The Auxiliary Territorial Service', pp. 201–4; TNA, WO 287/199, 'Barrack synopsis (war)', May 1943; F. A. E. Crew (ed.), *The Army Medical Services: administration*, vol. 2 (London: HMSO, 1955), pp. 124–6, 462. It should be noted that these square footages did vary to some extent over the course of the war. For example, both soldiers and auxiliaries were allocated 45 square feet until 1942, when the male scale was reduced to 30.

29. TNA, AIR 2/5868, DDWAAF(O) to Head of S11, 6 Apr. 1945.

30. TNA, WO 277/6, 'The Auxiliary Territorial Service', p. 205; IWM, Peyman, Documents.9600, 'In my officer's uniform', undated, p. 26.

31. Crew, *The Army Medical Services: administration*, vol. 2, p. 463.

32. Waller and Vaughan-Rees, *Women in uniform*, p. 62; MOA, 'General picture of WAAF life', p. 9; IWM, Scovell, Documents.6785, pp. 157–8.

33. IWM, Scovell, Documents.6785, p. 158.

34. RAFM, Woodhead, X002-5638, box 1, 'As we knew them', ch. vii, 'The WAAF is taken for granted', p. 11.

35. B. Cartland, *The years of opportunity 1939–1945* (London: Hutchinson & Co, 1948), pp. 146–7.

36. IWM, Hill, Documents.4782, pp. 48–9.

37. Costello, *Love, sex and war*, p. 190.

38. Pile, *Ack-Ack*, pp. 368–81; Pile, 'The anti-aircraft defence of the United Kingdom from 28 July 1939 to 15 April 1945', pp. 5991–2; M. Thomson, 'Christian Fraser-Tytler', obituary, *Independent*, 19 July 1995, p. 12; Bidwell, *The Women's Royal Army Corps*, p. 89.

39. Pile, *Ack-Ack*, p. 379.

40. Douie, *The lesser half*, p. 36; TNA, WO 32/10030, select committee on national expenditure (sub-committee on army services), 'Auxiliary Territorial Service', memorandum by War Office, 27 May 1940; Escott, *Women in air force blue*, p. 141; NMRN, WRNS collection, RNM 1988/350/72, 'Debate on navy estimates 1943', by DWRNS, undated, p. 1; TNA, T 189/12, annex 1 to 'Statement for the Royal Commission on Equal Pay'.

41. Crew, *The Army Medical Services: administration*, vol. 2, p. 464.

42. Ibid., pp. 461, 464–5.
43. RAFM, Woodhead, X002-5638, box 1, 'As we knew them', ch. vii, 'The WAAF is taken for granted', p. 10; TNA, T 189/7, Royal Commission on Equal Pay: first memorandum of evidence submitted by the Treasury, 26 Jan. 1945; N. Sher, 'An investigation into the causes of delayed menstruation, and its treatment in the Women's Auxiliary Air Force' (MD thesis, University of Glasgow, 1944), pp. 26–7. It should be recorded that the cash ration allowance for women members of the forces who, for various reasons, were not provided with service rations and had to buy their own meals from catering institutions, had been set at four-fifths of the corresponding male rates. However, in 1944 this ration allowance was brought up to the servicemen's rate. See 'Service pay and allowances', *Times*, 12 July 1944, p. 2.
44. Escott, *Women in air force blue*, p. 141.
45. IWM, Hazell, Documents.7535, p. 32.
46. IWM, Littlejohn, Documents.2879, pp. 6–7.
47. Quoted in Waller and Vaughan-Rees, *Women in uniform*, p. 65.
48. IWM, McMurdo, Documents.3575, pp. 20–1.
49. IWM, Documents.1553, WAAF file, M. Winter, undated, p. 9.
50. TNA, AIR 2/9422, 'Auxiliary Territorial Service', by W. H. T. Ottley, July 1943; TNA, T 189/7, Royal Commission on Equal Pay: first memorandum of evidence submitted by the Treasury; *Royal Commission on Equal Pay 1944–46*, p. 19; H. Smith, 'The problem of "equal pay for equal work" in Great Britain during World War II', *Journal of Modern History*, vol. 53, no. 4 (1981), p. 655. It should be noted that 'immobile' Wrens were paid at a lower rate than those who were 'mobile' and the pay of WRNS officers was broadly equivalent to the corresponding grades in the ATS and WAAF.
51. TNA, ADM 116/4723, select committee on national expenditure (sub-committee on army services), 'Statement of pay, allowances and conditions of service of men and women (both civilians and uniformed) in receipt of weekly wages in war department establishments', memorandum by War Office, undated [end of 1941]. Also see TNA, T 189/12, Royal Commission on Equal Pay, 'Letter from Adjutant-General supplementing oral evidence', by WGM, 30 July 1945; and NMRN, WRNS collection, RNM 1988/350/57, inter-departmental committee on post-war pay, allowances and pensions, report of the working party on the emoluments of the women's services, 21 May 1946, p. 2.
52. Pile, *Ack-Ack*, p. 187.
53. TNA, ADM 1/14075, letter from Commander-in-Chief, the Nore, to Secretary of the Admiralty, 4 Sept. 1943.
54. RAFM, Woodhead, X002-5638, box 1, 'As we knew them', ch. vii, 'The WAAF is taken for granted', p. 12.
55. Stone, 'The integration of women into a military service', pp. 131–2; NAM, Coulshed, 9401-243-158, Goldman, 'The utilization of women in combat', p. 58; Summerfield, *Reconstructing women's wartime lives*, pp. 127–8.
56. Gwynne-Vaughan, *Service with the army*, p. 142.
57. Mathews, *Blue tapestry*, pp. 80–1. In 1942, the *Economist* commented that one of the contributory factors in this inequality over pay was 'the reluctance of women who occupy leading positions in the war effort, especially in the women's Services, to "make trouble"'. See 'Two-Thirds of a Man', *Economist*, 5 Sept. 1942, p. 298.
58. *Parliamentary debates*, vol. 391, 3 Aug. 1943, cols. 2111–14. It might be noted here, and Summerskill alluded to this, that American women serving in the UK with the US Women's Army Corps enjoyed equal pay with their male counterparts. It seems,

however, that this was not a particular gripe of British servicewomen. See TNA 189/ 12, Royal Commission on Equal Pay, 'Discussion with the Adjutant-General to the Forces'.

59. *Parliamentary debates*, vol. 391, 3 Aug. 1943, col. 2114.
60. TNA, AIR 2/9422, 'Auxiliary Territorial Service', by W. H. T. Ottley; TNA, AIR 2/ 9422, brief for the 'women's day' debate in the House of Commons on Tuesday 3 August 1943, 31 July 1943.
61. *Parliamentary debates*, vol. 391, 3 Aug. 1943, cols. 2193–6.
62. Ibid., col. 2195.
63. Quoted in Waller and Vaughan-Rees, *Women in uniform*, p. 15.
64. Ibid., p. 151.
65. Summerfield, *Reconstructing women's wartime lives*, pp. 63–5.

Medical Matters

1. F. A. E. Crew, *The Army Medical Services: administration*, vol. 1 (London: HMSO, 1953), p. 209; Crew, *The Army Medical Services: administration*, vol. 2, p. 424; Rexford-Welch, *The Royal Air Force Medical Services*, vol. 1, *administration*, pp. 73–4, 449–50; J. L. S. Coulter, *The Royal Naval Medical Services*, vol. 1, *administration* (London: HMSO, 1954), pp. 77, 83; TNA, WO 277/6, 'The Auxiliary Territorial Service', pp. 209–11; TNA, AIR 10/5546, 'The Women's Auxiliary Air Force', pp. 38–9.
2. Crew, *The Army Medical Services: administration*, vol. 2, p. 424.
3. Wellcome Library, Camden, London (WL), papers of the Medical Women's Federation, SA/MWF/C.179, letter from Medical Secretary, Medical Women's Federation, to Leslie Hore-Belisha, 6 Dec. 1937; WL, SA/WMF/B.2/10, 'Medical women and national defence: a memorandum submitted to the Secretary of State for War in March 1939 by the council of the Medical Women's Federation', *The Medical Women's Federation Quarterly Review* (July 1939), pp. 47–51; Crew, *The Army Medical Services: administration*, vol. 1, pp. 206–9; M. Harrison, *Medicine and victory: British military medicine in the Second World War* (Oxford: Oxford University Press, 2004), p. 34.
4. WL, SA/MWF/C.179, letter from H. J. Creedy to the Secretary, British Medical Association, 21 Sept. 1939.
5. Rexford-Welch, *The Royal Air Force Medical Services*, vol. 1, *administration*, pp. 73–4; WL, SA/MWF/B.2/24, A. Winner, 'Women doctors in the armed forces in the Second World War', *Journal of the Medical Women's Federation*, vol. 49, no. 2 (April 1967), p. 104; WL, SA/MWF/C.222, E. D. Fenwick, 'Work of medical women in the RAF' in Medical Women's International Association, *Women doctors at work during the Second World War* (Stockholm: Albert Bonniers, 1948), p. 57.
6. Crew, *The Army Medical Services: administration*, vol. 1, p. 209; Crew, *The Army Medical Services: administration*, vol. 2, p. 424; Rexford-Welch, *The Royal Air Force Medical Services*, vol. 1, *administration*, pp. 74, 449; WL, SA/MWF/B.2/24, A. Winner, 'Women doctors in the armed forces in the Second World War', pp. 104, 106.
7. WL, SA/MWF/A.4/9, minutes of a meeting of the committee on medical women and war services, 15 Aug. 1941; Crew, *The Army Medical Services: administration*, vol. 1, p. 210.

8. WL, SA/MWF/C.179, 'Medical Women's Federation, memorandum for presentation to the Army Council', by Clara Stewart, 17 Sept. 1941; Crew, *The Army Medical Services: administration*, vol. 1, p. 211.

9. WL, SA/MWF/C.183, letter from S. Arnett to women medical officers, 30 Oct. 1941; WL, SA/MWF/A.4/9, minutes of a meeting of the London members of the committee on medical women and war services, 29 Jan. 1942; Crew, *The Army Medical Services: administration*, vol. 1, pp. 211-13.

10. C. Stewart, letter, *British Medical Journal*, 18 Apr. 1942, pp. 505-6; WL, SA/MWF/C.185, 'Memorandum for the BMA services committee', undated; Mathews, *Blue tapestry*, pp. 81-2.

11. Stewart, letter, *British Medical Journal*.

12. C. Stewart, letter, *British Medical Journal*, 4 July 1942, p. 23; Crew, *The Army Medical Services: administration*, vol. 1, pp. 213-14.

13. Crew, *The Army Medical Services: administration*, vol. 1, p. 214.

14. WL, SA/MWF/C.184, '"With" and not "in"', undated; WL, SA/MWF/C.185, 'Memorandum for the BMA services committee'.

15. WL, SA/MWF/C.185, 'Memorandum for the BMA services committee'. Also see E. Moberly Bell, *Storming the citadel: the rise of the woman doctor* (London: Constable & Co., 1953), pp. 185-7.

16. WL, SA/MWF/B.2/24, A. Winner, 'Women doctors in the armed forces in the Second World War', p. 105; Rexford-Welch, *The Royal Air Force Medical Services*, vol. 1, *administration*, p. 74; Coulter, *The Royal Naval Medical Services*, vol. 1, *administration*, p. 83. Women also served in the WAAF and WRNS as orthoptists. See A. V. MacLellan, *Orthoptics: the early years: recollections and a personal account* (Keighley, West Yorkshire: Ann Macvie Publishing, 2006). I am grateful to Elizabeth Crang for bringing this book to my attention.

17. Crew, *The Army Medical Services: administration*, vol. 2, pp. 427-9, 435, 439-41; Rexford-Welch, *The Royal Air Force Medical Services*, vol. 1, *administration*, pp. 445-9; Coulter, *The Royal Naval Medical Services*, vol. 1, *administration*, pp. 77-80; TNA, WO 277/6, 'The Auxiliary Territorial Service', pp. 212-14; TNA, AIR 10/5546, 'The Women's Auxiliary Air Force', pp. 39-42; *Report of the committee on amenities and welfare conditions in the three women's services*, pp. 28-9; L. Rees, 'Neurosis in the women's auxiliary services', *British Journal of Psychiatry*, vol. 95, issue 401 (1949), pp. 880-96.

18. Whateley, *As thoughts survive*, p. 114.

19. Soames, *A daughter's tale*, p. 218.

20. Crew, *The Army Medical Services: administration*, vol. 2, pp. 429-31; Rexford-Welch, *The Royal Air Force Medical Services*, vol. 1, *administration*, pp. 448-49; Coulter, *The Royal Naval Medical Services*, vol. 1, *administration*, pp. 80-1; TNA, WO 277/6, 'The Auxiliary Territorial Service', pp. 214, 228-9; TNA, AIR 10/5546, 'The Women's Auxiliary Air Force', p. 40.

21. WL, papers of the Research Board for the Correlation of Medical Science and Physical Education, SA/RBC/C.7/5, 'Report of services sub-committee: part iii – the wounded and the disabled: the Auxiliary Territorial Service', undated; Crew, *The Army Medical Services: administration*, vol. 2, pp. 429-32; J. Anderson, 'British women, disability and the Second World War', *Contemporary British History*, vol. 20, no. 1 (2006), pp. 42-43; J. Anderson, *War, disability and rehabilitation in Britain: 'soul of a nation'* (Manchester: Manchester University Press, 2011), pp. 161-2.

22. Crew, *The Army Medical Services: administration*, vol. 2, pp. 431–4; TNA, WO 277/6, 'The Auxiliary Territorial Service', pp. 214–15, 229; C. Large, letter, *The Lancet*, 15 Apr. 1944, p. 517.

23. *Report of the committee on amenities and welfare conditions in the three women's services*, p. 30; Crew, *The Army Medical Services: administration*, vol. 2, pp. 465–6; TNA, WO 277/6, 'The Auxiliary Territorial Service', pp. 234–5; TNA, AIR 2/6402, 'Women's services welfare and amenities committee: memorandum by DGMS, Air Ministry: medical services for the Women's Auxiliary Air Force', 27 Mar. 1942, p. 2.

24. *Report of the committee on amenities and welfare conditions in the three women's services*, p. 30; RAFM, Trefusis Forbes, AC 72/17/1, box 6, 'Report of the committee on amenities and welfare conditions in the three women's services', undated, p. 15.

25. Settle, *All the brave promises*, p. 48.

26. Quoted in G. J. DeGroot, 'Lipstick on her nipples, cordite in her hair: sex and romance among British servicewomen during the Second World War' in DeGroot and Peniston-Bird (eds.), *A soldier and a woman*, p. 114; IWM, Wallace, Documents.1161, p. 17.

27. Mathews, *Blue tapestry*, p. 119. It might be noted that both Rewcastle and Laughton Mathews were Roman Catholics. See 'Dr G. Rewcastle', obituary, *Times*, 22 Feb. 1951, p. 8; Thomas, 'Mathews, Dame Elvira', *ODNB*. Whilst free condoms were made available by the military authorities to British servicemen overseas (and occasionally to units at home), no provision seems to have been made for servicewomen. When rumours began to circulate in the United States that contraceptives were being distributed to the US Women's Army Corps (and one WRNS officer, Betty Hodges, claimed that they were issued 'as a matter of course' to the American women's services) such was the official concern that President Roosevelt was forced to repudiate them. See J. Marshall, 'Prevention of venereal disease in the British army' in H. Letheby Tidy (ed.), *Inter-Allied Conference on War Medicine 1942–1945* (London: Staples, 1947), pp. 261; Crew, *The Army Medical Services: administration*, vol. 2, pp. 232–3; Rexford-Welch, *The Royal Air Force Medical Services*, vol. 1, *administration*, p. 402; S. C. Rexford-Welch (ed.), *The Royal Air Force Medical Services*, vol. 3, *campaigns*, (London: HMSO, 1958), pp. 518–19; Coulter, *The Royal Naval Medical Services*, vol. 1, *administration*, p. 222; M. E. Treadwell, *United States Army in World War II: special studies: the Women's Army Corps* (Washington DC: Center of Military History, United States Army, 1991), pp. 201–5, 616–18; IWM, Hodges, Documents.8249, p. 67.

28. *Report of the committee on amenities and welfare conditions in the three women's services*, pp. 27–8.

29. TNA, T 189/12, 'Memorandum for the Royal Commission on Equal Pay', appended to 'Statement for the Royal Commission on Equal Pay'.

30. TNA, T 189/10, 'Question 4', app. 'd', 'Work and remuneration of women in the Auxiliary Territorial Service'; Crew, *The Army Medical Services: administration*, vol. 2, p. 460.

31. F. A. E. Crew, 'The Army Medical Services' in A. S. MacNalty and W. F. Mellor (eds.), *Medical services in war: the principal medical lessons of the Second World War* (London: HMSO, 1968), p. 89.

32. Rexford-Welch, *The Royal Air force Medical Services*, vol. 1, *administration*, pp. 467, 471; S. C. Rexford Welch, 'The Royal Air Force Medical Services' in W. F. Mellor (ed.), *Casualties and medical statistics* (London: HMSO, 1972), pp.

466, 601–6. These figures are arrived at by isolating the under forty-eight-hour sickness rates from the total WAAF sickness rates.

33. Rexford-Welch, *The Royal Air Force Medical Services*, vol. 1, *administration*, pp. 467–8.

34. Coulter, *The Royal Naval Medical Services*, vol. 1, *administration*, pp. 84–5.

35. Rexford-Welch, *The Royal Air Force Medical Services*, vol. 1, *administration*, p. 469.

36. F. P. Ellis, 'The Royal Naval Medical Service: medical statistics' in Mellor (ed.), *Casualties and medical statistics*, pp. 78–9; H. G. Mayne, 'The Army Medical Services' in Mellor (ed.), *Casualties and medical statistics*, pp. 446, 448, 452; Rexford-Welsh, 'The Royal Air Force Medical Services', pp. 596, 630, 632.

37. Rexford-Welsh, 'The Royal Air Force Medical Services', p. 630.

38. H. Croft, 'Emotional women and frail men: gendered diagnostics from shellshock to PTSD, 1914–2010' in A. Carden-Coyne (ed.), *Gender and conflict since 1914: historical and interdisciplinary perspectives* (Basingstoke: Palgrave Macmillan, 2012), pp. 114–15.

39. Rees, 'Neurosis in the women's auxiliary services', pp. 887–8; D. N. Parfitt, 'Psychoneurosis in RAF ground personnel', *Journal of Mental Science*, vol. 90, issue 379 (Apr. 1944), p. 571; S. I. Ballard and H. G. Miller 'Psychiatric casualties in a women's service', *British Medical Journal*, 3 Mar. 1945, p. 294.

40. 'Medical Women's Federation: social medicine in women's services', *The Lancet*, 22 Sept. 1945, p. 371; TNA, AIR 10/5546, 'The Women's Auxiliary Air Force', p. 41; Coulter, *The Royal Naval Medical Services*, vol. 1, *administration*, p. 85; IWM, papers of J. L. D. Fairfield, Documents.8448, box P372, file JLDF7/8, 'Mothers and woman power in relation to the women's services', by Dr Letitia Fairfield, 1942, p. 2; IWM, Fairfield, Documents.8448, box P372, file JLDF7/8, 'Notes for hygiene lectures to recruits (ATS)', May 1941; IWM, Fairfield, Documents.8448, box P372, file JLDF7/8, 'Care of feet in the ATS', 24 Dec. 1941.

41. Crew, *The Army Medical Services: administration*, vol. 2, pp. 457–8; TNA, WO 277/6, 'The Auxiliary Territorial Service', pp. 232–3; Rexford-Welch, *The Royal Air Force Medical Services*, vol. 1, *administration*, p. 460; TNA, AIR 10/5546, 'The Women's Auxiliary Air Force', p. 41; 'Medical Women's Federation', p. 371.

42. NAM, Cowper, 9401-247-572, draft memoir, undated, pp. 125–6; TNA, AIR 10/ 5546, 'The Women's Auxiliary Air Force', p. 41; S. C. Rexford-Welsh, 'The Royal Air Force Medical Services' in MacNalty and Mellor (eds.), *Medical Services in war*, p. 266. An investigation of ATS recruits found that incidences of infestation were higher among the lowest intelligence groups. See R. H. Ahrenfeldt, *Psychiatry in the British army in the Second World War* (London: Routledge & Kegan Paul, 1958), pp. 82–3.

43. Crew, *The Army Medical Services: administration*, vol. 2, p. 459; Rexford-Welch, *The Royal Air Force Medical Services*, vol. 1, *administration*, p. 460; TNA, WO 277/6, 'The Auxiliary Territorial Service', p. 233; TNA, AIR 10/5546, 'The Women's Auxiliary Air Force', p. 41; IWM, Fairfield, Documents.8448, 'Notes for hygiene lectures to recruits (ATS)'.

44. Crew, *The Army Medical Services: administration*, vol. 2, p. 455; TNA, WO 277/6, 'The Auxiliary Territorial Service', p. 223.

45. Sher, 'An investigation into the causes of delayed menstruation, and its treatment in the Women's Auxiliary Air Force', pp. 1, 20–5; also see *Report of the committee on amenities and welfare conditions in the three women's services*, p. 28.

46. Crew, *The Army Medical Services: administration*, vol. 2, p. 455; Sher, 'An investigation into the causes of delayed menstruation, and its treatment in the Women's Auxiliary Air Force', pp. 25–6; Coulter, *The Royal Naval Medical Services*, vol. 1, *administration*, p. 85.

47. Crew, *The Army Medical Services: administration*, vol. 2, p. 455; Sher, 'An investigation into the causes of delayed menstruation, and its treatment in the Women's Auxiliary Air Force', p. 21.

48. IWM, Fairfield, Documents.8448, box P372, file JLDF7/8, 'Notes for a lecture on special problems (for officers and NCOs of the ATS)', undated.

49. Crew, *The Army Medical Services: administration*, vol. 2, p. 456; Sher, 'An investigation into the causes of delayed menstruation, and its treatment in the Women's Auxiliary Air Force', p. 21; S. C. Rexford-Welch (ed.), *The Royal Air Force Medical Services*, vol. 2, *commands*, (London: HMSO, 1955), p. 460.

50. Crew, *The Army Medical Services: administration*, vol. 2, p. 456.

51. Ibid., pp. 461–2.

52. Rees, *The shaping of psychiatry by war*, pp. 94–5.

53. Crew, *The Army Medical Services: administration*, vol. 2, p. 455; Escott, *Women in air force blue*, p. 141; IWM, papers of M. J. James, Documents.2557, 'An account of life in the forces: Wrens 1942–1946', 1993, p. 43.

54. Taylor, *Women who went to war*, p. 43.

55. Escott, *Women in air force blue*, p. 141; Ashbee, *For the duration*, p. 28.

56. Crew, *The Army Medical Services: administration*, vol. 2, pp. 455–6; TNA, WO 277/6, 'The Auxiliary Territorial Service', p. 223; Rexford-Welch, *The Royal Air Force Medical Services*, vol. 2, *commands*, pp. 41–2.

57. IWM, Lane, Documents.137, p. 38.

58. IWM, papers of V. C. Cole, Documents.3374, untitled manuscript, 8 Sept. 1986, p. 54.

59. Crew, *The Army Medical Services: administration*, vol. 2, pp. 456.

60. Calvert, *Bull, battle-dress, lanyard & lipstick*, pp. 60–1.

61. Crew, *The Army Medical Services: administration*, vol. 2, p. 457.

62. S. O. Rose, 'Sex, citizenship, and the nation in World War II Britain', *The American Historical Review*, vol. 103, no. 4 (1998), pp. 1164–5; S. O. Rose, *Which people's war? National identity and citizenship in Britain 1939–1945* (Oxford: Oxford University Press, 2003), pp. 79–81.

63. RAFM, Trefusis Forbes, AC 72/17/1, box 7, 'Talk by the DWAAF to officers at Air Ministry', 26 Jan. 1940, p. 3.

64. Crew, *The Army Medical Services: administration*, vol. 2, p. 440, 448–50, 456; TNA, WO 277/6, 'The Auxiliary Territorial Service', pp. 215, 217, 222–4.

65. Costello, *Love, sex and war*, pp. 89–90.

66. TNA, WO 163/94, 'Hospital charges: other ranks', by AG, 17 May 1944; TNA, WO 163/94, minutes of the 163rd meeting of the executive committee of the Army Council, 26 May 1944; TNA, WO 163/53, 'War Office progress report', Sept. 1944; Crew, *The Army Medical Services: administration*, vol. 2, pp. 452–3; TNA, WO 277/6, 'The Auxiliary Territorial Service', p. 226. Pregnant auxiliaries who required hospital treatment also faced stoppages of pay, but these were abolished in 1944.

67. Rexford-Welch, *The Royal Air Force Medical Services*, vol. 1, *administration*, pp. 446–7; TNA, AIR 10/5546, 'The Women's Auxiliary Air Force', p. 42–3.

68. TNA, AIR 2/6402, 'Women's services welfare and amenities committee: memorandum by DGMS, Air Ministry: medical services for the Women's Auxiliary Air Force', p. 6.

69. TNA, ADM 1/11837, 'Women's Royal Naval Service: instructions for officers in charge of units', Admiralty, 1940, p. 4; Coulter, *The Royal Naval Medical Services*, vol. 1, *administration*, p. 86.
70. Crew, *The Army Medical Services: administration*, vol. 2, p. 457.
71. Ibid., p. 231; Costello, *Love, sex and war*, p. 20; Rexford-Welch, 'The Royal Air Force Medical Services' in Mellor (ed.), *Casualties and medical statistics*, p. 620.
72. Rexford-Welch, *The Royal Air Force Medical Services*, vol. 1, *administration*, pp. 461–2; RAFM, Woodhead, X002-5638, box 2, AHB monograph, 'Venereal disease to follow chapter ix', pp. 1–3.
73. Rexford-Welch, *The Royal Air Force Medical Services*, vol. 1, *administration*, p. 461; RAFM, Woodhead, X002-5638, box 2, AHB monograph, 'Venereal disease to follow chapter ix', p. 1.
74. Rexford-Welch, *The Royal Air Force Medical Services*, vol. 2, *commands*, p. 667.
75. Rexford-Welch, *The Royal Air Force Medical Services*, vol. 1, *administration*, p. 463.
76. Ibid., pp. 462, 473.
77. *Regulations for the Auxiliary Territorial Service 1941*, pp. 105–6; TNA, AIR 2/4460, 'Notes for the guidance of WAAF officers in dealing with pregnant women', Air Ministry, 1942, p. 2; TNA, AIR 2/4460, 'Report on meeting held at the Ministry of Labour concerning the care of women discharged from the services on grounds of pregnancy', by Squadron Officer M. A. Cumella, 22 Feb. 1943; TNA, AIR 2/4460, 'Scheme for provision of maternity care for unmarried ex-service women', 23 Apr. 1943; TNA, ADM 1/11837, 'Women's Royal Naval Service: instructions for officers in charge of units', Admiralty, 1940, p. 4.
78. Crew, *The Army Medical Services: administration*, vol. 2, p. 443; Rexford-Welch, *The Royal Air Force Medical Services*, vol. 1, *administration*, p. 463; TNA, ADM 182/133, 'WRNS – officers and ratings – pregnancy', confidential Admiralty Fleet Order 939, 14 May 1942.
79. Crew, *The Army Medical Services: administration*, vol. 2, pp. 443–4, 449–50; Crew, 'The Army Medical Services', p. 88; TNA, WO 277/6, 'The Auxiliary Territorial Service', p. 220; TNA, AIR 2/4460, letter from Director-General, Army Medical Services, to the Deputy Director of Medical Services, headquarters, Home Commands, 10 Dec. 1940.
80. TNA, AIR 2/4460, letter from Director-General of Medical Services to all principal medical officers at home, and Senior Medical Officer, No. 44 Group, 20 Dec. 1941; Crew, *The Army Medical Services: administration*, vol. 2, p. 445.
81. Crew, *The Army Medical Services: administration*, vol. 2, p. 443; RAFM, Woodhead, X002-5638, box 2, AHB monograph, 'Pregnancy to follow chapter ix', p. 1.
82. War Office, *Statistical report on the health of the army 1943–1945* (London: HMSO, 1948), p. 15.
83. Crew, *The Army Medical Services: administration*, vol. 2, p. 447.
84. S. Ferguson and H. Fitzgerald, *Studies in the Social Services* (London: HMSO and Longmans, Green and Co., 1954), p. 115; P. Thane and T. Evans, *Sinners? Scroungers? Saints? Unmarried motherhood in twentieth-century England* (Oxford: Oxford University Press, 2012), p. 65.
85. Quoted in Harris, *Women at war*, p. 34.
86. IWM, papers of O. J. Noble, Documents.685, 'Winged interlude', undated, p. 13.
87. Crew, *The Army Medical Services: administration*, vol. 2, pp. 440, 445, 448; TNA, WO 277/6, 'The Auxiliary Territorial Service', pp. 217, 221; Rexford-Welch, *The*

Royal Air Force Medical Services, vol. 1, *administration*, pp. 464–5; RAFM, Woodhead, X002-5638, box 2, AHB monograph, 'Pregnancy to follow chapter ix', pp. 5–6; TNA, AIR 2/4460, letter from A. T. Harris to the Under-Secretary of State, Air Ministry, 11 Sept. 1944; TNA, AIR 2/4460, 'Memorandum for the information of Her Majesty the Queen on the disposal and welfare arrangements for WAAF personnel discharged on grounds of pregnancy', by Lady Welsh, 5 Mar. 1945, p. 7.

88. IWM, Hill, Documents.4782, p. 58.

89. RAFM, papers of S. M. Drake-Brockman, B1761, 'Memoirs of the Women's Auxiliary Air Force (1940–1946)', undated, p. 87.

90. RAFM, Trefusis Forbes, AC 72/17/1, box 7, 'Talk by the DWAAF to officers at Air Ministry', p. 3.

91. IWM, Fairfield, Documents.8448, box P372, file JLDF7/8, 'The well-being of ATS discharged for "family reasons"', War Office, undated, passim; TNA, AIR 2/4460, 'Notes for the guidance of WAAF officers in dealing with pregnant women', passim; TNA, AIR 2/4460, letter from E. K. Stopford to W. Taylor, 3 Apr. 1941; TNA, AIR 2/4460, letter from Vera Laughton Mathews to J. Trefusis Forbes, 4 Jan. 1943; TNA, AIR 2/4460, 'WAAF personnel – release on account of pregnancy', extract from Air Ministry Confidential Order No. 12, 1943; TNA, AIR 2/4460, 'Report on meeting held at Ministry of Health on 19 February 1943 concerning the care of women discharged from the services on grounds of pregnancy'; TNA, AIR 2/4460, letter from E. A. Shearing to all commands at home, 17 May 1943; TNA, AIR 2/4460, 'Notes for guidance of matrons of ante and post-natal hostels when dealing with cases admitted under the Ministry of Health scheme for maternity care for ex-servicewomen', 28 Apr. 1944; TNA, ADM 1/11837, 'Women's Royal Naval Service: instructions for officers in charge of units', Admiralty, 1940, pp. 4–5; Crew, *The Army Medical Services: administration*, vol. 2, pp. 447–8, 451. It was estimated in 1943 that about half of unmarried pregnant members of the ATS could not be persuaded to return to their homes. See TNA, AIR 2/4460, Ministry of Health: conference with representatives of the women's services held on 19 February 1943.

92. Summerskill, *A woman's world*, p. 75.

93. Cartland, *Years of opportunity*, pp. 150–1.

94. Rexford-Welch, *The Royal Air Force Medical Services*, vol. 1, *administration*, p. 466.

95. TNA, AIR 2/4460, minutes of meeting, directors of the three women's services, 23 Dec. 1942; TNA, AIR 2/4460, 'Report on meeting held at the Ministry of Health on 19 February 1943 concerning the care of women discharged from the services on grounds of pregnancy'; TNA, AIR 2/4460, Ministry of Health: conference with representatives of the women's services held on 19 February 1943; TNA, AIR 2/4460, DWAAF confidential memorandum no. 14 (revised), Apr. 1944; *Report of the committee on amenities and welfare conditions in the three women's services*, pp. 32, 57; Whateley, *As thoughts survive*, pp. 45–6; Ferguson and Fitzgerald, *Studies in the Social Services*, pp. 115–26. I am grateful to Professor Pat Thane for bringing the material on the government scheme in this latter volume to my attention.

96. TNA, AIR 2/4460, 'Maternity care for ex-servicewomen', 28 Mar. 1945. During the first year of the scheme, one in three applications came from women whose parents had refused all responsibility for their daughters. One Ministry of Health official described this as 'a surely deplorable misconception of the duties of parenthood'. See Ferguson and Fitzgerald, *Studies in the Social Services*, p. 120.

97. TNA, AIR 2/4460, letter from A. T. Harris to the Under-Secretary of State, Air Ministry, 11 Sept. 1944.
98. Ibid.
99. TNA, AIR 2/4460, Wing Officer M. A. Cumella to DWAAF, 22 Sept. 1944.
100. TNA, AIR 2/4460, letter from E. A. Shearing to the Air Officer Commanding-in-Chief, Bomber Command, 24 Oct. 1944.
101. TNA, AIR 2/4460, letter from A. T. Harris to the Under-Secretary of State, Air Ministry, 6 Nov. 1944.

Off Duty

1. Waller and Vaughan-Rees, *Women in uniform*, p. 64; IWM, Documents.1553, ATS file, J. Skyes, undated, p. 2; J. Highfield, WW2 people's war, www.bbc.co.uk/history/ww2peopleswar/stories/21/a6000021.shtml (accessed 30 Jan. 2013).
2. IWM, Documents.1553, WAAF file, Hobson, p. 9.
3. IWM, McMurdo, Documents.3575, p. 54.
4. IWM, papers of K. F. Angus, Documents.10762, 'Remembered with advantages', undated, p. 105.
5. Waller and Vaughan-Rees, *Women in uniform*, p. 151.
6. Calvert, *Bull, battle-dress, lanyard & lipstick*, p. 49.
7. RAFM, Trefusis Forbes, AC 72/17, box 9, 'Progressive training: the discussion group', report attached to letter from Group Officer E. F. Dacre to the Director, WAAF, 17 Apr. 1943.
8. N. Scarlyn Wilson, *Education in the forces 1939–46: the civilian contribution* (London: Evans Brothers, 1949), p. 91.
9. T. Mason and E. Riedi, *Sport and the military: the British armed forces 1880–1960* (Cambridge: Cambridge University Press, 2010), pp. 247–8.
10. IWM, Goossens, Documents.2139, p. 8.
11. IWM, Kup, Documents.507, p. 10.
12. IWM, Documents.1553, ATS file, J. Sykes, undated, p. 4.
13. IWM, papers of C. M. Lowry, Documents.2283, untitled manuscript, undated, pp. 34–5. Also see Waller and Vaughan-Rees, *Women in uniform*, pp. 152–3.
14. Quoted in ibid., p. 153.
15. Quoted in C. Drifte, *Women in the Second World War* (Barnsley: Remember When, 2011), p. 109.
16. Quoted in Waller and Vaughan-Rees, *Women in uniform*, p. 158.
17. IWM, papers of J. R. O. S. Demey, Documents.1101, 'Down memory lane 1940–1946', 1986, p. 34.
18. IWM, McMurdo, Documents.3575, pp. 33–4.
19. Quoted in Taylor, *Women who went to war*, p. 230.
20. Waller and Vaughan-Rees, *Women in uniform*, p. 163.
21. C. Langhamer, '"A public house is for all classes, men and women alike": women, leisure and drink in Second World War England', *Women's History Review*, vol. 12, no. 3 (2003), pp. 423–4, 430–1, 437; D. W. Gutzke, *Women drinking out in Britain since the early twentieth century* (Manchester: Manchester University Press, 2014), p. 57.
22. IWM, papers of D. J. Carter, Documents.4483, 'A time to tell: my life in the ATS', by Joan Zeepvat, undated, p. 11.
23. IWM, papers of F. Stone, Documents.1100, 'Turns the wheel slowly', undated, p. 75.
24. Quoted in P. Lewis, *A people's war* (London: Thames Methuen, 1986), p. 134.

290 / Notes to Pages 146-149

25. Wyndham, *Love lessons and love is blue*, p. 221. Apparently, Oscarine was so named because her mother started to give birth to her during a matinée performance of Oscar Wilde's *The Importance of Being Earnest*.
26. DeGroot, 'Lipstick on her nipples', p. 112.
27. Francis, *The flyer*, pp. 35–6, 121.
28. RAFM, Trefusis Forbes, AC 72/17/1, box 6, 'Notes for the guidance of WAAF administrative officers on hygiene and health of WAAF personnel', app. 'b' to women's services welfare and amenities committee, memorandum by DGMS, Air Ministry, medical services for the Women's Auxiliary Air Force, 27 Mar. 1942. The Markham report drew attention to the habit of drinking and remarked that 'alcohol has become a symbol of conviviality for women no less than men'. See *Report of the committee on amenities and welfare conditions in the three women's services*, pp. 50–1.
29. Whateley, *As thoughts survive*, p. 114.
30. 'Smoking in the ATS', *Times*, 29 Mar. 1944, p. 2.
31. *Parliamentary debates*, vol. 398, 4 Apr. 1944, col. 1785.
32. Whateley, *As thoughts survive*, p. 114.
33. P. Tinkler, *Smoke signals: women, smoking and visual culture in Britain* (Oxford: Berg, 2006), pp. 147–8.
34. D. Reynolds, *Rich relations: the American occupation of Britain, 1942–1945* (London: Harper Collins, 1995), p. 224. Also see G. Smith, *When Jim Crow met John Bull: black American soldiers in World War II Britain* (London: I. B. Tauris, 1987), pp. 54–82.
35. Quoted in Reynolds, *Rich relations*, p. 225; TNA, CO 876/14, 'Notes on relations with coloured troops (not to be published)', MGA Southern Command to all district commanders, 7 Aug. 1942, p. 2; TNA, CO 876/14, 'United States coloured troops in the United Kingdom', memorandum by the Secretary of State, 3 Oct. 1942; TNA, PREM 4/26/9, 'United States negro troops in the United Kingdom', War Office, 25 Nov. 1942. Also see NAM, Cowper, 9401-247-575, WRAC history, pp. 380–1.
36. Settle, *All the brave promises*, pp. 49–50.
37. W. Webster, *Mixing it: diversity in World War Two Britain* (Oxford: Oxford University Press, 2018), pp. 17–18, 210–11.
38. M. Berger, 'US soldier spanks Mary Churchill as retort to jest over his big feet', *New York Times*, 1 Aug. 1942, p. 13.
39. CAC, Churchill, CHAR 20/64/46–53, letter from G. Gough to Mr and Mrs Churchill, 12 Nov. 1942; CAC, Churchill, CHAR 20/64/46–53, newspaper cutting entitled 'Yank spanks Mary Churchill', 1 Aug. 1942; CAC, Churchill, CHAR 20/64/46–53, note by J. M. M. (John Martin), 6. Aug. 1942.
40. *Regulations for the Auxiliary Territorial Service 1941*, p. 78; TNA, ADM 116/5102, Admiralty Fleet Order 4351/42, WRNS regulations and instructions, 3 Sept. 1942; Nicholson, *Kiss the girls goodbye!*, p. 31; S. Duncan, WW2 people's war, www.bbc.co.uk/history/ww2peopleswar/stories/59/a4137059.shtml (accessed 30 Jan. 2013).
41. Kirkham, 'Beauty and duty', p. 25.
42. IWM, papers of K. M. Cove, Documents.1947, 'Memoir of life in the Women's Auxiliary Air Force 1942–1946', Mar. 1992, p. 19.
43. IWM, Carter, Documents.4483, p. 16.
44. IWM, Brisley-Wilson, Documents.4009, p. 23.
45. IWM, papers of B. G. Rhodes, Documents.3226, 'When granny wore navy blue', c. 1970, p. 151.
46. MOA, 'General picture of WAAF life', p. 4.

47. IWM, Hazell, Documents.7535, pp. 64–5.
48. MOA, 'Women in wartime 1939–1945', box 3, 32-3-E, 'Cosmetics in the WAAF', by N. Masel, 23 Sept. 1941.
49. Scott, *They made invasion possible*, p. 70.
50. IWM, Lowry, Documents.2283, p. 60.
51. Nicholson, *Kiss the girls goodbye!*, p. 31; Whateley, *As thoughts survive*, p. 45. The provision of hairdressers, it was calculated, would also help to improve the 'head hygiene' problem.
52. NMRN, WRNS collection, RNM 1991/24/103, letter from Nancy Hunt to Director WRNS, 1987, 9 Feb. 1987.
53. TNA, WO 277/6, 'The Auxiliary Territorial Service', p. 99; Mary Thomson, interview with the author, 17 July 2003.
54. Francis, *The flyer*, p. 76.
55. M. A. Liskutin, *Challenge in the air: a Spitfire pilot remembers* (London: William Kimber, 1988), p. 82.
56. Lamb, *I only joined for the hat*, p. 22.
57. Quoted in Waller and Vaughan-Rees, *Women in uniform*, p. 157.
58. IWM, Hazell, Documents.7535, p. 157.
59. Quoted in D. Sheridan (ed.), *Wartime women: an anthology of women's wartime writing for Mass-Observation 1937–45* (London: Mandarin, 1991), p. 187. Corinna Peniston-Bird indicates that some wartime servicewomen found civilian men unmanly. See C. Peniston-Bird, 'Classifying the body in the Second World War: British men in and out of uniform', *Body & Society*, vol 9, issue 4 (2003), pp. 41–2.
60. MOA, 'Women in wartime 1939–1945', 32-3-E, 'The Great Digby Man-Chase', by N. Masel, 28 Dec. 1941, pp. 1–8 (reproduced as MOA, 'The Great Man-Chase', file report 1031, 5 Jan. 1942, pp. 2–6); A. Calder and D. Sheridan (eds.), *Speak for yourself: a Mass Observation anthology, 1937–49* (London: Jonathan Cape, 1984), pp. 130–4.
61. Wyndham, *Love lessons and love is blue*, pp. 193, 217–18.
62. IWM, McMurdo, Documents.3575, pp. 39–42.
63. Calvert, *Bull, battle-dress, lanyard & lipstick*, p. 56.
64. RAFM, Trefusis Forbes, AC 72/17/1, box 10, 'Talk by the Director', 20 Dec. 1939, p. 3; Gwynne-Vaughan, *Service with the army*, p. 144; IWM, Lowry, Documents.2283, p. 61.
65. IWM, Documents.1553, ATS file, Sykes, p. 4.
66. Quoted in Summerfield, *Reconstructing women's wartime lives*, p. 279.
67. Quoted in Waller and Vaughan-Rees, *Women in uniform*, p. 158.
68. De Courcy, *Debs at war*, p. 157.
69. TNA, AIR 2/10919, letter from L. A. Pattinson, headquarters, Training Command, to Under-Secretary of State, Air Ministry, 9 Jan. 1941.
70. TNA, AIR 2/10919, A. W. Street to A/AMP, 28 Oct. 1943; TNA, AIR 2/10919, AMP to PUS, 4 Nov. 1943; TNA, AIR 2/10919, A. W. Street to AMP, 9 Nov. 1943.
71. TNA, AIR 2/10919, letter from A. W. Street to Air Officers Commanding-in-Chief, 8 Nov. 1943. These stipulations were to apply equally to 'association' between WAAF officers and airmen.
72. E. Taylor, *Forces sweethearts: service romances in World War II* (London: Robert Hale, 1990), p. 165.
73. IWM, Kup, Documents.507, p. 65.
74. Calvert, *Bull, battle-dress, lanyard & lipstick*, p. 55.
75. Quoted in De Courcy, *Debs at war*, p. 96.

76. IWM, papers of J. Sears, Documents.10354, 'Summer 1944 – some memories of a Wren', 7 Dec. 1976, p. 5.
77. Ashbee, *For the duration*, p. 26.
78. Calvert, *Bull, battle-dress, lanyard & lipstick*, pp. 14, 93.
79. Quoted in DeGroot, 'Lipstick on her nipples', p. 113; IWM, Goossens, Documents.2139, p. 11.
80. IWM, papers of N. C. Walton, Documents.1109, 'Memories of WAAF service 1942–1946', 1988, p. 13.
81. IWM, Cole, Documents.3374, p. 38.
82. Mathews, *Blue tapestry*, p. 121.
83. RAFM, Trefusis Forbes, AC 72/17/1, box 4, letter from K. Trefusis Forbes to Sir Philip Joubert, 21 May 1943; TNA, AIR 2/8793, minutes of the 4th meeting of the WAAF Advisory Council, 2 June 1943. In her evidence to the Markham committee in 1942, Trefusis Forbes acknowledged that the 'emotional strain' and 'atmosphere of danger' experienced by Waafs involved in operations did encourage 'living for the moment': 'your airwoman may be awfully fond of an airman; she knows he has gone out night after night, and the chances are that sooner or later he will not come back, so dash it, you might as well'. See LSE, Markham 24/22, women's services welfare and amenities committee, minutes of evidence, 27 Mar. 1942, p. 29.
84. TNA, AIR 2/8793, minutes of the 4th meeting of the WAAF Advisory Council. Lesley Hall has written of a historical 'double moral standard which permitted sexual peccadilloes to men, while punishing the slightest deviation from chastity in women.' See L. A. Hall, *Sex, gender and social change in Britain since 1880* (Basingstoke: Palgrave Macmillan, 2013), p. 29.
85. TNA, AIR 2/8793, minutes of the 13th meeting of the WAAF Advisory Council, 5 Jan. 1945; TNA, AIR 2/4460, 'Memorandum for the information of Her Majesty the Queen on the disposal and welfare arrangements for WAAF personnel discharged on grounds of pregnancy', by Lady Welsh, 5 Mar. 1945, pp. 11–13.
86. RAFM, Woodhead, X002-5638, box 2, AHB monograph, 'Conclusions', p. 2. Also see chapter on 'Guidance on moral welfare', pp. 1–2.
87. Mathews, *Blue tapestry*, pp. 119–20.
88. Ashbee, *For the duration*, pp. 102–3.
89. Ibid., pp. 136–40.
90. Quoted in De Courcy, *Debs at war*, p. 97.
91. Whateley, *As thoughts survive*, pp. 56–7.
92. Nicholson, *Kiss the girls goodbye!*, p. 32; Douie, *Daughters of Britain*, p. 29.
93. Douie, *Daughters of Britain*, p. 29; WO 32/10663, letter from R. F. Adam to Sir Geoffrey Ince, 6 Dec. 1944
94. RAFM, Trefusis Forbes, AC 72/17/1, box 1, 'Discipline', undated; Escott, *Women in air force blue*, p. 103.
95. Mathews, *Blue tapestry*, p. 132.
96. Quoted in Taylor, *Forces sweethearts*, p. 165.
97. NAM, Cowper, 9401-247-575, WRAC history, p. 332; Whateley, *As thoughts survive*, pp. 119–20; Cartland, *The years of opportunity*, pp. 163–4; TNA, WO 277/4, 'Army welfare', compiled by Brigadier M. C. Morgan, War Office, 1953, p. 163.

98. IWM, Hodges, Documents.8249, p. 21.

99. IWM, McMurdo, Documents.3575, p. 57.

100. Beck, *A WAAF in Bomber Command*, p. 57.

101. Francis, *The flyer*, p. 79; Barnett, *Lambs in blue*, p. 58; S. P. MacKenzie, *Flying against fate: superstition and allied aircrews in World War II* (Lawrence: University of Kansas Press, 2017), p. 63.

102. D. Stafford-Clark, 'Morale and flying experience: results of a wartime study', *British Journal of Psychiatry*, vol. 95, issue 398 (1949), p. 16.

103. Smith, *Why did we join?*, p. 100.

104. C. Hodgkinson, *Best foot forward: the autobiography of Colin Hodgkinson* (London: Corgi, 1977), pp. 178–80.

105. Quoted De Courcy, *Debs at war*, p. 95.

106. Quoted in Costello, *Love, Sex and* War, pp. 79–80.

107. IWM, Littlejohn, Documents.2879, pp. 29–30.

108. MOA, 'ATS', file report 955, Nov. 1941, p. 2.

109. IWM, Documents.1553, ATS file, B. Rose, 2 Aug. 1988, p. 15.

110. *Parliamentary Debates*, vol. 400, 25 May 1944, col. 913.

111. IWM, Documents.1553, WRNS file, J. Dunhill, 3 July 1988, p. 4.

112. IWM, Walton, Documents.1109, p. 13.

113. IWM, Noble, Documents.685, pp. 3–4.

114. Quoted in Waller and Vaughan-Rees, *Women in uniform*, pp. 164–5.

115. Calvert, *Bull, battle-dress, lanyard & lipstick*, pp. 58–9.

116. Quoted in S. Neild and R. Pearson, *Women like us* (London: The Women's Press, 1992), p. 52.

117. IWM, papers of M. Herterich, Documents.9909, 'Cotton-waste soldier girls', 2000, p. 4.

118. IWM, McMurdo, Documents.3575, pp. 25–6.

119. Quoted in De Courcy, *Debs at war*, p. 160.

120. E. Vickers, 'Infantile desires and perverted practices: disciplining lesbianism in the WAAF and ATS during the Second World War', *Journal of Lesbian Studies*, vol. 13, issue 4 (2009), p. 433; E. Vickers, *Queen and country: same-sex desire in the British armed forces, 1939–45* (Manchester: Manchester University Press, 2013), p. 55.

121. Crew, *The Army Medical Services: administration*, vol. 2, p. 454; TNA, WO 277/6, 'The Auxiliary Territorial Service', p. 227.

122. IWM, Fairfield, Documents.8448, box P372, file JLDF7/8, 'A special problem', by Letitia Fairfield, Mar. 1941.

123. RAFM, Trefusis Forbes, AC 72/17/1, box 5, DWAAF to DDWAAF and P & MS, 8 Oct. 1941; Stone, 'The integration of women into a military service', p. 170; Vickers, 'Infantile desires', p. 435. In the WRNS, it seems that lesbian women were posted to different bases if discovered. See Roberts, *The WRNS in wartime*, p. 202.

124. Vickers, 'Infantile desires', pp. 437–8; Vickers, *Queen and country*, p. 130.

125. Vickers, *Queen and country*, p. 144.

126. Vickers, 'Infantile desires', pp. 431, 435–6, 439; Vickers, *Queen and country*, pp. 123–4, 129.

127. A. L. Winner, 'Homosexuality in women', *The Medical Press and Circular*, vol. 217 (1947), p. 220.

128. Quoted in Neild and Pearson, *Women like us*, p. 59.

Overseas Service

1. TNA, WO 277/6, 'The Auxiliary Territorial Service', pp. 39–41, 77–83, 103–16; TNA, AIR 10/5546, 'The Women's Auxiliary Air Force', pp. 105, 112–27; TNA, ADM 234/219, 'The Women's Royal Naval Service', pp. 66, 80–1, 95–9.

2. TNA, WO 277/6, 'The Auxiliary Territorial Service', app. vi, p. 278; TNA, AIR 10/5546, 'The Women's Auxiliary Air Force', app. 5, p. 139; TNA, ADM 234/219, 'The Women's Royal Naval Service', p. 100.

3. TNA, AIR 10/5546, 'The Women's Auxiliary Air Force', p. 117.

4. TNA, AIR 2/4815, AMP to AMSO, Vice-CAS, US of S, S of S, PUS, Dec. 1941.

5. TNA, AIR 2/5018, DGO to AMP, 26 July 1943; TNA, AIR 2/5018, S11 to AMP, 18 Nov. 1943; TNA, AIR 2/5018, DWAAF to D of M, 22 Nov. 1943; TNA, AIR 2/5018, AMP to S of S, 22 Jan. 1944; TNA, AIR 2/5018, A. Sinclair to AMP, 24 Jan. 1944.

6. TNA, AIR 10/5546, 'The Women's Auxiliary Air Force', p. 105.

7. TNA, WO 32/10663, 'Policy regarding employment of WRNS and WAAF overseas', app. 'a' to 'Employment of ATS overseas', by AG, 7 Mar. 1944.

8. TNA, WO 32/10663, 'Compulsory posting of ATS overseas', brief for S of S, 5 Nov. 1944; TNA, WO 32/10663, 'Policy regarding employment of WRNS and WAAF overseas'.

9. Rexford-Welch, *The Royal Air Force Medical Services*, vol. 1, *administration*, p. 451.

10. Mathews, *Blue tapestry*, pp. 148–9; Stuart Mason, *Britannia's daughters*, pp. 82–3.

11. TNA, ADM 1/18880, minute by Head of N, 18 Jan. 1944; TNA, ADM 1/18880, minute by Head of N, 25 Jan. 1944; Mathews, *Blue tapestry*, p. 149.

12. TNA, WO 32/10663, letter from B. C. T. Paget to Under-Secretary of State, War Office, 6 July 1943.

13. TNA, WO 32/10663, 'Employment of ATS in European theatres of war', by AG, 31 Aug. 1943. The Japanese were widely regarded as fanatical, cruel and inhuman. See, for example, MOA, 'People's attitude with regard to fighting the Japanese after the European war is over', file report 1887, 31 Aug. 1943, p. 1.

14. TNA, WO 32/10663, extract from the minutes of the 126th meeting of the executive committee of the Army Council, 3 Sept. 1943; TNA, WO 32/10663, 'Employment of ATS in European theatres of war', by AG, 2 Nov. 1943; TNA, WO 32/10663, extract from the minutes of the 137th meeting of the executive committee of the Army Council, 19 Nov. 1943 (and undated addition to the minutes).

15. TNA, WO 32/10663, FCB [Sir Frederick Bovenschen] to VCIGS, 27 Nov. 1943.

16. TNA, WO 32/10663, FCB to S of S, 22 Dec. 1943; TNA, WO 32/10663, minute by PJG, 23 Dec. 1943; TNA, WO 32/10663, extract from the minutes of the 142nd meeting of the executive committee of the Army Council, 31 Dec. 1943.

17. TNA, ADM 1/18880, minute by Head of N, 25 Jan. 1944; TNA, ADM 1/18880, minute by Head of CW, 26 Jan. 1944.

18. TNA, ADM 1/18880, AUW to Secretary, 24 Apr. 1944; TNA, ADM 1/18880, HVM to Second Sea Lord, 30 Apr. 1944; TNA, ADM 1/18880, minute by Head of N, 6 July 1945; TNA, AIR 2/8268, letter from E. A. Shearing to the Air Commander-in-Chief, Allied Expeditionary Air Force, 28 May 1944.

19. TNA, WO 163/449, standing committee on army post-war problems: regular women's service: final report of the sub-committee, 1 Apr. 1947, p. 9.

20. Whateley, *As thoughts survive*, p. 86. Whateley places the meeting in November 1943, but it appears to have taken place in January 1944.
21. TNA, AIR 10/5546, 'The Women's Auxiliary Air Force', p. 108–9.
22. Mason, *Britannia's daughters*, pp. 45–6. A RNLI lifeboat, *Aguila Wren*, was built in memory of the lost WRNS personnel. It served at Aberystwyth, and later at Redcar, between 1951 and 1972. It was said to have been launched fifty-three times and saved thirty-eight lives. See National Historic Ships UK www .nationalhistoricships.org.uk/register/2242/aguila-wren (accessed 4 May 2013).
23. Quoted in Mason, *Britannia's daughters*, p. 103; Mathews, *Blue tapestry*, p. 146.
24. Mathews, *Blue tapestry*, p. 147.
25. IWM, papers of M. Pratt, Documents.8241, 'Recollections of a wartime Wren', undated, p. 9. HMS *Chitral* was in fact an armed merchant cruiser.
26. Bidwell, *The Women's Royal Army Corps*, pp. 95–100; TNA, WO 277/6, 'The Auxiliary Territorial Service', pp. 78–9, 103; A. Granit-Hacohen (translated by O. Cummings), *Hebrew women join the forces: Jewish women from Palestine in the British forces during the Second World War* (London: Valletine Mitchell, 2017), pp. 115–16; M. Abbasi, 'Palestinians fighting against Nazis: the story of the Palestinian volunteers in the Second World War', *War in History*, vol. 26, issue 2 (2019), pp. 242–5; E. Herlitz, 'ATS and WAAF in World War II', Jewish Women's Archive, jwa.org/encyclopedia/article/ats-and-waaf-in-world-war-ii (accessed 21 Mar. 2013).
27. TNA, WO 277/6, 'The Auxiliary Territorial Service', p. 103; Granit-Hacohen, *Hebrew women join the forces*, p. 274–5.
28. NAM, papers of T. Taylor, 9802-141-8, 'ATS drivers in the Middle East', by T. Taylor, undated, p. 2.
29. Bidwell, *The Women's Royal Army Corps*, pp. 97–8; NAM, Cowper, 9401-247-575, WRAC history, pp. 304–6, 320; NAM, Cowper, 9401-247-264-4/5, letter from Belinda Buxton to Julia Cowper, 11 Apr. 1956; Granit-Hacohen, *Hebrew women join the forces*, pp. 40–1, 264–7.
30. TNA, WO 277/6, 'The Auxiliary Territorial Service', pp. 103–4; NAM, Taylor, 9802-141-7-9, 'ATS drivers in the Middle East', pp. 1, 3; Granit-Hacohen, *Hebrew women join the forces*, p. 211.
31. TNA, WO 277/6, 'The Auxiliary Territorial Service', p. 103.
32. D. N. Izraeli, 'Gendering military service in the Israeli defence forces' in DeGroot and Peniston-Bird (eds.), *A soldier and a woman*, p. 258; Granit-Hacohen, *Hebrew women join the forces*, pp. 369, 373.
33. TNA, WO 277/6, 'The Auxiliary Territorial Service', pp. 82, 109.
34. B. Bousquet and C. Douglas, *West Indian women at war: British racism in World War II* (London: Lawrence & Wishart, 1991), pp. 3, 50, 82–95; T. Kushner, '"Without intending any of the most undesirable features of a colour bar": race science, Europeanness and the British armed forces during the twentieth century', *Patterns of Prejudice*, vol. 46, nos. 3–4 (2012), pp. 350, 354.
35. Bousquet and Douglas, *West Indian women at war*, pp. 52, 55; TNA, CO 968/81/4, letter from A. J. K. Pigott to N. L. Mayle, 17 Feb. 1943.
36. Bousquet and Douglas, *West Indian women at war*, pp. 29, 50–2; C. Jones, 'West Indian women at war' in D. Dabydeen, J. Gilmore and C. Jones (eds.), *The Oxford companion to Black British history* (Oxford: Oxford University Press, 2007), pp. 520–3.
37. Bousquet and Douglas, *West Indian women at war*, pp. 2–3, 52–3, 94–103.
38. Quoted in ibid., p. 103; TNA, CO 968/81/4, letter from P. J. Grigg to O. Stanley, 19 May 1943.

39. Bousquet and Douglas, *West Indian women at war*, pp. 2, 107. The Air Ministry and the Admiralty also seem to have done their best to exclude black colonial recruits from the WAAF and the WRNS. See Bousquet and Douglas, *West Indian women at war*, pp. 91–3; and TNA, ADM 234/219, 'The Women's Royal Naval Service', pp. 51–2.

40. Quoted in D. Bean, *Jamaican women and the world wars: on the front lines of change* (Cham, Switzerland: Palgrave Macmillan, 2018), p. 199.

41. Bousquet and Douglas, *West Indian women at war*, pp. 114–15; Bean, *Jamaican women and the world wars*, p. 213.

42. Quoted in P. Fryer, *Staying power: the history of black people in Britain* (London: Pluto Press, 2010), p. 363.

43. RAFM, Woodhead, X002-5638, box 1, 'As we knew them', ch xvii, 'The WAAF in the Middle Eastern and Far Eastern theatres', p. 11.

44. NMM, DAU 161, 'Compulsory service overseas', undated; TNA, AIR 2/5018, extract from parliamentary debates, House of Commons official report, 20 Oct. 1943; TNA, WO 32/10663, 'Policy regarding employment of WRNS and WAAF overseas'; TNA, ADM 234/219, 'The Women's Royal Naval Service', p. 81; Wadge, *Women in uniform,* p. 75. A married woman was not excluded from the obligation to serve overseas but could claim exemption if 'her husband objects' or if she had 'set up home' in the UK with her husband and he was unlikely to be called up. See ADM 1/17177, 'WRNS – compulsory overseas service', 2 Jan. 1945.

45. TNA, AIR 2/9278, 'Item 6: compulsory posting of ATS overseas', brief, 6 Nov. 1944; TNA, AIR 2/9278, E. A. Shearing to DPR, 20 Dec. 1944; TNA, AIR 2/5018, E. A. Shearing to PS to S of S, 12 Jan. 1945; TNA, AIR 10/5546, 'The Women's Auxiliary Air Force', p. 106.

46. TNA, WO 32/10663, 'Employment of ATS overseas', by AG, 7 Mar. 1944; TNA, WO 32/10663, extract from the minutes of the 152nd meeting of the executive committee of the Army Council, 10 Mar. 1944; TNA, WO 32/10663, letter from G. W. Lambert to Commanders-in-Chief, 28 Mar. 1944.

47. TNA, WO 32/10663, AG to S of S, 7 Oct. 1944.

48. TNA, WO 32/10663, 'War Cabinet: compulsory posting of ATS overseas', brief for S of S, 5 Nov. 1944.

49. TNA, CAB 66/57, 'Compulsory posting of ATS overseas', by PJG, 1 Nov. 1944.

50. TNA, CAB 65/44, conclusions of a meeting of the War Cabinet, 13 Nov. 1944.

51. TNA, WO 32/10663, draft letter from S of S to Ernest Bevin, undated; TNA, WO 32/10663, 'Compulsory posting of ATS overseas', draft memorandum by S of S, undated.

52. TNA, WO 32/10663, 'Compulsory posting of ATS overseas', draft memorandum by S of S.

53. TNA, WO 32/10663, AG to ACS, 20 Nov. 1944; TNA, WO 32/10663, letter from R. F. Adam to Sir Godfrey Ince, 6 Dec. 1944; TNA, PREM 3/506/4, letter from Ernest Bevin to Prime Minister, 13 Dec. 1944; CAB 65/44, conclusions of a meeting of the War Cabinet, 18 Dec. 1944.

54. CAC, Churchill, CHAR 1/381/45–49, letter from WSC to Randolph Churchill, 23 Nov. 1944; Soames, *A daughter's tale*, pp. 322–3.

55. *Parliamentary debates*, vol. 406, 21 Dec. 1944, cols. 1957–8; *Parliamentary debates*, vol. 399, 9 May 1944, col. 1729. The conditions and amenities in these latter areas were clearly not deemed suitable for servicewomen.

56. Whateley, *As thoughts survive*, pp. 152–3.

57. *Parliamentary debates*, vol. 407, 24 Jan. 1945, col. 866.

58. *Parliamentary debates*, vol. 407, 24 Jan. 1945, cols. 843–6, 857, 865, 871–3, 877, 880.
59. *Parliamentary debates*, vol. 407, 24 Jan. 1945, col. 845.
60. *Parliamentary debates*, vol. 407, 24 Jan. 1945, cols. 849, 860, 883–94.
61. *Parliamentary debates*, vol. 407, 24 Jan. 1945, col. 854.
62. TNA, WO 32/10663, 'Employment of ATS overseas', notice board information, summary of ACI 370 of 1945, issued 7 Apr. 1945; WO 277/6, 'The Auxiliary Territorial Service', p. 102.
63. Whateley, *As thoughts survive*, pp. 155–6.
64. Ibid., p. 157.
65. Rosenzweig, 'The construction of policy for women in the British armed forces 1938–1945', pp. 122–5.
66. LSE, Markham 24/28, letter from E. M. Bowker to Mrs Whateley, undated [1945].
67. LSE, Markham 24/28, report of a visit by Miss Markham and Mrs Stocks to ATS units at SHAEF and 21 Army Group, May 1945, pp. 5–7.
68. LSE, Markham 24/28, letter from Ronald Adam to Miss Markham, 29 June 1945.
69. Whateley, *As thoughts survive*, p. 188.
70. Ibid., p. 189.
71. TNA, WO 277/6, 'The Auxiliary Territorial Service', pp. 39–41, 77–83, 102–16; TNA, AIR 10/5546, 'The Women's Auxiliary Air Force', pp. 117–27; TNA, ADM 234/219, 'The Women's Royal Naval Service', appendices, 'WRNS personnel overseas – August, 1945 – officers' and 'WRNS personnel overseas – August, 1945 – ratings'; Wadge, *Women in uniform*, pp. 133–6.
72. TNA, ADM 234/219, 'The Women's Royal Naval Service', p. 84; Mathews, *Blue tapestry*, pp. 196–7; NMRN, WRNS collection, RNM 1988/350/72/1, 'Notes for naval estimates for the year ending 31 January 1944', by DWRNS, undated, p. 1; Roberts, *The WRNS in wartime*, p. 175.
73. J. Schwarz, 'A bird's eye view of the Yalta conference by a Wren', WW2 people's war, www.bbc.co.uk/history/ww2peopleswar/stories/12/a4336012.shtml (accessed 17 July 2013).
74. Barnett, *Lambs in blue*, pp. 102–3. Also see 'Two girls on a war mission', WW2 people's war, www.bbc.co.uk/history/ww2peopleswar/stories/01/a4264201.shtml (accessed 19 Aug. 2013).
75. IWM, papers of D. E. Smith, Documents.2379, 'A short account of two years in Europe: 1944–1946', undated, p. 1.
76. IWM, Documents.1553, WRNS file, J. Dinwoodie, undated, p. 9.
77. TNA, AIR 10/5546, 'The Women's Auxiliary Air Force', pp. 117–18.
78. Quoted in V. Lynn, *Unsung heroes: the women who won the war* (London: Sidgwick and Jackson, 1990), p. 106.
79. Quoted in Taylor, *Women who went to war*, p. 58.
80. TNA, WO 277/6, 'The Auxiliary Territorial Service', pp. 40–1; Gwynne-Vaughan, *Service with the army*, pp. 124–5; Bidwell, *The Women's Royal Army Corps*, pp. 49–50; Wadge, *Women in uniform*, p. 134.
81. P. Hall, *What a way to win a war: the story of No. 11 Coy. M.T.C, and 5-0-2 M.A. C., A.T.S, 1940–1945* (Tunbridge Wells: Midas Books, 1978), p. 100.
82. IWP, papers of E. J. F. Knowles, Documents.1798, 'Underage and overseas', undated, p. 11. Also see E. Watkins, *Cypher officer in Cairo, Kenya, Caserta* (Brighton: Pen Press Publishers, 2008), pp. 9–10.
83. Quoted in Drifte, *Women in the Second World War*, p. 28. As an aside, in early 1943 Pat Hall was among a party of twenty ATS women in Egypt who were taken on one of the first tours of the El Alamein battlefield, which was still strewn with

wrecked vehicles and uncleared minefields. 'In the high cold wind', she noted, 'we had to be particularly careful to hang on to our caps as an ATS cap badge found in later years on the site of a minefield might have given an erroneous twist to the history of the battle.' See Hall, *What a way to win a war*, pp. 111–12.

84. TNA, WO 277/6, 'The Auxiliary Territorial Service', p. 108; Bidwell, *The Women's Royal Army Corps*, p. 110.

85. TNA, WO 277/6, 'The Auxiliary Territorial Service', pp. 114–15;

86. Quoted in Saywell, *Women in war*, p. 26.

87. Ibid., p. 27.

88. TNA, WO 277/6, 'The Auxiliary Territorial Service', p. 115. Another one was claimed.

89. Pile, *Ack-Ack*, p. 376.

90. Hall, *What a way to win a war*, pp. 107–8.

91. Ibid., pp. 106–7.

92. Quoted in Saywell, *Women in war*, p. 27.

93. IWM, Documents.1553, WAAF file, Winter, p. 22.

94. IWM, Documents.1553, WRNS file, P. Taylor, undated, pp. 6, 8.

95. IWM, Documents.1553, WAAF file, E. Shaw, undated, pp. 5, 7.

96. IWM, papers of E. W. Dunkley, Documents.12470, 'As I remember it', Apr. 2001, p. 3.

97. Watkins, *Cypher officer*, p. 54.

98. IWM, Ackroyd, Documents.660, 'Memories of WRNS days, 1943–45', by D. Smith, 20 Nov. 1990, p. 11. Joan Russell recalled that in Colombo she and her fellow Wrens had to be accompanied by a male escort when going out for an evening and signed out of their quarters. This procedure, she surmised, must have become garbled in the telling because when an American aircraft carrier arrived in the harbour, the ship's company turned up at the camp gates shouting 'We Wanna Wren'. It seems that 'word had gone around that if you wanted a Wren you signed for one like a parcel and she was presumably supposed to be handed over like a parcel.' See IWM, Ackroyd, Documents.660, letter from Joan Russell to Miggs Ackroyd, 10 June 1989.

99. IWM, Wright, Documents.4298, p. 87.

100. IWM, Martin, Documents.11884, p. 30.

101. IWM, Mannock, Documents.7538, pp. 66–7.

102. NMM, DAU 173, 'Early notes on Kilindini', by Third Officer Todd, 11 Feb. 1944.

103. Quoted in De Courcy, *Debs at war*, p. 97.

104. NMRN, WRNS collection, RNM 1988/350/18/77, B. Platts, 'I was there', *The Wren*, no. 249 (1970), p. 38.

105. IWM, Orde, Documents.6468, p. 189.

106. Barnett, *Lambs in Blue*, p. 132.

107. IWM, Hodges, Documents.8249, p. 75.

108. TNA, ADM 1/25860, letter from Dorothy Mackenzie, Office of Flag Officer, Levant and Eastern Mediterranean, to the Superintendent, WRNS, Western Approaches, 16 June 1944. In 1944, the Home Office knew of 'only 12 to 20 cases' of illegitimate children born overseas to servicewomen. See TNA, Home Office papers (HO), 213/179, meeting in Sir Alexander Maxwell's room on 30 Mar. 1944.

109. TNA, ADM 1/25860, letter from Admiralty to Commanders-in-Chief British Pacific Fleet, East Indies Fleet, Mediterranean, South Atlantic, and Flag Officer Commanding West Africa, 6 June 1945.

110. IWM, Documents.1553, WRNS file, D. Baldwin, 1 Apr. 1987, p. 4.

111. IWM, Wright, Documents. 4298, p. 86.

112. De Courcy, *Debs at war*, p. 116.

113. IWM, Mannock, Documents.7538, p. 120.
114. Ibid.
115. Ibid., pp. 120–1.
116. TNA, ADM 1/15101, 'WRNS: wearing of plain clothes overseas', by VLM, 18 Mar. 1944. Also see Rosenzweig, 'The construction of policy for women in the British armed forces 1938–1945', pp. 126–8.
117. TNA, ADM 1/15101, minute by DWRNS, 10 Apr. 1944.
118. TNA, ADM 1/15101, minute by DWRNS, 2 Mar. 1944.
119. TNA, ADM 1/15101, 'WRNS: wearing of plain clothes overseas'.
120. TNA, ADM 1/15101, letter from Admiralty to Commanders-in-Chief Canadian North West Atlantic, Eastern Fleet, Mediterranean and South Atlantic, 28 June 1944.
121. TNA, ADM 1/15101, CFISBC Mediterranean to Admiralty, 6 Sept. 1944.
122. TNA, ADM 1/15101, letter from J. H. D. Cunningham to the Admiralty, 24 Sept. 1944. Also see Q. Colville, 'Jack Tar and the gentleman officer: the role of uniform in shaping the class- and gender-related identities of British naval personnel, 1930–1939' in *Transactions of the Royal Historical Society*, 6th series, vol. 13 (Cambridge: Cambridge University Press, 2003), p. 116.
123. TNA, ADM 1/15101, letter from J. F. Somerville to the Admiralty, 15 Aug. 1944.
124. Ibid.
125. TNA, ADM 1/15101, minute by DWRNS, 7 Oct. 1944; TNA, ADM 1/15101, letter from Admiralty to Commanders-in-Chief Canadian North West Atlantic, East Indies Station, Mediterranean, South Atlantic and British Admiralty Delegation, HMS *Sakar*, 29 Nov. 1944.
126. TNA, ADM 1/15101, minute by WRNS, 3 Mar. 1945.
127. IWM, Hodges, Documents.8249, pp. 86–7.
128. A. Sebba, *Laura Ashley: a life by design* (London: Weidenfeld and Nicolson, 1990), pp. 23–5; NMRN, WRNS collection, RNM 1991/24/128, M. Mellor, 'Life with Laura', 1988, p. 2; 'In the WRNS with Laura Ashley', WW2 people's war, www .bbc.co.uk/history/ww2peopleswar/stories/46/a2939646.shtml (accessed 12 Sept. 2013).
129. IWM, McMurdo, Documents.3575, p. 139.
130. NAM, papers of D. Dixon, 9802-64-2-2, 'W/246131 Cpl. Dixon, D. ATS', Sept. 1987, pp. 2, 12.
131. Mack, *Dancing on the waves*, p. 162.
132. TNA, ADM 1/16195, minute by PAS(NP), 26 Mar. 1945.

Demobilisation and the Creation of the Permanent Women's Services

1. TNA, WO 277/12, 'Manpower problems', p. 65; TNA, AIR 41/65, 'Manning: plans and policy', pp. 255–63.
2. *Re-allocation of man-power between the armed forces and civilian employment during the interim period between the defeat of Germany and the defeat of Japan*, cmd. 6548 (London: HMSO, 1944), passim; Ministry of Labour and National Service, *Release and resettlement: an explanation of your position and rights* (London: HMSO, 1945), pp. 3–6, 9–10, 17–21, 24–5; TNA, LAB 76/13, 'Women's auxiliary services', p. 86; 'Priority for married women – not men', *Daily Mail*, 22 Sept. 1944, p. 1. In the WRNS, immobile personnel were to be treated for release purposes like mobiles, but if their local naval base closed down and they became redundant they were to be released 'in excess of establishment' irrespective of age and length of service. See NMM, DAU 152, 'Histories of special

subjects 1939–1945', BR 1075, 'Demobilization of the navy 1945–1948', Admiralty, 1957, p 7.

3. *Re-allocation of man-power*, p. 4; Ministry of Labour and National Service, *Release and resettlement*, pp. 9–10.

4. P. Summerfield, '"It did me good in lots of ways": British women in transition from war to peace' in C. Duchen and I. Bandhauer-Schöffmann (eds.), *When the war was over: women, war and peace in Europe, 1940–1956* (London: Leicester University Press, 2000), p. 17. Also see J. Swindells, 'Coming home to heaven: manpower and myth in 1944 Britain', *Women's History Review*, vol. 4, no. 2 (1995).

5. P. Allatt, 'Men and war: status, class and the social reproduction of masculinity' in E. Gamarnikow, D. Morgan, J. Purvis and D. Taylorson (eds.), *The public and the private* (London: Heinemann, 1983), passim; TNA, WO 277/6, 'The Auxiliary Territorial Service', pp. 172–9; *Report of the committee on amenities and welfare conditions in the three women's services*, pp. 43–4.

6. Army Bureau of Current Affairs, 'Women's place . . .', *Current Affairs*, no. 61, War Office, 29 Jan. 1944, pp. 3, 5.

7. Ibid., pp. 9–10. There were said to have been difficulties in interesting members of the ATS in current affairs. Indeed, a survey undertaken at one ATS training centre revealed that 70 per cent of the recruits did not realise that they had the right to vote. Hawkins and Brimble, *Adult education: the record of the British army*, p. 148.

8. TNA, WO 32/11573, minutes of the 6th meeting of the inter-services committee on educational and vocational training, 8 Sept. 1944.

9. IWM, De Wolff, Documents.742, pp. 101–2.

10. NAM, papers of H. J. Impson, 8310–148, 'Donnington group: opening of the ATS home training and handicraft centre by Lieut-General D. G. Watson', 20 Sept. 1944.

11. NMM, DAU 166, WRNS bi-monthly statement on the manpower situation, 1 May 1946; NMM, DAU 162/2, 'Education and resettlement education', Admiralty, 17 Feb. 1947, p. 66; Fletcher, *The WRNS*, pp. 90–1.

12. Scarlyn Wilson, *Education in the forces 1939–46*, pp. 94–5.

13. Escott, *Women in air force blue*, p. 235.

14. Ibid; IWM, De Wolff, Documents.742, p. 102. Kathleen Cove trained as a WAAF instructor in economics for the release period but was asked if she would teach domestic science instead, such was the demand for these courses. She declined on the grounds that 'at this time I could just about boil an egg or toast some cheese'. See IWM, Cove, Documents.1947, pp. 25–6, 30.

15. Watkins, *Cypher officer*, p. 171.

16. 'The Women's Auxiliary Air Force', *The Royal Air Force Quarterly*, vol. 16 (1944–45), p. 216.

17. IWM, papers of M. R. Mills, Documents.6503, 'Women soldiers: a memoir of the ATS', 1991, pp. 44–5.

18. TNA, WO 277/6, 'The Auxiliary Territorial Service', pp. 118–19; TNA, AIR 41/65, 'Manning: plans and policy', pp. 264–6, 268–9; Escott, *Women in air force blue*, pp. 236–8; NMM, DAU 152, Histories of special subjects 1939–1945, BR 1075, 'Demobilization of the navy 1945–1948', pp. 16–17, 29; Fletcher, *The WRNS*, p. 80.

19. IWM, Stone, Documents.1100, pp. 101–3; Peake, *Pure chance*, pp. 144–5.

20. Peake, *Pure chance*, p. 144.

21. RAFM, Woodhead, X002 5638, box 1, 'As we knew them', ch. xix, 'Releases and conclusion', pp. 3–4.

22. TNA, WO 277/12, 'Manpower problems', p. 70. Also see Sheridan (ed.), *Wartime women*, p. 235.
23. TNA, AIR 10/5546, 'The Women's Auxiliary Air Force', p. 56; TNA, WO 277/6, 'The Auxiliary Territorial Service', p. 119; *Parliamentary debates*, vol. 415, 8 Nov. 1945, c. 1601.
24. Whateley, *As thoughts survive*, p. 186.
25. WO 277/6, 'The Auxiliary Territorial Service', p. 119; NMM, DAU 152, 'Histories of special subjects 1939–1945', BR 1075, 'Demobilization of the navy 1945–1948', p. 46.
26. Ministry of Labour and National Service, *Release and resettlement*, p. 10.
27. TNA, AIR 10/5546, 'The Women's Auxiliary Air Force', p. 56.
28. Whateley, *As thoughts survive*, p. 180.
29. R. Pope, 'The planning and implementation of British demobilisation, 1941–1946' (PhD thesis, the Open University, 1985), p. 278; J. A. Crang, 'Welcome to civvy street: the demobilisation of the British armed forces after the Second World War', *The Historian*, no. 46 (summer 1995), pp. 18–21; A. Allport, *Demobbed: coming home after the Second World War* (London: Yale University Press, 2009), p. 48.
30. Central Statistical Office, *Fighting with figures*, table 3.7, p. 42; *Ministry of Labour and National Service: report for the years 1939–1946*, p. 151.
31. TNA, WO 277/12, 'Manpower problems', p. 78.
32. Scott, *They made invasion possible*, p. 147; D. Sheridan, 'Ambivalent memories: women and the 1939–45 war in Britain', *Oral History* (Spring 1990), p. 34; Stone, 'The integration of women into a military service', p. 135.
33. *Parliamentary debates*, vol. 391, 3 Aug. 1943, c. 2127.
34. Mass Observation, *The journey home* (London: John Murray, 1944), p. 59.
35. Ibid., p. 60. Also see S. Todd, *Young women, work, and family in England 1918–1950* (Oxford: Oxford University Press, 2005), p. 142.
36. Wyndham, *Love lessons and love is blue*, p. 394.
37. Quoted in Escott, *Women in air force blue*, p. 238.
38. IWM, Documents.1553, WRNS file, Dunhill, pp. 4–5; Waller and Vaughan-Rees, *Women in uniform*, p. 189.
39. IWM, Myler, Documents.7972, pp. 97–8.
40. IWM, Documents.1553, WRNS file, Sealey, p. 7.
41. Quoted in Waller and Vaughan-Rees, *Women in uniform*, p. 188.
42. Mack, *Dancing on the waves*, p. 186.
43. IWM, Hazell, Documents.7535, p. 271.
44. NMRN, WRNS collection, RNM 1994/422, quoted in 'Happy memories of HMS *Tormentor* 1940–1946: a brief history', by K. Scott, undated, p. 217.
45. H. Forrester, *Lime street at two* (London: Harper Collins, 1994), p. 431.
46. TNA, CAB 66/33, 'Future of the women's services', by Deputy Prime Minister, 13 Jan 1943; *Report of the committee on amenities and welfare conditions in the three women's services*, p. 53; TNA, CAB 65/33, conclusions of a meeting of the War Cabinet, 20 Jan. 1943.
47. TNA, CAB 92/112, report of the committee on the women's services, 24 June 1943, pp. 1–3.
48. TNA, CAB 92/112, minutes of a meeting of the committee on the women's services, 21 May 1943; TNA, CAB 92/112, report of the committee on the women's services, p. 3.
49. TNA, CAB 92/112, minutes of a meeting of the committee on the women's services, 7 May 1943.

50. Ibid; TNA, CAB 92/112, report of the committee on the women's services, p. 3.
51. TNA, CAB 92/112, report of the committee on the women's services, p. 3.
52. TNA, CAB 92/112, minutes of a meeting of the committee on the women's services, 20 April 1943.
53. TNA, CAB 92/112, report of the committee on the women's services, p. 4.
54. Ibid., p. 5.
55. TNA, CAB 65/35, conclusions of a meeting of the War Cabinet, 5 July 1943; TNA, AIR 2/7824, extract from Hansard, 22 July 1943.
56. TNA, AIR 2/7824, committee appointed by the Air Member for Personnel to discuss the policy for the manning of the post-war Royal Air Force: 6th interim report: Women's Auxiliary Air Force, Dec. 1944.
57. Ibid.
58. TNA, AIR 2/7824, 'Future of the WAAF', by AMP, 31 Jan. 1945; TNA, AIR 2/7824, extract from the conclusions of the 5th meeting of the Air Council post-war planning committee, 7 Feb. 1945.
59. TNA, AIR 2/7824, 'Future of the WAAF', by AMP, 20 June 1945.
60. TNA, AIR 2/7824, extract from the conclusions of a meeting of the Air Council, 17 July 1945.
61. TNA, AIR 2/7824, 'Future of the women's services', by the Secretary of State for Air, Aug. 1945; Sherit, 'The integration of women into the Royal Navy and the Royal Air Force', pp. 34–6; Sherit, Women on the front line, pp. 36–8.
62. TNA, WO 32/13160, army post-war problems, committee to consider the future of the women's services in the post-war army, 23 Feb. 1945; TNA, WO 32/13160, minutes of the 197th meeting of the executive committee of the Army Council, 19 Jan. 1945.
63. TNA, WO 32/13160, 'The future of the women's services', by DATS and DD of O (ATS), undated; TNA, WO 32/13160, army post-war problems, 'Future of the women's services', 17 May 1945; TNA, WO 32/13160, extract from the minutes of the 32nd meeting of the standing committee on army post-war problems, 31 May 1945.
64. TNA, WO 163/97, 'Provision of a permanent regular women's service as part of the post-war army', 12th interim report of the standing committee on army post-war problems, Aug. 1945.
65. TNA, WO 163/97, minutes of the 226th meeting of the executive committee of the Army Council, 10 Aug. 1945.
66. TNA, WO 32/13160, extract from the minutes of the 39th meeting of the standing committee on army post-war problems, 6 Sept. 1945; TNA, AIR 2/7824, letter from A. C. W. Drew to G. S. Whittuck, 11 Sept. 1945; TNA, AIR 2/7824, 'Future of the WAAF', by AMP, 11 Jan. 1946; Sherit, 'The integration of women into the Royal Navy and the Royal Air Force', pp. 36–7; Sherit, Women on the front line, pp. 38–9.
67. TNA, ADM 1/18957, board reconstruction committee: naval personnel reconstruction committee, 1st interim report, 7 Aug. 1945.
68. TNA, T 189/12, 'Statement for the Royal Commission on Equal Pay'.
69. TNA, ADM 1/17791, minute by DWRNS, 29 Aug. 1945.
70. TNA, AIR 2/7824, letter from B. C. Harvey to G. S. Whittuck, 10 Sept. 1945; Sherit, 'The integration of women into the Royal Navy and the Royal Air Force', pp. 37–8; Sherit, Women on the front line, pp. 39–40.
71. TNA, AIR 2/7824, extract from the minutes of the 6th meeting of the inter-service consultative body on post-war organisational and administrative problems, 3 Oct. 1945.

72. TNA, AIR 2/7824, 'Future of the WAAF', by AMP, 11 Jan. 1946.
73. TNA, AIR 2/7824, extract from the conclusions of a meeting of the Air Council, 15 Jan. 1946; Sherit, 'The integration of women into the Royal Navy and the Royal Air Force', pp. 38–9; Sherit, *Women on the front line*, p. 40.
74. TNA, ADM 116/5725, The future of the Women's Royal Naval Service, minutes of a meeting, 8 Nov. 1945; TNA, ADM 116/5725, minute by USN, 8 Jan. 1946; TNA, ADM 116/5725, note on the future of the women's services, by ACNP, 28 Mar. 1946; TNA, ADM 116/5725, draft paper for DC [defence committee] on women's services, Apr. 1946.
75. TNA, ADM 116/5725, minute by AVA, 4 Mar. 1946; TNA, ADM 116/5725, telegram from First Lord to Henry Markham, 17 Apr. 1946.
76. TNA, ADM 116/5725, extract from the minutes of a meeting of the Admiralty Board, 17 Apr. 1946; TNA, ADM 116/5725, telegram from Markham to First Lord, 27 Apr. 1946; TNA, ADM 116/5725, telegram from First Lord to Markham, 29 Apr. 1946; Sherit, 'The integration of women into the Royal Navy and the Royal Air Force', pp. 39–40; Sherit, *Women on the front line*, p. 41.
77. TNA, PREM 8/835, 'Organisation of the women's services in peace', joint memorandum by the Parliamentary Secretary of the Admiralty, the Secretary of State for War and the Under-Secretary of State for Air, 8 May 1946.
78. TNA, AIR 2/7824, 'Organisation of the women's services in peace', brief for defence committee by S.11, 10 May 1946; TNA, AIR 2/7824, extract from the minutes of the 16th meeting of the defence committee, 17 May 1946; TNA, PREM 8/835, JCE to Prime Minister, 15 May 1946.
79. *Parliamentary debates*, vol. 423, 30 May 1946, col. 1338; Ministry of Labour and National Service, *Call-up to the forces in 1947 and 1948*, Cmd. 6831 (London: HMSO, 1946).
80. Mathews, *Blue tapestry*, pp. 276–7.
81. Ibid., p. 276. Also see Sherit, *Women on the front line*, p. 25.
82. TNA, PREM 8/835, extract from parliamentary debate on 'women's auxiliary services (continuance)', 20 Nov. 1946, col. 859.
83. TNA, PREM 8/835, 'Future of women's services', by the First Lord of the Admiralty, the Secretary of State for War and the Under-Secretary of State for Air, undated; TNA, ADM 1/20316, 'Titles of the women's services', by cabinet section, 6 Mar. 1947; TNA, WO 32/12618, 'Future title of the ATS', by AG, 11 Mar. 1947; TNA, WO 32/12618, minutes of the 300th meeting of the executive committee of the Army Council, 14 Mar. 1947.
84. TNA, PREM 8/835, CRA to Minister Without Portfolio, 29 Oct. 1946.
85. TNA, PREM 8/835, CRA to First Lord of the Admiralty, Secretary of State for War, Secretary of State for Air, 4 Nov. 1946.
86. TNA, AIR 19/742, draft minutes of a special meeting of the Air Council, 5 Feb. 1948; TNA, AIR 19/742, letter from J. S. Orme to Sir Alan Lascelles, 12 Feb. 1948.
87. TNA, WO 32/12618, 'Title of army women's service', by Secretary of State for War, 29 Apr. 1947; TNA, WO 32/12618, 'Future title of the ATS', by AG, 26 Aug. 1947; TNA, WO 32/12618, 'Title of the women's service in the army', by Secretary of State for War, 12 Jan. 1948; TNA, WO 32/12618, extract from the minutes of the 343rd meeting of the executive committee of the Army Council, 6 Feb. 1948; TNA, WO 32/12618, letter from Sir Alan Lascelles to General Sir James Steele, 5 Feb. 1948; Sherit, 'The integration of women into the Royal Navy and the Royal Air Force', pp. 45–8; Sherit, *Women on the front line*, pp. 50–2.

88. TNA, WO 32/12618, letter from A. E. B. Johnston, M. Swinton and H. Gwynne-Vaughan to the Under-Secretary of State, War Office, 10 Feb. 1948.
89. TNA, WO 32/12618, letter from E. B. B. Speed to H. Gwynne-Vaughan, 11. Feb. 1948.
90. 'Girls like WRAF but they're not keen on WRAC', *Daily Mirror*, 14 Feb. 1948, p. 1.
91. Noakes, *Women in the British army*, pp. 149–52. Also see Gould, 'The women's corps', pp. 384–8.
92. TNA, WO 32/13173, DATS to AG, 22 Apr. 1948.
93. TNA, WO 32/13689, 'The defensive role in war of the Women's Royal Army Corps', by J. E. C. McCandlish, 18 July 1949.
94. TNA, WO 32/13173, DSD to DPA, 14 June 1949.
95. *Parliamentary debates*, vol. 995, 2 Dec. 1980, col. 127; Terry, *Women in khaki*, pp. 214–21. Also see K. Sherit, 'Combatant status and small arms training: developments in servicewomen's employment', *British Journal for Military History*, vol. 3, no. 1 (2016).
96. Peake, *Pure chance*, p. 172.
97. Ibid., pp. 174–5.
98. *Army and Air Force (Women's Service): a Bill to enable women to be commissioned and enlisted for service in His Majesty's land and air forces, and for purposes connected therewith* (London: HMSO, 1947); *Parliamentary debates*, vol. 446, 6 Feb. 1948, cols. 2046–8; 'Inauguration of WRAC and WRAF', *Times*, 1 Feb. 1949, p. 2; 'Future of the WRNS', *Times*, 31 Jan 1949, p. 2.
99. The WRAC was augmented by the Women's Royal Army Corps (Territorial Army); the WRAF by the Women's Royal Auxiliary Air Force and the Women's Royal Air Force Volunteer Reserve; and the WRNS by the Women's Royal Naval Reserve and the Women's Royal Naval Volunteer Reserve. See 'WRAC permanent staff', *Times*, 9 May 1949, p. 4; Escott, *Women in air force blue*, p. 240; 'RAF's part at coronation', *Times*, 16 Mar. 1953, p. 4; Fletcher, *The WRNS*, p. 93; 'Recruiting for WRNVR', *Times*, 4 Feb. 1952, p. 2.
100. TNA, WO 32/13160, 'Comparative statement of the main related points in the draft schemes proposed by the Admiralty, War Office and Air Ministry', app. 'a' to inter-service working party on the permanent women's services, 16 Aug. 1947; TNA, WO 163/238, Sub-committee on the regular women's service: interim report, app. 'a' to standing committee on army post-war problems: regular women's services, 18 Oct. 1946. Sherit argues that 'WRAF' was largely an administrative term, rather than an organisation, within the post-war RAF. See Sherit, 'Combatant status and small arms training', p. 73.
101. TNA, AIR 2/13967, *Women's Royal Air Force: careers for women*, Air Ministry, 1951; Escott, *Women in air force blue*, p. 253; TNA, Ministry of Information papers (INF), INF 13/272, *Serve with the Royal Navy in the WRNS*, Admiralty and Central Office of Information, 1952; Stuart Mason, *Britannia's daughters*, p. 98; 'Recruiting "not satisfactory"', *Times*, 17 Mar. 1949, p. 2; TNA, WO 32/12615, 'Women's Royal Army Corps: recruiting instruction no. 1: enlistment from civilian life', 27 Jan. 1949; TNA, INF 2/86, *The Women's Royal Army Corps*, undated [c. 1949]. It is likely that the three services categorised their types of work differently, so the figures are not necessarily strictly comparable.
102. TNA, AIR 2/13967, *Women's Royal Air Force*; TNA, INF 13/272, *Serve with the Royal Navy in the WRNS*; 'Future of WRNS', *Times*, 31 Jan. 1949, p. 2; TNA, WO 32/12615, 'Women's Royal Army Corps'; TNA, INF 2/86, *The Women's Royal Army Corp*.

103. Peake, *Pure chance*, pp. 164–5.
104. Sherit, 'The integration of women into the Royal Navy and the Royal Air Force', table 3.1, p. 100.
105. *Parliamentary debates*, vol. 435, 1 Apr. 1947, cols. 1955–6; *Parliamentary debates*, vol. 446, 6 Feb. 1948, cols. 2051–2; L. V. Scott, *Conscription and the Attlee governments: the politics and policy of national service 1945–1951* (Oxford: Clarendon Press, 1993), pp. 104–6. The National Service (No. 2) Act was repealed on 1 Jan. 1949. See TNA, LAB 76/13, 'Women's auxiliary services', p. 138.
106. *Parliamentary debates*, vol. 435, 1 Apr. 1947, cols. 1955–6.
107. TNA, AIR 2/13804, 'WRAF organisation and administration', Air Ministry Order A337, 14 June 1951; TNA, AIR 2/13967, *Women's Royal Air Force*; TNA, INF 13/272, *Serve with the Royal Navy in the WRNS*; TNA, INF 2/86, *The Women's Royal Army Corp*. The WAAF 'administrative' officer branch was, however, eliminated in the post-war WRAF and officers had to perform both administrative and substitution roles. See J. A. Fountain, 'Modern jobs for modern women' (PhD thesis, University of Illinois, 2015), pp. 51–2; Sherit, 'The integration of women into the Royal Navy and the Royal Air Force', p. 72; and Sherit, *Women on the front line*, p. 73.
108. Sherit, 'The integration of women into the Royal Navy and the Royal Air Force', p. 12; Sherit, *Women on the front line*, p. 44; Bidwell, *The Women's Royal Army Corps*, p. 137.
109. TNA, WO 32/15616, letter from M. S. Chilton to General Officers Commanding-in-Chief, Home Commands, 2 Dec. 1954; Bidwell, *The Women's Royal Army Corps*, p. 134; Fountain, 'Modern jobs for modern women', p. 93–4; IWM, Barker, Documents.13791, pp. 174–82.
110. TNA, CAB 129/31, 'Rates of pay, pensions and gratuities for the permanent women's forces', by Minister of Defence, 7 Dec. 1948; TNA, ADM 116/5579, extract from the conclusions of a meeting of the cabinet, 9 Dec. 1948; *Pay, retired pay, service pensions and gratuities for members of the women's services*, Cmd. 7607 (London: HMSO, 1949), p. 3; Sherit, 'The integration of women into the Royal Navy and the Royal Air Force', pp. 78–5; Sherit, *Women on the front line*, pp. 74–80.
111. *Parliamentary debates*, vol. 457, 10 Nov. 1948, col. 1647; TNA, WO 32/21705, 'Discipline – Women's Royal Army Corps', memorandum by Director of Personal Services, 26 Jan. 1949; *Parliamentary debates*, vol. 461, 23 Feb. 1949, cols. 1848–9; TNA, WO 32/13679, K. A. Jackman to JAG, 24 Jan. 1949; TNA, AIR 2/10254, PI to DPS and DWAAF, 14 Dec. 1948; Fountain, 'Modern jobs for modern women', pp. 62–71.
112. TNA, ADM 1/21217, letter from Commander-in-Chief, Plymouth, to Secretary of the Admiralty, 23 Sept. 1948; TNA, ADM 1/21217, minute by DWRNS, 30 Sept. 1948.
113. NMRN, WRNS collection, RNM 1988/350/57, working party on WRNS permanent rating force, draft report on structure of and conditions of service for the permanent WRNS rating force, 17 Dec. 1946; TNA, AIR 2/9838, principal personnel officers committee, 'Discipline in the women's services', by the Joint Secretary, 21 July 1947; *Parliamentary debates*, vol. 446, 6 Feb. 1948, col. 2049.
114. Stuart Mason, *Britannia's daughters*, p. 109; Fountain, 'Modern jobs for modern women', pp. 71–2; Sherit, 'The integration of women into the Royal Navy and the Royal Air Force', pp. 45, 160–3; Sherit, *Women on the front line*, pp. 47–9, 133–4.

115. TNA, WO 32/13699, 1st report of the committee on post-war dress for QARANC and WRAC, 2 Apr. 1949.
116. 'New WRAC uniform', *Times*, 5 Nov. 1949, p. 2; Fountain, 'Modern jobs for modern women', pp. 122–5.
117. TNA, AIR 2/12601, letter from N. M. Salmon to Victor Stiebel, June 1952; TNA, AIR 2/12601, 'New pattern WRAF No. 1 dress, officers and airwomen', by AMP, 2 July 1953.
118. TNA, AIR 2/12601, letter from Anne Stephens to N. M. Salmon, 8 Dec. 1952.
119. TNA, AIR 2/12601, 'New pattern WRAF No. 1 dress, officers and airwomen', note by AMP, 2 July 1953; TNA, AIR 2/12601, extract from the minutes of a meeting of the Air Council, 20 July 1953; TNA, AIR 2/12601, DWRAF to AMP, 18 Aug. 1953.
120. 'New uniforms for WRAF', *Times*, 12 Feb. 1954, p. 5; Fountain, 'Modern jobs for modern women', pp. 110–17.
121. TNA, ADM 1/26660, letter from Commodore, RN barracks, Portsmouth, to Commander-in-Chief, Portsmouth, 25 Nov. 1950.
122. TNA, ADM 1/26660, letter from Mary Lloyd to Mr Rickards, 5 Dec. 1950; TNA, ADM 1/26660, Director of Victualling to ACST, 6 Dec. 1950.
123. TNA, ADM 1/26660, Assistant Chief of Supplies and Transport to Director of Victualling, 13 Dec. 1950.
124. Jarrett, *British naval dress*, pp. 136–7; 'Queen and duchess saw it first', *Daily Mirror*, 21 Sept. 1951, p. 1; Fountain, 'Modern jobs for modern women', pp. 131–2.
125. In 1960, a mess dress for WRAC officers was unveiled which was arguably more glamorous. Designed by Owen Hyde-Clark of the House of Worth, it featured 'a slim cream and gold lamé Empire gown, with small sleeves, square neck, a fish-tail pleat at the floor-length hem and a long green silk sash fastened to the shoulder by a single rank-marked epaulette, then falling to the ground and ending in a gold fringe'. One contemporary newspaper report remarked that it 'casts aside all semblance of uniform and comes right out on the side of glamour'. See E. Ewing, *Women in uniform through the ages* (London: B. T. Batsford, 1975), p. 137; and 'Evening glamour for WRAC officers', *Glasgow Herald*, 27 July 1960, p. 5.

Conclusion

1. See, for example, J. Liddington, *The long road to Greenham: feminism and anti-militarism in Britain since 1820* (London: Virago, 1989), pp. 130–71; Pugh, *Women and the women's movement*, pp. 103–7; and S. Bruley, *Women in Britain since 1900* (Basingstoke: Macmillan, 1999), pp. 88–9.
2. RAFM, Woodhead, X002-5638, box 2, AHB monograph, ch. iii, 'WRAF forerunner of the WAAF', p. 4.
3. RAFM, Woodhead, X002-5638, box 2, AHB monograph, ch. ii, 'Inherent difficulties', p. 5.
4. A. De Courcy, *Circe: the life of Edith, Marchioness of Londonderry* (London: Sinclair-Stevenson, 1992), p. 80; Urquhart, 'Stewart, Edith'; Londonderry, *Retrospect*, p. 104; Izzard, *A heroine in her time*, pp. 87–91, 109, 126; Creese, 'Vaughan, Dame Helen', *ODNB*. It might be noted in this regard that Mary Allen was a former suffragette who had been a member of the militant Women's Social and Political Union. She had been imprisoned several times for her suffragette activities. Vera Laughton Mathews had also been a member of the WSPU and chaired the St Joan's Social and Political Alliance (formerly the

Catholic Women's Suffrage Society) in the inter-war years. She vividly recalled that at the age of twenty she had been spat upon in the street by passers-by whilst selling the *Suffragette* newspaper. See Douglas, *Feminist freikorps*, p. 16; Thomas, 'Mathews, Dame Elvira', *ODNB*; and Mathews, *Blue tapestry*, pp. 28–9, 45.

5. Izzard, *A heroine in her time*, p. 271. In the mid-1930s Londonderry had written admiringly of Hitler but also pressed for the utilisation of women in the armed forces. It seems likely that, like her husband, she believed that making friends with Germany and rearmament were, as Ian Kershaw has noted, 'complementary strands of the same policy'. See I. Kershaw, *Making friends with Hitler: Lord Londonderry and Britain's road to war* (London: Penguin, 2005), pp. 155, 340; and M. Pugh, *'Hurrah for the blackshirts!': fascists and fascism in Britain between the wars* (London: Jonathan Cape, 2005), p. 271.

6. Peake, *Pure chance*, pp. 18, 33–49. The WAAF section officer played by Susannah York in Harry Saltzman's 1969 film *The Battle of Britain* was based on Peake.

7. C. Dobinson, *AA Command: Britain's anti-aircraft defences of World War II* (London: Methuen, 2001), p. 473. This story of gender advance correlates with the views of Arthur Marwick and others that the war had a significant impact on the status of women. See, for example, A. Marwick, 'People's war and top people's peace? British society and the Second World War' in A. Sked and C. Cook (eds), *Crisis and controversy: essays in honour of A. J. P. Taylor* (London: Macmillan, 1976), pp. 161–2; G. Williams, *Women and work* (London: Nicholson & Watson, 1945), pp. 11–13, 96–7.

8. Calculations based on Central Statistical Office, *Fighting with figures*, p. 39.

9. Escott, *Women in air force blue*, p. 96.

10. TNA, AIR 41/65, 'Manning: plans and policy', p. 215.

11. TNA, CAB 44/48, 'History of AA Command', p. 124.

12. G. Forty, *British army handbook 1939–1945* (Stroud: Sutton, 1998), pp. 164–5.

13. CAC, Churchill, CHAR 20/232/4–6, appendix to note from John Anderson to Prime Minister, 12 July 1945.

14. V. Laughton Mathews, 'The Women's Royal Naval Service in the war', *Royal United Service Institution Journal*, vol. 91 (1946), p. 92; TNA, ADM 234/219, 'The Women's Royal Naval Service', pp. 91–2.

15. Mason, *Britannia's daughters*, p. 80.

16. CAC, Churchill, CHAR 20/232/10, 'Man-power', note by the Prime Minister, 5 July 1945.

17. CAC, Churchill, CHAR 20/232/4–6, note from John Anderson to Prime Minister, 12 July 1945. In fact, it was argued that 'the need to adopt a detailed demobilisation scheme for the Women's Auxiliary Services was the final testimony to their indispensability to the Armed Forces'. See TNA, LAB 76/13, 'Women's auxiliary services', pp. 85–6.

18. Stone, 'The integration of women into a military service', p. 95.

19. Quoted in Sheridan, 'ATS women', p. 67. Also see Sheridan, 'Ambivalent memories', p. 34.

20. Quoted in Drifte, *Women in the Second World War*, p. 128.

21. RAFM, papers of M. Burns, X003-0303/001, 'The WAAF during wartime', 18 July 2001, p. 4.

22. Quoted in Summerfield, *Reconstructing women's wartime lives*, p. 292.

23. IWM, Wright, Documents.4298, p. 44.

24. Robinson, *Sisters in arms*, p. 13.

25. Barnett, *Lambs in blue*, pp. 37–8.

26. IWM, Lane, Documents.137, p. 36.
27. Summerfield, *Reconstructing women's wartime lives*, p. 268.
28. TNA, WO 166/11252, war diary of HQ 103 AA Bde, entry for 11 May 1943; S. Snelling, 'Seventy years on, ATS girls meet again', *EDP Weekend*, 5 May 2012, p. 6. Available at www.stephensnelling.com/articles.html (accessed 16 Jan. 2019); 'Horror of air raid lives on', *Great Yarmouth Mercury*, 22 Oct. 2009. Available at www.greatyarmouthmercury.co.uk (accessed 16 Jan. 2019). Burial calculations are based on the cemetery records of the Commonwealth War Graves Commission: www.cwgc.org (accessed 16 Jan. 2019).
29. IWM, 'War memorials register'. Available at www.iwm.org.uk (accessed 16. Jan 2019).
30. 'Flowers, messages of sympathy sent by WACS, WAVES' and 'Members of British contingent perish in auto crash', *Washington Post*, 17 Nov. 1943, p. 1B; 'WAAFS buried in Arlington', *Washington Post*, 20 Nov. 1943, p. 3; 'WAAFS buried at capital', *New York Times*, 20 Nov. 1943, p. 13. Another Waaf, Section Officer Dorothy Rodwell, was seriously injured in the crash.
31. Pushman, *We all wore blue*, pp. 116–18. It seems likely that Pushman was describing the raid on Cardiff on 18 May 1943 that killed three WAAF balloon operators of 953 Squadron. If this is the case, the 'corporal' referred to was Leading Aircraftswoman Lilian Sarah Ellis who was awarded the British Empire Medal for 'outstanding leadership, coolness and courage'. See 'Injured WAAF raid heroine', *Citizen*, 24 Dec. 1943, p. 8. Also see TNA, AIR 27/2302, Operations record book, No. 953 Squadron, 1940–5.
32. Beauman, *Partners in blue*, p. 165.
33. M. R. Higonnet and P. L-R. Higonnet, 'The Double Helix' in M. R. Higonnet, J. Jenson, S. Michel and M. C. Weitz (eds), *Behind the lines: gender and the two world wars* (New Haven and London: Yale University Press, 1987), pp. 34–5. In similar terms, Dorothy Sheridan has written of 'challenge and containment' in the ATS. See Sheridan, 'ATS women', p. 67. More broadly, Sonya Rose contends that the war 'opened up new opportunities for women to exercise their obligations as citizens' but 'gender difference continued to be a fundamental principle of wartime policies'. See Rose, *Which people's war?*, p. 122.
34. TNA, WO 32/13160, 'The future of the women's services', by DATS and DD of O (ATS), undated.
35. *Parliamentary debates*, vol. 376, 9 Dec. 1941, col. 1492.
36. For an overview of 'difference feminism', see J. S. Goldstein, *War and gender: how gender shapes the war system and vice-versa* (Cambridge: Cambridge University Press, 2001), pp. 38–49. Julie Fountain has also written of 'conservative feminism' to denote women who were motivated by duty and citizenship and did not explicitly pursue a feminist agenda, but nevertheless sought wider opportunities and recognition within the existing system. See Fountain, 'Modern jobs for modern women', pp. 16, 224.
37. Mathews, *Blue tapestry*, pp. 125, 127.
38. Whateley, *As thoughts survive*, p. 49.
39. RAFM, Trefusis Forbes, AC 72/17/1, box 4, 'Women's Auxiliary Air Force organisation with particular reference to the duties and status of the WAAF directorate', by Squadron Officer Charis Rowley, 26 Apr. 1941.
40. Goldsmith, *Women at war*, p. 57. It is possible that Knox was seeking to reassure the public that women were not being defeminised in the ATS, but her comments could be interpreted as a disservice to the contribution of servicewomen to the wartime armed forces.
41. M. Thomson, interview with the author, 31 July 2002.

42. Rees, *The shaping of psychiatry by war*, pp. 94–5

43. TNA, AIR 10/5546, 'The Women's Auxiliary Air Force', p. 46.

44. IWM, Fairfield, Documents.8448, 'Mothers and woman power in relation to the women's services', p. 3; IWM, Fairfield, Documents.8448, box P372, file JLDF7/8, letter from Alex Hood to Dr Fairfield, 30 June 1942.

45. 'Princess and the WRAC', *Times*, 28 Mar. 1949, p. 6.

46. Mack, *Dancing on the waves*, pp. 9, 13. Also see Roberts, *The WRNS in wartime*, p.184.

47. MOA, 'Women in wartime 1939–1945', box 1, 32-1-F, 'MO report on ATS', by K. Mortimore, 17 Oct. 1941; MOA, 'ATS', file report 955, pp. 2–12; Some of these workplace issues have been highlighted more recently in *Speak out: sexual harassment report 2015* (Ministry of Defence, 2015).

48. IWM, Gray, Documents.5561, p. 10.

49. IWM, Documents.1553, ATS file, J. Stewart, undated, p. 4. Also see Stanley, *Women and the Royal Navy*, p. 102.

50. A. Kessler-Harris, 'The long history of workplace harassment', *Jacobin*, 23 Mar. 2018. Available at www.jacobinmag.com/2018/03/metoo-workplace-discrimination-sexual-harassment-feminism (accessed 9 Feb. 2019).

51. RAFM, Brooks, B3940, 'A Waaf's tale', p. 5.

52. IWM, Documents.1553, ATS file, C. Poolman, undated, p. 3.

53. Costello, *Love, sex and war*, p. 80. In regard to the ATS, instructions were issued to group commanders in 1941 that in suspected cases of rape or criminal assault, medical evidence was to be obtained as soon as possible and that help should be obtained from the army medical branch and the Judge Advocate General's office. With the arrival of greater numbers of foreign troops and increasing numbers of cases, new advice was issued in 1943 which indicated that the civil police should deal with these offences and instructed the ATS officer on the spot to inform the local police, ascertain if the woman was to be examined by a police surgeon and ensure that she was made comfortable whilst minimising the damage to the evidence on her clothes or person. See Crew, *The Army Medical Services: administration*, vol. 2, pp. 453–4.

54. Noakes, *Women in the British army*, p. 156. Also see Fountain, 'Modern jobs for modern women', pp. 221–2.

55. 'Audrey Roche', obituary, *Daily Telegraph*, 6 Feb. 2009, p. 37; G. Liardet, 'Exhibition salutes the Wrens', *Times*, 14 Mar. 2003, p. 45; TNA, ADM 1/12218, message 1215C/5 July from C-in-C Mediterranean; TNA, ADM 1/12218, 'Recommendation for decoration or mention in despatches', 12 Oct. 1942; TNA, ADM 1/12218, note by Vice-Admiral, chairman, honours and awards committee, 17 Dec. 1942; IWM, Audrey Silvia Roche (oral history), 13126, reels 2–4, 1993. For some weeks after the sinking, Roche suffered from insomnia and also needed to be coaxed to swim again in the sea.

APPENDIX

Table 1: Strength of the women's auxiliary services

Year	ATS	WAAF	WRNS
1939 Dec	23,900	8,800	3,400
1940 Mar	...	8,900	4,400
June	31,500	11,900	5,600
Sept	36,100	17,400	7,900
Dec	36,400	20,500	10,000
1941 Mar	37,500	27,000	12,300
June	42,800	37,400	15,100
Sept	65,000	64,100	18,000
Dec	85,100	98,400	21,600
1942 Mar	111,100	110,800	24,800
June	140,200	125,700	28,600
Sept	162,200	141,500	33,500
Dec	180,700	166,000	39,300
1943 Mar	195,300	180,100	45,000
June	210,300	181,600	53,300
Sept	212,500	180,300	60,400
Dec	207,500	176,800	64,800
1944 Mar	206,200	175,700	68,600
June	199,000	174,400	73,500
Sept	198,200	171,200	74,000
Dec	196,400	166,200	73,400
1945 Mar	195,300	159,700	73,200
June	190,800	153,000	72,000

Source: Central Statistical Office, *Fighting with figures* (London: HMSO, 1995), p. 39. These figures include women locally enlisted abroad.

Table 2: WAAF: annual rates of venereal disease

Year	Average strength	Cases	Rates per 1,000 per annum
1939	2,300	1	0.40
1940	13,085	15	1.15
1941	48,182	137	2.84
1942	127,781	496	3.88
1943	178,689	424	2.37
1944	173,066	355	2.05
1945	142,045	299	2.11

Source: S. C. Rexford-Welch (ed.), *The Royal Air Force Medical Services*, vol. 1, *administration*, (London: HMSO, 1954), p. 473.

Table 3: WAAF: source of venereal infection: consorts

	1942	1943	1944
	per cent	per cent	per cent
RAF	43	40	34
Army	21	26	18
Royal Navy	6	10	8
Civilians	23	13	7
Allies, Dominions, etc.	7	11	33

Source: S. C. Rexford-Welch (ed.), *The Royal Air Force Medical Services*, vol. 1, *administration*, (London: HMSO, 1954), p. 474.

Table 4: ATS and WAAF pregnancies (married and unmarried): rates per 1,000 per annum

Year	ATS	WAAF
1942	55.23	46.2
1943	68.89	67.7
1944	89.87	89.7

Source: compiled from War Office, *Statistical report on the health of the army 1943–1945* (London: HMSO, 1948), p. 17; S. C. Rexford-Welch (ed.), *The Royal Air Force Medical Services*, vol. 1, *administration* (London: HMSO, 1954), p. 474. The ATS figure for 1942 is based on statistics from July to December.

Table 5: ATS: discharges of married and single pregnant women: average annual rates, July 1943–December 1944

Age group	Married (per 1,000 of married strength)	Single (per 1,000 of single strength)
Under 19	448	27
19–21	587	31
22–24	466	27
25–27	335	27
28–30	267	24
31–33	175	23
34–36	109	21
37 and above	35	9
All ages	409	28

Source: TNA, T 189/10, 'Question 3', app. 'c' to 'Work and remuneration of women in the Auxiliary Territorial Service', War Office, 1945; TNA, T 189/12, Royal Commission on Equal Pay, 'Letter from Adjutant-General supplementing oral evidence', by WGM, 30 July 1945. Widows are included in the figures for single women.

BIBLIOGRAPHY

Unpublished sources

Archives

The National Archives of the UK:

Admiralty papers: ADM 1, ADM 116, ADM 178, ADM 182, ADM 234.
Air Ministry papers: AIR 2, AIR 6, AIR 8, AIR 10, AIR 19, AIR 24, AIR 27, AIR 41, AIR 58, AIR 72.
Cabinet papers: CAB 21, CAB 44, CAB 57, CAB 65, CAB 66, CAB 92, CAB 98, CAB 129.
Colonial Office papers: CO 876, CO 968.
Home Office papers: HO 213.
Ministry of Information papers: INF 2, INF 13.
Ministry of Labour papers: LAB 76.
Prime Minister's papers: PREM 3, PREM 4, PREM 8.
Records of the Government Social Survey Department: RG 23.
Treasury papers: T 189.
War Office papers: WO 32, WO 73, WO 163, WO 165, WO 193, WO 277, WO 287.

Imperial War Museum:

Ackroyd papers, Angus papers, Ball papers, Barker papers, Brisley-Wilson papers, Britten papers, Brookes papers, Bryce papers, Bywater papers, Carter papers, Cole papers, Cove papers, Coyne papers, Demey papers, De Wolff papers, Dunkley papers, Fairfield papers, Forsdyke papers, Goossens papers, Gray papers, Hazell papers, Herterich papers, Hill papers, Hodges papers, Holbrook papers, Hunter papers, James papers, Knowles papers, Kup papers, Lambert papers, Lane papers, Littlejohn papers, Lodge papers, Lowry papers, Macbeth papers, Mannock papers, Martin papers, McMurdo papers, Mills papers, Myler papers, Noble papers, Orde papers, Pearson papers, Peyman papers, Pratt papers, Rhodes papers, Scovell papers, Sears papers, Smith papers, Stallard papers, Stewart papers, Stone papers, Wallace papers, Walton papers, Wheatley papers, Wright papers; 'ATS reports on job analyses, 1944–1946'; 'Material contributed for the book women in uniform 1939–45'; Audrey Silvia Roche (oral history).

Churchill Archives Centre:

Churchill papers, Hore-Belisha papers, Spencer-Churchill papers.

Liddell Hart Centre for Military Archives:

Adam papers.

London School of Economics, Women's Library:

Markham papers.

The Mass Observation Archive:

FR 757, FR 955, FR 1031, FR 1083, FR 1887, TC 'Women in wartime 1939–1945'.

National Army Museum:

Button papers, Coulshed papers, Cowper papers, Dixon papers, Gwynne-Vaughan papers, Impson papers, Taylor papers; press cutting from the *Daily Mirror*.

National Maritime Museum:

HMS *Dauntless* papers.

National Museum of the Royal Navy:

Wren collection.

Royal Air Force Museum:

Brooks papers, Drake-Brockman papers, Hickes papers, Trefusis-Forbes papers, Woodhead papers.

Wellcome Library:

Research Board for the Correlation of Medical Science and Physical Education papers; Women's Medical Federation papers.

Published sources

Government, service and other official publications

Army and Air Force (Women's Service): a Bill to enable women to be commissioned and enlisted for service in His Majesty's land and air forces, and for purposes connected therewith (London: HMSO, 1947).

Army Bureau of Current Affairs, 'Women's place … ', *Current Affairs*, no. 61, War Office, 29 Jan. 1944.

Central Statistical Office, *Fighting with figures* (London: HMSO, 1995).

'Corporal (now Assistant Section Officer) Joan Daphne Mary Pearson, Women's Auxiliary Air Force', *London Gazette*, 19 July 1940.

Instructions for American servicemen in Britain 1942 (Washington DC: War Department, 1942; Oxford: Bodleian Library, 2004).

Manual of Air Force law (London: HMSO, 1939).

Ministry of Labour, *Report of the commission of enquiry appointed by the Minister of Labour to enquire into the Women's Army Auxiliary Corps in France* (London: HMSO, 1918).

Ministry of Labour, *National service: a guide to the ways in which the people of this country may give service* (London: HMSO, 1939).

Ministry of Labour and National Service, *Release and resettlement: an explanation of your position and rights* (London: HMSO, 1945).

Ministry of Labour and National Service, *Call-up to the forces in 1947 and 1948*, Cmd. 6831 (London: HMSO, 1946).

Ministry of Labour and National Service: report for the years 1939–1946, Cmd. 7225 (London: HMSO, 1947).

Parliamentary debates (House of Commons), 5th series.

Pay, retired pay, service pensions and gratuities for members of the women's services, Cmd. 7607 (London: HMSO, 1949).

Pile, F., 'The anti-aircraft defence of the United Kingdom from 28 July 1939 to 15 April 1945', *Supplement to the London Gazette*, 18 Dec. 1947.

Re-allocation of man-power between the armed forces and civilian employment during the interim period between the defeat of Germany and the defeat of Japan, Cmd. 6548 (London: HMSO, 1944).

Report of the committee on amenities and welfare conditions in the three women's services, Cmd. 6384 (London: HMSO, 1942).

Royal Commission on Equal Pay 1944–46: report, Cmd. 6937 (London: HMSO, 1946).

Speak out: sexual harassment report 2015 (Ministry of Defence, 2015).

Strength and casualties of the armed forces and auxiliary services of the United Kingdom 1939 to 1945, Cmd. 6832 (London: HMSO, 1946).

The statutes: third revised edition, vol. 10, *from the forty-first and forty-second to the forty-sixth and forty-seventh years of Queen Victoria AD 1878–1883* (London: HMSO, 1950).

Twelfth report from the select committee on national expenditure (London: HMSO, 1940).

War Office, *Regulations for the Auxiliary Territorial Service* (London: HMSO, 1941).

War Office, *Statistical report on the health of the army 1943–1945* (London: HMSO, 1948).

Journals and newspapers

Abbasi, M., 'Palestinians fighting against Nazis: the story of the Palestinian volunteers in the Second World War', *War in History*, vol. 26, issue 2 (2019).

Anderson, J., 'British women, disability and the Second World War', *Contemporary British History*, vol. 20, no. 1 (2006).

Aspden, R., 'War through women's eyes', *New Statesman*, 16 Mar. 2009.

'ATS killed in action', *Times*, 21 Apr. 1942.

'Audrey Roche', obituary, *Daily Telegraph*, 6 Feb. 2009.

Ballard, S. I. and Miller, H. G., 'Psychiatric casualties in a women's service', *British Medical Journal*, 3 Mar. 1945, p. 294.

Berger, M., 'US soldier spanks Mary Churchill as retort to jest over his big feet', *New York Times*, 1 Aug. 1942.

Campbell, D'A., 'Women in combat: the World War II experience in the United States, Great Britain, Germany, and the Soviet Union', *Journal of Military History*, vol. 57, no. 2 (1997).

'Candidates for ATS commissions', *Times*, 3 Aug. 1943.

'Chief controller Knox resigns', *Times*, 21 Oct. 1943.

Condell, D., 'Daphne Pearson: first woman to receive a gallantry award in the Second World War', *Guardian*, 31 July 2000.

'Constance Babington Smith', obituary, *Daily Telegraph*, 9 Aug. 2000.

'Court Circular', *Times*, 21 Nov. 1947.

Crang, J. A.,'Welcome to civvy street: the demobilisation of the British armed forces after the Second World War', *The Historian*, no. 46 (Summer 1995).

Cumming, B., 'The only WAAF to go on a wartime bombing raid', *Flightlines* (March/April 2018).

Danchev, A. and Todman, D. (eds.), *War diaries 1939–1945: Field Marshal Lord Alanbrooke* (London, Weidenfeld and Nicolson, 2001).

'Daphne Pearson GC', obituary, *Daily Telegraph*, 26 July 2000.

'Daphne Pearson GC', obituary, *Times*, 26 July 2000.

DeGroot, G. J., '"I love the scent of cordite in your hair": gender dynamics in mixed anti-aircraft batteries during the Second World War', *History*, vol. 82, no. 265 (1997).

DeGroot, G. J., 'Whose finger on the trigger? Mixed anti-aircraft batteries and the female combat taboo', *War in History*, vol. 4, no. 4 (1997).

'Dr G. Rewcastle', obituary, *Times*, 22 Feb. 1951.

Elliot, P., 'The RAF's first women pilots', *Air Clues*, vol. 44, no. 5 (1990).

'Elspeth Green', obituary, *Daily Telegraph*, 30 Aug. 2006, p. 21.

'Evening glamour for WRAC officers', *Glasgow Herald*, 27 July 1960.

'Flowers, messages of sympathy sent by WACS, WAVES' and 'Members of British contingent perish in auto crash', *Washington Post*, 17 Nov. 1943.

'Future of WRNS', *Times*, 31 Jan 1949.

'Girls like WRAF but they're not keen on WRAC', *Daily Mirror*, 14 Feb. 1948.

Halley, J. J., 'Operation Outward: the Royal Navy's strategic air command', *Aviation News Magazine*, vol. 15, no. 1 (1986).

'Her act of courage means everything to the Bond family: she ignored flames and bombs to rescue man who would become helicopter king', *Daily Mail*, 15 May 1995.

'Horror of air raid lives on', *Great Yarmouth Mercury*, 22 Oct. 2009. www.greatyarmouthmercury.co.uk

'How the "call-up" affects the women of Britain: an official explanation of registration and compulsory call-up', *Times*, 24 Feb. 1942.

'I see life ... by Charles Graves', *Daily Mail*, 16 Jan. 1940.

'Inauguration of WRAC and WRAF', *Times*, 1 Feb. 1949.

'Injured WAAF raid heroine', *Citizen*, 24 Dec. 1943.

J. W. N [Naylor, Lieut-Col. J. W.], '"Mixed" batteries', *Journal of the Royal Artillery*, vol. 69, no. 3 (1942).

Kessler-Harris, A., 'The long history of workplace harassment', *Jacobin*, 23 Mar. 2018. www.jacobinmag.com/2018/03/metoo-workplace-discrimination-sexual-harassment-feminism

Kirkham, P., 'Beauty and duty: keeping up the (home) front', in Kirkham, P. and Thoms, D. (eds.), *War culture: social change and changing experience in World War Two* (London: Lawrence and Wishart, 1995).

Kirkham, P., 'Keeping up home front morale: "beauty and duty" in wartime Britain', in Atkins, J. M. (ed.), *Wearing propaganda: textiles on the home front in Japan, Britain, and the United States, 1931–1945* (New Haven, CT: Yale University Press, 2005).

Kushner, T., '"Without intending any of the most undesirable features of a colour bar": race science, Europeanness and the British armed forces during the twentieth century', *Patterns of Prejudice*, vol. 46, nos. 3–4 (2012).

Langhamer, C., '"A public house is for all classes, men and women alike": women, leisure and drink in Second World War England', *Women's History Review*, vol. 12, no. 3 (2003).

Large, C., letter, *The Lancet*, 15 Apr. 1944.

Laughton Mathews, V., 'The Women's Royal Naval Service in the war', *Royal United Service Institution Journal*, vol. 91 (1946).

Liardet, G., 'Exhibition salutes the Wrens', *Times*, 14 Mar. 2003.

Lingwood, L., 'Test performances of ATS recruits from certain civilian occupations', *Occupational Psychology*, vol. 26, no. 1 (1952).

Londonderry, E., 'National efficiency: a plea for the organisation of women', *The Nineteenth Century and After*, vol. 115 (1934).

'Medical Women's Federation: social medicine in women's services', *The Lancet*, 22 Sept. 1945.

Mercer, E., 'A woman psychologist at war', *The Psychologist*, vol. 4, no. 9 (1991).

Mercer, E. O., 'Psychological methods of personnel selection in a women's service', *Occupational Psychology*, vol. 19, no. 4 (1945).

'Muriel Petch: WAAF sergeant and "ops room" plotter at RAF Hornchurch who helped win the Battle of Britain', obituary, *Independent*, 21 Apr. 2014.

'New conditions for WRNS', *Times*, 26 Jan. 1943.

'New uniforms for WRAF', *Times*, 12 Feb. 1954.

'New WRAC uniform', *Times*, 5 Nov. 1949.

Nicholson, H., 'A disputed identity: women conscientious objectors in Second World War Britain', *Twentieth Century British History*, vol. 18, no. 4 (2007).

Noakes, L., 'Demobilising the military women: constructions of class and gender in Britain after the First World War', *Gender & History*, vol. 19, no. 1 (2007).

'Oldest ATS' age is a secret', *Daily Mirror*, 12 Mar. 1945.

Parfitt, D. N., 'Psychoneurosis in RAF ground personnel', *Journal of Mental Science*, vol. 90, issue 379 (Apr. 1944).

Peniston-Bird, C., 'Classifying the body in the Second World War: British men in and out of uniform', *Body & Society*, vol 9, issue 4 (2003).

Peniston-Bird, C., 'Of hockey sticks and Sten guns: British auxiliaries and their weapons in the Second World War', *Women's History Magazine*, issue 76 (Autumn, 2014).

'Princess and the WRAC', *Times*, 28 Mar. 1949.

'Priority for married women – not men', *Daily Mail*, 22 Sept. 1944.

'Queen and duchess saw it first', *Daily Mirror*, 21 Sept. 1951.

'RAF's part at coronation', *Times*, 16 Mar. 1953.

Raphael, W., 'An autobiography', *Occupational Psychology*, vol 38. no. 1 (1964).

'Recruiting for WRNVR', *Times*, 4 Feb. 1952.

'Recruiting "not satisfactory"', *Times*, 17 Mar. 1949.

Rees, L., 'Neurosis in the women's auxiliary services', *British Journal of Psychiatry*, vol. 95, issue 401 (1949).

Rollin, H. R., 'Trade training failures in the WAAF: factors in predisposition and precipitation', *British Journal of Medical Psychology*, vol. 20, issue 1 (1944).

Rose, S. O., 'Sex, citizenship, and the nation in World War II Britain', *The American Historical Review*, vol. 103, no. 4 (1998).

Sainsbury, A. B., 'Daphne Pearson', obituary, *Independent*, 31 July 2000.

Schwarzkopf, J., 'Combatant or non-combatant? The ambiguous status of women in British anti-aircraft batteries during the Second World War', *War & Society*, vol. 28, no. 2 (2009).

'Service pay and allowances', *Times*, 12 July 1944.

Sheridan, D., 'Ambivalent memories: women and the 1939–45 war in Britain', *Oral History* (Spring 1990).

Sherit, K., 'Combatant status and small arms training: developments in servicewomen's employment', *British Journal for Military History*, vol. 3, no. 1 (2016).

Smith, H., 'The problem of "equal pay for equal work" in Great Britain during World War II', *Journal of Modern History*, vol. 53, no. 4 (1981).

Smith, H. L., 'The womanpower problem in Britain during the Second World War', *The Historical Journal*, vol. 27, no. 4 (1984).

'Smoking in the ATS', *Times*, 29 Mar. 1944.

Snelling, S., 'Seventy years on, ATS girls meet again', *EDP Weekend*, 5 May 2012. www.stephensnelling.com/articles.html

Stafford-Clark, D., 'Morale and flying experience: results of a wartime study', *British Journal of Psychiatry*, vol. 95, issue 398 (1949).

Stewart, C., letters, *British Medical Journal*, 18 Apr. 1942, 4 July 1942.

Stone, T., 'Creating a (gendered?) military identity: the Women's Auxiliary Air
Force in Great Britain during the Second World War', *Women's History
Review*, vol. 8, no. 4 (1999).

Summerfield, P. and Crockett, N., '"You weren't taught that with the welding":
lessons in sexuality in the Second World War', *Women's History Review*, vol.
1, no. 3 (1992).

Summerskill, E., 'Conscription and women', *The Fortnightly*, vol. 151 (March
1942).

Swindells, J., 'Coming home to heaven: manpower and myth in 1944 Britain',
Women's History Review, vol. 4, no. 2 (1995).

'The Women's Auxiliary Air Force', *The Royal Air Force Quarterly*, vol. 16
(1944–45).

Thomson, M., 'Christian Fraser-Tytler', obituary, *Independent*, 19 July 1995.

Trefusis Forbes, K. J., 'Women's Auxiliary Air Force', *Flying and Popular
Aviation* (Sept. 1942).

'Two-Thirds of a Man', *Economist*, 5 Sept. 1942.

Vernon, P. E., 'Psychological tests in the Royal Navy, army and ATS',
Occupational Psychology, vol. 21, no. 2 (1947).

Vickers, E., 'Infantile desires and perverted practices: disciplining lesbianism in
the WAAF and ATS during the Second World War', *Journal of Lesbian
Studies*, vol. 13, issue 4 (2009).

'Waaf-cuddling WO is sentenced – reduced to ranks', *Daily Mirror*, 3 Oct. 1944.

'WAAFS buried at capital', *New York Times*, 20 Nov. 1943.

'WAAFS buried in Arlington', *Washington Post*, 20 Nov. 1943.

Whateley, L., 'The work of the Auxiliary Territorial Service in the war', *Royal
United Service Institution Journal*, vol. 91 (1946).

Wickham, M., 'Follow-up of personnel selection in the ATS', *Occupational
Psychology*, vol. 23, no. 3 (1949).

Winner, A. L., 'Homosexuality in women', *The Medical Press and Circular*, vol.
217 (1947).

'Women are not killers – ATS Chief', *Courier and Advertiser*, 1 Oct. 1942.

'Women who are helping in Britain's war effort', *The Sphere*, 18 Oct.1941.

'Women's Auxiliary Air Force', *Times*, 3 July 1939.

'WRAC permanent staff', *Times*, 9 May 1949.

Books

Adie, K., *Corsets to camouflage: women and war* (London: Coronet, 2004).

Ahrenfeldt, R. H., *Psychiatry in the British army in the Second World War*
(London: Routledge & Kegan Paul, 1958).

Allatt, P., 'Men and war: status, class and the social reproduction of masculinity' in Gamarnikow, E., Morgan, D., Purvis, J. and Taylorson, D. (eds.), *The public and the private* (London: Heinemann, 1983).

Allen, M. S., *Lady in blue* (London: Stanley & Co., 1936).

Allport, A., *Demobbed: coming home after the Second World War* (London: Yale University Press, 2009).

Allport, A., *Browned off and bloody-minded: the British soldier goes to war, 1939–1945* (London: Yale University Press, 2015).

Anderson, J., *War, disability and rehabilitation in Britain: 'soul of a nation'* (Manchester: Manchester University Press, 2011).

Ashbee, F., *For the duration: a light-hearted WAAF memoir* (Syracuse, New York: Syracuse University Press, 2012).

Babington Smith, C., *Evidence in camera: the story of photographic intelligence in the Second World War* (Stroud: Sutton Publishing, 2004).

Barnett, C., *Engage the enemy more closely: the Royal Navy in the Second World War* (London: Penguin Books, 2000).

Barnett, R., *Lambs in blue: the experiences of three lasses from Tyneside in the wartime WAAF* (Bognor Regis: Woodfield Publishing, 1999).

Bean, D., *Jamaican women and the world wars: on the front lines of change* (Cham, Switzerland: Palgrave Macmillan, 2018).

Beck, P., *A WAAF in Bomber Command* (London: Goodall Publications, 1989).

Bentley Beauman, K., *Partners in blue: the story of women's service with the Royal Air Force* (London: Hutchinson, 1971).

Bentwich, N., *I understand the risks: the story of refugees from Nazi oppression who fought in the British forces in the World War* (London: Victor Gollancz, 1950).

Bet-El, I. R., *Conscripts: forgotten men of the Great War* (Stroud: Sutton, 1999).

Bidwell, S., *The Women's Royal Army Corps* (London: Leo Cooper, 1977).

Bishop, P., *Air force blue: the RAF in World War Two: spearhead of victory* (London: William Collins, 2017).

Blake, J. W., *Northern Ireland in the Second World War* (Belfast: Blackstaff Press, 2000).

Bousquet, B. and Douglas, C., *West Indian women at war: British racism in World War II* (London: Lawrence & Wishart, 1991).

Boyle, A., *Trenchard: man of vision* (London: Collins, 1962).

Braybon, G. and Summerfield, P., *Out of the cage: women's experience in two world wars* (London: Pandora, 1987).

Bruley, S., *Women in Britain since 1900* (Basingstoke: Macmillan, 1999).

Bullock, A., *The life and times of Ernest Bevin*, vol. 2, *Minister of Labour 1940–1945* (London: Heinemann, 1967).

Calder, A. and Sheridan, D. (eds.), *Speak for yourself: a Mass Observation anthology, 1937–49* (London: Jonathan Cape, 1984).

Calvert, D., *Bull, battle-dress, lanyard & lipstick* (Bognor Regis: New Horizon, 1978).

Cartland, B., *The years of opportunity 1939–1945* (London: Hutchinson & Co, 1948).

Castle, B., *The Castle diaries 1964–1976* (London: Papermac, 1990).

Cazalet-Keir, T., *From the wings* (London: The Bodley Head, 1967).

Clayton, A., *The enemy is listening: the story of the Y Service* (Manchester: Crécy Books, 1993).

Collette Wadge, D., *Women in uniform* (London: Sampson Low, Marston, 1946).

Colville, Q., 'Jack Tar and the gentleman officer: the role of uniform in shaping the class-and gender-related identities of British naval personnel, 1930–1939' in *Transactions of the Royal Historical Society*, 6th series, vol. 13 (Cambridge: Cambridge University Press, 2003).

Cooper, A., *Wot! No engines? Royal Air Force glider pilots in Operation Varsity* (Bognor Regis: Woodfield Publishing, 2012).

Cormack, A., *The Royal Air Force 1939–45* (Oxford: Osprey, 1990).

Corrigan, I., '"Put that light out!" The 93rd Searchlight Regiment Royal Artillery' in Lee, C. and Strong, P. E. (eds.), *Women in war* (Barnsley: Pen & Sword, 2012).

Costello, J., *Love, sex and war: changing values 1939–45* (London: Pan, 1986).

Coulter, J. L. S., *The Royal Naval Medical Services*, vol. 1, *administration* (London: HMSO, 1954).

Cowper, J. M., 'Women in the fighting services' in Thursfield, H. G. (ed.), *Brassey's annual: the armed forces year-book 1957* (London: William Clowes & Sons, 1957).

Crang, J. A., *The British army and the people's war 1939–1945* (Manchester: Manchester University Press, 2000).

Crew, F. A. E., *The Army Medical Services: administration*, vol. 1 (London: HMSO, 1953).

Crew, F. A. E. (ed.), *The Army Medical Services: administration*, vol. 2 (London: HMSO, 1955)

Crew, F. A. E., 'The Army Medical Services' in MacNalty, A. S. and Mellor, W. F. (eds.), *Medical services in war: the principal medical lessons of the Second World War* (London: HMSO, 1968).

Croft, H., 'Emotional women and frail men: gendered diagnostics from shell-shock to PTSD, 1914–2010' in Carden-Coyne, A. (ed.), *Gender and conflict since 1914: historical and interdisciplinary perspectives* (Basingstoke: Palgrave Macmillan, 2012).

De Courcy, A., *Circe: the life of Edith, Marchioness of Londonderry* (London: Sinclair-Stevenson, 1992).

De Courcy, A., *Debs at war 1939–45: how wartime changed their lives* (London: Weidenfeld and Nicolson, 2005).

DeGroot, G. J., 'Lipstick on her nipples, cordite in her hair: sex and romance among British servicewomen during the Second World War' in DeGroot, G. J. and Peniston-Bird, C. (eds.), *A soldier and a woman: sexual integration in the military* (London: Longman, 2000).

Dobinson, C., *AA Command: Britain's anti-aircraft defences of World War II* (London: Methuen, 2001).

Douglas, R. M., *Feminist freikorps: the British Voluntary Women Police 1914–1940* (Westport, Conn: Praeger 1999).

Douie, V., *The lesser half* (London: Women's Publicity Planning Association, 1943).

Douie, V., *Daughters of Britain: an account of the work of British women during the Second World War* (Oxford: George Ronald, 1950).

Drifte, C., *Women in the Second World War* (Barnsley: Remember When, 2011).

Dunbar, J., *Laura Knight* (London: Collins, 1975).

Dunlop, T., *The Bletchley girls: war, secrecy, love and loss: the women of Bletchley Park tell their story* (London: Hodder, 2015).

Eforgan, E., *Leslie Howard: the lost actor* (London: Vallentine Mitchell, 2010).

Ellis, F. P., 'The Royal Naval Medical Service: medical statistics' in Mellor, W. F. (ed.), *Casualties and medical statistics* (London: HMSO, 1972).

Escott, B. E., *Women in air force blue: the story of women in the Royal Air Force from 1918 to the present day* (Wellingborough: Patrick Stephens, 1989).

Ewing, E., *Women in uniform through the ages* (London: B. T. Batsford, 1975).

Fennell, J., *Fighting the people's war: the British and Commonwealth armies and the Second World War* (Cambridge: Cambridge University Press, 2019).

Ferguson, S. and Fitzgerald, H., *Studies in the Social Services* (London: HMSO and Longmans, Green and Co., 1954).

Field, G. C., *Blood, sweat, and toil: remaking the British working class, 1939 1945* (Oxford: Oxford University Press, 2011).

Fletcher, M. H., *The WRNS: a history of the Women's Royal Naval Service* (London: Batsford, 1989).

Forrester, H., *Lime street at two* (London: Harper Collins, 1994).

Forty, G., *British army handbook 1939–1945* (Stroud: Sutton, 1998).

Francis, M., *The flyer: British culture and the Royal Air Force, 1939–1945* (Oxford: Oxford University Press, 2008).

Fraser, D., *And we shall shock them: the British army in the Second World War* (Sevenoaks: Sceptre, 1988).

French, F., *Raising Churchill's army: the British army and the war against Germany 1919–1945* (Oxford: Oxford University Press, 2000).

Fryer, P., *Staying power: the history of black people in Britain* (London: Pluto Press, 2010).

Furse, K., *Hearts and pomegranates: the story of forty-five years, 1875–1920* (London: Peter Davies, 1940).

Goldsmith, M., *Women at war* (London: Lindsay Drummond, 1943).

Goldstein, J. S., *War and gender: how gender shapes the war system and vice-versa* (Cambridge: Cambridge University Press, 2001).

Granit-Hacohen, A., (translated by Cummings, O.), *Hebrew women join the forces: Jewish women from Palestine in the British forces during the Second World War* (London: Valletine Mitchell, 2017).

Gutzke, D. W., *Women drinking out in Britain since the early twentieth century* (Manchester: Manchester University Press, 2014).

Gwynne-Vaughan, H., *Service with the army* (London: Hutchinson, 1942).

Hall, A. (ed.), *We, also, were there: a collection of recollections of wartime women in Bomber Command* (Braunton, Devon: Merlin Books, 1985).

Hall, L. A., *Sex, gender and social change in Britain since 1880* (Basingstoke: Palgrave Macmillan, 2013).

Hall, P., *What a way to win a war: the story of No. 11 Coy. M.T.C., and 5-0-2 M. A.C., A.T.S., 1940–1945* (Tunbridge Wells: Midas Books, 1978).

Halsall, C., *Women of intelligence: winning the Second World War with air photos* (Stroud: Spellmount, 2012).

Harris, C., *Women at war in uniform 1939–1945* (Stroud: Sutton Publishing, 2003).

Harris, H., *The group approach to leadership testing* (London: Routledge & Kegan Paul, 1949).

Harrison, M., *Medicine and victory: British military medicine in the Second World War* (Oxford: Oxford University Press, 2004).

Hawkins, T. H. and Brimble, L. J. F., *Adult education: the record of the British army* (London: Macmillan & Co, 1947).

Higonnet, M. R. and Higonnet, P. L-R., 'The Double Helix' in Higonnet, M. R., Jenson, J., Michel, S. and Weitz, M. C. (eds.), *Behind the lines: gender and the two world wars* (New Haven and London: Yale University Press, 1987).

Hodgkinson, C., *Best foot forward: the autobiography of Colin Hodgkinson* (London: Corgi, 1977).

Houston, R., *Changing course: the wartime experiences of a member of the Women's Royal Naval Service, 1939–1945* (London: Grub Street, 2005).

Howard, R., *In search of my father: a portrait of Leslie Howard* (New York: St Martin's Press, 1981).

Hubback, R., *Winifred Raphael (1898–1978)* (London: CFT, 1983).

Izraeli, D. N., 'Gendering military service in the Israeli defence forces' in DeGroot, G. J. and Peniston-Bird, C. (eds.), *A soldier and a woman: sexual integration in the military* (London: Longman, 2000).

Izzard, M., *A heroine in her time: a life of Dame Helen Gwynne-Vaughan, 1879–1967* (London: Macmillan, 1969).

Jackson, L.A., *Women police: gender, welfare and surveillance in the twentieth century* (Manchester: Manchester University Press, 2006).

Jarrett, D., *British naval dress* (London: J. M. Dent, 1960).

Johnson, K. and Gallehawk, J., *Figuring it out at Bletchley Park 1939–1945* (Redditch: Book Tower Publishing, 2007).

Jones, C., 'West Indian women at war' in Dabydeen, D., Gilmore, J. and Jones, C. (eds.), *The Oxford companion to Black British history* (Oxford: Oxford University Press, 2007).

Joubert de la Ferté, P., *The forgotten ones: the story of the ground crews* (London: Hutchinson & Co., 1961).

Kershaw, I., *Making friends with Hitler: Lord Londonderry and Britain's road to war* (London: Penguin, 2005).

Lamb, C., *I only joined for the hat: redoubtable Wrens at war: their trials, tribulations and triumphs* (London: Bene Factum Publishing, 2007).

Lant, A., *Blackout: reinventing women for wartime British cinema* (Princeton: Princeton University Press, 1991).

Lewis, P., *A people's war* (London: Thames Methuen, 1986).

Liddington, J., *The long road to Greenham: feminism and anti-militarism in Britain since 1820* (London: Virago, 1989).

Lindsay, D., *Forgotten general: a life of Andrew Thorne* (Salisbury: Michael Russell, 1987).

Liskutin, M. A., *Challenge in the air: a Spitfire pilot remembers* (London: William Kimber, 1988).

Londonderry, Marchioness of, *Retrospect* (London: Frederick Muller, 1938).

Lynn, V., *Unsung heroes: the women who won the war* (London: Sidgwick and Jackson, 1990).

Macintyre, D., *U-boat killer: fighting the U-boats in the Battle of the Atlantic* (London: Cassell, 2002).

Mack, A., *Dancing on the waves* (Little Hatherden, near Andover: Benchmark Press, 2000).

MacKenzie, S. P., *Flying against fate: superstition and allied aircrews in World War II* (Lawrence: University of Kansas Press, 2017).

Mackesy, K., *The searchers: radio intercept in two world wars* (London: Cassell, 2004).

MacLellan, A. V., *Orthoptics: the early years: recollections and a personal account* (Keighley, West Yorkshire: Ann Macvie Publishing, 2006).

Markham, V. R., *Return passage: the autobiography of Violet. R. Markham* (London: Oxford University Press, 1953).

Marshall, J., 'Prevention of venereal disease in the British army' in Letheby Tidy, H. (ed.), *Inter-Allied Conference on War Medicine 1942–1945* (London: Staples, 1947).

Marwick, A., 'People's war and top people's peace? British society and the Second World War' in Sked, A. and Cook, C. (eds.), *Crisis and controversy: essays in honour of A. J. P. Taylor* (London: Macmillan, 1976).

Mason T. and Riedi, E., *Sport and the military: the British armed forces 1880–1960* (Cambridge: Cambridge University Press, 2010).

Mass Observation, *The journey home* (London: John Murray, 1944).

Mathews, V. L., *Blue tapestry* (London: Hollis & Carter, 1948).

Mayne, H. G., 'The Army Medical Services' in Mellor, W. F. (ed.), *Casualties and medical statistics* (London: HMSO, 1972).

Messenger, C., *Call to arms: the British army 1914–18* (London: Weidenfeld and Nicholson, 2005).

Minney, R. J., *The private papers of Hore-Belisha* (London: Collins, 1960).

Minney, R. J., *Carve her name with pride: the story of Violette Szabo* (London: George Newnes, 1956; Barnsley: Pen & Sword, 2011).

Moberly Bell, E., *Storming the citadel: the rise of the woman doctor* (London: Constable & Co., 1953).

Morden, B. C., *Laura Knight: a life* (Pembroke Dock, Pembrokeshire: McNidder & Grace, 2014).

Morgan, D. and Evans, M., *The battle for Britain: citizenship and ideology in the Second World War* (London: Routledge, 1993).

Natzio, G., 'Homeland defence: British gunners, women and ethics during the Second World War' in Lee, C. and Strong, P. E. (eds.), *Women in war* (Barnsley: Pen & Sword, 2012).

Neild, S. and Pearson, R., *Women like us* (London: The Women's Press, 1992).

Nicholson, J., *Kiss the girls goodbye!* (London: Hutchinson & Co., 1944).

Nicholson, V., *Millions like us: women's lives in war and peace 1939–1949* (London: Viking, 2011).

Noakes, L., *Women in the British army: war and the gentle sex 1907–1948* (London: Routledge, 2006).

Palmer, K., *Women war artists* (London: Tate Publishing, 2011).

Page, G. (ed.), *We kept the secret: now it can be told: some memories of Pembroke V Wrens* (Wymondham, Norfolk: Geo. R. Reese, 2002).

Parker, H. M. D., *Manpower: a study of war-time policy and administration* (London: HMSO, 1957).

Parkin, D., 'Women in the armed services, 1940–5' in Samuel, R. (ed.), *Patriotism: the making and unmaking of British national identity*, vol. 2, *Minorities and outsiders* (London: Routledge, 1989).

Parkin, S., *A game of birds and wolves: the secret game that won the war* (London: Sceptre, 2019).

Payne, D., 'The bombes' in Hinsley, F. H. and Stripp, A. (eds.), *Codebreakers: the inside story of Bletchley Park* (Oxford: Oxford University Press, 1993).

Peake, F., *Pure chance* (Shrewsbury: Airlife, 1993).

Pearson, D., *In war and peace: the life and times of Daphne Pearson GC: the first woman to receive the George Cross* (London: Thorogood, 2001).

Philo-Gill, S., *The Women's Army Auxiliary Corps in France, 1917–1921* (Barnsley: Pen & Sword, 2017).

Pile, F., *Ack-Ack: Britain's defence against air attack during the Second World War* (London: George Harrap, 1949).

Pimlott, B., *The Queen: a biography of Elizabeth II* (London: Harper Collins, 1996).

Popham, H., *The FANY in peace & war: the story of the First Aid Nursing Yeomanry 1907–2003* (London: Leo Cooper, 2003).

Pryce-Jones, D., *Unity Mitford: a quest* (London: Phoenix Giants, 1995).

Prysor, G., *Citizen sailors: the Royal Navy in the Second World War* (London: Penguin Books, 2012).

Pugh, M., *Women and the women's movement in Britain 1914–1959* (London: Macmillan, 1992).

Pugh, M., *'Hurrah for the blackshirts!': fascists and fascism in Britain between the wars* (London: Jonathan Cape, 2005).

Pushman, M. G., *We all wore blue* (London: Robson Books, 1994).

Rees, J. R., *The shaping of psychiatry by war* (London: Chapman and Hall, 1945).

Redford, D., *A history of the Royal Navy: World War II* (London: I. B. Tauris, 2014).

Rexford-Welch, S. C. (ed.), *The Royal Air Force Medical Services*, vol. 1, *administration* (London: HMSO, 1954).

Rexford-Welch, S. C. (ed.), *The Royal Air Force medical services*, vol. 2, *commands* (London: HMSO, 1955).

Rexford-Welch, S. C. (ed.), *The Royal Air Force Medical Services*, vol. 3, *campaigns* (London: HMSO, 1958).

Rexford Welch, S. C., 'The Royal Air Force Medical Services' in MacNalty, A. S. and Mellor, W. F. (eds.), *Medical services in war: the principal medical lessons of the Second World War* (London: HMSO, 1968).

Rexford Welch, S. C., 'The Royal Air Force Medical Services' in Mellor, W. F. (ed.), *Casualties and medical statistics* (London: HMSO, 1972).

Reynolds, D., *Rich relations: the American occupation of Britain, 1942–1945* (London: Harper Collins, 1995).

Rice, J., *Sand in my shoes: coming of age in the Second World War: a WAAF's diary* (London: Harper Perennial, 2007).

Roberts, H., *The WRNS in wartime: the Women's Royal Naval Service 1917–45* (London: I. B. Tauris, 2018).

Robinson, V., *Sisters in arms* (London: Harper Collins, 1996).

Rose, S. O., *Which people's war? National identity and citizenship in Britain 1939–1945* (Oxford: Oxford University Press, 2003).

Saywell, S., *Women in war* (Tunbridge Wells: D. J. Costello, 1987).

Scarlyn Wilson, N., *Education in the forces 1939–46: the civilian contribution* (London: Evans Brothers, 1949).

Schweitzer, P., Hilton, L. and Moss, J. (eds.), *What did you do in the war, mum?* (London: Age Exchange Theatre Company, 1993).

Scott, L. V., *Conscription and the Attlee governments: the politics and policy of national service 1945–1951* (Oxford: Clarendon Press, 1993).

Scott, P., *They made invasion possible* (London: Hutchinson, 1944).

Sebba, A., *Laura Ashley: a life by design* (London: Weidenfeld and Nicolson, 1990).

Settle, M. L., *All the brave promises: the memories of Aircraftwoman 2nd Class 2146391* (London: Heinemann, 1966).

Sheridan, D. (ed.), *Wartime women: an anthology of women's wartime writing for Mass-Observation 1937–45* (London: Mandarin, 1991).

Sherit, K., *Women on the front line: British servicewomen's path to combat* (Stroud: Amberley, 2020).

Smith, C., *The hidden history of Bletchley Park: a social and organisational history, 1939–1945* (Basingstoke: Palgrave Macmillan, 2015).

Smith, E., *Why did we join? A former Waaf remembers service life in World War II* (Bognor Regis: Woodfield, 2003).

Smith, G., *When Jim Crow met John Bull: black American soldiers in World War II Britain* (London: I. B. Tauris, 1987).

Soames, M., *A daughter's tale: the memoir of Winston and Clementine Churchill's youngest child* (London: Doubleday, 2011).

Spain, N., *Thank you – Nelson* (London: Hutchinson/Arrow Books, c. 1950).

Stanley, J., *Women and the Royal Navy* (London: I. B. Tauris, 2018).

Stern, G. B., *Trumpet voluntary* (London: Cassell and Co., 1944).

Stocks, M., *My commonplace book* (London: Peter Davies, 1970).

Stuart Mason, U., *Britannia's daughters: the story of the WRNS* (London: Leo Cooper, 1992).

Summerfield, P., *Reconstructing women's wartime lives: discourse and subjectivity in oral histories of the Second World War* (Manchester: Manchester University Press, 1998).

Summerfield, P., '"It did me good in lots of ways": British women in transition from war to peace' in Duchen, C. and Bandhauer-Schöffmann, I. (eds.), *When the war was over: women, war and peace in Europe, 1940–1956* (London: Leicester University Press, 2000).

Summerfield, P., '"She wants a gun not a dishcloth!": gender, service and citizenship in Britain in the Second World War' in DeGroot, G. J. and Peniston-Bird, C. (eds.), *A soldier and a woman: sexual integration in the military* (London: Longman, 2000).

Summerfield, P., 'Women and war in the twentieth century' in Purvis, J. (ed.), *Women's history: Britain 1850–1945: an introduction* (London: Routledge, 2000).

Summerfield, P. and Peniston-Bird, C., *Contesting home defence: men, women and the Home Guard in the Second World War* (Manchester: Manchester University Press, 2007).

Summers, J., *Fashion on the ration: style in the Second World War* (London: Profile Books, 2016).

Summerskill, E., *A woman's world* (London: Heinemann, 1967).

Sumner, I., *The Royal Navy 1939–45* (Oxford: Osprey, 2001).

Taylor, E., *Women who went to war 1938–1946* (London: Grafton Books, 1989).

Taylor, E., *Forces sweethearts: service romances in World War II* (London: Robert Hale, 1990).

Terraine, J., *The right of the line: the Royal Air Force in the European war 1939–1945* (Sevenoaks: Sceptre, 1988).

Terry, R., *Women in khaki: the story of the British woman soldier* (London: Columbus Books, 1988).

Thane, P. and Evans, T., *Sinners? Scroungers? Saints? Unmarried motherhood in twentieth-century England* (Oxford: Oxford University Press, 2012).

Tinkler, P., *Smoke signals: women, smoking and visual culture in Britain* (Oxford: Berg, 2006).

Todd, S., *Young women, work, and family in England 1918–1950* (Oxford: Oxford University Press, 2005).

Treadwell, M. E., *United States Army in World War II: special studies: the Women's Army Corps* (Washington DC: Center of Military History, United States Army, 1991).

Vernon, P. E. and Parry, J. B., *Personnel selection in the British forces* (London: University of London Press, 1949).

Vickers, E., *Queen and country: same-sex desire in the British armed forces, 1939–45* (Manchester: Manchester University Press, 2013).

Vogeleisen, R., *In their own words: women who served in World War II* (Cirencester: Mereo Books, 2015).

Waller, J. and Vaughan-Rees, M., *Women in uniform 1939–45* (London: Papermac, 1989).

Ward, I., *FANY invicta* (London: Hutchinson, 1955).

Watkins, E., *Cypher officer in Cairo, Kenya, Caserta* (Brighton: Pen Press Publishers, 2008).

Webster, W., *Mixing it: diversity in World War Two Britain* (Oxford: Oxford University Press, 2018).

Whateley, L., *As thoughts survive* (London: Hutchinson, 1949).

Williams, A., *Operation crossbow: the untold story of photographic intelligence and the search for Hitler's V Weapons* (London: Preface, 2013).

Williams, G., *Women and work* (London: Nicholson & Watson, 1945).

Winterbotham, F. W., *The ultra secret* (London: Weidenfeld and Nicolson, 1974).

Wyndham, J., *Love lessons and love is blue* (London: Mandarin, 1995).

Theses

Ellin, D., 'The many behind the few: the lives and emotions of Erks and WAAFs of RAF Bomber Command 1939–1945' (PhD thesis, University of Warwick, 2015).

Fountain, J. A., 'Modern jobs for modern women' (PhD thesis, University of Illinois, 2015).

Gould, J. M., 'The women's corps: the establishment of women's military services in Britain' (PhD thesis, University of London, 1988).

Pope, R., 'The planning and implementation of British demobilisation, 1941–1946' (PhD thesis, the Open University, 1985).

Rosenzweig, J., 'The construction of policy for women in the British armed forces 1938–45' (M.Litt thesis, University of Oxford, 1993).

Sher, N., 'An investigation into the causes of delayed menstruation, and its treatment in the Women's Auxiliary Air Force' (MD thesis, University of Glasgow, 1944).

Sheridan, D., 'ATS women: challenge and containment in women's lives in the military during the Second World War' (MA thesis, University of Sussex, 1988).

Sherit, K. L., 'The integration of women into the Royal Navy and the Royal Air Force, post-World War II to the mid 1990s' (PhD thesis, King's College, London, 2013).

Stone, T., 'The integration of women into a military service: the Women's Auxiliary Air Force in the Second World War' (PhD thesis, University of Cambridge, 1998).

Films

The Gentle Sex, directed by Leslie Howard. Two Cities/Concanen, 1943.

Websites

Oxford Dictionary of National Biography (www.oxforddnb.com):

Beardwood, L., 'Ellis, Mary Baxter (1892–1968)'.
Citrine, 'Haslett, Dame Caroline Harriet (1895–1957)', rev. Putnam Symons, E.
Creese, M. R. S., 'Vaughan, Dame Helen Charlotte Isabella Gwynne- (1879–1967)'.
Escott, B. E., 'Welsh, Dame (Ruth) Mary Eldridge (1896–1986)'.
Foot, M. R. D., 'Szabo, Violette Reine Elizabeth (1921–1945)', rev. Brown, R.
Grigg, J., 'Keir, Thelma Cazalet- (1899–1989)', rev. Matthew, H. C. G.

Jackson, A., 'Stewart, Charles Stewart Henry Vane-Tempest-, 7th marquess of Londonderry (1878–1949)'.

Jones, H., 'Markham, Violet Rosa (1872–1959)'.

Linklater, M., 'Elliot, Katharine, Baroness Elliot of Harwood (1903–1994)'.

Mathews, V. L., 'Furse, Dame Katharine (1875–1952)', rev. McConnell, A.

Stewart, J., 'Summerskill, Edith Clara, Baroness Summerskill (1901–1980)'.

Stone, T., 'Forbes, Dame (Katherine) Jane Trefusis (1899–1971)'.

Sutherland, D., 'Stocks, Mary Danvers, Baroness Stocks (1891–1975)'.

Thomas, L., 'Mathews, Dame Elvira Sibyl Maria Laughton (1888–1959)'.

Urquhart, D., 'Stewart, Edith Helen Vane-Tempest-, marchioness of Londonderry (1878–1959)'.

Others:

www.bbc.co.uk/history/ww2peopleswar

www.cwgc.org

www.iwm.org.uk

www.jwa.org

www.nationalhistoricships.org.uk

INDEX

References to figures are in *italics* and tables from the appendix are shown in **bold**.

accommodation
  additional amenities for service-
    women, 116–117
  ATS recruits at a hutted camp, *116*
  challenges of, 115, 117–118
  personal modifications to, 117
Allen, Mary, 8, 12
Army and Air Force (Women's Service)
    Act, 228
Assheton committee, 214
Assheton, Ralph, 212
Attlee, Clement, 39–40, 212, 225
Auxiliary Territorial Service (ATS). *See
    also* Gwynne-Vaughan, Dame
    Helen; Knox, Jean; Whateley, Leslie
ATS military policewoman, *101*
attitudes of conscripts, 37
ban on combatant roles, 68–69
ban on smoking in uniform, 147
barrack nights, 141–142
bravery awards for gunners, 73, 88
in combat zones, 187–190
compulsory overseas postings,
    182–183
culture shock of basic training, 47–49
disciplinary challenges for, 102–103

early days of, 16–17
first female chief for, 17
foot health of recruits, *130*, **130**
formation of, 15–16
The Gentle Sex (promotional film),
    37–38
guidelines for the overseas deployment
    of servicewomen, 175–177
gunners deployed overseas, 189–190
gunners in Anti-Aircraft Command,
    70, 72, 91, 95, **237**
home management training, 204
Home Training and Handicraft
    Centre, 204
image problem of for recruitment, 30,
    32, 37–38
job categories, 61–62, 63
as members of the armed forces, 93,
    95–96
numbers of servicewomen, 2–3, **310**
occupational hierarchies, 63–64
officer training, 53, 54–55
officer guidance on dealing with same-
    sex relationships, 172–173
officer selection system, 57
Palestine branch, 179–180

powers of ATS officers, 96
Princess Elizabeth in, 3, 4, 42, 243
proposed integration of gunners into
    the army, 74
proposed revisions to the disciplinary
    code, 103
recruitment campaign for, 34
recruitment office, 29
recruitment shortfall, 31, 34
recruits at a hutted camp, *116*
as a regular force, post-war, 212–214,
    217–219, 221
relations with the Territorial Army,
    16–17
romances with servicemen, 154–157
rumours of immorality in, 32, 34,
    41–42, 72–73
searchlight regiment, 76–77
selection system, 55
servicewomen applying make-up, *149*
servicewomen compared to service-
    men, 90–91
status of female medical officers, 93
telephonists, Germany, *199*
tensions with FANY, 19
uniform, 29–30, 32–34, 44–45,
    46–48, 112
voluntary recruitment, 27–28
wartime organisational structure, 26
wedding dress service, 163
well-being administration, 26
West Indian women in, 180–182,
    181
awards, military
    ATS gunners, 73, 88
    Daphne Pearson, 1–2, 2, 4–6, *6*,
    gendered perceptions of bravery,
        245–247
    Roche, Audrey, 245–247, *246*
    for servicewomen, 87–88

Baxter Ellis, Mary, 15, 19
Bevin, Ernest
    on compulsory overseas postings, 183
    on female conscription, 34–35

review of amenities for women
    recruits, 38–39
Bletchley Park, 88–90
Boyle, Belinda, 11, 12

Cartland, Barbara, 117, 138, 163
Cazalet-Keir, Thelma, 39, 40, 212
Churchill, Clementine, 127
Churchill, Diana, 3
Churchill, Mary, 3, 4, 75, 127, 148, 183
Churchill, Sarah, 3
Churchill, Winston
    daughters in the services, 3
    on demobilisation, 237
    on female conscription, 35
    on the future of the women's ser-
        vices, 214
    on overseas service, 183
    on the Warrender Committee, 40
    watching an anti-aircraft demonstra-
        tion, *75*
    WRNS cypher officers, 186–187
Committee of Imperial Defence (CID)
    lack of need for a women's reserve,
        10–11, 12
    War Office's overruling of, 15
conscription
    allocation to war work, 36–37
    attitudes of conscripts, 37
    and discipline charges in the WAAF,
        99–102
    and discipline charges in the
        WRNS, 108
    to the men's services, 37
    regulations for women, 36
    shift to conscription, 31, 34–36

deaths
    of ATS gunners, 73
    'jinxed' airwomen, 165–166
    of servicewomen, 3, 238–241
    of servicewomen overseas,
        178–179, 239
Defence (Women's Forces) Regulations,
    95, 97

demobilisation
  aspirations of servicewomen, 208–209
  clothing grant, 202, 207
  education schemes, 202–204
  home management training, 203–204
  from overseas service, 205–206
  priority for married servicewomen,
    202, 206–207
  readjustment to civilian life, 209–212,
    237–238
  release schemes, 201–202, 205–206,
    207–208, 237
  resumption of married life, 209–210
  war gratuity payments, 207
discipline
  ATS as members of the armed forces,
    93, 95–96
  ATS military policewoman, 101
  civilian status of servicewomen and,
    93–94
  of conscripts vs. volunteers, 99–102, 108
  disciplinary challenges for the ATS, 102
  disciplinary challenges for the WAAF,
    99–103
  Markham report recommendations,
    103, 108
  military status of the WAAF, 95–96
  moves to strengthen the regulations,
    94–95
  non-military status of WRNS, 97–98,
    108–111
  for overseas servicewomen, 97
  powers of female officers, 96
  in the regular services, 229–230
  revisions to the ATS code, 103
  revisions to the WAAF code, 103–108
  under the service acts, 96–97
  uniform infractions, 46–47
  WRNS exemption from the Naval
    Discipline Act, 93, 97–98, 108–111,
    158, 229–230

education. See also training
  demob home management training,
    203–204, 205
  during off duty leisure time, 142–143
  health and sex education, 127–128
  on women's roles, post-war, 202–203
Elizabeth II, 3, 4, 42, 243
Emergency Powers (Defence) Act, 94
Emergency Service, 11–12, 13, 16, 20

Fairfield, Dr Letitia, 172–173, 243
feminism
  'A Woman Has a Right to a Career'
    slogan, 203
  debates on post-service roles, 202–203
First Aid Nursing Yeomanry (FANY),
  7, 19
food
  food standards, 118–120
  mealtime in a WRNS mess, 119
  ration entitlements, 118
Furse, Dame Katharine, 21–22, 236

George VI, 24
Grigg, Sir James, 71, 103, 106, 147, 177,
  180, 182–183
Gwynne-Vaughan, Dame Helen
  on an ATS officer selection panel, 57
  campaigning for a women's reserve,
    14, 236
  as chairman of the Emergency
    Service, 11
  as chairman of the Women's
    Legion, 10
  as Director of the ATS, 17–18, 18, 32
  introduction to George VI, 24
  officer training section within the
    Women's Legion, 10, 11
  on servicewomen's pay, 121

Harris, Sir Arthur, 139–140
health. See also medical provisions
  discharges of single and married preg-
    nant women, 312
  fears of sterility, 132
  foot health, 130
  head infestations, 130–131
  health and sex education, 127–128

incidences of venereal disease,
134–135, 311
levels of minor sickness, 128–129
menstrual disorders, 131–132
mental health issues, 47–48,
129–130
pregnancy rates, 135–136, 311
provisions for unmarried expectant
mothers, 137–140
sanitary towel use, 132–133
treatment of venereal diseases,
133–134
Hore-Belisha, Leslie, 14, 15, 16
Howard, Leslie, 37–38

Joubert de la Ferté, Sir Philip, 20, 26, 71,
95, 100–102

Knox, Jean
as Director of the ATS, 32, 33
on female combatant roles, 69–70
gendered perception of women's
services, 242
on loyalty to the ATS, 75–76
on a regular ATS, 213
resignation of, 76
Knox, Sir Harry, 10, 14

Laughton Mathews, Vera
as Director of the WRNS, 23, 23,
24, 82
on female combatant roles, 69
on gender myths, 90
gendered perception of women's services, 242
on inappropriate sexual behaviour,
159–160, 161
loss of servicewomen overseas,
178–179
on military status for WRNS, 97–98,
108, 109–110, 111
omission from the presentation to
George VI, 24
on the provision of contraceptives to
WRNS, 128

on a regular WRNS, 213, 221,
224–225
on servicewomen's pay, 121
uniform protocols overseas, 195–196
on women in the services, 79
leisure activities
amateur dramatics, 143
ban on smoking in uniform, 147
barrack nights, 141–142
camaraderie, 142
dances, 143–145, 149, 159, 195
drinking in pubs, 145–146
education schemes, 142–143
interracial relationships with
American GIs, 147–148
off-duty servicewomen overseas,
190–193
personal grooming, 148–150
sports, 143, 144
Liddell, Sir Clive, 14
Lloyd, Mary, 234
Loch, Lady Margaret, 12–13
Londonderry, Edith Vane-Tempest-
Stewart, Marchioness of
the 'Ark' social circle, 15
campaign for a women's reserve,
13–14, 236
as founder of the Women's Legion, 8,
9

MacDonald, Ramsay, 8, 10
Markham report, 40–42, 103, 108,
139, 212
Markham, Violet, 41, 104, 185–186,
212, 213–214
McMurdo, Eileen (ATS), 45–46, 49,
118–120, 141, 154–157,
170–171, 199
medical provisions. *See also* health
care facilities, 126–127
foot health, 130
status of female medical officers,
124–126
men's services
conscription, 37

men's services (cont.)
  differences with the regular women's
    services, 229–230
  feelings of disempowerment, 190
  morale boost from the presence of ser-
    vicewomen, 150
  release schemes, 202
  resistance to mixed-sex training, 51
  voluntary recruitment, 30
  workplace relations with service-
    women, 78–79, 81–83
military authorities, 250
  amenities for women in the services,
    38–39
  consultation on the post-war future of
    the women's services, 212–214
  joint consultation on regular services,
    221–225
  lack of interest in a women's reserve,
    10–11, 13–14
  on a regular ATS, 212–214,
    217–219, 221
  on a regular WAAF, 212–217, 221
  on a regular WRNS, 212–214, 219–222
  remit of the (new) Women's Legion,
    8–11, 12–14
  revised position on a women's reserve,
    14–15
Ministry of Labour
  national service handbook, 22
  pressure on recruitment to the ATS, 34
  provision of womanpower via the
    Labour Exchange, 11, 13–15, 21
Mitford, Unity, 11–12
morality
  deployment of servicewomen overseas,
    184, 185–186
  rumours of immorality in the ATS, 32,
    34, 41–42, 72
  social stigma of venereal disease,
    133, 134
Mosley, Sir Oswald, 12

officers
  ATS officer selection scheme, 57–59

ATS officer training, 53–55
  guidance on dealing with same-sex
    relationships, 172–173
  powers of ATS officers, 96
  powers of WAAF officers, 96
  relations between servicewomen and
    female officers, 86–87
  status of female medical officers,
    124–126
  tensions between female officers,
    86–87
  training section of the Women's
    Legion, 10, 11
  WAAF officer training, 51–52, 54
  WRNS officer training, 52–53,
    53, 54
  WRNS officers' mess dress, 233, 234
overseas service
  ATS gunners, 189–190
  ATS Palestine branch, 179–180
  in combat zones, 187–190
  compulsory overseas postings of the
    ATS, 182–186
  compulsory overseas postings of the
    WAAF, 182, 183
  demobilisation, 205–206
  deployment of the ATS abroad,
    175–178
  deployment of the WRNS abroad,
    175, 176
  discipline for servicewomen
    overseas, 97
  enlistment of local women into the
    services, 179–182
  firearms training for service-
    women, 188
  in Germany, 198–200, 199, 200
  guidelines for the deployment of
    servicewomen, 174–178
  loss of servicewomen overseas,
    178–179, 239
  and male servicemen's feelings of
    disempowerment, 190
  moral reservations about, 184,
    185–186

numbers of servicewomen, 174
occupational roles, 186
off duty activities, 190–193
opportunities to wear civilian clothes,
194–195
relationships with local men, 194
sexual harassment during, 193–194
troopship transport for, 178–179
uniform protocols for WRNS,
195–198
WAAF in the Middle East, 174–175,
187, 188, 190–191, 192, 205–206
West Indian women in the ATS,
180–181, 181
working conditions, 187
WRNS cypher officers, 186–187

pay
disposable income, 122–123
for female medical officers, 124
inequalities in service pay, 120–122
levels of, 120
pay scale for regular servicewomen,
227–228, 229
war gratuity payments, 207
Wrens receive their pay, 122
Peake, Felicity (formerly Hanbury),
227–228, 236
Pearson, Daphne, 1–2, 2, 4–6,
6
Pile, Sir Frederick
ATS clerk for, 94
ATS searchlight units, 77–78
on integration of the ATS with the
army, 74, 76
on servicewomen's pay, 120
on the success of the operational role of
the ATS, 78, 189–190
utilisation of ATS gunners, 70–71,
78, 118
watching an anti-aircraft demonstration, 75

Queen Mary's Army Auxiliary Corps,
8

recruitment
ATS recruitment office, 28
image problem of the ATS, 30, 32–34,
37–38
recruitment shortfall to the ATS,
31, 34
shift to conscription, 31, 34–36
social pressures against volunteering,
31–32
uniform considerations, 29–30, 32
volunteers to the ATS, 27–31
volunteers to the men's services, 30
volunteers to the WAAF, 27–31
volunteers to the WRNS, 27–31, 36
WRNS recruitment poster, 29
regular services
a regular ATS, 212–214, 217–219, 221
a regular WAAF, 212–217, 221
a regular WRNS, 212–214, 219–222
consultation on the post-war future of
the women's services, 212–214
differences with the men's services,
229–230
disciplinary codes for, 229–230
gender tensions within, 245
joint consultation on regular services,
221–225
pay scale for, 227–228, 229
titles for, 225–226
uniforms, 230–234
weapons training for, 226–227
Reinstatement in Civil Employment
Act, 201
Roche, Audrey, 245–247, 246
romantic and sexual relationships
bereavement, 163–166
between commissioned and non-
commissioned ranks, 157–158,
161
discharges of single and married
pregnant women, 312
discussions on illegitimate pregnancies
in the WRAF, 227
inappropriate sexual behaviour,
158–160

romantic and sexual relationships (cont.)
  incidence of venereal disease,
    134–135, 160
  interracial relationships with
    American GIs, 147–148
  lesbian servicewomen, 169–173
  with local men on overseas post-
    ings, 194
  marriages to servicemen, 162–163
  off duty activities overseas, 191–193
  parental involvement in service-
    women's love lives, 162
  pregnancy rates, 135–136, 311
  provision for unmarried expectant
    mothers, 137–140, 160
  psychological benefits of, 166
  resumption of married life, 209–210
  romances with servicemen,
    154–157, 166
  sexual harassment, 166–169,
    193–194, 244–245
  WAAF romances with servicemen,
    151–154, 166
  wedding dress service, 163

Salmon, Nancy, 230
selection. See also training
  challenges of, 55
  for officer training, 57–59
  selection system, 55–57
Sinclair, Sir Archibald, 39, 40
Somerville, Sir James, 196–198, 197
Stephens, Anne, 230–232
Stocks, Mary, 40, 185–186
Summerskill, Dr Edith, 40, 41, 69,
    121–122, 138, 184

Territorial Army, 16–17
Thomson, Mary, 73, 80–81, 81, 114, 243
training. See also selection
  basic training centres, 43–44
  culture shock of, 46–49
  demob home management training,
    203–204

esprit de corps with the men's services,
    49–50
  induction process, 44–45
  military instruction, 45–46
  officer cadet training, 51–55
  resistance to mixed-sex training, 51
  specialist training, 50–51
  Women's Legion officer training,
    10, 11
Trefusis Forbes, Jane
  as Director of the WAAF, 20, 21, 91
  on female combatant roles, 70
  gendered perception of women's ser-
    vices, 242
  guidance on dealing with same-sex
    relationships, 173
  introduction to George VI, 24
  on a regular WAAF, 213
  request for trousers for the WAAF, 113
  social stigma of venereal disease, 133
  treatment of Waafs, 48–49
  on unmarried expectant mothers,
    137–138
  WAAF code of discipline, 103
Tyrwhitt, Mary, 70, 226

uniforms
  of the ATS, 29–30, 32, 44, 46–47,
    112
  ATS ban on smoking in, 147
  modifications for servicewomen, 112
  personal modifications of, 114–115
  in place of wedding dresses, 163
  and recruitment choices, 29–30, 32
  regular services, 230–234
  rules over appearance, 148
  trousers for the WAAF, 112–114
  uniform protocols overseas, 194–198
  of the WAAF, 44–45, 112
  of the WRAC, 230, 233
  of the WRAF, 230–233
  of the WRNS, 112, 115
United States of America (USA)
  dances at American bases, 145

improper behaviour of GIs, 167,
  168
interracial relationships with
  servicewomen, 147–148
Mary Churchill and a GI incident, 148
West Indian ATS servicewomen in
  Washington DC, 180

Warrender Committee, 39–40
weapons
  ban on servicewomen using firearms,
    36, 45, 71
  firearms training for overseas service-
    women, 188
  firearms training for servicewomen,
    68–69
  non-combatant status and, 69–70,
    71
  training for the regular services,
    226–227
  weapons training for the WRAC,
    226–227
welfare
  calls for an independent inquiry into,
    39–40
  the Markham report, 40–42, 103, 108,
    139, 212
  Warrender committee, 39–40
Welsh, Lady Mary
  as Director of the WAAF, 92
  on living conditions, 116
  on a regular WAAF, 91–92, 216
  WAAF code of discipline, 104, 105
Whateley, Leslie
  ban on smoking in uniform, 147
  on compulsory overseas postings, 184,
    185, 186
  on the demob clothing grant, 207
  as Deputy-Director of the ATS, 33–34
  gendered perception of women's ser-
    vices, 242
  image of, 77
  on loyalty to the ATS, 76
  parental involvement in service-
    women's lives, 126–127, 162

on perceptions of women in the services, 17, 61
on the rate of demobilisation, 207–208
on a regular ATS, 218
transport for overseas deployment, 178
Women's Army Auxiliary Corps
  (WAAC), 7
Women's Auxiliary Air Force (WAAF)
  attitudes of conscripts, 37
  basic training, 43–44
  bereavement, 164–166
  compulsory overseas postings,
    182, 183
  culture shock of basic training, 48–49
  Director of (DWAAF), 20, 25, 91
  disciplinary challenges, 99–102, 130
  domestic nights, 141–142
  esprit de corps with the men's services,
    49–50
  formation of, 19–21
  in Germany, 200
  home management training, 204
  identification of a German V-1 flying
    bomb, 88
  inappropriate sexual behaviour,
    160–161
  incidence of venereal disease,
    134–135, 311
  Indian servicewomen, 181–182
  inter-rank relationships, 157–158,
    161
  jinxed servicewomen, 165–166
  job categories, 20, 60–61, 62, 63, 64
  levels of minor sickness, 128–129
  military status of, 95–96
  numbers of servicewomen, 2–3, 310
  occupational hierarchies, 63–65
  officer cadet training, 51–52, 54
  officer guidance on dealing with same-
    sex relationships, 173
  postings to the Middle East, 174–175,
    187, 188, 190–191, 192, 205–206
  powers of WAAF officers, 96
  prohibited roles, 68

Women's Auxiliary Air Force (cont.)
 provision for unmarried expectant
  mothers, 139–140
 as a regular force, post-war,
  212–217, 221
 relations with the aircrews, 83–86, 85
 revisions to the disciplinary code,
  103–108
 romances with servicemen,
  151–154, 166
 servicewomen compared to servicemen, 91–92
 tensions between female officers,
  86–87
 treatment of venereal diseases, 134
 trousers for the WAAF, 112–114
 uniforms, 44–45, 112
 voluntary recruitment, 27–31
 WAAF aircraft plotters, 63–64, 65
 WAAF police, 104
 Waafs on parade, 48
 wartime organisational structure, 25,
  26–27
 well-being administration, 25, 27
women's auxiliary services
 campaigning for the formation of,
  235–236
 during the First World War, 7
 early feminism in, 9
 female identity within, 243–244
 gendered perceptions of, 241–243
 key military functions of, 236–237
 and military career opportunities, 236
 post-First World War, 7–8, 235
 post-war continuation of, 212
Women's Legion
 Dame Helen Gwynne-Vaughan's
  chairmanship of, 10
 during the First World War, 7
 flying section, 12–13, 15
 officers' training section, 10, 11
 remit of the (new) Women's Legion,
  8–11, 12–14
 The Marchioness of Londonderry in
  the uniform, 9

Women's Reserve, 8, 12
Women's Royal Air Force (WRAF)
 discussions on illegitimate pregnancies, 227
 during the First World War, 7
 inauguration of, 228
 as the name for the regular service, 225
 uniform, 230–233
Women's Royal Army Corps (WRAC)
 inauguration of, 228
 as the name for the regular service,
  225–226
 uniform, 230, 233
 weapons training for, 226–227
Women's Royal Naval Service (WRNS)
 applications to, 22
 as a regular force, post-war
 basic training, 43
 compulsory overseas postings,
  182, 184
 cypher officers overseas, 186–187
 deployment abroad, 175, 176
 Director of (DWRNS), 23, 24, 25–26
 domestic skills training, 204, 205
 during the First World War, 7
 early days of, 24
 esprit de corps with the Royal Navy, 49
 formation of, 21–24
 inappropriate sexual behaviour,
  159–160, 161
 inauguration as a regular force, 228
 inspection by Sir James Somerville, 197
 job categories, 60, 61, 62, 63
 loss of servicewomen overseas,
  178–179
 mealtime in a WRNS mess, 119
 non-military status of WRNS, 97–98,
  108–111
 numbers of servicewomen, 2–3,
  310
 officer cadet training, 52–53, 53, 54
 officers' mess dress, 233, 234
 recruitment poster, 29
 as a regular force, post-war, 212–214,
  219–222

rules governing visits to warships, 81–82
servicewomen compared to servicemen, 90
uniforms, 112, 115
voluntary recruitment, 27–31, 36
wartime organisational structure, 25–26
well-being administration, 26
women learning Morse code, 50
Wrens receive their pay, 122
Woodhead, Constance (WAAF), 43–44, 61, 79, 83, 86–87, 106, 117, 120–121, 160–161, 175, 181–182, 206, 207, 235
work
ATS gunners deployed overseas, 189–190
ATS gunners in Anti-Aircraft Command, 70–74, 72, 91, 95, 237
ATS searchlight duties, 76–78
ban on combatant roles, 68–70
at Bletchley Park, 88–90

courage and bravery, 73, 87–88
early roles available, 3, 15, 20, 60
expanded job categories, 60–63, 62
'feminine' military jobs, 66, 67, 68
key wartime roles of, 236–237
occupational hierarchies, 63–65
occupational roles overseas, 186
in the regular services, 228
in the secret war, 88
of servicewomen compared to servicemen, 90–92
prohibited roles, 68
proposed integration of gunners into the army, 74–76
relations between servicewomen and female officers, 86–87
sexual harassment, 79–81
skill and intuition, 88
WAAF aircraft plotters, 63–64, 65
Waafs' relations with the aircrews, 83–86, 85
working conditions overseas, 187
workplace relations with servicemen, 78–79, 81–83

.

Printed by Printforce, United Kingdom